The Welfare of Children

The Welfare of Children

Duncan Lindsey

New York   Oxford
OXFORD UNIVERSITY PRESS
1994

Oxford University Press

Oxford   New York   Toronto
Delhi   Bombay   Calcutta   Madras   Karachi
Kuala Lumpur   Singapore   Hong Kong   Tokyo
Nairobi   Dar es Salaam   Cape Town
Melbourne   Auckland   Madrid

and associated companies in
Berlin   Ibadan

Published by Oxford University Press, Inc.,
198 Madison Avenue, New York, New York 10016-4314

Oxford is a registered trademark of Oxford University Press

Library of Congress Cataloging-in-Publication Data
Lindsey, Duncan.
The welfare of children / Duncan Lindsey.
p.   cm.   Includes bibliographical references (p.337) and index.
ISBN 0-19-508518-3
1. Child welfare—United States—History.
2. Child welfare—North America—History.
3. Child abuse—United States—Prevention—Finance.
4. Child abuse—North America—Prevantion—Finance.
I. Title.
HV741.L527   1994   362.7'0973—dc20   93-40132

9   8   7   6   5   4   3
Printed in the United States of America
on acid-free paper

In memory of
Martin Luther King, Jr.

Acknowledgments

I have struggled with the issues examined here for the last two decades. During this period, I have had the fortune of founding and editing *Children and Youth Services Review*, the major research journal in the child welfare field. This experience has placed me near the center of a broad professional debate during a period of great creative ferment. The ideas and approaches debated in the *Review's* pages have been the wellspring of my own thinking and have driven the analysis presented here. I am grateful to all who have participated.

I began writing this book at the Child Welfare Research Center at the University of California at Berkeley where I was a visiting scholar during the 1990-91 academic year. Berkeley was an extraordinary place—a vibrant research community. It was the ideal environment to pursue the development of this study. I was hosted by Rick Barth, one of the foremost contributors of our time. The delight at Berkeley for me was getting to know Eileen Gambrill, whose compassion and intellectual leadership affected not only me, but a generation of scholars in social work. Two other people made Berkeley a special place. Neil Gilbert, a perspicacious scholar, unafraid of controversy, has a gift for invigorating intellectual debate and infusing it with a measure of good humor. Harry Specht is a good friend and extraordinary dean. One has only to spend a short time at Berkeley to see how profound his influence has been in creating a community of scholars. Jill Duerr Berrick, Mark Courtney, and Mary Ann Mason also contributed each in his or her own way. No discussion of my time at Berkeley would be complete without thanking George Bennett, with whom I spent many hours in coffee-houses and over meals discussing child welfare.

The University of Oregon has allowed me to pursue the study of child welfare in a learned community situated in a beautiful setting. I have been at the university for more than a decade and a half. My debts are too numerous to mention. I want to acknowledge the contribution of Marie Harvey, Wes Hawkins, Michele Hawkins, the late Richard J. Hill, and Paul Olum. I also want to thank Kevin Concannon, Art Emlen, Sally Fullerton, Madeline Hartman, Judy Hibbard, Mary Ickes, Steve Ickes, Marty Kaufman, Virginia Low, Paul Nicholson, Joan Shireman, and Ira Weise.

This study was completed at the Faculty of Social Work at the University of Toronto. My close friends Lynn McDonald and Nico Trocmé have been a source of inspiration and knowledge. I also want to thank Margot Breton, Adrienne Chambon, Joyce Cohen, David Hulchanski, Howard Irving, Don Meeks, Joe Michalski, Cheryl Regehr, and Kwok Kwan Tam.

As I finish this study I begin at the School of Public Policy and Social Research at the University of California at Los Angeles. I want to thank Rosina Becerra, Ted Benjamin, Diane de Anda, Jeanne Giovannoni, Zeke Hasenfeld, Alfreda Iglehart, Harry Kitano, James Lubben, Mitch Maki, Jack Rothman, and others for their warm welcome.

While writing this book I have sent versions to various friends and colleagues. I am grateful to those who took time out of their busy schedule to read and comment on the developing study. Victor Groze, Elizabeth Hutchison, Alfred Kadushin, Thomas McDonald, LeRoy Pelton, and Ted Stein read several versions of the full study, providing comments as the work unfolded. Their detailed analyses and contributions were substantial. Several other colleagues were most generous with their interest and concern. I particularly want to thank Marianne Berry, Douglas Besharov, Sheldon Danziger, Robert Dingwall, David Fanshel, David Gil, Jeanne Giovannoni, Malcolm Hill, Alfred J. Kahn, Sheila B. Kamerman, Stuart Kirk, Henry S. Maas, Kristie Nelson, Rosemary Sarri, Michael Sherraden, Ann W. Shyne, Cecelia Sudai, Michael Wald, and Stan Witkin.

This book took shape with the help of Howard H. Wade. Before it was drafted Howard and I debated and discussed these issues for endless hours. While assembling the study Howard's editorial assistance was tremendous. I cannot adequately express my gratitude for his contributions both as architect and builder of what you now see as a book.

In addition, I have had the great fortune of working with David Roll at Oxford University Press. The book that emerged following his editorial leadership is considerably different from what I started with. I am grateful for his tireless effort and encouragement.

In preparing this study I have taken a particular perspective that has been shaped by my upbringing. When I was less than a year old my mother was left to raise my twin brother and me by herself. We were mischievous and troublesome children. We had no idea of the difficulties and risks our mother confronted. I remember looking up at her as she tackled the world with each boy holding onto a hand. And what did the child welfare system offer? Throughout this study I have tried to view the child welfare system from the perspective of the families and children being served.

I recognize the influence my mother has had. Her love has been the most important ingredient of this study. I am eternally grateful for all she has taught me and for all she has done. It has taken many years to realize the sacrifices she made to raise my brother and me. But now I am beginning to understand and appreciate all she has done. I hope in some small way this book is a testament to that understanding.

My family has been my been my haven. They have provided the context for everything I do, including the writing of this book. My brother Buck and I have engaged in a dialogue since we could first talk and which continues to this day. His careful reading and critique of the ideas presented here have been essential. My wife Debbie, more than anyone, has nurtured and encouraged this study. Our children Ethan and Sierra debated many of the issues discussed here. I owe so much of my understanding of children and young people to them. They have been the source of my inspiration and perseverance in completing this study. Other family members who have shared their views with me include Jerry McDaniel, Paul and Paula McDaniel, John and René McDaniel, Jenny Lindsey, Merlin Kaufman, Dana Diller, Marci and Eric Skinner, and Danny Kaufman. I would also like to thank Garrett and Sean Lindsey, Aaron, Anne Marie, and Rebecca McDaniel, and all our children.

My wife's mother, Betty McDaniel, has been a child welfare social worker (MSW from the University of Chicago) throughout her career. Her life has been dedicated to children. She has lived what she believes and has provided an example for all who know her of heartfelt commitment.

I have dedicated this book to the memory of Martin Luther King, Jr. No one in my lifetime has had more of an influence on making the world we live in a better place for all. His commitment to change and the character of his leadership represent the highest ideals. His loss remains difficult to reconcile. Martin Luther King, Jr. (1963, 128), used to tell a story of a young freedom marcher in Birmingham which provides the allegory for this study:

A child of no more than eight walked with her mother one day in a demonstration. An amused policeman leaned down to her and said with mock gruffness, "What do you want?"

The child looked into his eyes, unafraid, and gave her answer. "F'eedom," she said.

She could not even pronounce the word, but no Gabriel trumpet could have sounded a truer note.

Hers is the quest of child welfare.

Contents

The Welfare of Children

1

Introduction

The Talmud, emphasizing the importance of each individual life, says, "If during the course of your own life, you have saved one life, it is as if you have saved all humankind." Few occupations give us the opportunity of participating in the saving of a life. The everyday life of the child welfare worker is concerned with just that—reclaiming a child for life.

Alfred Kadushin, *Child Welfare Services*

When we examine how a society cares for its children we are peering directly into the heart of a nation. Today, the United States, the wealthiest country in the world, has more children living in poverty than any other industrialized nation. Millions of children wake up to dangerous neighborhoods, dilapidated and violent schools, impoverished and stressful homes, and futures devoid of opportunity. While poverty has essentially been eliminated for groups such as the elderly, it continues to blight the lives of millions of children. Further, the country that pioneered strategies to prevent child abuse and now spends more money fighting it than do all other industrialized countries has the highest rate of child abuse. In fact, more children are reported for child abuse and neglect in the United States than all the other industrialized nations combined.

In our society we assign primary responsibility for the care and nurturing of children to the family, which is understood as a haven in an often uncaring and impersonal world. Collective responsibility for children has been restricted to reclaiming children from situations where the family has been unable to meets its obligation. This approach was adequate during a period when most families were able to meet the needs of their children. However, in North America major social change during the last several decades has left large numbers of families unable to meet those needs. Although the TV family of the 1950s where the father goes off to work while the mother stays home with the children still dominates our imagination, the lone-mother struggling to support her children is today quite literally the more common family structure. For the millions of children living in such families, poverty is the prevailing condition.

Impoverished families who are unable to meet the needs of their children are, in overwhelming numbers, relying on the child welfare system for help. Yet the child welfare system has been transformed and is no longer able to cope with the problems of child poverty. From its inception the child welfare system has focused on the children left out. In the early years orphanages and foster families cared for abandoned and neglected children. As long as the problems could be confined to a limited, "residual" group of children, services could be developed to meet their needs. In recent decades, the economic hardship and social changes experienced by so many families has unraveled that system. As a consequence, the residual approach within which child welfare operates no longer makes sense. The avalanche of child abuse and neglect reports in the last decade has transformed the child welfare system into a child protection system directed toward investigating child abuse reports and occasionally removing children from families and placing them in foster care. Child welfare social workers spend most of their time investigating reports of child abuse, trying to rescue children from crises, when they should be working in a framework that will effectively prevent those crises.

What should be done? Should we stress "family values" and hope that everything will work out? Should we continue to blame parents? We do that already but to no avail. Perhaps, as many would like to think, the child welfare professionals are the real culprits. If only they could... well, do their job more effectively. But social workers are not miracle workers, and it is hard to imagine how they could do more, given their crushing caseloads and shrinking resources. Daily struggling to aid multitudes of children caught in a web of social disintegration, poverty, substance abuse, and despair, most are doing all that is humanly possible. Increasingly, child abuse regulations are placing them in a position where they can do little more than conduct criminal abuse investigations—something for which most have neither the training nor aptitude.

The problem is, in fact, with the perspective that guides current understanding of what can be accomplished. The residual approach to child welfare demands that aid should be invoked only after the family is in crisis and other immediate support groups (kin, neighborhood) fail to meet a child's minimal needs. From this perspective the child welfare agency becomes the site of triage, a battlefront hospital where casualties are sorted and only the most seriously wounded receive attention. But because the damage to children is so great by the time they enter the system, the number who survive and benefit is minimal. A growing proportion of children are being left to fend for themselves in an increasingly competitive high-technology market economy.

By every standard this residual perspective and the system it has spawned has failed to make progress for children. While the system has seen periods of progress, overall it has not adapted to the major demographic and structural changes that have occurred. In critical ways, the system lacks the instruments to effectively solve the problems confronting children today. While the residual approach may stave off the most brutal and horrific instances of abuse and poverty, it cannot return the millions of children who live in poverty into the economic and social mainstream. Approaches that may have been appropriate one hundred, fifty, or even thirty years ago are no longer effective today.

It is significant to note that the situation children face is not tolerated in other areas of our society. For example, government policies and programs ensure collective action to provide the technology, infrastructure, and resources that businesses require to compete in the global economy. Entrepreneurs and investors routinely look to government to provide a suitable environment for their economic enterprises. Likewise, senior citizens have been able, through Social Security, to see poverty ended among their ranks.

The problems that confront the public child welfare system are not insurmountable. As I demonstrate in this study, children can be helped. Safety and opportunity for children can be assured. The high rates of poverty among children that have persisted during the last several decades can be eliminated. All of this is possible given strategies that account for new realities.

I have divided this book into two parts. Part I provides a history of the child welfare system in North America, examining the major institutions that developed over the years to carry out society's collective responsibilities toward children. I examine the residual model, which is the form collective responsibility for children has taken from the time the field emerged around 1850, until now. I trace the development of the child welfare system, analyzing the changes both in our society and in the practice of child welfare that have led to the problems we now face.

I also provide an overview of what researchers have learned about the effectiveness of child welfare programs, research that has shaped the system that exists today. When we understand the knowledge base that informs child welfare practice in North America and the assumptions that underlie the approaches that have been taken to the problems, we are ready to examine the limits of current practices and look toward long-term solutions. Thus, Part I provides the necessary foundation for understanding and critically assessing the public child welfare system.

Part II points the way toward long-term solutions. I examine the situation of children in North America and ask how adequately the public child welfare system has addressed their needs, especially in an advanced global economy in the post industrial society. In these chapters I step back from approaches that have dominated our child welfare system in the past in order to examine the root causes of the problem. My goal is to explore the kinds of structural approaches and investments in our human infrastructure that may help to break the cycle of child poverty and neglect.

I provide a review of the major programs and policies that affect children. During the last two decades little progress has been achieved toward reducing child poverty or child abuse. In fact, the percentage of children living in poverty has increased. Thus, I examine approaches that would permit substantial advances against such problems.

The two parts are interdependent. While the second part speaks to the heart of the matter, it nevertheless rests upon a conceptual foundation established by the first. Understanding the history of child welfare enriches the discussion of long-term solutions I feel are necessary and suitable for the problems we face going into the twenty-first century. If you are not interested in the historical development of the child welfare system, but would like to examine various approaches designed to ameliorate child poverty, begin with Part II. Later, if interest leads you, return to Part I.

The child welfare system we know today emerged in its current form during the 1850s. Chapter 2 begins the story.

Part I

The Child Welfare System in North America

The maltreatment syndrome of children is an intolerable disease and can be eradicated through definite measures and through cooperative integrated efforts by the medical, social and legal disciplines of our society.

V. J. Fontana and D. J. Besharov, *The Maltreated Child*

Motivated by a sense of moral responsibility and compassion, like the charity movement that preceded it, child welfare has historically responded to the needs of dependent and neglected children with common sense, energy and practicality. Lacking a tradition of scientific research, help relied on good intentions and high moral purpose. This approach was satisfactory for only so long in an age of research and science. My interest in Part I is to examine what is known from research in the field of child welfare. Has a credible and serviceable knowledge base developed that would permit building an effective child welfare service system?

The Medical Model

There are certain historical and present day parallels between the child welfare and the medical profession. Prior to the late 1800s the medical profession was essentially nonscientific. Medical practice was transformed into a respected profession because of the development of scientific knowledge and technology for the treatment of medical problems. Physicians were authorized to prescribe treatment regimens based on to their professional judgement as to what would work for a given patient with a particular set of problems (Starr, P., 1982).

Where is the child welfare field in the development of a scientifically validated knowledge base? Part I examines the current state of knowledge development in the child welfare field. As with medicine, so it is possible in child welfare to develop scientifically tested programs and intervention

7

strategies, a technology, that will allow for better service to children and families in need (Desowitz, 1987; Lindblom and Cohen, 1979). I examine the progress made in this regard.

Chapter 2 reviews the first century of research in child welfare (roughly 1850 to 1950). After World War II a new era of commitment to child welfare research emerged along with the development of institutions to support the research institutions required for knowledge development. Chapter 3 examines the fundamental research developed since the 1970s with a particular focus on the major child welfare demonstration programs. These programs paved the way for comprehensive child welfare service delivery reform. The requisite knowledge for achieving major improvements in the child welfare field were now, as Lisbeth Schorr (1989) asserts, "within our reach."

While major advances were occurring in service delivery reform for the child welfare system, a new problem was emerging that required attention. After World War II mothers began a long steady entry back into the labor force that would continue for the next four decades. Although education (and thus child care) was provided for children from ages six to eighteen, very little was available for mothers of children under six. Yet increasingly women with preschool children were expected to work outside the home. The failure to provide universal day care placed increasing demands on these women. In Chapter 4 I examine the changing portrait of families and how the child welfare system adapted to these.

In 1962, C. Henry Kempe and his colleagues published the epic "Battered Child Syndrome" in the *Journal of the American Medical Association*. The study reported on hundreds of children under three years of age who had been "battered." These children had serious injuries—broken bones or cranial injuries—that were inadequately or inconsistently explained. The dramatic image of infants being battered horrified and galvanized the public into demanding action. Those responsible for the battering and abuse were seen as reprehensible parents. Abusers needed to be punished and controlled and their children needed to be protected.

With the prestige of the medical profession behind them, child protection advocates led efforts to pass mandatory child abuse reporting legislation. The result of this legislation was a meteoric rise in child abuse reports. Before 1962 there were about 10,000 reports of child abuse a year in the United States. Shortly after passage of the mandated reporting legislation the number of reports increased to more than half a million. In 1992 the number increased to almost 3 million. Efforts to address the demands created by these reports has resulted in a complete refocusing of the child welfare system from disadvantaged children to children reported for abuse. In Chapter 5 I examine the transformation of the public child welfare system into a child protection system and discuss the implications and consequences.

Mandated child abuse reporting has changed the case finding approach used by the public child welfare system. In Chapter 6 I examine why children come into care. I look at the factors that influence decision making and the provision of foster care services. One of the startling findings is the role of poverty and the importance of parents having an adequate income. Nevertheless, child abuse has remained the principal focus in decision-making.

After the passage of mandatory child abuse reporting laws, concern with child abuse has taken center stage. Efforts to protect children from alleged physical and sexual assault have absorbed virtually all the resources of the child welfare system. In Chapter 7 I question the soundness of this approach. Concern with child abuse has been driven by the brutality of severe physical and sexual assault of children and the horror of child abuse fatalities. Yet, the number of child abuse fatalities is relatively small and not apparently influenced by the efforts of the child protection system. I argue that the proper place for the investigation and prosecution of child abuse fatalities and severe physical and sexual assault of children is with the police and the judicial system. Responsibility for receiving, investigating, and prosecuting cases of severe child abuse requires coercive intervention and needs to be clearly assigned to the police. If the police were to play their appropriate role, then the child welfare system could return to its original mandate—to serve disadvantaged and deprived children. Placing responsibility for protection with a helping profession like social work mires the profession in a morass it cannot solve. Child welfare social workers lack the investigative training and coercive authority required to deal with severe physical and sexual assault of children. This properly belongs to the police who have the training and authority.

Taken as a whole Part I provides the necessary understanding of the field and background information required to develop broad policy initiatives in the child welfare field. It is written for those who have an interest in understanding how the child welfare system emerged and why it has come to take the form it has. It provides an understanding of the problem that the solutions in Part II address.

2

Development of the System

Of Child-Birth. When labour proves tedious and difficult; to prevent inflammations, it will be proper to bleed... She should lose at least half a pound of blood from the arm. Her drink ought to be barley water sharpened with juice of lemon.

William Buchan, M.D., *Domestic Medicine*

Prior to the midnineteenth century the practice of medicine was essentially nonscientific, which is to say that the causes of most medical problems were unknown. It wasn't until the last half of the nineteenth century that germs, viruses, and the host of genetic and functional causes of illness were discovered. Even the mechanisms associated with obvious traumas were known only in a very gross way: "broken bones heal correctly only if reset properly and immobilized." The medical profession was, by and large, restricted to minor symptomatic treatment where that was possible, and palliative "supportive therapy" that consisted primarily of comforting and giving hope. Seriously ill people went to the hospital, such as it was, to die. The beds were arranged so the patients could see the altar and join in the celebration of daily mass. Instead of nurses, the hospital staff was comprised of nuns. The staff administered medicine made from herbs gathered from the wild or cultivated in the convent gardens to relieve the suffering of the patients in their final days.

Given this state of medical development, it was not surprising that even mild illnesses and injuries could turn fatal, especially among the poor. A fall from a roof, resulting only in broken bones, could mean death a few days later. A minor flesh wound in war often festered into an injury that took the soldier's life. What today might be regarded as a routine complication of child birth frequently carried away the mother. A mild flu or cold could escalate into a fever that within hours or days consumed the patient.

Throughout the nineteenth century, and as late as the first decades of the twentieth century, large numbers of children lost their parents in just this fashion, and so became wards of the state. In 1920, there were more than 750,000 orphaned children in the United States, a number that would

11

decline to less than 2,000 fifty years later. Until the mid-nineteenth century, provision for the welfare of orphaned or abandoned children took the form of institutional custodial care. Children were lodged, as had been the practice since the seventeenth century in Europe, in infirmaries and almshouses (poorhouses) alongside the aged, infirm, and insane. The circumstances in which young children were condemned to live were frequently appalling:

> In no less than three different infirmaries, we found little boys confined, for constraint or punishment, with the insane. In one instance, a little deaf and dumb boy was locked in a cell, in the insane department, opposite a cell in which a violently insane woman was confined. This woman had been casting her own filth, through the shattered panels of her door, at this little boy, the door of whose cell was all bespattered. He was crying bitterly, and, on being released, made signs indicating that he was very hungry. He was locked here to prevent him from running off. This little boy is something over 10 years of age. His father was killed in the war of the rebellion; his mother is an inmate of a lunatic asylum. He (the boy) is of sound body and mind. (*Children in Ohio Infirmaries*, 1867, Albert G. Byers, Secretary of Ohio Board of State Charities, p. 249)

> Last spring I was much attracted by a little girl in the poorhouse, three years old, whose parents were respectable people. The father had been drowned, the mother had an arm so wasted by rheumatism that she was unable to support herself and child. Notwithstanding the painful surroundings, she being one of three respectable women in a room otherwise filled with women of bad character, the love of the mother and child, the one so tender and patient, the other so clinging and affectionate, brought a redeeming flood of light into the darkened room. Shortly after, the mother died. Last autumn I saw the little girl. In the interval she had changed to stone. Not a smile nor a word could be drawn from her. The bright look had faded utterly. She was now under the care of the old pauper-woman. I had known this old woman for more than a year, and ought not therefore to have been surprised at the change in little Mary, and yet I did not recognize the child at first. I could not believe such a change possible... A member of our Committee on Children, Mr. Charles L. Brace, when informed of the condition of these children, offered, as Secretary of the Children's Aid Society, to take all these children, including the little babies, free of charge, and provide them with [foster] homes in the West. But the superintendents declined this offer. They wished the children to remain in the county, where, as they said, they could see them themselves, look after them, know what became of them. Alas! we know only too well what becomes of children who live and grow up in the poorhouse. (*Children in Westchester County Poorhouse*, New York, 1872,

Miss Schuyler, State Charities Aid Association, First Annual Report, 1873, p. 251)

Investigations and exposés of the conditions of almshouses gave rise to a reform movement to remove children from such unsuitable conditions and to place them in more humane surroundings, such as children's orphanages and asylums. Orphanages were large custodial institutions that provided food and shelter to sometimes hundreds of children of all ages in a single building. Although expensive to operate, they nevertheless removed children from the abuse, neglect, and despair of the almshouses, to an environment where their needs could be more adequately addressed. Many children entered the orphanage as infants and left as young adults. Although orphanages were regarded as cold, people-processing institutions lacking the warmth and loving care of family life, they continued to proliferate through out the 1800s, until by the end of the century they housed in excess of 100,000 children.

Foster care offered an alternative. In New York in 1853, Charles Loring Brace believed a better way could be found to provide for the children and youth found wandering aimlessly along the streets of New York City. As a young Yale educated theologian, Brace founded the Children's Aid Society and developed the "placing-out system" (or foster care) as an alternative to life in large custodial institutions such as orphanages and almshouses (Brace, 1859). Arguing for the relative advantage of foster home care, Brace began sending children from the streets of New York to farm homes in Ohio, Michigan, Illinois, and Indiana. Children were sent in groups of about a hundred each to designated places where farmers and their families would gather to receive them. By 1875, 35,000 children had been removed from the streets of New York City and placed out in this way (Bruno, 1957, 57). Between the period 1853 to 1890 the Children's Aid Society alone placed more than 92,000 children from the almshouses, orphanages and slums of New York City to family farms in the Midwest (Leiby, 1978).

Brace argued that placing children with farm families provided those families with needed labor while also providing the children with wholesome work and a caring family. Placing children out represented more than just care and provision of orphaned and abandoned children—it represented an avenue of upward mobility and an avenue for children to escape poverty. Brace (1880) wrote, "The very constitution, too, of an agricultural and democratic community favors the probability of a poor child's succeeding. When placed in a farmer's family, he grows up as one of their number, and shares in all the social influences of the class. The peculiar temptations to which he has been subject—such, for instance, as stealing and vagrancy—are reduced to a minimum; his self-respect is raised, and the chances of success held out to a laborer in this country, with the influence of school and religion soon raise him far above the class from which he sprang."

Brace's experiment with sending orphaned and abandoned children to foster families in the Midwest was favorably received by many people concerned with the problem of orphaned children, and became widely used. In 1891, J. J. Kelso developed the "placing out" approach in Canada and founded the Toronto Children's Aid Society. By the turn of the century the emerging "system" of child welfare consisted not only of numerous large custodial orphanages, but of many foster care agencies like the Children's Aid Societies established by Brace and Kelso that sought to place orphaned and abandoned children out with farm families.[1]

As far away as Australia, Frances Power Cobb argued for following the approach developed by Brace. In 1864 she pleaded to have children removed from the adult institutions:

> The sick, the healthy, the sane, the insane, the aged and the young, the unfortunate and the criminal, all are gathered together under one roof, bringing all to the one sad level, cannot we scatter and lose these unfortunate children among our healthy and industrious population instead of fostering them in the hotbed of their own moral diseases? Let us at least take them out of the town. In the country they could be removed from sight and sound of evil among their elders. (Cited in Picton and Boss, 1981, 23)

However, not all the children who were placed out to foster homes or confined in orphanages were orphaned or abandoned. Clements, who examined the history of children in foster care in late nineteenth century Philadelphia, found that most came from families who were either "too poor or too vicious" to care for them. The children were removed from lone-mothers too poor to properly care for them and placed in "good" Christian homes in the country, which were viewed as providing a clean wholesome environment far removed from the deleterious influences of the urban squalor they came from.[2]

---

1. J. J. Kelso has been viewed as the chief architect of Ontario's, and to a lesser extent, Canada's child welfare system (Bellamy and Irving, 1986; Jones and Rutman, 1981).

The children were returned home only when the mother was able to demonstrate she had the economic resources to properly care for the child (Gordon, 1988). Costin (1992, 191) cites a letter from the period (1916) that indicates the patronizing and authoritative attitudes of child welfare workers:

Dear Sir,

During the last week we have heard from several neighbors and numerous friends of yours that you have been drinking a great deal. We also heard that you are partly to blame for your wife's recent conduct [due to your alcoholism]... We urge you to stop drinking, as we are seriously thinking that the home environment is not what it should be for the children.

We hope you will give us no further opportunity to warn and reprimand you.

Very truly yours,
The Associated Charities

Over the years, as the number of orphans declined, foster care would come to serve primarily children whose mothers were viewed as being unable to properly provide for them.

It should be noted that the primary concern was not to assist the mothers, but to aid the children. The bias throughout North America during this period derived from the Puritan tradition that viewed the poor and unemployed as "lazy" and "undeserving" (Sinanoglu, 1981), while mothers of children born out of wedlock were "sinful." Thus, the children placed in foster homes were being rescued by the early social reformers from an immoral and unhealthy environment to an environment where clean air, middle-class values, and strong religious guidance were believed to be abundant. [3]

---

2. Preceding the development of family foster care was the policy of sending vagrant and homeless street children from Britain to colonies around the world. In *Lost Children of the Empire*, Bean and Melville (1989) trace the sending of 150,000 children from the dangers of the streets of England's urban center squalor to new opportunities in Canada, Australia, South Africa, and the American colonies.

3. The effort to rescue children from "unsuitable" conditions also characterized the wave of child exports from England during the same period (roughly 1850 to 1950). Altogether about 150,000 homeless and wayward youth were gathered up in urban centers of England and sent to rural farm outposts in Canada, the United States, South Africa, and Australia (Bean and Melville, 1989).

Early Residual Approach to Child Welfare

It is important to note that from the beginning the problem of orphaned and abandoned children was viewed from a *residual perspective*.[4] Without family or resources, abandoned or orphaned children constituted the social "leftovers" (or residual children) who had fallen beyond the economic and social pale. That this may have happened through no fault of their own was of no consequence. They were to be provided for, if at all, as inexpensively and conveniently as possible, enough to satisfy the social conscience but no more. At best, child welfare services were viewed as a grudging handout. As Kadushin and Martin (1988, 673) noted, "In general... arrangements to provide institutional care for children were made for the convenience of the community, not out of the concern for the individual child. Provision of minimal care in the cheapest way was considered adequate care."

Within this residual perspective, numerous internal debates would arise. One question that arose early on (Wolins and Piliavin, 1964) was: Which was better, foster care or life in an orphanage? Later, when the number of orphans and orphanages declined, and foster care emerged as the dominant choice of child welfare intervention, the questions would become: How effective is foster care? How and when should it be used? How can children be kept out of it? As we shall see, such questions would guide the direction of research in the field for the next century. The underlying premise, however, that neglected, abandoned, and orphaned children were a social problem to be dealt with in a residual fashion, would continue unexamined.

In the late nineteenth century those who operated orphanages were, not surprisingly, critical of the placing-out system. Was foster care, they asked, really an improvement over an orphanage? Custodial institutions offered professional attention to the particular needs of the children, which foster families, lacking the training, could not provide. Children placed in orphanages were not dispersed all over the country where their care could not be supervised. The proponents of institutional care were concerned that chil-

---

4. The residual perspective views state intervention as a measure of last resort, and only after the resources of the family, kinship network and neighborhood have been exhausted (Wilensky and Lebeaux, 1965). The residual approach holds that individuals who need help should look first to their family and kinship networks and then to their friends and immediate community. Only if all these sources of support fail should the individual turn to the wider society (government) for help. When the government does help, the residual approach suggests it should be minimal, time-limited, and confined to highly selective forms of help directed to specific categories of need.

dren placed out in foster homes were too often viewed by their caretakers as indentured servants or even slaves. And, no doubt, some farm families certainly exploited their foster children for their labor.

On the other side, foster care advocates argued that placing out provided a nonrestrictive family home environment in which the children might receive love and care in a manner not found in orphanages. Such arguments were, of course, based not on empirical research but on common-sense views of what was best for children. While Brace received support from New York City officials who facilitated his efforts by pointing to the decline in the number of juveniles arrested—from 5,880 in 1860 to 1,666 in 1876— others were concerned about where these juveniles were ending up. In 1879, at a national conference on social work, Albert G. Byers of Ohio claimed that Brace simply dumped carloads of delinquents in the midwest without concern for the welfare of either the children or the states receiving them. John Early, of Indiana, echoed Byers concern and declared that many of the children sent from New York ended up in state penitentiaries. Every placed out child from New York that he knew about, with the exception of one, Early said, had gone "to the bad." In 1882, at a national social work conference, a delegate from North Carolina claimed that the farmers receiving the children used them as slaves.

In 1876, stung by accusations by the New York Prison Association that midwestern prisons were filled with former wards of his placing-out system, Brace sponsored a series of studies to investigate the allegations. He assigned investigators to visit prisons and reformatories in Illinois, Indiana, and Michigan. In 1894, after several years of tracking down and interviewing thousands of people who had been involved in the experiment, he was able to proclaim, "It was found that in Michigan and Illinois, where 10,000 children had been sent for foster care placement, not a single boy or girl could be found in all their prisons and reformatories!" (Brace, 1894, 348).

In 1894, Hastings Hart, secretary of the Minnesota State Board of Charities, examined the fates of 340 children sent from New York in the previous three years. According to Hart, more than 58 percent of the children either turned out badly or could not be located. Hart found that a few seriously delinquent children had been sent out, perhaps without the knowledge of the Children's Aid Society, but sent nonetheless. In addition, Hart found that many children had been hastily placed without adequate supervision to ensure their protection. Hart concluded his study with recommendations that would prevent the placing out of dangerous children and insure the proper protection of all children once they were placed.

Brace responded to these criticisms by improving the procedures used to place children. Yet, it was long after Brace's death before the Children's Aid Society implemented procedures to ensure supervision of children placed out in distant farm homes. What eventually distinguished foster care, as initiated by Brace and Kelso, and which improved and strengthened over time, from indentured servitude, was that the children were placed in homes where a Children's Aid Society caseworker had conducted a "home study" to make sure the family would provide a suitable home for the child placed in their care. In addition, the Children's Aid Society periodically reviewed the homes where the children were placed to monitor their progress. If children were exploited or mistreated, they would, at least in theory, be removed and placed in another more suitable home.

Although questions on the placing out system lingered, no significant studies on the effectiveness of foster care versus institutional care, or for that matter any aspect of the emerging child welfare "system," were undertaken for some 25 years following publication of the last Brace-sponsored studies (Wolins and Piliavin, 1964). Then, in 1924, Theis published a study entitled, *How Foster Children Turn Out*, which examined a sample of 797 children who at one time had been placed in foster care. After interviewing two thirds of the children Theis concluded that, "of those whose present situation is known 77.2 percent are `capable' persons, individuals able to manage their affairs with average good sense and who live in accordance with good standards in their communities" (p. 161). In other words, foster care, Theis concluded, did not prevent children from becoming capable members of the community.

An immediate criticism of Theis' study, one reflected in the foreword by Holmer Folks, was that it lacked a comparison group of children in institutional care. In 1930, Trotzkey rectified this in a study that included a sample of 1,214 foster children and a comparison group of 2,532 children in institutional care. Trotzkey examined the physical and psychological development of the children and concluded that "both types of care are doing good work and are needed." Trotzkey argued against the critics of institutional care and suggested that to abolish institutions would result in "a distinct and irreparable loss both to the child and the community." (Trotzkey, 1930, 107)

Following the studies by Theis and Trotzkey, no other significant research on foster care would be attempted for another twenty-five years. Not until the early 1950s would a consistent effort at conducting research in child welfare emerge. However, to guide the research efforts the child welfare field would need to develop a consensus on its purpose and domain.

Once a definition was agreed upon practitioners and researchers could begin developing the necessary scientifically tested knowledge base required for professional practice and effective services.

Cementing the Traditional Approach to Child Welfare

By the turn of the century, the child welfare system had begun shifting from mere institutional care of children[5] to a broader definition of what child welfare should involve. In the United States, the Children's Bureau, for example, established in 1910, focused on the development of health and safety standards for children, and was active in promoting labor standards to end the exploitation of children as a cheap labor source (Bradbury, 1962; see Schnell, 1987 for similar efforts in Canada). The Bureau also promoted the passage of mother's pension programs to provide income protection to families headed by mothers.[6] The great depression saw social welfare become an institutionalized function of government. The Social Security Act undertook to provide income protection for the elderly (Old Age Assistance), the disabled (Aid to the Permanently and Totally Disabled [APTD]), and families headed by mothers (Aid to Dependent Children [ADC]).

The modern child welfare system emerged as a major public institution during the 1950s when child welfare agencies became professional state agencies providing foster care and an assortment of other services such as adoption.[7] In 1956, the United States Children's Bureau reported that 5,628 staff were employed in public child welfare agencies (Low, 1958). Six states had more than 200 child welfare workers, while only eight states had less than twenty-five staff.[8] During the 1950s thirty-five states and the Dis-

---

5. During the last half of the nineteenth century public responsibility for neglected and abandoned children became formalized in the provision of institutional care with orphanages, asylums, and reformatories. Almost three quarters of children served by public child welfare agencies were cared for in orphanages. In 1882, Hastings Hart presented a census of public institutions for children (Bruno, 1957, 69). According to Hart the total number of children in public and private institutions was 100,000. There were 74,000 children in orphanages, 15,000 were in reformatories, 5,000 in institutions for the feebleminded, 4,500 in institutions for the deaf, and 1,500 in institutions for the blind.

6. In 1922, in the second year of her directorship of the Children's Bureau, Grace Abbott outlined the three major goals of the Bureau: 1) legislation to protect children for exploitation in the labor market, 2) implementation of maternal and infant services (Sheppard-Towner Act), and 3) "protection of children from the devastating influence of the economic depression which the country was experiencing at the time" (Bruno, 1957, 157).

Figure 2.1 Full-time Professional Employees of Public Child Welfare Agencies, 1955-1977

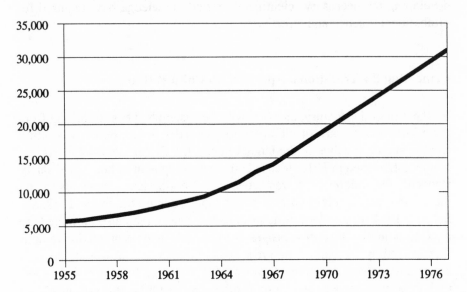

trict of Columbia passed their first legislation giving local public welfare agencies responsibility for child welfare services. Within the next decade the staff of public child welfare agencies in the United States nearly tripled (see Figure 2.1). By 1977, the professional employees in state and local child welfare agencies in the United States had doubled again to more than 30,000. In Ontario, Canada, the number of child welfare positions increased by 71 percent between 1966 and 1980 (Hepworth, 1982, 36-38).

---

7. Foster care has historically been the major expenditure for child welfare agencies. In 1956, 72 percent of total spending for child welfare services by state and local agencies in the United States went for foster care payments (Low, 1958). Analyzing the annual reports of the Ministry of Human Resources in British Columbia between 1978 to 1981, Callahan reported, "that funds for 8,700 children in care demanded at least 65 percent of the budget while preventive programs including day care, rehabilitation, special services, and home-makers for 25,000 children received the remaining 35 percent" (1985, 23).

8. Only six states had more than 200 child welfare workers, while eight states had less than 25 staff and another eight states had less than 50 staff. Further, one-half of the counties in the United States had no child welfare worker (more than one quarter of all children lived in these counties). In 1956, DeFrancis reported that thirteen states made no legal provision for child protective services.

As early as 1934 professional organizations attempted to define the child welfare field. By 1957, Hagan could write: "Child welfare in social work deals with the problems of the child that result when the needs which parents are ordinarily expected to meet are either unmet or inadequately met." The Child Welfare League of America's (1959) task force on defining child welfare services echoed Hagan's definition.

In 1967, Alfred Kadushin, one of the great theorists in the field, published *Child Welfare Services*, his seminal textbook on child welfare. His work, which reflected an encyclopedic knowledge of the research in child welfare at the time, expanded and elaborated on the definition of child welfare proposed by other professionals. It would determine the direction of child welfare for the next three decades. To Kadushin, the child welfare system existed within the traditional residual orientation:

> The approach suggesting that child welfare services are responsible primarily in those situations in which the usual normative social provisions are failing to meet the child's needs adequately is generally called a residual or minimalist orientation to social services... A residual orientation may leave the child without protection until such harm has been done since it is essentially crisis-oriented and reactive rather than proactive, remedial rather than preventive in approach... It is frequently termed a "deficit model," in that it is focused on family breakdown... The aim of this book is todescribe the residually oriented activities that child welfare services actually do perform. (Kadushin and Martin, 1988, 7-8)[9]

Operating from within the residual perspective, Kadushin maintained that child welfare social workers must look to and understand the parent/child relationship, because it was from problems in this relationship that the need for social work intervention arose. The child welfare system was:

> a network of public and voluntary agencies in social work practice that specialize in the prevention, amelioration, or remediation of social problems related to the functioning of the parent-child relationship network through

---

9. Kadushin and Martin (1988) recognized "the contrasting developmental orientation suggests that child welfare services are social utilities, like public schools, libraries, and parks (Wilensky and Lebeaux, 1958)" (p. 24). Such services, then, should be made available to all children in all families and should be appropriately helpful to all. Child welfare services, rather than being only for the "poor, the troubled, the dependent, the deviant and the disturbed," should also be directed to "average people under ordinary circumstances" to meet "normal living needs" (Schorr, 1974; Kahn and Kamerman, 1975, Kahn, 1976)." Nevertheless, Kadushin preferred the residual model.

the development and provision of specific child welfare services: services to children in their own home, protective services, day care, homemaker service, foster family care, services to the unwed mother, adoption services, and institutional child care. (Kadushin and Martin, 1988, 24)

According to Kadushin, child rearing was the responsibility of parents. He identified a number of role responsibilities that parents had in raising their children. If all went minimally well in these responsibilities, there would be no need for state involvement.[10] He also identified circumstances in which parents failed to fulfill their responsibilities, and which would require the intervention of public child welfare.[11]

The child welfare system helped parents meet their responsibilities through the provision of supportive and supplementary services or, when that was not possible, by removing the children and providing substitute care. Kadushin viewed the child welfare system as a three-tiered system that offered services designed to help the family—to provide services that would assist parents in meeting their obligations to their children. Kadushin identified three levels of intervention to characterize the hierarchy of services child welfare agencies provided:

- *Supportive.* Direct service programs, such as counseling in the home to help parents fulfill their parental responsibilities, were designed to strengthen and preserve the family.
- *Supplementary.* The provision of income assistance (AFDC) or in-kind services, such as homemaker services and day care, would help parents carry out their parental role responsibilities.
- *Substitute.* If the parent was unable to meet the essential parental role responsibilities, even with the provision of supportive and supplementary services, services to temporarily replace (or substitute for) the biological parent, such as foster family care, group care, residential treatment and, when appropriate, adoption would be provided.

---

10. The role responsibilities of the parent include providing: (1) income (for food shelter, clothes, etc.); (2) emotional security and love; (3) discipline; (4) protection from harm and danger; (5) education; and (6) socialization.

11. Problems of role functioning are categorized by Kadushin as: (1) parental role unoccupied, e.g., death of parent; (2) parental incapacity, e.g., serious illness, drug addiction; (3) parental role rejection, e.g., neglect or abandonment; (4) intrarole conflict, e.g., neither parent takes responsibility for care and discipline; (5) interrole conflict, e.g., competing demands prevent adequate care of child; (6) child incapacity, e.g., autism, epilepsy, brain injury; (7) deficiency of community resources, e.g., unemployment, economic depression.

Although the traditional model proposed a three tier service approach, the residual perspective had the effect of ratcheting the system down to making foster care the heart of the child welfare system. The residual model, especially in difficult economic times, required limiting services to the most serious cases. Too quickly, the child welfare system became a crisis intervention service where only the most seriously harmed children received attention. The needs of families that did not require the child to be removed would have to wait. Supportive services such as counseling and parent training were usually the first to be cut. Likewise, supplementary services such as day care never became a principal concern. While Kadushin was concerned with these in his textbook, in practice, they were rarely provided by child welfare agencies.

Today, the child welfare system is concerned primarily with supportive and substitute care services. Although originally viewed as central to child welfare, income maintenance programs (such as AFDC and social assistance) are viewed as outside the domain of public child welfare (Steiner, 1976, 36-39). Although Kadushin, in his early formulations, was concerned with the importance of income security programs like AFDC, he eventually came to view income security programs and issues of economic well being as outside the scope of the child welfare social worker.[12] Income maintenance and child welfare are now provided by separate agencies and departments, with little formal connection between the two.

The residual perspective has always assumed that the troubles of those families served by the child welfare system derive either from unknown causes or from shortcomings in the parents (that is, a moral, psychological, physiological, or otherwise personal failing) that must be addressed through casework. As Martin (1985, 53) observes, "The residual perspective incorporates the psychological rationale. Underpinning this ideological set is the belief that our society offers opportunities for all families to provide for the physical, emotional, and social needs of their children and, consequently, that failure in these tasks is a failure of the parent(s) or possibly the family as a whole. Service intervention is thus focused on seeking change at the individual or family level." The child is seen as needing protection from these failings. Foster care emerged as the major tool the child welfare system uses to deal with parental and family problems. The agency removes

---

12. This can be seen by Kadushin's treatment of AFDC in the first edition of his classic textbook (1967). Originally, Kadushin included a major chapter on AFDC. In the fourth edition (1988) this chapter was discontinued.

the child and then watches and hopes that the family will sufficiently heal itself to take the child home again. Only occasionally are services provided to the parent.

As a result of the arguments of Kadushin and other child welfare theorists the residual perspective was cemented into place as the underlying premise on which the entire edifice of traditional child welfare practice rested. During the formative years of the profession, it provided the framework, the essential background assumptions, for essentially all research that would occur. It shaped the questions to be asked. It narrowed the aspirations and opportunities the child welfare system might have. The major textbooks in the field still advocate the residual approach (Kadushin and Martin, 1988; McGowan and Meezan, 1983). McGowan and Meezan (1983, 505) argue:

> We believe it is unrealistic to expect the child welfare field to expand its boundaries to the point where it could assume the responsibility of providing for the welfare of all children, and we would urge a renewed emphasis on its original function of providing services to children whose developmental needs cannot be fully met by their own families, even with the assistance of the community support services available to all families and children. In other words, we view child welfare as essentially a residual service system.

Why did Kadushin and his colleagues choose to define child welfare within a residual perspective? Its major advantage is that it allows the profession to target services to those most in need. In this sense, the residual perspective differentiated child welfare from other activities that were supportive of the welfare of children such as the Girls Scouts, Campfire Girls, and the Boy Scouts. Child welfare was directed toward disadvantaged children. Thus, the choice of the residual perspective was in large measure pragmatic. There were many children who could benefit from publicly supported programs (Zeitz, 1964). If services were made available to all children, the amount available to any one child would be limited. Further, it was believed that disadvantaged children were more deserving of the limited resources of child welfare than were others.

The choice of the residual perspective was also in keeping with cherished belief in protecting the privacy of the family. Within this view, "the State should not interfere in the rearing of children unless it can be shown that the child is exposed to a serious risk of harm" (Archard, 1993, 122). The residual perspective conforms to this view. Involvement of agents of the public child welfare system are invoked only when the child is at risk of harm because of parental failures. As Goldstein, Freud, and Solnit (1979, 9) argue: "The child's need for safety within the confines of the family must be met by law through its recognition of family privacy as the barrier to state intrusion upon parental autonomy, a child's entitlement to autonomous parents, and privacy—are essential ingredients of 'family integrity.'"

The decision of Kadushin and others in the child welfare field to stay with the residual perspective was in keeping with the history of the field. Yet, as we shall learn, this decision was to have profound consequences for the growth and development of the profession.

Development of Institutional Support for Research in Child Welfare

From the start of the century to the years immediately following World War II child welfare social workers had been working to establish themselves as "professionals" responsible for the organization and management of child serving institutions (both foster and institutional care). Their efforts, as we have just seen, were mainly organizational. The charity movement provided its own motive and rationale for child welfare staff in the early period. Little or no scientific research had been undertaken to justify or guide their actions. Following the war this came to be regarded as a great lack, since, with the impetus and prestige given science and technology by the war, a coherent scientific knowledge base was something increasingly necessary for any group wanting to regard itself as "professional" and "scientific."

One reason for the dearth of research in child welfare is that before 1948 no professional journal that might attract research existed. In that year, the Child Welfare League changed its *Bulletin*, which to that time had been essentially a newsletter discussing professional matters, into a professional journal entitled *Child Welfare*. The editor observed, "This first issue of *Child Welfare*... marks our rededication to better services for children. The content is particularly appropriate, for each article tells of efforts of social agencies that promise decidedly better service." (Gordon, 1948, 10)

The following year *Child Welfare* published an article entitled "The Challenge to Research" by Gunnar Dybwad (1949, 9), in which the author began: "If we pose as our first question, 'Why do we need research?' the simplest answer might be: To explain and evaluate what we have done in the past; to be able to defend or even to understand what we are doing now; and to plot the guideposts of future planful action." It was, however, difficult to conduct major empirical studies without proper funding. Dybwad (1949,

10) pointed out that, "In 1947 the Army and Navy together spent $500 million for research, and the Department of Agriculture spent $13 million, of which no less than $1,300,000 worth of research was spent on cows; as contrasted to $50,000 available to the Children's Bureau for research (1/26th of the amount spent for research on cows)." Unrecognized by Dybwad, such fiscal imbalance was merely a reflection of the continuing residual perspective with which society regarded neglected or abandoned children. As social leftovers, it was only fitting they receive the meagerest allotment.

Although Dybwad chafed at the lack of money, he was aiming in another direction: "As social workers, we must either relinquish the claim of constituting a professional group, or we must acknowledge that one of the basic criteria of a profession is its use of scientific analysis in constant self-evaluation." Dybwad's plea for research was being echoed in the broader field of social work (Abbott, 1942; French, 1949; Karpf, 1931; Todd, 1919). Since the early formation of the profession, social work had been concerned with the development of a method or approach that would allow it to persuade the general public that practitioners should be relied on to solve the problems of the disadvantaged and the poor. The primary method developed by social work was casework. Casework procedures were particularly suited to the needs of child welfare social workers, since they allowed for the careful tracking of children who became the responsibility of the state. Casework procedures were used to conduct "home studies" to determine the suitability of a prospective foster home. Once children were in care, casework provided a method for monitoring the progress of children.

The casework method promoted by Mary Richmond in the early decades of the century emphasized systematic, efficient and accurate record keeping along with an attitude of scientific investigation and understanding of the clients' problems.[13] Along with developing a professional approach, Rich-

---

13. The social work profession emerged from a dialectic between its two major theorists—Jane Addams and Mary Richmond. At the turn of the century there was considerable debate as to the best method or approach for social work. Jane Addams (1910) developed the settlement movement at the Hull House. The settlement house movement advocated a broader community organization and social change approach. Addams (1902) was critical of the approach taken by Richmond because it established the caseworker in a role of "moral guardian" to the disadvantaged and poor. Although this concern was appropriate to understanding the problems of the poor, the needs of orphaned and abandoned children required adult supervision and intervention. Addams also criticized the "negative, pseudo-scientific spirit" of the casework approach. Wenocur and Reisch (1989) argue that the casework approach advocated by Richmond prevailed, owing in part to its sponsorship by the powerful elites such as the Russell Sage Foundation and universities.

mond identified the need for social work to specify its knowledge base. For Richmond the focus of casework was the individual and his or her problems. Knowledge and theory about human behavior were viewed as central to effective casework practice. In 1917, Richmond published her *Social Diagnosis*, which symbolized the transition "from Darwin to Freud, from environmentalism to the psyche [which] had startling consequences" for the social work field (Wenocur and Reisch, 1989, 69).

Richmond's emphasis on the psychological problems of the disadvantaged and poor offered charity workers the opportunity to move "beyond benevolence and morality into the sanctified realm of scientific expertise" (Wenocur and Reisch, 1989, 59). But where and how to focus the research? Children who had been orphaned and placed in foster homes did not require psychological treatment. Fortunately for Richmond, the fundamental premise of child welfare social work was changing. Because of advances in medical care and the broad improvement in living conditions, the number of orphans in the United States began declining sharply. In 1920 there were 38 million children and 750,000 orphans. By 1962 the number of children had increased to 66 million, and the number of orphans had dropped to 2,000. Despite this, the number of children in foster care had increased, from 73,000 in 1923 to 177,000 in 1962. No longer was foster care or institutional care being provided primarily to orphaned children. The children now being served by public child welfare were coming to the attention of the child welfare system for very different reasons. What were the psychological, sociological, political, and economic reasons that these children were being placed in foster care? The early research comparing foster care with institutional care had made no attempt to address such questions. The 1950s began with a call for research to find the answers.

In 1956, the *Social Service Review* published the "Proceedings of the Conference on Research in the Children's Field." Present were many who would participate in constructing an empirical knowledge base for child welfare and serve as architects of the changing child welfare system. Alfred Kahn (1956, 343) concluded his presentation to the Conference:

The writer remembers the poet's theme that "free [people] set themselves free." We should do what we can to facilitate research and to create the necessary structures and institutions. But we must do more, as educators, as members of professional associations, and as practitioners, to assure that we become, and help prepare others to become, the kind of social workers who will undertake research because they need to and want to. Such social workers will themselves create the necessary practical arrangements.

Such was the clarion call for the development of a scientific knowledge base that would support, justify, and direct the practice of child welfare. In all of it, however, the assumption that child welfare was a perennial social phenomenon that must be viewed and dealt with in a residual manner continued unchallenged (Brieland, 1965).

The Golden Age of Research in Child Welfare

The most important study to signal the new era of research in child welfare came from two researchers at the School of Social Welfare at the University of California, Berkeley—Henry Maas and Richard Engler, one a social worker, the other sociologist.

Maas and Engler conducted an in-depth study of the public and voluntary child welfare system in the United States. In 1959, after several years of exhaustive study and research they published *Children in Need of Parents*, the first large scale examination of foster care as it operated in a representative sample of communities. Maas and Engler found that children removed from their biological parents and placed with a foster family on what was to be a "temporary" basis often lingered in foster care for an indeterminate number of years. Further, most children even experienced multiple placements. Joseph H. Reid (1959) of the Child Welfare League of America, in the study's call for action, noted that of the 268,000 children in foster care, "roughly 168,000 children [were] in danger of staying in foster care throughout their childhood years. And although in a third of the cases at least one parent did visit the child, in approximately half the parents visited infrequently or not at all."

Since the early 1900s the number of orphans had been steadily declining, so that by mid-century foster care was being provided to children with one or more living parents. Foster care had changed from serving orphaned children to serving "neglected children."

Maas and Engler reported neglect and abandonment as the most common reason, followed by death, illness and economic hardship, and marital conflict, as the reasons for placement in foster care (see Table 2.1). (Although we will not examine the issue at this point, it is important to note that *no mention was made of child abuse* as a causative factor.)

In reviewing the original data collected by Maas and Engler, Dwight Ferguson (1961, 2) observed that "there was a direct relationship between the proportion of children who came into foster care because of economic hardship and the size of the AFDC grant." Those families who received a

Table 2.1 Factors Causing Foster Care Placement of Children in the Maas and Engler Study (1959)

Causative Factor	Referrals (%)
Neglect and abandonment	29
Death, illness and economic hardship	25
Marital conflict	10
Unwed motherhood	9
Psychological problems	4
other	24

Note: No mention of child abuse.

sufficient AFDC grant were able to adequately care for their children and thus were less likely to have their children removed. However, when the grant was too small, the families were in danger of losing their children. Ferguson complained, "Children are being separated from their parents where the primary problem in the family is economic hardship" (1961, 2).

Foster care was now commonly viewed as a temporary boarding arrangement for children while their parents could address severe personal, financial, or relationship problems (with orphaned children being placed through adoptive services). The intent was to provide casework services to the parents in order to permit reunification with their child.

The average time spent for children in foster care in the Maas and Engler study was three years. Apparently child welfare agencies sought to aid distressed families by removing the children until the families could demonstrate an ability to adequately provide for them. However, few biological families were able to show enough improvement to warrant returning the children. Thus, the children lingered in "temporary" foster care for long periods of time, often extending over many years. Joseph Reid termed such children languishing in foster care *orphans of the living*.

Not only did Maas and Engler provide a critical analysis of the foster care system that had developed in the United States, they provided the first comprehensive scientific look at the nation's child welfare system. They investigated the system at eight broadly representative sites. With national statistics on the child welfare system lacking, their data permitted the first general understanding of how foster care was working across the United

Table 2.2 Length of Time in Foster Care Reported in Published Studies

Wires and Drake (1952)			Shyne and Schroeder (1978)	
5 years or less	65%		Up to 1 year	29
6 to 10 years	26		1 to 4 years	36
11 to 15 years	9		4 or more years	34
Maas and Engler (1959)			Tatara and Pettiford (1985)	
Up to 1.5 years	28		Up to 1 year	37
1.5 to 5.5 years	44		1 to 2 years	20
5.5 years and over	28		2 to 5 years	22
			5 or more years	18
Jeter (1960)				
Up to 1.25 years	31		Goerge (1990)	
1.25 to 5.25	41		See Figure 6.1	
5.25 years and over	27			
Fanshel and Shinn (1978)				
Up to 1 year	24			
1 to 2	13			
2 to 3	8			
3 to 4	9			
4 to 5	7			
5 or more years	39			

States. The research revealed that foster care was no longer a service provided to orphaned children, but rather had been transformed into a holding service provided to living parents who, for a variety of reasons, were unable to care for their children. Further, foster care often became long-term substitute care.

In 1962 in a national survey of child welfare agencies across the United States., Helen Jeter of the Children's Bureau corroborated many of Maas and Engler's findings. Based on data collected from forty-two states, Jeter estimated that 115,168 children were in foster care and 63,391 children were living in institutions (51,000 in private voluntary institutions for dependent and neglected children). When she compared the length of time in care for the national sample with the representative sample in the Maas and Engler study, Jeter found them similar (see Table 2.2).

Table 2.3 Problems Presented by Children Receiving Child Welfare Services in the Jeter Study (1960)

Problem	Referrals (%)
Neglect, abuse or exploitation of child	36
Parents not married to each other	7
Child in need of guardianship	8
Illness of parent	9
Interpersonal relationships	9
Child's behavior or condition	17
Financial need of family	5
Unemployment	2
Other	8

Moreover, few of the children were orphaned. Only 14 percent of the children had lost one or both parents (compared to 23 percent in 1945), while only 1 percent had lost both parents. Clearly, most of these children had been lingering in foster care for years even though they had living parents. They were being treated like orphans even though they were not. Clearly, they had become in Reid's term *orphans of the living.*

In addition, the Jeter study, reported before the "discovery of the battered child syndrome" by Kempe and his colleagues (1962), found wide variations in the use of foster care, some states having foster care placement rates four times greater than other states. As did Maas and Engler, Jeter examined children's "reason for placement." While children were entering foster care for a variety of reasons (Table 2.3), little was being done to address those reasons. As Maas and Engler had found, children were placed in foster care and simply left there.

Attachment Theory

Shortly after Maas and Engler published their research on children in foster care, Harry Harlow (1958, 1961; Harlow and Zimmerman, 1959) at the University of Wisconsin Primate Center in Madison began a series of experiments with monkeys that would have profound implications for understanding the potential harm of long term foster care. Although Harlow was probably unaware of the Maas and Engler study and had little interest in foster care, his work would have major implications for understanding the impact of foster care on children.

An experimental psychologist, Harlow wanted to understand the importance of a mother's nurturing on the growth and development of a child. He examined what happened to an infant monkey that was raised in a wire cage that provided necessary physical nourishment but did not permit any emotional interaction or attachment with other monkeys. The monkey's cage allowed it to see and hear other monkeys but did not allow any physical contact. Harlow observed that the infant raised in the isolated cage suffered from intense neurotic behavior when compared to an infant monkey raised with a cloth surrogate mother. When placed with other monkeys, the isolated monkey would spend most of its time huddled in a corner, rocking and clasping itself. The monkey raised with the cloth surrogate did not develop the same problems. Further, the effects of social isolation continued for the experimental monkey into adulthood.

Harlow's experiments provided dramatic evidence of the importance of parental affection and care to the developing child. The research emphasized the importance of providing children with parental nurturing. Children growing up in institutions or in a series of foster homes were deprived of the essential bonding and attachment that comes from a parent.

The implications of this were further examined by the research of John Bowlby (1965, 1973 and 1980) who discovered that children who had been separated from their parents during the second or third year of life (because of war or other reasons), suffered severe distress. Most had been cared for in hospitals or residential nurseries without a mother or mother substitute. According to Bowlby (1969), the "loss of the mother" during this early period of life generated "depression, hysteria, or psychopathic traits in adults." From his extensive research Bowlby concluded that disruption of the continuity of the emotional relationship with the parent seriously disrupts the normal development of a child.[14]

The significance of Harlow and Bowlby's research for the child welfare field was obvious. Children deprived of parental love and affection not only suffered from stunted psychological development but also experienced distorted and harmful developmental consequences. Their research was interpreted by developmental and child psychiatrists to mean that removing children from their parents, for whatever reason, was harmful to their development (Goldstein, Freud and Solnit, 1973; Johnson and Fein, 1991). Foster

---

14. Several modern investigators have questioned the research by Bowlby. Rutter (1981) and Clarke and Clarke (1976) have questioned the importance of mother-infant bonding postulated by Bowlby. Also see Johnson and Fein (1991).

care could no longer be considered a harmless intervention applied for the benefit of the child. If used inappropriately, it could cause severe psychological harm. Further, the multiple placements many children experienced were especially harmful. Maas and Engler (1959, 1) had observed from their research that "Children who move through a series of families are reared without close and continuing ties to a responsible adult have more than the usual problems in discovering who they are. These are the children who learn to develop shallow roots in relationships with others, who try to please but cannot trust, or who strike out before they can be let down. These are the children about whom we were most concerned."

The line of research by Bowlby laid the foundation for the permanency planning movement, which would follow a decade later and which would emphasize the importance of ensuring that all children have a sense of permanency in their life. Children must not be left to drift in foster care because such drift would detrimentally impact their emotional and psychological development. Despite this, caseworkers in child welfare agencies continued to believe that foster care, in and of itself, was not necessarily harmful to all children. Who was right? Was foster care, by its very nature, harmful or not? What exactly was the impact of foster care on children and did it influence their development? To answer these questions, longitudinal research on the impact of foster care was necessary.

Longitudinal Study of Children in Foster Care

In 1963 the Child Welfare League of America and the National Association of Social Workers sponsored an Institute on Child Welfare Research in Amherst, Massachusetts, which became a catalyst for basic research on foster care to be carried out by researchers in the School of Social Work at Columbia University (Norris and Wallace, 1965). The resulting study was *Children in Foster Care: A Longitudinal Investigation*, by David Fanshel and Eugene Shinn. This study provided basic empirical research that laid the ground work for subsequent demonstration programs in child welfare.

In 1965 Fanshel and Shinn examined a sample of 659 children who entered foster care in New York over a five-year period. The researchers found a system that was not guided by any systematic scientific knowledge or principles. Although most children who came into foster care eventually left, they spent years in foster care before getting out. In most cases, the home situation they returned to had not improved. In fact, the economic situation had, in many of the families, deteriorated.

The study focused on the impact of foster care on the psychological and social development of children. Using a battery of psychological, intellectual, and emotional measures, the study provided a careful, objective, and comprehensive assessment of the impact of foster care on children. Fanshel and his colleagues found little evidence that foster care had a detrimental impact on children in terms of personality, intellectual growth, or social development and behavior. In fact, most children appeared to improve slightly while in foster care.

The study revealed that the most important determinant of how well children did in foster care was *parental visiting*. Those children who were visited by their parents while in foster care showed greater improvement and were most likely to be restored to their parent(s) than were children who were rarely visited by their parent(s). As did Maas and Engler and Jeter, Fanshel and Shinn found that many children remained in foster care more than five years. In addition, many of the children had experienced multiple placements.

According to Fanshel and Shinn (1978), "Of those children who remained in foster care after five years, more than half had not been visited by their parents for more than a year."[15] Here again were the orphans of the living decried in the Maas and Engler study. Fanshel and others began to ask why, in the absence of contact with their parents, were children being kept in foster care. Foster care was not a treatment modality. Rather, it was viewed as the least restrictive form of out-of-home care, intended only for a temporary period.

The practice of placing-out children had been seen by Brace and his contemporaries as a "permanent solution," even though the Children's Aid Society retained custody of the placed children. Many of the children placed out were orphaned or abandoned and unlikely to return home. Current foster care, on the other hand, was different. Since the 1950s, central to the definition of foster care was the assumption that the child should be reunited with its family as soon as the parent could solve the problems that led to placement (see Goldstein, Freud and Solnit, 1973).

In 1972 and 1975, Shirley Jenkins and Elaine Norman conducted a collateral study on the same sample of children examined by Fanshel. Jenkins

---

15. In a review of the foster care system in New York City by the National Black Child Development Institute it was found that 55 percent of the children who entered care in 1986 were still there four and a half years later. They also reported that only 30 percent of Black children who entered in 1986 had been discharged with no return during this period (Children's Defense Fund, 1983, 43).

and Norman were concerned with filial deprivation—that is, the impact on parents of having their children taken away. What feelings did they experience? How did they cope with the loss? What services were provided? After all, if their children were being removed, it made sense to assume that services would be provided that would enable them to get their children back.

Jenkins and Norman found, not surprisingly, that the mothers experienced enormous sadness and emotional pain at the loss of their children, which lasted for years. Further, the child welfare agencies provided few services to the mothers. Little effort was made to address the problems that had led to the children's removal. Despite this, most of the children were returned to their parents, even though their circumstances had changed little, and in many cases had even deteriorated.

Overall, the studies illuminated an almost Kafkaesque system, in which removal of children from their parents merely aggravated individual pain and suffering, which the agencies seemed neither to understand nor appreciate. There was little evidence that systematic efforts were being made to restore foster care children to their parents. The primary method used to restore children consisted of casework. Since few children were being returned home expeditiously, it was reasonable to question the effectiveness of casework services.[16]

The Effectiveness of Casework

The core skill available to the child welfare social worker operating within the residual model was the casework method, which allowed the social worker to examine the child's problem and to develop a plan to address the child's needs. Casework proceeded on the assumption that underlying the family were certain fundamental "psychodynamic" principles of human relationship and being, both individual and collective, which in the case of

---

16. As with any professional discipline, the child welfare field during this time wished to emphasize the depth and breadth of its knowledge base (Costin and Rapp, 1984). But the fact was that child welfare had not built an empirically validated knowledge base as was found in physics, chemistry or public health. The nature of the discipline did not permit the discovery of immutable laws of nature that could be formalized into exact mathematical equations (see Ravetz, 1971; Glazer, 1974) Nor had child welfare developed any powerful theoretical approaches (as in economics, sociology and psychology) that provided new insight and understanding into the areas of child welfare. Although the introductory textbooks at the time created the impression that there was, as it were, almost a highly developed knowledge base, child welfare was and remains essentially a young and undeveloped field.

the troubled family had gone awry. The caseworker's task was to unravel the complexities of these problems—social and psychological—and so help the family reestablish a stable functionality (Richmond, 1917).

During the early seventies a spate of empirical studies began evaluating and reporting on the effectiveness of the casework approach. One of the earliest studies to examine the effectiveness of casework services for children was conducted by Powers and Witmer (1951). Their evaluation of the Cambridge Somerville Youth Study has been identified as the first to use a control group design (Fischer, 1973). Powers and Witmer examined the effectiveness of intensive casework services in preventing delinquency among young boys. The study compared an experimental group of 325 pre-delinquent boys who received direct individualized casework services with a matched control group of 325 boys. The experimental group received treatment for an average of almost five years (mean length of contact equaled four years and ten months). The caseworkers involved in the study believed that their efforts had substantially helped most of the boys. However, when the outcome was measured in terms of court records, police reports, ratings of social adjustment, and psychological inventories, and compared to the matched control group, no significant differences were found between the boys who received services and those who did not on all of the study's major criteria. Fifteen years after Powers and Witmer, McCabe (1967) conducted a similar experiment that targeted small-group services on parents and children and found no significant difference on overall outcome measures.

One of the most ambitious studies to examine the effectiveness of social casework methods was carried out by Meyer, Borgatta and Jones (1965). Working with about 400 girls identified through tests administered when they entered a vocational high school in New York as "potential problems," the researchers used trained social workers in an agency specializing in services to delinquent girls to provide social casework services. This large experiment lasted six years and involved 189 referrals to the casework agency and 192 controls. The services included both individual and casework services. During the first year, the program consisted primarily of group treatment for the girls. The investigators examined a broad spectrum of outcome indicators encompassing school behavior (including grades and highest grade completed), personality and sociometric measures, and ratings completed by the caseworkers and the girls. Most of the girls received services over a three year period, although one subgroup received services for two years. After examining all of the outcome data, the investigators

(Meyer, Borgatta, and Jones, 1965) reported, "the conclusion must be stated in the negative when it is asked whether social work intervention with potential high school girls was... effective."

The early evaluation studies of the effectiveness of casework services to reduce or prevent delinquency among children and adolescents thus found no significant differences between experimental groups receiving treatment compared to control groups. Although casework services were apparently not effective with these children, it was reasoned that they would be effective if directed toward providing services to the family. Two evaluation studies illustrate the outcome with this population.

In 1968 Brown reported on an experiment that provided intensive casework services to a population of AFDC recipients. From a group of 1,200 AFDC recipients the investigators randomly selected a group of fifty low-income multiproblem families and compared them with two randomly selected control groups of fifty families who received the usual services of the public welfare agency. In addition to the usual services of the public welfare agency, the experimental families received intensive services from professionally trained caseworkers who had reduced caseloads. The program lasted more than two and half years. At the end of the treatment the investigators found no significant differences between the experimental group and the two control groups on the major outcome measures. In fact, the study found little movement on the measures of family functioning among any of the groups.

In 1970, Mullin, Chazin, and Feldstein reported a similar study designed to test the effectiveness of intensive professional casework services in changing the family functioning of public assistance families. The eighty-eight randomly selected experimental group families were chosen from new public assistance families and compared with sixty-eight randomly selected control group families. Intensive casework services were provided to the experimental group for a period of up to two years. At the conclusion of the study the investigators found no significant differences between the experimental and control groups.

In 1971, Blenkner, Bloom, and Nielsen reported one of the most discouraging findings from their research on the impact of casework services. Beginning with a group of 164 elderly referred to a community agency because they were having difficulty caring for themselves, the investigators randomly assigned 76 to an experimental group and 88 to a control group. The experimental group received intensive casework services from professional caseworkers while the control group received routine community services from a variety of agencies. On outcome, measures derived from interviews and observation ratings found no significant differences between the experimental and control group. On measures of concrete assistance and relief of stress to the family of the elderly, the experimental group performed better. However, the improved situation for the experimental group could be explained by their higher rate of institutionalization.

The higher rate of institutionalization for the experimental group concerned the investigators and led them to consider the hypothesis that the intensive casework services may have accelerated the elderly participants' decline. Thus, they conducted a five-year follow-up, in which they reported significant differences between the experimental and control groups on rates of institutionalization and death. Although outcome measures are debated, there is no question that survival was the ultimate criterion variable. Those elderly persons receiving intensive casework services died significantly sooner than those who were not receiving services, raising troubling doubts about the beneficial impact of casework services for this population.

Evaluation Reviews

Making sense of the evaluation studies that began with Powers and Witmer required comprehensive analysis of the studies' essential findings. By identifying common themes revealed in many studies reviewers endeavored to assess the overall effectiveness of casework services. The published reviews provided an overview, allowing caseworkers to see, as it where, the forest for the trees.

In 1972, Mullen and Dumpson reviewed thirteen evaluation studies of social work intervention conducted during the 1960s. Four of these studies found no significant difference between the groups receiving intervention services and those not. Two studies reported limited gains and seven reported findings supportive of hypotheses of gains made by individuals receiving treatment compared with control groups not receiving treatment. However, for those studies reporting positive results the gains were modest and the overall distributions leaned toward nonsuccess.

In January 1973, Joel Fischer published a comprehensive review of all evaluation studies reported in major social work journals, doctoral dissertations and unpublished agency monographs completed between 1930 and 1970. More than seventy studies on the effectiveness of casework interventions with a variety of client populations were located and examined in detail. Although many of the studies contained useful information, most failed to include a control group that would have gauged the impact of the casework method. This was a critical factor because the central requirement of experimental research is that a controlled environment be established where a group receiving treatment be compared to a control group not receiving treatment. The critical requirement of an evaluation study is the inclusion of a control group (Metcalf and Thornton, 1992). Those studies that did not include a control group were thus excluded from Fischer's review, leaving only eleven studies. Six of the eleven dealt with children as clients and three with low income multiproblem families. According to Fischer, the overall outcome of these eleven scientifically acceptable research and evaluation studies was clear: "None of the studies revealed that their program had any significant effect on the clients when outcome measures for experimental and control groups were compared (p. 10)...This review of the available controlled research strongly suggests that at present lack of evidence of the effectiveness of professional casework is the rule rather than the exception" (p. 19). In fact, Fischer observed that in about half of the eleven studies clients receiving casework services tended to deteriorate.

Several months earlier Segal (1972) had published similar findings from his review of social work therapeutic interventions, especially with poor clients. Segal concluded that "the evidence with respect to the effectiveness of social work therapeutic intervention remains equivocal. The trends in the data, however, point strongly in the negative direction" (p. 15).

In summary, the research was showing that the therapeutic interventions used by caseworkers with troubled families were having little or no measurable beneficial effect. All three major reviews concluded that no substantial evidence existed demonstrating the effectiveness of casework methods.

Nevertheless, the debate about the effectiveness of social casework intervention continued. In 1980, Reid and Hanrahan published a review of twenty-two controlled experimental studies of direct practice reported since the Mullen and Dumpson, Fischer, and Segal reviews. Their findings were more encouraging: "No recent study that involved a comparison between treated and untreated groups failed to yield at least some positive effects of social work intervention" (1980, 331). Yet even this cautious optimism was met with skepticism from others regarding the significance of the difference observed (Fischer, 1983; Epstein, 1983).

In 1985, Rubin reviewed twelve research studies that appeared after the Mullen and Dumpson, Fischer, and Segal reviews and that included random assignment to control or nonequivalent control groups (see Campbell and Stanley, 1963). As with the Reid and Hanrahan review, Rubin found "further grounds for optimism about the effective forms of practice." But again, several authors were critical of Rubin's review. Ezell and McNeece (1986) challenged Rubin's optimistic conclusion, citing that his review was based on studies in which casework intervention had not been performed *by actual social workers*. The issue involves the definition of casework around which there has always been substantial disagreement (Fischer, 1971). Although, as Hartman (1971) has pointed out, "no one has been elected to determine the definition" of casework, it can be defined simply as the services provided by professional caseworkers. In fact, this is the definition Fischer used to identify the studies for his review.

Ezell and McNeece observed that of the twelve studies Rubin reviewed, interventions in three "were conducted by social work students, social workers were in the minority of workers in two other studies, and there was no mention of social work involvement in five other studies. Another study provided a complete description of the therapists, and none were social workers. There were only two studies in which the majority of personnel delivering a service or providing therapy were social workers, and in one of those, there were no significant differences between the experimental and comparison groups!" (p. 402) (See Rubin, 1986 for his response.)

On balance it is fair to indicate that there has been limited evidence of the effectiveness of casework intervention. As reviews by Thomlison (1984) and Sheldon (1986) suggested, social workers need to take seriously the importance of identifying what works and what doesn't on the basis of rigorous empirical research. Examining the second wave of experimental evaluations of casework intervention conducted since the reviews by Fischer and Segal, Sheldon (1986, 238) cautions,

> It will be seen that, although there are some strong signs that social work is increasingly able to demonstrate its effectiveness, it may be doing so, in the case of a few studies, at the expense of general relevance. Were it to continue, this would be a profound mistake. It would invite the conclusion that when social workers conducted large-scale experiments on problems of genuine concern to the community, they did rather poorly; when they moved on to much smaller scale problems and used less strict tests of outcome, they did rather better.

The evaluation studies have not produced definitive evidence of the effectiveness of social welfare casework as applied to the problems laid at the doorstep of the profession (Lindsey and Kirk, 1992).[17] Part of the problem relates again to limitations of the residual perspective. The casework evaluation studies have, in the main, failed to consider the fact that individuals selected to receive casework services often confront structural and institutional barriers that the caseworker has little or no means of changing. Further, providing individuals with casework services whose problems are not strictly personal often stigmatize them.

Family Preservation: Intensive Casework Services During Crisis

The most recent effort to assess the impact of casework has occurred with the evaluations of family preservation services. As a result of the findings from research on the importance of parental bonding and attachment, the emphasis in modern child welfare has centered on preventing children from being removed from their families. Thus, the fundamental axiom of family preservation, as with all of modern child welfare, is that children should be kept with their biological family whenever possible. The concern is that too many children are removed when, instead, intensive services from a child welfare caseworker might be able to prevent placement. The earliest research to test this intensive casework approach to avert placement was reported by Homebuilders in the state of Washington (Kinney, Madsen, Fleming, and Haapala, 1977). It is important to stress that what is unique with "family preservation" is not its goal but the method used to achieve it—intensive casework services.

Homebuilders developed an approach that allowed for intensive case management services provided by a professional caseworker with a limited

---

17. The concern with the effectiveness of social intervention programs has not been limited to clinical work (Berlin, 1992). After reviewing a number of social experiments Rossi and Wright (1984, 331) wrote that the main lesson learned from research "is that the expected effects of social programs hovers around zero, a devastating discovery for the social reformers." While the negative income tax experiments that shaped Rossi's view produced only minor results, it does not follow that social programs in general can be expected to have little effect. Critics were concerned that a negative income tax would greatly reduce the work effort of those who received a guaranteed minimum income. Further, Rossi's (1987) "iron law" fails to explain the success of the many social programs that have worked well. Since 1930, Social Security in Britain and North America has raised millions out of poverty. The GI Bill in the United States allowed hundreds of thousands of men and women to obtain a college education who might otherwise have never set foot on a campus. In the United States Medicare and Medicaid provides a much needed, although inadequate, safety net for the elderly, while in Britain and Canada national health care provides needed health care on a universal basis. Business and industry lobby for programs to create incentives to invest in new machinery and research. Few challenge the role of government policies to support industry. Finally, as we shall see in Chapter 8, government policies and programs can have substantial influence on the distribution of wealth and income.

case load—usually no more than five active cases at a time. In addition, services were provided within 24 hours and at the convenience of the family being served. Services were viewed as crisis intervention and concentrated within four to six weeks. Homebuilders attempted to identify children who were in imminent need of placement and targeted services to them in order to prevent placement. The early success reported by Homebuilders were remarkable—more than 97 percent avoided placement (Kinney et al., 1977). This spectacular success rate is reminiscent of that reported by Brace (where he reported that not one child in 10,000 he placed in foster care ended up in jail, prison, or a reformatory).

The enthusiastic supporters and advocates of family preservation have consistently reported favorable results but with major design limitations (Rossi, 1994). The early research design limitations of Homebuilders were corrected with the use of a matched control group in the Washington and Utah studies reported by Fraser and colleagues (1991). The methodological flaw of these later evaluation studies, however, centered on the absence of a control group for the Washington study and a "crippled" overflow control group (nonresponse for a third of the control group) for the Utah study with small sample sizes (27 families in the control condition). But the more fundamental limitation is that these studies represent "advocacy research" rather than conventional impartial science (see Gilbert, 1994 for a discussion of "advocacy research"). As such, the research effort of family preservation advocates has been to prove the effectiveness of this approach rather than to critically assess its impact.

In recent years there have been more than 35 evaluations of family preservation in one form or another.[18] The essential requirement of an unbiased test of an experimental study is, as we learned from Fischer's (1973) work, the use of a randomized control group.[19] In this regard, three "intensive

---

18. These studies include: Bergquist, Szwejda, and Pope, 1993; Berry, 1990, 1991, 1992; Chess et al., 1993; Collier and Hill, 1993; Cunningham and Smith, 1990; Feldman, 1990 and 1991; Fraser, Pecora, and Haapala, 1991; Halper and Jones, 1981; Henggler et al., 1992; Hennepin County Community Services Department, 1981; Jones, Neuman, and Shyne, 1976; Kinney et al., 1977; Kinney et al., 1991; Landsman, 1985; Lewis, 1994; Lyle and Nelson, 1983; Magura, 1981; McDonald and Associates, 1990; Meezan and McCroskey, 1993; Michigan Department of Social Services, 1993; Mitchell, Tovar, and Knitzer, 1989; Nelson, Emlen, Landsman, and Hutchinson, 1988; Nelson and Landsman, 1992; Pecora, Fraser, and Haapala, 1991 and 1992; Scannapieco, 1994; Schafer and Erickson, 1993; Schuerman et al., 1991, 1992 and 1993; Schwartz and AuClaire, 1989; Schwartz, AuClaire, and Harris, 1991; Szykula and Fleischman, 1985; Thieman, Fuqua, and Linnan, 1990; University Associates, 1992 and 1993; Wells and Whittington, 1993; Wheeler, 1992; Wheeler et al., 1992; Willems and DeRubeis, 1981; Wood, Barton, and Schroeder, 1988; and Yuan et al., 1990.

casework" family preservation studies stand out for their use of randomized control groups with sufficient sample size to test for experimental effects. In California, New Jersey, and Illinois randomized experimental designs were used with sample sizes in the experimental conditions of 338, 117, and 995 respectively. These three studies provide the most rigorous and unbiased tests of family preservation and all have found small or insignificant differences as a result of intensive casework services.

The Illinois Study. Although there have been many tests of intensive casework services, the most comprehensive test of family preservation approach has been the Illinois study. A team of child welfare researchers at Chapin Hall at the University of Chicago developed the most comprehensive examination of the family preservation approach. Family preservation was understood as intensive casework services provided to a family where there was a likelihood a child might be removed. Services were provided by a caseworker who was limited to five cases at any one time, whereas the normal caseload for caseworkers in the control group was fifty cases. Families were provided with services within 24 hours and their caseworkers met with them at a time and place convenient to the family.

The Illinois study stands out for its care in documenting exactly what services the experimental group received in comparison to the control group. It involved multiple sites with data collected over a three year period. Families in the experimental condition received almost *ten* times more contact hours with a caseworker. Even after receiving far more casework services the researchers found no significant advantages for the experimental families (Schuerman et al., 1993).

Summarizing the overall findings from the enormous effort to assess the impact of intensive casework services in child welfare it is reasonable to suggest that the more rigorous has been the research design, the more convincing has been the evidence that these services have failed to produce significant improvements for clients.[20] Schuerman and colleagues (1993) conclude, "We find little evidence that family preservation programs result in substantial reductions in the placement of children. Claims to the con-

---

19. With the increased use of statistical designs to evaluate programs a skepticism toward research in social work has developed. As critics of the positivist approach point out, research is not the use of statistical procedures to *prove* a particular point of view. Rather, research is the impartial search for truth and the use of investigative methods designed to limit the influence of personal bias (Cournand and Meyer, 1976; Lindsey, 1978). Research must also allow for the refutation of one's program or point of view (Mahoney, 1976).

trary have been based largely on non-experimental studies which do not provide sufficient evidence of program effects."[21] Yet, family preservation may also be viewed as a philosophy of service—children should be kept out of foster care whenever possible. As Peter Rossi (1994) observes, the basis for family preservation's success has more to do with faith or "advocacy research" than science. In the absence of evidence of its effectiveness, it is remarkable to observe the support intensive casework services under the banner of family preservation has received at the federal level.

Long-term Impact of Foster Care: The concern about the effectiveness of casework raised by the review studies extended itself quite naturally to foster care. What was foster care's impact on children? What became of the many thousands of young people who had been submerged for so many years in the foster care system? Did they become productive well-adjusted adults? Too often the answer was "no" (Kendrick, 1990). Sosin, Piliavin and Westerfelt (1991) studied the long-term homeless in Minneapolis and found that 39 percent had experienced foster or institutional care as children. Corbit (1985) interviewed "street kids" in Calgary and found that 90 percent had been in foster care (crown wards). Hepworth (1985, 38) observes, "It is

---

20. The 1994 Federal budget provides 60 million in 1994, rising to 240 million in fiscal 1998 for states to use to establish family preservation services. Most recent federal and state initiatives seem to be guided by this essentially residual approach even though numerous empirical studies have failed to provide evidence of meaningful success (Rossi, 1992a,b; Schuerman et al., 1993; Yuan, 1990). Adams (1992) has indicated that much of the success achieved by advocates of this approach has derived from the leveraging of substantial funding from two large private foundations. Many of these evaluation studies have been funded by the benefactors of this approach. Yet, still the findings have been equivocal. Rossi (1994) summarizes, "The existing studies all show that there are at best marginal differences in post treatment placement rates or in improved families and more frequently no differences at all between experimental group and control groups families." The main research in support of family preservation comes from two studies conducted in Utah and Washington. Although an impressive amount of data were collected in these studies they were, according to Rossi, "badly flawed." Reviewing the results of the Washington and Utah research reported by Fraser, Pecora, and Haapala (1991) in their *Families in Crisis*, Rossi (1994) asks, "Given what these studies have shown, why is it that the child welfare establishment still enthusiastically advocates family preservation? Analogously, why do otherwise competent and surely intelligent persons publish a volume based on fatally flawed data in order to advance the 'family preservation movement'? Are we witnessing another triumph of faith over data?"

21. To explain the absence of experimental advantage even with almost ten times more contact with social workers, Schuerman and colleagues offer two main suggestions. First, it is very difficult to identify children in imminent need of placement and to target services to this group. Second, many of the problems the families served face, such as severe poverty and social dislocation, are not amenable to casework services.

a sad fact that many children graduate from child welfare services to training schools and even ultimately to prison; this is particularly true for native
children (Native Council of Canada, 1978)." Kendrick (1990, 69) is even
more discouraged with the child protection system that "turns out uneducated, unemployed, confused, and isolated young people."

Summary and Conclusion

Child welfare arose in the latter half of the nineteenth century as a societal
response to the needs of children whose parents had died, abandoned or
were unable to care for them. It began with orphanages that provided food
and shelter and limited instruction. Soon after, "placing out" or foster care
emerged as a response to the high cost and limited public satisfaction with
large state-operated orphanages. Foster care provided a more family-like
setting, was less restrictive, and less expensive. Shifting the care of children
from large custodial institutions into foster family boarding homes was
viewed as progressive reform.

With the decline in the number of orphans, child welfare agencies
expanded their focus to a broader concern for the welfare of impoverished
and neglected children. They provided services to children whom, it was
believed, were not adequately cared for by their parent(s) and needed to be
removed to substitute care. Over time these residual services evolved into a
safety net to protect those children who were at greatest risk of harm
through abandonment or neglect.

By 1950 foster care became the major service provided by public child
welfare agencies. At about the same time an effort to develop an understanding of foster care was initiated. Leaders in child welfare called for
research and empirical studies that would examine its effects. One of the
first studies, that by Maas and Engler (1959), indicated that children temporarily placed in foster care underwent numerous placements and lingered in
care for years. Nevertheless, later research found little evidence of a distinc-
tively harmful effect resulting from foster care (Fanshel and Shinn, 1978).
The research by Jenkins and Norman (1972, 1975) found that those who
suffered most were mothers who had their children taken from them. These
women experienced years of sadness and grief that was only relieved when
their children returned. Fanshel and Shinn (1978) found that one of the most
important variables determining a child's progress while in foster care was
the extent of parental visiting, which affected both the length of stay and
how well the child adjusted while in foster care.

Along with the basic research on the impact of foster care, this period also gave rise to the use of experimental research designs to examine the effectiveness of casework intervention in social work. In the long view of history, one of the major achievements during the 19th Century centered around the advances in medicine. Using the methods of science, medicine developed an understanding of the principles of germ theory, the functioning of the circulation system, the biochemical nature of the human body, and the overall functioning of the human organism. During the same period medical science developed vaccinations, surgical techniques, and medical treatments to heal and cure the sick. The principal scientific method used to test medical treatments was the experimental design. Medical treatments were tested by randomly assigning individuals to experimental and control groups and exposing the experimental group to treatment, while the control group was not exposed. After the treatment was administered and allowed to have an effect, individuals were assessed to see if there was a difference between the experimental and control group. If the treatment was effective, then those in the experimental group would have improved relative to those in the control group.

When the central method of social work—casework—was examined using experimental designs with random assignment to experimental and control groups, it did not produce significant change.[22] Yet casework was not a treatment method. It was not developed as a curative process. Rather, casework was essentially a case management approach designed to assess client needs, identify available resources and monitor client progress. It was an individual case accounting and planning method suited to the needs of the residual approach.

Overall, the basic research conducted during the early history of child welfare provided a framework for understanding the child welfare system and the efficacy of approaches designed to serve children. The stage was set for a new direction in research: How might the system be improved and reformed?

---

22. The discouraging findings from experimental research did not result in a fundamental questioning of the essential method of intervention—casework—as might be expected. Instead, in the years that followed the disappointing findings, there has emerged a distrust of the scientific method and a questioning of its relevance to social work. Convinced of the efficacy of its current involvement with clients, many in social work questioned the definition of effectiveness and the use of experimental and empirical research approaches to the field (Goldstein, 1992; Heineman, 1981). In recent years these scholars have argued that social work has a different philosophical basis than other "science based" professions, that it is more like an art and finds its place in the humanities more than the sciences (England, 1986).

3

Child Welfare Reform through Research and Demonstration: Permanency Planning

Of all the children we studied, better than half of them gave promise of living a major part of their childhood years in foster families and institutions. Among them were children likely to leave care only when they came of age, often after having had many homes—and none of their own—for ten or so years.

Henry Maas and Richard Engler, Jr., *Children in Need of Parents*

In a market economy consumers hold power because of their ability to choose one product or service over another. The problem in the social services, and child welfare in particular, is that free-market forces do not operate. Instead of freely choosing from among a spectrum of services, clients have only once choice, for which they must qualify. Decisions regarding the type and character of services offered reside with the agency providing them, a circumstance that too often voids accountability to the client. In the absence of a market mechanism that would make the social service delivery system accountable, the child welfare system has had to rely on other ways to achieve accountability. As we have seen, evaluation research studies emerged as one solution to accountability—the best method for monitoring the success or failure of child welfare programs.

During the 1970s several major demonstration programs in child welfare challenged the prevailing view that social programs were likely to have only limited impact. These research projects, motivated by a collective need in the profession to force accountability, instituted changes in the child welfare delivery system, afterwards carefully monitoring the outcomes. The studies demonstrated that the existing child welfare system could, through institutional and structural reform based on research, be made more effective at reduced cost. The studies were significant because they illustrated the means by which effective reform could be instituted.

47

The traditional child welfare system described by Kadushin and Martin (1988) could be viewed as a social service organization where children and their parents: (1) entered the system, (2) received care and services, and then (3) left. The federal demonstration projects of the seventies focused on each of these phases (see Figure 3.1). In this chapter we examine three major federally funded research and demonstration programs that were part of a broad movement toward permanency planning and are illustrative of the research of the period. The Comprehensive Emergency Services (CES) program focused on the first phase, proposing major changes to the way children entered the system. The second demonstration program, the Alameda Project, examined what changes could be made in casework services provided to children and families once they entered care. The third study, the Oregon Project, examined how children exit foster care and investigated strategies for reducing the number of children lingering in foster care.

Exposing the Problem

In 1970, the Urban Institute sponsored a study by Marvin Burt and Louis Blair to examine child welfare services for neglected and abused children. Using a systems approach, the study (Burt and Blair, 1971) examined the adequacy of the ongoing child welfare service delivery system. The investigators felt that the system was not functioning well, and they hoped to identify problems and devise, institute, and test workable solutions (Gruber, 1978; Vasaly, 1976). The site chosen for the study was Nashville-Davidson county, Tennessee, considered to be a fairly typical urban child welfare system. What was true here, would likely be true nationwide.

The study (Burt and Blair, 1971) began with a descriptive survey of the county's child welfare services and how they were being delivered. What the investigators in Nashville-Davidson county found was a fragmented and uncoordinated federation of state, local, and voluntary agencies. No single agency had the authority to ensure that the problems of children and families were being effectively and comprehensively served. Children were often shuttled from the police to the courts to the social service agency and then into a mix of out-of-home care facilities. At any one time, no one could explain why one child was being treated differently than another. Little continuity existed. Child welfare services consisted of a hodgepodge of different agencies providing services to selected categories of needs. Children

Figure 3.1 The Structure of the Child Welfare System

1	⇒	2	⇒ 3
Entry		Services	Exit
Decision Making		Foster Care for the Child	Restoration
Diversion		Services to the Biological	Parent Adoption
Emergency Services		to Facilitate Restoration	Long-term Care

and families were dealt with when they seemed to match a particular category of problem, otherwise they were dismissed, or dealt with summarily in a manner that did not fit the circumstance. For example, the mother of two is suddenly hospitalized. The father, a trucker, is currently away from home. Called to the home by neighbors, the police have no other choice but to take the children into custody and initiate court action placing them in state custody. In a short time, the children have ended up who knows where, perhaps in a foster home, perhaps in a residential, locked-door treatment facility.

Further, most children and families in Nashville-Davidson county had initial contact with the service delivery system after normal office hours. Nevertheless, no emergency services existed except what the police might offer. Consequently, more children were getting into the child welfare system than should have gotten in. Once in, the bureaucratic door closed behind them, and they found it hard to get out. Bureaucratic inertia suddenly asserted itself. Procedures had to be followed. Forms filled out. Hearings held. Interviews. More forms. No one wanted to take responsibility for releasing the children back into a possibly dangerous home environment. The burden of proof shifted from the agency, which, in its view, had acted correctly in removing the children, to the parents who must now prove definitively why their children should be allowed to return home. The system designed to serve children and families had lost sight of its mission.

The Comprehensive Emergency Services System

Burt and Blair (1971) concluded their study, entitled *Options for Improving the Care of Neglected and Dependent Children*, with a proposal for the development of a comprehensive child welfare emergency services program. Essentially, the proposal had two goals: (1) to bring about a successful coordination and reorganization of child services, and (2) to expand existing service programs to include a comprehensive emergency service system. The aim was to screen out people who did not need to get in, while providing more comprehensive services for those who did.

With support from federal, state and local government, the reforms were tested by CES, which was implemented in Nashville-Davidson County, Tennessee in April 1972 (Burt and Bayleat, 1978). In accord with its goals, the project provided for 1) a centralized coordination of service delivery and 2) the implementation of an emergency services system. The emergency services system encompassed four units:

1. Twenty-four hour emergency intake allowed for both coordination of services and provision of care on a twenty-four-hour, seven-days-a-week basis.
2. Emergency caretaker service for children temporarily left without supervision because of an unforeseen circumstance or emergency, caretakers would be available to stay at the home with the children until the parent was able to return. Every attempt would be made to keep the child at home and out of the service delivery system when appropriate.
3. Emergency homemaker service for those children or families where extended in-home care was needed, a twenty-four-hour emergency homemaker service was developed.
4. Emergency foster homes so that every effort would be made to return children home as quickly as possible. Short term foster family care would be provided only until children could be returned home or placed elsewhere.

In part, the CES system (Burt and Blair, 1971) was viewed as a diversion program for neglected and abused children, to substantially reduce the number of children inappropriately entering into the foster care system. It was designed to ensure retention of children in their own home or, if that was not possible, their return home at the earliest possible time in order that they not enter into the system and find it difficult to exit. Using baseline data obtained during the first study, the demonstration project staff were able to assess the changes that came about as a result of the project's structural and institutional reforms.

The CES project had several specific objectives that were ideally suited for measurement. The first objective was to "reduce the number of neglect and dependency petitions filed and the number of children entering into the system by screening out those cases where a petition was not justified" (Burt and Blair, 1971, 25). Figure 3.2 shows that the number of petitions

Figure 3.2 The Impact of the CES System on Child Placements

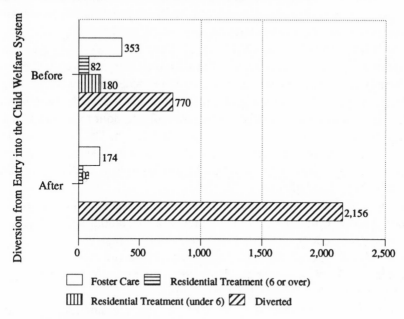

Source: Burt and Blair (1977, 52).

dropped sharply from 602 in 1969-70, before the program started to 226 in 1973-74, two years later. This was achieved largely by screening the number of petitions sworn out and averting or preventing the inappropriate placement of children in care. The number of cases where a petition was not sworn out in response to a complaint increased from 770 in 1969-70 to 2,156 in 1973-74, an increase of 180 percent (Figure 3.2). Thus, although the number of potential entrants increased threefold, the number actually admitted to the system dropped by two-thirds.

The second objective of the CES program, reminiscent of the current family preservation programs, was to keep children in their own home whenever possible (Forsythe, 1992; McGowan, 1990). Again, the results were substantial. As seen in Figure 3.2, the number of children removed from their homes and placed in substitute care declined from 353 in 1969-70 to 174 in 1973-74, a decline of about 50 percent. Further, the number of children placed in residential facilities was reduced from 262 to 35 (a decrease of more than 85 percent), and the number of children under six who were admitted dropped from 180 to 0 (see Figure 3.2). Clearly, the demonstration program altered both the type and number of services delivered. The use of residential treatment was almost eliminated, while the use of foster care was dramatically reduced. In brief, the program was highly successful in averting placement.

The third objective of the CES program was to ensure that children were placed in safe, stable environments. The aim of diverting children whenever possible from substitute care back to their home would have been pointless if the child had simply shown up again seeking admittance due to continuing abuse or neglect (essentially creating a revolving door to service). In the CES program, however, this did not appear to happen. The number of children for whom petitions were initially filed and who, because of abuse or neglect, turned up again by the end of the following year declined from 196 in 1969-70 to 23 in 1973-74.

Finally, the CES project sought to be cost-effective. In this regard, despite start-up costs, the program achieved a substantial net savings over previous years' budgets. Further, if one considers that the direct savings reported did not include the amortized savings of foster care payments that would have been required for children kept in long term foster care, the program achieved substantial long-term savings.

As a result of the success of the CES project, the authors of the study developed training materials to allow for the dissemination of the approaches they used (National Center for Comprehensive Emergency Service to Children, 1976). The CES staff developed a variety of casework approaches to better serve families entering the system. The availability of the training materials facilitated the implementation of the program's achievements beyond Nashville-Davidson county.

There is little doubt that the coordination of services and the implementation of the CES system brought about by the CES program substantially improved the care of neglected and dependent children in Nashville-Davidson county. The question is why this approach—which proved so effective—was not widely adopted and implemented elsewhere.[23] One can only wonder. As Carol Meyer (1984, 499) observed, "The research in child welfare has been prodigious and exemplary... In view of these potential strengths, one might ask why this field, particularly foster care, stays the same no matter what is learned empirically."

The CES program was a precursor to the family preservation services approach. The success of the approach used in the CES program no doubt explains the current interest in family preservation programs. Family preservation is essentially an "emergency services" system with a greater role for child welfare social work professionals.[24] The CES relied on paraprofessional homemakers and caretakers to provide services. Most of the direct services provided to families came from persons with no training in social work. In contrast, family preservation services are usually provided by trained social workers with limited case loads (two or three families receiving intensive services for a two- or three-month period).[25]

The concern with the CES approach was to make sure that children who did not need to enter the foster care system were protected from inappropriate placement. Burt and Bayleat (1978) believed that too many children who did not need to be placed in foster care were entering the system because of the failure to provide emergency services at a time of crisis. They believed that once children entered the system it became more difficult to reverse the process. Efforts had to be taken to ensure that children didn't enter into care in the first place. What is most remarkable about the CES program is its spectacular results. Before the program's implementation 46 percent of the children who came to the attention of child welfare authorities were placed in foster care. After the CES system was implemented the rate of placement dropped to 8 percent, a more than fivefold decrease in the rate of placement. It would be hard to imagine a more dramatic reduction in placement rates.

The major criticism of the CES system was that in the process of reducing the number of children who were inappropriately being placed in foster care, it may have denied services to many children who should have otherwise received services. This same concern is echoed by critics of family preservation services (Wald, Carlsmith, and Leiderman, 1988). As a conse-

---

23. In 1976 the General Accounting Office (GAO) conducted a study of the impact of research supported by the Administration for Children, Youth, and Families (ACYF) on public child welfare agencies. The report found that most of the research had not seemed to influence the policy or practice of the public agencies. When contacted, most of the agencies reported not being familiar with the ACYF funded research. Of particular concern to the GAO was the lack of knowledge regarding the CES project that the ACYF had funded. The GAO called for both (1) increased efforts to involve agency personnel in the research process (through participation in the setting of priorities and the selection of projects for funding) and (2) for the ACYF to make greater efforts to disseminate the results of funded research.

24. Family preservation programs focus on identifying children in imminent need of placement. These are generally families in crisis who might have their children removed if they do not receive needed services to help them through their crisis (Wells and Biegel, 1991).

25. The current popularity of family preservation services is partly explained by the substantial funding and support received from two large private foundations—the Anne E. Casey Foundation and the Edna McConnell Clark Foundation (Adams, 1992).

quence, these children, although denied access to services at first approach, will show up again in a sort of revolving-door phenomenon. To the extent this criticism was true it would show up in recidivism statistics. However, the data collected in follow-up studies indicate that the rate of recidivism actually declined after the implementation of the CES system.

From a methodological perspective, the major drawback of the CES study involves the limitation of a before and after quasi-experimental design. The study did not use a randomized control group design and thus other factors could partly explain the changes observed by the researchers. However, it would be difficult to suggest that the dramatic reduction observed was the result of alternative explanations not controlled by the research design. The results of the Comprehensive Emergency Services indicate the potential achievements possible through the family preservation services approach (if. Nelson et al., 1988).

The Alameda Project

While the Comprehensive Emergency Services system attempted to modify the intake process in order to prevent the inappropriate placement of children in foster care, the Alameda Project focused on the delivery of effective services to the client after entry. The Alameda Project had three major objectives. First, it attempted to increase the continuity of care for children taken into care. Of major concern was the apparent lack of vigorous interest among caseworkers in returning children to their biological family. Too many children, after coming into foster care, were cast adrift. According to project investigators Theodore Stein, Eileen Gambrill, and Kermit Wiltse, three social work researchers at the University of California at Berkeley's School of Social Welfare, the caseworker's primary responsibility was to "gather objective data demonstrating that the initial problems requiring placement have been resolved and that a child may be returned to his or her parents or, in the absence of such resolution, that alternative planning for the child occur" (1978, 77). As we learned from Jenkins and Norman (1972) this was too often not happening.

Coupled with this, the Alameda Project was concerned about the dearth of services to the biological family. The fundamental research in the foster care field by Fanshel, Jenkins, and their colleagues at Columbia University had shown that services (or an absence thereof) to the biological family was crucial in restoring the child to the family (Fanshel and Shinn, 1978, 521-522). In addition, Fanshel's longitudinal research indicated that the best predictor of restoration was the extent of parental visits. Consequently, the Alameda Project placed an emphasis on ensuring parental visits in order to facilitate restoration.

Second, the Alameda Project wished to compare the effectiveness of a systematic case management procedure including behavioral intervention methods, with conventional casework methods (Gambrill and Stein, 1981). Until now, casework had involved limited systematic planning. Many children had failed to have case plans developed. Part of the proposed systematic case management procedure involved using "contracts" with biological parents to encourage the visiting that had proven so important to the eventual restoration of their children. When children came into care, the experimental caseworkers would work with the biological parent to develop a contract that outlined the expectations, procedures and responsibilities of the agency. In addition, the contract would spell out the actions the parent would take in order to have their children reunited with them. This included a visitation schedule as well as other provisions that varied from case to case. The parents realized up front what conditions they must satisfy to have their children returned.

Thus, the strategy of the Alameda Project was to involve the biological parent in the process that would lead to restoration. At the same time, problems in the family that had necessitated the substitute care were identified and became the target of behavioral intervention and change. The primary task of the caseworker was to provide the services the biological parent needed in order to have their child reunited.

Finally, the project design specified that responsibility for each case was to be divided between two social workers: One worker concentrated on problems within the biological family, while the other worker served the child and the foster family. Thus the third objective of the Alameda Project was to assess the value of dividing services among two workers monitoring the success of casework in both areas. Casework has long been viewed as most useful when provided to the biological parent. After all, it was the problems of the parent(s) that led to placement. The child usually only required casework monitoring to ensure that he or she was adjusting to the foster placement and was being properly cared for by the foster family. The task of casework in the Alameda Project was to assist the parent in solving the problems that led to the removal of their children. Although the idea seemed obvious, the emphasis of child welfare services too often concentrated on the child while the parent was left to take care of her or himself.

Quasi Experimental Design. To prepare caseworkers for the experiment, the project staff first underwent training in the use of systematic case management procedures, including the use of behavioral intervention methods (Stein and Gambrill, 1976). The project was then implemented in Alameda County, California, using a quasi experimental design.[26] The sample consisted of children assigned to either the experimental group or the control group. Children in the experimental group would be served by the experimental staff according to the experimental guidelines developed by the project. The control group represented children served in the usual way by workers not associated with the project.

In light of previous studies questioning the effectiveness of casework services, the results of the Alameda Project were impressive. As can be seen in Figure 3.3, at the end of the second year of the project 60 percent of the experimental group children had been restored to their families, compared to only 32 percent of those in the control group. Further, 15 percent of those in the experimental group had been adopted, whereas only 9 percent of those in the control group had been adopted. At the end of the experimental period, 57 percent of the children in the control group remained in long-term foster care, compared to only 21 percent in the experimental group. Clearly, the Alameda Project staff had greater success in achieving their goal of restoring children to their biological homes, or providing them with some sense of permanency—that is, through adoption—than did the conventional foster care program.

For young people entering the substitute care system, the casework management methods developed by the Alameda Project were extremely effective in restoring children to their families. As well, the behavioral intervention methods pioneered in this application to child welfare services represented the application of a promising technology for improving the effective delivery of service by trained workers.

An often overlooked component of the Alameda Project was its quasi-experimental design methodology. If we are to develop an empirical knowledge base in the child welfare field, then wider use of this approach in research and evaluation is critical. It represented a significant advance over the design used in the CES system.

---

26. Quasi-experimental designs allow for conducting an experiment without the standard requirement of random assignment to experimental and control groups. Quasi experimental designs allow for the use of matched control groups for comparions and the use of modified statistical tests that take into account the fact that the experimental and control groups were not randomly assigned (Campbell and Stanley, 1963; Bawden and Sorenstein, 1992).

Figure 3.3 Outcomes of the Alameda Project

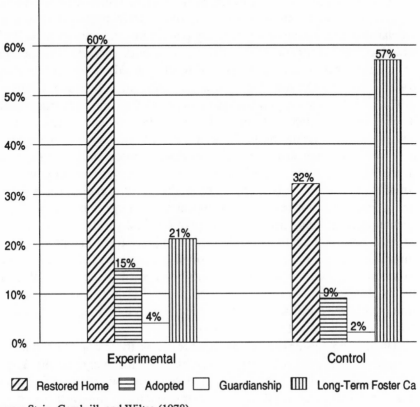

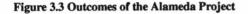

Source: Stein, Gambrill, and Wiltse (1978).

The Alameda Project was not without critics (Firestone-Seghi, 1979). Probably the most important limitation of the study resulted from its departure from pure random assignment. At the beginning cases were volunteered for the groups. These initial cases were supplemented by new cases that were randomly assigned to either the experimental or control group. However, the experimental and control group did differ on important dimensions that need to be considered in assessing the study.[27]

27. One essential difference between the experimental and control groups was that only 6 percent of the experimental group was over twelve years old, while 22 percent of the control group was over twelve. The Oregon Project (Emlen, et al., 1977) indicated that children over twelve were more difficult to place and thus did not include them in their demonstration effort to achieve permanency.

The Oregon Project

Whereas the Comprehensive Emergency Services project examined reform of the intake and entry system and, like family preservation services, emphasized prevention of unnecessary placement, and the Alameda Project examined programmatic changes in the casework services provided once children enter into care, the Oregon Project focused on how children leave foster care. The Oregon Project was a collaboration between Victor Pike (1976, 1977) of the Oregon Children's Services Division and Arthur Emlen, a social work researcher at Portland State University. The project examined strategies for reducing the backlog of children who accumulated in foster care for the relative lack of just such systematic interventions as those used in the Alameda Project. Studies of the foster care system had consistently found that, despite the best efforts of workers and agencies, some families and parents did not respond. An unwarranted large number of children accumulated in long-term foster care. No one had yet developed a strategy to either restore them to their families, or to place them in a permanent setting. The children too often simply drifted in long term foster care for years experiencing multiple placements and being denied the sense of permanency children find in their own home. Instead of just lamenting the situation of children adrift in the foster care system, Victor Pike urged concerted effort to end the plight of these children.

Underlying the desire for permanency was the recognition that long-term foster care was undesirable, even harmful, for many reasons. First, as the work by Bowlby (1958, 1969), and later Harlow (1958, 1961) pointed out, the denial of parental love and compassion can diminish the capacity for these qualities in children raised in foster care. Second, foster care had never been regarded as a therapeutic modality, only a temporary way of getting the children out of harm's way. That the family problems that had initiated it remained unresolved was a telling comment upon the effectiveness of the practice methods used by the child welfare system (Knitzer, Allen, and McGowan, 1978). Third, children were not necessarily safer in foster care. In fact, studies have suggested that foster care is often more dangerous than the family the child is removed from (Bolton, Laner, and Gai, 1981; Pryor, 1991; Spencer and Knudsen, 1992). Finally long-term foster care was expensive. Cost to the state of maintaining a child in long-term foster care is approximately $15,000 per year (Fanshel and Shinn, 1972; Forsythe, 1992). In this regard, the study came to be of particular interest to legislators, who were eager to find ways to reduce costs, while also improving the child welfare system.

Faced with more than 4,400 children in foster care in Oregon, the project staff initiated a study of the barriers to "permanency planning." They developed strategies designed to place the child permanently, either with the biological family or with an adoptive family. Faced with a "backlog of children whose status in foster care was indeterminate, drifting, and vague, [the project focused] sharply on the goal of achieving an alternative to foster care that had greater prospects for permanence." (Emlen et al., 1977, 1)

An initial study by Emlen in 1976 had identified the absence of an organized and coordinated effort to get children out of care as being the major problem to permanent placement: "The foster care system does tend to favor the maintenance of relationships in foster care, and the use of foster care itself as a treatment or care setting, rather than the planning necessary to secure the child's future in a family...Indecisiveness and deeply ingrained attitudes favor the maintenance of placement in foster care. A strong commitment from caseworkers and all levels of the state agency, as well as from other institutions and society at large, is needed to change the character of foster care practice." (Emlen et al., 1977, 44)

Following this lead, the Oregon Project staff designed a procedure for screening the children currently in care to identify those who appeared likely candidates for long-term placement. The goal was, by concerted effort, to establish a permanent placement for these children rather than allowing them to drift in care. The screening criteria posed four questions that, based upon previous experience, would likely identify children headed for long-term care.

- Had the child been in care more than one year? If so, the child was likely to be headed for long-term foster care unless something was done. The average length of time for children in foster care was more than twenty-nine months. Research had indicated that with each subsequent year in foster care, a child's probability of leaving diminished (Fanshel, 1971; Goerge, 1990; Maas and Engler, 1959). Half of the children selected by the screening process had been in foster care for more than two years before the project began (mean time in care equaled twenty-nine months). Most of the children had experienced multiple placements: 33 percent had one placement, 30 percent had two placements, and 37 percent had three or more placements.

- Was the child unlikely to return home? Did difficult, unresolved problems still remain with the biological family which would indicate that the child was likely to continue in care?

- Was the child adoptable? One of the purposes of this project was to identify those children who were adoptable or who would be returned home.
  In this sense, the project focused on those most likely to benefit from
  permanency planning efforts.
- Was the child less than twelve years old? The project focused on children under twelve because they were considered the most readily adoptable.

Terminating Parental Rights

With some parents the issue of restoring their children too often culminated
in a dead end. As we have seen, many biological parents received, except in
the case of the Alameda Project, few services. However, even when services
were provided some parents showed little interest in having their children
returned. What could the caseworker do when the parent(s) did not want to
cooperate in devising ways that would allow their children to return home?
Was there a limit on the efforts to be made by the caseworker?

To provide caseworkers with the tools necessary to achieve permanent
placements for children, the Oregon Project developed procedures that
would free children for adoption when their parents showed a marked lack
of interest in having them restored Pierce, 1982). One of the most important
was the right of the caseworker to petition to terminate parental rights. Historically, termination of parental rights had been viewed as a last resort that
should be invoked only under the most extreme circumstances. As Hewitt
(1983, 229) observed:

> Termination proceedings are among the most dramatic actions the state can
> take against its citizens. A termination of parental rights is the ultimate legal
> infringement on the family... There are few state-imposed deprivations
> more unyielding and personal than the permanent and irrevocable loss of
> one's children. Termination of parental rights is even more severe than a
> criminal sanction. Only the death penalty is a more severe intrusion into per-
> sonal liberty.

Prior to the implementation of the Oregon Project, some legislative
groundwork for the Termination of Parental Rights (TPR) had been established. The guidelines establishing the circumstances required to prepare a
TPR petition included:

- If a parent who had abandoned the child could not be contacted after searching strenuously for six months, or
- If the parent had deserted the child for more than one year and could not be found, or
- If after deserting a child for more than a year, if the parent is found, it would be necessary to determine if placement with the child would be detrimental to the child, or
- If the parent suffers a condition that is seriously detrimental to the child and is not remediable, or
- If a parent with no diagnosable condition continually fails to perform minimally to work toward change that would lead to the restoration of the child.

To put teeth into the warnings by the child welfare caseworkers that they would take decisive action on behalf of the child if parent(s) did not demonstrate a sincere commitment to working for conditions in which the child might return home, the Project staff worked to strengthen and clarify the termination of parental rights statutes. Termination had long been a neglected area of child welfare. The law surrounding termination had been the principle domain of the legal community. Child welfare caseworkers only rarely called upon termination proceedings for the most severe cases of abuse or circumstances involving felony behavior on the part of parents (i.e., drug trafficking, serious sexual assault, severe physical harm, etc.).

Like the Alameda Project, the Oregon Project staff developed a training program and materials to aid the project social workers (Downs and Taylor, 1978; Pike and Downs, 1977; Regional Research Institute for Human Services, 1978). The training focused on what rules and procedures might best get children out of long-term care and into permanent placement. In a way, the project staff represented a special "strike force" given the task of finding permanent placements for the backlog of children in the foster care system. Their major new weapon was the threat of termination of parental rights if the parents did not cooperate.

How successful was the Oregon Project? During a three-year period beginning in November of 1973 the staff worked with 509 children selected using the screening procedure to identify those likely to drift in care from the 2,283 children in foster care. By October 31, 1976, permanent plans had been implemented for 72 percent of these children (see Table 3.1). Twenty-seven percent had been restored to their biological family. A surprising 52

Table 3.1 Results of the Oregon Project

	Plan Implemented	In Progress	Total	(%)
Restoration	131	5	136	(27)
Adoption				
by foster parents	96	63		
by new parents	88	20		
	----	----		
	184	83	267	(52)
Contractual foster care	37	3	40	(8)
Relatives	15	1	16	(3)
Plan not successful			50	(10)

	367	92	509	

Source: Emlen et al., 1977, from Table 1.1, p. 5.

percent were freed for adoption and either had been adopted or were in the process of being adopted. This represented an unheard of level of success in freeing children for adoption. Overall, 90 percent of the children in the Oregon Project either had plans for permanency implemented or the plans were in progress. Clearly, the backlog of children in the foster care system was being shifted out of temporary care into a permanent setting.

Although the Oregon Project did not have a comparison or control group, it was evident that the progress achieved was greater than would otherwise have been achieved using normal procedures. When compared to children in other nonexperimental counties, the Oregon Project children were more rapidly and frequently placed in permanent settings. In counties where the project was implemented, the average daily population of children in foster care dropped by 31 percent, compared to only a 4 percent reduction in nonproject counties. Most of the drop was attributed to the success of putting children in permanent placements.

Although the Oregon Project did not have a comparison or control group, it was evident that the progress achieved was greater than would otherwise have been achieved using normal procedures. When compared to children in other nonexperimental counties, the Oregon Project children were more rapidly and frequently placed in permanent settings. In counties where the project was implemented, the average daily population of children in foster care dropped by 31 percent, compared to only a 4 percent reduction in nonproject counties. Most of the drop was attributed to the success of placing children in permanent placements.

In addition to providing children with a sense of permanency, the Oregon Project resulted in considerable financial savings. A cost analysis estimated that the project saved more than a million dollars in foster care payments alone (even without amortizing the expected care payments of the project cases over their projected career in foster care). It is important to note that although initially the project was not cost effective, "the cumulative savings from decreased payments overtook the cumulative expenses of operating the Project in January, 1977" (Emlen et al., 1977, 89).

Conceptual Base for Reform

Overall, the Comprehensive Emergency Services Program (Nashville), the Alameda Project, and the Oregon Project showed that comprehensive improvements to the child welfare services system could be achieved (Lindsey, 1982). Further they provided a clear picture of what kinds of achievable reforms were necessary. Emergency services were needed to divert inappropriate cases from substitute care to appropriate emergency services or to prevent inappropriate placements. For children appropriately placed in foster care, the delivery system had to ensure that they be restored to their homes as soon as possible. Consequently, efforts to achieve restoration had to be the central concern of child welfare caseworkers. And finally, for those children who remained in foster care for more than a year and who seemed likely to continue in foster care for a long period, case workers trained in systematic case management procedures needed to take decisive action either to restore the children to their biological family or to find an appropriate permanent alternative.[28]

---

28. As a result of the success of these three demonstration program, training materials were developed to facilitate dissemination of these successful strategies to child welfare professionals (National Center for Comprehensive Emergency Service to Children, 1976; Regional Research Institute for Human Services, 1978; Stein and Gambrill, 1976). The National Institute for Advanced Studies assembled a comprehensive syllabus for these programs and other important studies (Children's Bureau, 1980; cf. Cohen and Westhues, 1990).

With the results of these demonstration programs the child welfare field had developed the technology to permit a substantial reduction of the number of children in foster care. The CES system produced a fivefold decrease in the rate of foster care placements. The Alameda Project was able to achieve a rate of restoring children to their biological parents within the first year almost twice as high as the rate achieved by an equivalent control group (60% versus 32%). The Oregon Project, working with children who had been in foster care for more than one year and who seemed likely to remain in care for years to come, was able to find permanent placements for almost 80 percent of these children within three years (with 27% reunited and 52% adopted). The stage was set for major child welfare reform. In combination the reforms could achieve a substantial reduction in the number of children entering care. They would quickly return home those fewer children who did enter care by providing services to the biological parent. And they would ensure that children who remained in care after one year would have permanent plans for their care implemented. By conservative estimate the cumulative impact of these reforms could likely reduce the number of children in foster care by more than 90 percent. The result would not deny needed services to any child but would ensure appropriate and effective service delivery informed by the scientific research.

Permanency Planning

The single unifying theme among the demonstration projects was the concept of permanency planning, which postulated the importance that foster care be temporary and that children either be returned to their biological family, or placed in adoption, as soon as possible. No longer should children enter foster care inappropriately, drift in care once they had entered, and remain in care for years on end with little effort made to restore them.

If a child was unlikely to be restored to his or her biological parent, permanency planning required that a concerted effort be made to find the child a permanent home. Systematic case management (scientific casework) for the child should work toward either restoration with the biological family or termination of parental rights, thus freeing the child for adoption. The child should not be allowed to drift in foster care (Rowe and Lambert, 1973). Clearly the children in the Fanshel and Shinn (1978) study who had been in foster care for more than five years had been essentially abandoned by their biological parents needed a more permanent solution.

Further, foster care was not a treatment modality. It did not provide a cure to children. The goal of foster care, as expressed by Jenkins (1974, 4) "is not upward mobility for the lower-class child, but typically the return of the child to the same milieu from which he [or she] came." It was, as the Alameda Project so eloquently demonstrated, only an adjunct service the caseworker could use to assist the parent with problems that prevented her from inadequately providing for her child. The caseworkers' objective, as delineated in the Alameda Project, was to achieve reunification. If this could not be achieved, the child should be freed for adoption. The Oregon Project had shown how this could happen.

Overall, the demonstration projects had shown that if the objectives of foster care were clear, the system could meet those objectives in an effective fashion. The studies demonstrated the potential of child welfare professionals to use research-based knowledge to achieve more effective social service programs. The projects indicated that substantial advance in science is spurred when measurable utility can be derived. In this regard, child welfare may well be at the forefront in demonstrating the usefulness of empirical knowledge from the social and behavioral sciences. Finally, the projects provided direction for comprehensive program reform of the foster care system at a national level.

The Adoption Assistance and Child Welfare Act (PL 92-272)

Following the success of the demonstration projects, child welfare professionals were for a time hopeful and expectant that fundamental reform guided by scientific research was not only possible but imminent. And with reform would come decreased numbers of children in foster care. In fact, the demonstration programs ushered in major federal child welfare legislation, particularly the *Adoption Assistance and Child Welfare Act* (PL 96-272) passed by the U. S. Congress in 1980 (Administration for Children, Youth, and Families, 1984). This act implemented the concept of permanency planning, providing federal funding to the states to support efforts to restore children to their biological parents or to free them for adoption using legal efforts to terminate parental rights. Research demonstrating how these efforts could be achieved had been published and was widely available. The permanency planning legislation required that states, through periodic review, demonstrate what efforts were being taken to reduce the number of children lingering in foster care. The legislation provided additional funding to facilitate these efforts.

Unfortunately, the actual funds to achieve these reforms were never provided (see Kamerman and Kahn, 1990).[29] Under the Reagan Administration, the 1980s were characterized by broad scale reductions in federal spending for social programs in the United States. Child welfare services saw a virtual end to support for major demonstration programs, even though these represented a proven technology to facilitate permanency planning and reduce the number of children in foster care. Following a brief decline, the number of children in foster care rose again. In 1977 the number of children in foster care in the United States was estimated at more than 500,000. Two years after the passage of the *Adoption Assistance and Child Welfare Act* the number of children in foster care had dropped to 262,000. However, beginning in 1982, the number of children in foster care had leveled off and begun to increase. It is estimated that by 1995, the number of children in foster care will again exceed 500,000 (see Figure 3.4).

The lack of vigorous federal support for "permanency planning" was by itself probably not sufficient to derail efforts to reform the child welfare system. Other forces emerged that would prove decisive. Beginning as early as the late forties, while social workers were attending to the problems of children in foster care, fundamental societal changes had begun occurring that were to shift the ground upon which the traditional approach to child welfare services rested. Even as Kadushin was codifying the traditional definition of child welfare as a "helping" institution indicating how it should function, and what it must strive to accomplish (within a residual framework), and even as the demonstration programs struggled to institute reforms that would allow child welfare to better fit that definition, the traditional approach was, almost without anyone noticing, being weakened by forces outside of its control. First, social forces were affecting the family that the traditional approach was unable to address. These social changes required structural change that were outside the residual and casework perspective of the traditional approach. They invoked a paradigm shift.[30] These changes are explored in detail in Chapter 4.

---

29. With the passage of the *Adoption Assistance and Child Welfare Act* in 1980, child welfare funding to provide for permanency planning was, according to Kamerman and Kahn (1990, 33), "to increase gradually from approximately $3 billion in fiscal year 1981 to approximately $3.7 billion in fiscal year 1985. Instead, by 1985 the combined funding was less than in 1981-$2.8 billion. In contrast to the expectations for implementing the 1980 reforms, in 1981 Title XX funds were cut from $3 billion to $2.4 billion and so service plans for children and families are not implemented and directives from judicial and other external reviews are not followed." Permanency planning legislation provided "a new philosophy and a service framework. The federal government did not, however, provide the resources on which all else was premised" (Kamerman and Kahn, 1990, 9).

Figure 3.4 Foster Care Population in the United States, 1972-1995

Children in Substitute Care

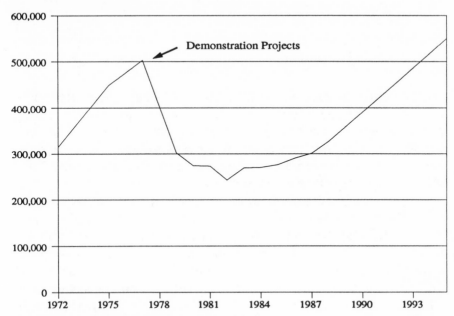

Note: Data for several years are interpolated.
Source: Tatara (1993); Pelton (1989).

---

30. The principle organizing framework for knowledge development in a field is termed a paradigm. It is used to define the domain of a field, suggest productive lines of inquiry, and indicate acceptable methods of analysis and research. Thomas Kuhn has examined the development of knowledge in several scientific fields and proposed that progress is determined, in large part, by the adequacy of their paradigms. Kuhn observed that often progress in scientific fields would be stalled by defunct paradigms that waited to be overturned. However, overturning the obsolete paradigm often required what amounted to a revolution in the scientific field. This is because a paradigm includes the fundamental assumptions which guide inquiry. As Kuhn (1962, 37) writes, "One of the things a scientific community acquires with a paradigm is a criterion for choosing problems that, while the paradigm is taken for granted, can be assumed to have solutions. To a great extent these are the only problems that the community will admit as scientific or encourage its members to undertake. Other problems, including many that had previously been standard, are rejected as metaphysical, as the concern of another discipline, or sometimes as just too problematic to be worth the time. A paradigm can, for that matter, even insulate the community from those socially important problems that are not reducible to the puzzle form, because they cannot be stated in the terms of the conceptual and instrumental tools the paradigm supplies." In a funadamental sense, the residual model is the paradigm which guides thinking and understanding in the child welfare field. The shift to protective services from the traditional approach was more a transformation of services than a paradigm shift.

Second, the rediscovery of child abuse and the passage of mandatory child abuse reporting legislation would lead to the transformation of the weakened and increasingly insufficient efforts of the traditional approach. These changes are the concern of Chapter 5.

Summary and Conclusion

Building upon the basic research of Maas and Engler, Fanshel, Jenkins, Bowlby, Harlow, and others, several demonstration programs that became part of the larger permanency planning movement were developed to limit the number of children getting into foster care, to speed the return of the child to the parents once admitted for care, and to reduce the number of children lingering in long-term foster care.

The success of these demonstration projects led to the widespread success of the permanency planning movement both in North America (Emlen et al., 1977, 118; Kendrick, 1990, 22) and throughout the world. Permanency planning postulated the importance of making foster care temporary and finding a permanent setting for the child. The success of these research projects led to the passage of major public policy reform (Adoption Assistance and Child Welfare Act of 1980; Barth and Berry, 1987). At the beginning of the 1980s the stage was set for comprehensive reform of the public child welfare system. Unfortunately, child welfare lacked a mechanism (either in the form of a free market or effective review procedures) to sustain and reward efforts to reduce the number of children entering the foster care system. After several years of success in reducing the number of children entering and remaining in foster care, the number children entering care stabilized and now has begun rising above pre-permanency planning movement levels.

Further, while the traditional approach was being enhanced by the permanency planning movement, other social changes were occurring that would undermine the traditional approach. In the next chapters we examine these changes.

4

The Changing Social Portrait
of Families

I must confess to you today that not long after talking about the dream, I started seeing it turn into a nightmare as I moved through the ghettos of the nation and saw my black brothers and sisters perishing on a lonely island of poverty in the midst of a vast ocean of material prosperity.

Martin Luther King, Jr., *Why We Can't Wait*

In a recent address to a conference on children's needs, a United States senator admitted he knew nothing about the subject [child care] and would have felt more comfortable discussing energy. Policy makers are simply not accustomed to thinking about children's needs in the same ways they think about missile development, dam construction, or even old-age assistance.

Hillary Rodham, "Children's Policies"

The traditional approach to child welfare located the problems of clients in the parent/child relationship (Kadushin and Martin, 1988). Hagan (1957) wrote: "Child welfare in social work deals with the problems of the child that result when the needs which parents are ordinarily expected to meet are either unmet or inadequately met." This traditional approach was developed at a time when the economy was expanding, the divorce rate was low, and children born out-of-wedlock were rare. However, broad social changes, which began just as the traditional approach was taking hold, began impacting families and created new problems that had little to do with the parent/child relationship, problems that were not amenable to being solved through the traditional child welfare approach.

During the fifties, sixties, and seventies, the typical nuclear family was portrayed in the popular media as a Norman Rockwell vision of four people—a mother, father, and two children—living comfortably in a modest suburban home. The father, who headed the household, worked eight to five in a white collar job, while the mother stayed home to raise the children.

The family ate together every evening and went to church on Sundays. Family aspirations included continued promotions for dad, a college education for the kids, and eventually retirement and grandchildren. Family problems centered around which youngster should cut the lawn, or use the family car on weekends. The economy was experiencing a long term upward trend. Real wages were rising. Society was perceived as moving inevitably through ever more wondrous technological innovations and home improvements toward a kind of utopia. Television, just then emerging as the dominant media, romanticized this ideal in such early shows as "Leave it to Beaver," "Father Knows Best," and "The Nelson Family." But even as families in North America were staring fondly at this image, the everyday reality was undergoing major changes.[31]

In fact, the changes had started years before during World War II, when women had come out of the parlors and kitchens to work in the defense plants building the planes, tanks, and munitions used by their husbands and sons to battle a bitter enemy. Between 1942 and 1945 almost five million women left the confines of their home for work in the factories and defense plants. Seventy percent of the new jobs had actually been "men's" work and the women taking them were paid the same wages that had previously been reserved for men (Polakow, 1993, 38). It was a new experience for women, who became pipefitters, welders, machinists, painters, carpenters, die cutters, plumbers—all the working roles that for generations had been held by men. In 1945, when victory brought the men back to reclaim their former positions of employment, women were thanked for their efforts and shunted back into the home to become mothers again. The substantial federal government child care subsidies which women enjoyed during the war were also ended. As Tobin, Wu, and Davidson (1989, 219) observed, "The full-time mother enjoyed her greatest popularity in America in the 1950s, an era in which large numbers of men returning from the war and needing jobs pressured society to endorse an ideology that would justify the expulsion of women from the work force."

For many women, however, the war experience had shattered the old conventional roles. They had tasted the independence, opportunity, and sense of achievement that working in the labor market afforded, and many

---

31. In 1961, 65 percent of Canadian families were characterized by a husband who went to work and a wife who stayed at home. In 1994, this traditional family structure represented 12 percent of all families. Further, by 1994 more than 70 percent of all Canadian children under six were in non-parental care arrangements on a regular basis (Rusk, 1994).

Figure 4.1 Percentage of U.S. Mothers with Children Under Age Six in Labor Force, 1950-1993

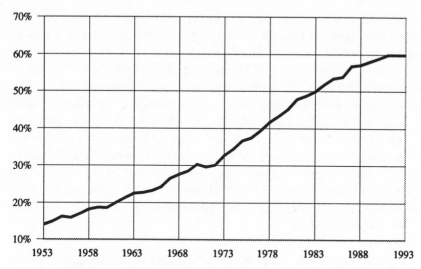

Source: Children's Defense Fund (1994); Maxwell (1990).

liked it (Kessler-Harris, 1982). Many women realized that, given the chance, they could succeed in whatever job they chose as well or better than a man. In the next decades women began entering the labor market in increasing numbers, many choosing to work even when they had children. In 1950 only 10 percent of mothers with children under six worked outside the home (Figure 4.1). By 1960 the numbers had increased to 20 percent, by 1970 to more than 30 percent, and by 1993 to 60 percent. By 1992 more than half of all mothers with infants less than one year old were employed outside the home.

The continuing entry of women, especially those with children, into the labor force, raised troubling questions: What will happen to the family with mothers working? Who will cook? Keep house? Wash, dress, and feed the children? On their face, the questions seemed straightforward and innocent, but underneath they spoke to social developments that were exceedingly complex, and held disruptive and ultimately decisive implications for family social structure—and for the traditional approach to child welfare which attempted to safeguard that structure. Forty years later the questions are still being asked, although many of the answers have already materialized, producing a family portrait decidedly different from early years.

Equitable Distribution of Household Chores

To confound this situation, parents, in the nearly four decades that these changes have been taking place, have largely failed to establish a new and equitable equilibrium in their family responsibilities. A 1985 survey by the Family Services Association of Toronto found that when both husband and wife worked full-time, the wife did twice as much housework as the husband and three times as much child care (Conway, 1990, 103). Hotschild and Machung (1989) conducted a longitudinal study of the sharing of domestic chores among two career families in the United States and found a similar pattern. Calasanti and Bailey (1991), examining the division of household tasks among working couples, found that in the United States women performed between 73 and 84 percent of all domestic labor. The issue of who is responsible for what household chores remains an area of conflict in many families.

Children Unsupervised. For child welfare one of the changes of particular concern is that with women working and child care difficult to find, many children have been left virtually unsupervised. The U.S. Census Bureau has estimated that approximately 2.1 million children under thirteen are left without adult supervision both before and after school (the so-called "latch-key children"). Pryor (1991) has observed that "child left unattended" is the major reason children are reported for child abuse in New York. In Canada, with approximately one tenth as many children, an estimated 360,000 children are regularly left without supervision by working parents both before and after school (Conway, 1990, 49). Many of these children have taken responsibility for managing household responsibilities. Market research in Canada found that 37 percent of children between the ages of six and eleven shop for the family or perform household chores before dinner, while 13 percent of children between ages six and fifteen make dinner for themselves most of the time, and 8 percent make dinner for the family (Mandell, 1988).

Divorce and Unwed Motherhood:
Two Paths to Becoming a Lone-Parent

Accompanying the entrance of women into the workforce have been other social developments that have further altered the family social equation. One

Figure 4.2 Number of Divorces and Children Involved, United States, 1950-1992

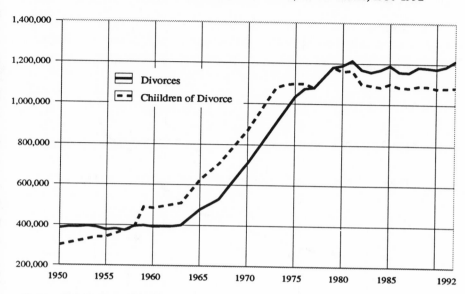

Source: U.S. Bureau of the Census.

is the rapid rise in the divorce rate during the mid 1960s, shortly after the widespread use of the birth control pill; the other is the steadily increasing number of children born to young women out of wedlock. Both have given rise to the social phenomenon of the lone-parent,[32] responsible for raising children by herself.

Between 1960 and 1992 the number of divorces in the United States tripled, from approximately 400,000 to more than 1,200,000 a year (see Figure 4.2). Almost one half of all marriages currently end in divorce. Moreover, in the last twenty-five years the number of children involved in divorce has tripled, although the overall child population has remained stable (Figure 4.2). In Canada there has been a sixfold increase in the divorce rate during the 25 year period from 1961 to 1986 (Adams, 1988).

---

32. The term "lone-parent" is widely used in Canada instead of the conventional term "single parent" popular in the United States. The rationale for using "lone-parent" stems from the fact that children are conceived by two parents. Single parent implies a status that is selected by the role occupant because of the freedom of relationships it permits. However, most lone-parents are simply parents who have taken responsibility to raise their children even when the other parent has departed. Thus, they are lone-parents. The child's other parent still has child care and child support responsibilities which are not relinquished to a single parent.

Figure 4.3 Annual Births to Unmarried Women, United States, 1950-1991

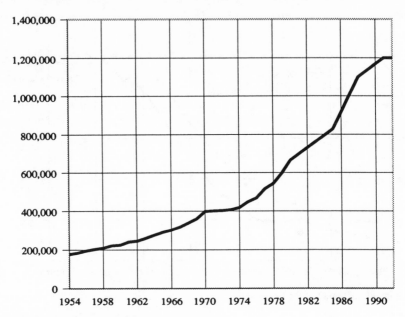

Note: Data for 1955, 1989, and 1990 are interpolated.
Source: Zill and Rogers (1988, 40); Murray (1993).

As for unmarried mothers, from 1950 to 1991 the number of children born out-of-wedlock in the United States increased from 142,000 to more than 1,200,000 per year (see Figure 4.3). The problem is particularly severe for teenagers (Bane and Jargowsky, 1988; Zill and Rogers, 1988). In 1985, more than 600,000 unmarried teenagers became pregnant in the United States.

The consequence of both the rising divorce rate and increased rate of children born out-of-wedlock has been a sharp increase in the number of lone-parent households, increasing from 2.8 million in 1960 to more than nine million in 1990, of which only 16 percent are headed by fathers. The percentage of children who lived with a never married mother was 4.2 percent in 1960; by 1970 the percent increased to 6.8 percent; and by 1980 to 14.6 percent. By 1990 more than 30 percent of all children lived with a never married parent (World Almanac, 1991, 944). The percentage of lone-mother families more than tripled since 1950. The rise in lone-mother families has been particularly steep for African-Americans and has now become the predominant family arrangement (see Figure 4.4).

Figure 4.4 Percentage of Lone-Mother Families in the United States, 1940-1991

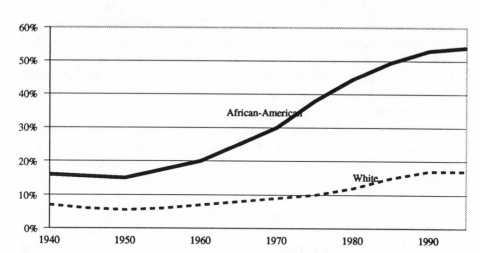

Source: McLanahan and Garfinkel (1993); U.S. Bureau of the Census.

Poverty: The Consequence of Being a Lone-Parent

Along with the rise in lone-parent families has come an increase in poverty rates. Lone-parents, the vast majority of whom are women, are almost always obliged to find work outside the home. To support their family they must shoulder the burden of two jobs—homemaker and employee outside the home (Armstrong and Armstrong, 1984). As they have attempted to do this, their economic situation has inevitably declined.

While it might be expected that after divorce, child support payments and alimony would equalize economic conditions for both father and mother, the actual consequence has been a downward economic plunge for the mother and children (whose care invariably falls to the mother), matched with improved economic circumstances for the father. Examining the economic situation of families after a divorce, Weitzman (1985, xii) found that the mother and children experienced a 73 percent decline in their standard of living, while the father's standard of living increased by 42 percent. Espenshade (1979, 623) has observed that following divorce, "In general, wives are left worse off than their former husbands. Not only are they usually the ones awarded custody of the children without commensurate financial help from fathers, but they generally face other impediments in the labor market to higher pay and adequate employment opportunities."

Examining the longitudinal data from the *Panel Study of Income Dynamics*, Duncan and Hoffman (1985) reported that one year after divorce, men see their income decline on average from $25,403 to $21,488, while the parent with the children (usually the mother) observes a decline from $23,213 to $13,822. Five years after the divorce the income for men was, on average, greater than before the divorce. For women, restoration to predivorce income almost always required remarriage. Women who did not remarry five years later averaged $15,178, compared to $22,871 for women who remarried. Further, Duncan and Hoffman (1985) observed that this occurred even though the percentage of women who worked more than 1,000 hours per year increased from 51 percent before the divorce to more than 73 percent after.

The declining support from income transfer programs such as AFDC and social assistance has exacerbated the problem. Too often, current income assistance programs have proven a trap for lone-parents. Eligibility and levels of support for AFDC have been tied, not to care and provision of children, but to labor force participation by the lone-parent outside the home. Consequently, lone-parents have faced a situation where program eligibility requirements have failed to make it cost-effective for them to leave public assistance. McLanahan and Garfinkel (1993, 23) observe that "single mothers with low earnings capacity in the U.S. are forced to choose between working full time, living at the poverty line and having no time for their children, or not working, living below the poverty line, and having time with their children."

The Feminization of Poverty: During the last several decades, while the work load carried by men has been decreasing, the work load for women has increased substantially. Besides greatly increasing their participation in the labor market, women continue to carry primary responsibility for childrearing and household chores. One would expect that as women worked longer their overall economic situation would improve. However, as women have taken on substantial new burdens, their economic situation has, in fact, deteriorated. In 1987, the median income of all two-parent families in the United States was $35,423, while that of families headed by a lone-mother was only $9,838. In Canada, the median income for a male head of household was 40,984 Canadian dollars, while for a female it was $21,415 (Hiller, 1991, 83).

This economic decline is not surprising. With only one potential wage earner, lone-mothers with children face major barriers to earning adequate income. Two-thirds of working women are secretaries or sales clerks, traditionally low paying jobs (Faludi, 1991).[33] In Canada, the two leading occupations for women in 1988 were clerical and sales (Statistics Canada, 1987). In 1985, Statistics Canada reported that a woman with a postsecondary degree (other than a university degree) earned $2,466 less than a man with less than a ninth-grade education. For those with a university degree, the typical man earned about $12,000 a year more than a woman (Statistics Canada, 1985). Overall, it has been estimated that in 1900, full-time working women earned 60 percent of the amount earned by men (Phillips and Phillips, 1983). In 1967, Statistics Canada reported that a woman working full time made about 58 percent of that earned by a man. By 1987, the percent had increased to 66 percent (Conway, 1990, 108).

This development has little to do with women's commitment to work, since both relative to men and overall, women are working more. Rather, the feminization of poverty is a product of policies and programs that have failed to provide for child care needs of women, protect their economic security, and ensure their equitable treatment in the labor market.

The result is that today lone-mothers and their children constitute the largest social group afflicted by poverty in both the United States and Canada. Currently, almost 60 percent of all households headed by lone-mothers in both the United States and Canada (66%) have income below the poverty line (National Council on Welfare, 1993, 20, table 14). Lone-mothers face enormous demands with almost no community or government support. In the United States their economic situation has led to more than one fifth of all children growing up in poverty. In Canada, as Eichler (1988, 404) observes, "A fifth of Canadian children are growing up in poverty—a truly obscene figure considering the fact that Canada ranks among the countries with the highest per capita income in the world."

The Responsibility of Fathers: Where are the fathers in this picture, who at the very least, should be expected to provide child support? Because child support collection in both the United States and Canada is a civil matter, responsibility for collecting it has fallen to the lone-mother. However, the courts have proven an ineffective tool for mothers to use in enforcing child support. Overall fathers have found the legal system, with all of its safeguards and protections, an easy enforcement mechanism to sidestep.[34] Since child support collection lacks reciprocity (that is, the mothers have

33. Conversely, less than 0.5 percent of top corporate managers are women (Faludi, 1991).

nothing to withhold from the nonpaying father), the consequences for fathers who avoid payment have been insignificant. If the father pays, it is more out of moral obligation than any legal coercion. Consequently, most mothers and their children have ended up going without child support, and either make do with less or work harder to make up the difference. Once in sole charge of the children, most mothers uphold their child care responsibilities, not for fear of being reported for child abuse and neglect, but because they love their children—a love that has sustained the species.

The situation for unwed mothers is even more difficult. Those women who elect not to terminate an unplanned pregnancy or give up the child for adoption assume an eighteen-year burden of raising the child on their own. Although a father has obviously been involved, before he can be compelled to pay child support, paternity must be established. Census studies have indicated that fewer than one in eight unwed fathers pay child support (Hacker, 1992, 88). For an unwed, uneducated teenage mother, the task of providing proper child care, maintaining a household, and working full-time in a job market that provides reduced opportunities for women is difficult to say the least.

Limits of the Residual Approach to Child Welfare

> In contemporary science fiction... many stories deal with desperate attempts to understand a world in which everything seems commonplace but some simple assumption is unstated... Interplanetary wars are fought until some child stumbles on the key. The situation in child welfare is not dissimilar. There are many problems and choices we understand; for better or worse, we are responsible for them. But [the residual approach] is laid on us by a history that may no longer be functional; it is maintained by its own tendency to perpetuate itself; one the whole we have not even known we were making a choice. Unfortunately, [the residual approach] means war, and the losers are always the same—children and the poor.
>
> Alvin Schorr, *Children and Decent People*

---

34. The Canadian Advisory Council on the Status of Women reported that 50 to 85 percent of divorced husbands and fathers default on child support payments (Conway, 1990, 125). The National Council on Welfare (1988) found that between 1987 and 1989 over 16,000 mothers and their children in Ontario received welfare as a result of support payment defaults. In 1989, only about 26 percent of court ordered child support payments in Ontario were complied with.

The traditional residual approach to child welfare focuses on the problems in the parent/child relationship and the provision of services to ameliorate those problems (Kadushin and Martin, 1988). However, the broad social changes that affected families, especially those served by the public child welfare system, had little to do with that relationship. Further, the problems created by these major social changes are not amenable to solution through the residual perspective. The main service provided by the residual child welfare system is foster care (Godfrey and Schlesinger, 1965). Yet, the provision of foster care doesn't address the problems women face as a result of their increased entry into the labor market. The residual approach doesn't address the problem of the increased divorce rate or the rise in single parent families (Longfellow, 1979). The residual approach simply provides a system to respond to the most egregious problems which result from these trends. The residual child welfare system provides a form of soft police who monitor, through the use of the child abuse reporting systems, the actions of poor mothers (or as Pelton (1989) asserts, the poorest of the poor) and removes children when failure to provide proper child care reaches an unspecified threshold for intervention. The residual approach doesn't provide for developing policies and programs that would prevent these egregious problems from occurring in the first place.

The residual perspective doesn't speak to the issues of the feminization of poverty or child poverty. Nor have social programs been developed that take proper consideration of the circumstances of lone-mothers. Eichler (1988, 404) has observed, "In Canada, mothers are economically penalized for giving birth, fathers are largely precluded from caring for the children full-time at any point in time, and the [residual system] as a whole has in no way adequately responded to the dramatic effects of a labour force participation of wives and mothers which has by now become the norm."

In North America children's programs have, at the federal level, historically suffered from benign neglect.[35] With the increasing number of women entering the labor force and thus unable to remain at home and care for their children, combined with the demand that lone-mothers enter the labor market, it is astonishing that greater attention has not been given to providing universal child care. It is an obvious policy need that has remained unaddressed since the 1950s. Women have been largely absent from the halls of legislatures, and their exclusion has not been without consequence. Family policy has relied on the concerns of predominantly male legislatures that have historically shown little interest in this area.[36]

Although the needs of children are frequently recognized, child policy has been limited to reforms of the residual system, usually after a tragic incident compels public concern. The traditional approach retains its hold even though the assumptions about family on which it is based have collapsed (Meissner, 1975). As Polakow (1993, 23) observes, "While families have changed in profound ways, particular myths of the family and consequently of motherhood have endured, myths that have placed mother in a specific domestic and social space in relation to husband, children and the state." The tenacious hold of these mythical views of the family have restricted progress toward solutions, especially in the area of child care.

The Child Care Example

Nowhere is neglect for children's issues more clearly demonstrated than in the area of child care—responsible, cost-effective care and supervision provided to preschool children so that their mothers can work. As we have

35. As an example, the provisions of maternity leave programs of European democracies allow mothers to maintain their jobs while bearing children (Conway, 1990; Eichler, 1988; Kamerman and Kahn, 1978). West Germany allows mothers six months at full pay. Sweden has a "parenthood insurance" program that provides twelve months at 90 percent pay (Liljestrom, 1978). Italy provides five months at 80 percent pay. Norway provides every working woman an eighteen-week leave at 90 percent pay (Henriksen and Holter, 1978). In Canada, women are entitled to eighteen weeks unpaid maternity leave. Unemployment insurance (UIC) guarantees women in Canada a compensated maternity leave of fifteen weeks at 60 percent pay (to a maximum of $363 in 1989). Until recently, the United States had no government provision for maternity leave. Hewlett (1991, 28) observes that the United States is the "only rich country that fails to provide new mothers with maternity benefits of job-protected leave." Alison Clarke-Stewart (1993, 148) adds, "The United States lags behind almost all other industrialized countries in the supply, quality, and affordability of day care. The United States, alone with South Africa among advanced industrialized nations, has no clear and integrated national policy to provide support and services for children and families." In 1993 the U.S. Congress enacted family leave legislation.

36. Government sets the rules the community will abide by in determining how re-sources (such as the Gross National Product) will be distributed. In a society where special interest politics shape governmental interests, those groups able to use their financial advantage to fund the campaigns of elected officials will likely see their interests protected and legislation which is favorable to protecting and improving their interests enacted. Likewise, those groups who are unable to make contributions to the campaigns of elected officials will likely see their interests go unprotected. Further, those groups, such as single mothers and the poor, who have historically recorded low voter turnout will be especially vulnerable. And most of all, those who do not vote—children—are unlikely to have their interests protected and will likely fare poorly in competition with others in the arena of political decision-making.

seen, the family has undergone major changes. The majority of mothers of children under six are now in the labor force. This has created an enormous need for child care services (Kamerman and Kahn, 1988a). Nevertheless, only a small fraction of children are accommodated by current programs. Emlen (1974, 91) observed, "In 1971 the children of working mothers numbered nearly 6 million under the age of 6 and 18 million between six and fourteen. The 440,000 children [under six] who received full-day day care are a small proportion... [less than one tenth]." Tobin, Wu, and Davidson (1989, 218-219) observed, "Unlike culturally similar Western European democracies, the United States government has failed to provide more than token support for child care. An exception is Head Start, a federal-and-state-supported program for children from disadvantaged homes. But at current funding levels Head Start has slots for less than 5 percent of the children it could potentially serve."

Government inaction in the area of child care has resulted in a hodge-podge of private child care facilities characterized by vast differences in quality—quality being accorded to those who can afford it. Tobin, Wu, and Davidson (1989, 218) observe, "Seventy six percent of American families [in the upper income brackets] have their young children in preschool as compared to forty percent of middle-income families and less than five percent of families earning less than ten thousand dollars. The well-to-do can easily afford good preschools while the middle class struggles to pay tuition and the poor most often are left with second-rate proprietary child centers, family care homes, and inadequate makeshift arrangements."

The public school system provides a caretaker function for children as soon as they turn six years old, since a child is taken care of most of the day by the school. This makes it easier for the mother to work and earn income. The problem of child care falls heaviest on the mother during the early years of the child's life—at a time when assistance with child care is most needed. However, the mother of a child younger than six is left to her own resources. In deciding whether to stay at home and provide children with the love and affection that so benefits them during their earliest years (Fraiberg, 1977; White, 1975), the mother must weigh the cost of child care against potential earnings in the labor market.

In Canada a recent report found that the average costs for full-time child care was approximately $75 a week per child (more in urban areas, less in rural), or about $300 a month (in U.S. dollars). For two children this amounts to about $600 a month. The cost of child care in the United States is similar. This cost is roughly the amount spent on public school education

(Lindsey, 1991b). For two-parent families, this cost is high but can be offset against additional income. Further, part of the costs are tax deductible. For lone-mothers this cost is often too great. As Tobin, Wu, and Davidson (1989, 207) observe, "At the minimum wage level in the United States, the cost of even inexpensive full-time preschool care for one child will eat up more than a third of her annual earnings. With two or more preschool-aged children the cost ratio makes working for a minimum wage and putting children in preschool an unattractive option. Salaries have to rise dramatically above minimum wage before putting two children in child care makes sense." They add that when two parents "balance the cost of paid child care against the loss of earnings and jeopardy to a career, it is almost always the wife's and not the husband's earnings and career that are at stake" (p. 207). Should the lone-mother spend the amount required for child care, she would have little money left over for rent and food.

The French Model

In contrast to Canada and the United States, France developed a universal child care system. After World War II the French built a comprehensive child care system to protect the children of women who went to work in the rebuilding and industrializing of France after the war. For the 4.5 million children under the age of six there is a vast constellation of child care programs (Greenhouse, 1993). For infants and toddlers, from three months old to three years of age, child care is provided in day care centers and day care homes. Day care homes are government-licensed baby sitters who look after young children in their own home. The day care home staff must pass medical and psychological tests and have their facilities regularly inspected.

For children from two and a half to five years of age subsidized preschools are provided. The preschools are normally open from 7 A.M. in the morning until 7 P.M. at night. Care is provided on a sliding scale basis. Annual costs range from $390 for poor families, $3,200 for middle class families, and $5,300 for upper income families. The remaining costs are subsidized by the French government at a cost of approximately $7 billion a year. As a result, more than 99 percent of three, four, and five-year old children attend preschool at no or minimal charge. This is sharp contrast to the United States and Canada. Stanley Greenhouse (1993, 59) writes, "Comparing the French system with the American system—if that word can be used to describe a jigsaw puzzle missing half its pieces—is like comparing a vintage bottle of Chateau Margaux with a $4 bottle of American wine."

Figure 4.5 Comparable Wages by Sex in the United States, 1992

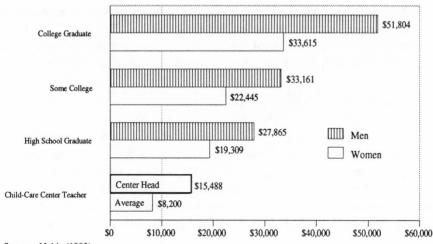

Sources: Noble (1993).

Child Care as a Public Priority

Although there is a broad consensus that care of children is vital, child care has not been recognized as such by the labor market (Holman, 1978 and 1988). Many women care for their children as full-time homemakers. In this effort they rely on the fairness and good will of their husbands to recognize the importance of their labor. Yet, the mother who stays home with her children is usually paid no income. Those who provide care for children in day care facilities are usually paid low salaries. The average salary for a child care worker in the United States is about $8,000 a year (Noble, 1993). The highest salary usually paid for the head teacher, requiring a college degree, at a child care center is about $15,500 (see Figure 4.5). This is less than one third of the income of the average college graduate. This salary structure would indicate that child care is not a high priority.

It seems incomprehensible that public policy during the last several decades has not adjusted to provide lone-mothers or working women with accessible, quality child care. Attempts have been made. In 1971, the United States Congress passed the Comprehensive Child Development Act, which President Nixon promptly vetoed, arguing that it would be a serious error to commit "the vast moral authority of national government to the side of communal approaches to child rearing over and against the family-centered approach." In reaction to the women's movement, critics have argued that women should be at home raising their children. Small children especially, these critics argue, need the close personal contact with the mother. This view has been primarily directed at two-parent households.

Ambivalence Toward Working Mothers

Should a woman with a preschool age child, given the choice, work or not? This question is the crux of the issue. On the one hand, mothers, even of young children, are encouraged to work outside the home, since their additional earnings, will help make the family self-sufficient (Kamerman and Kahn, 1988a). On the other hand, they are urged to stay home and devote time to their children. Tobin, Wu and Davidson (1989, 182) observe,

> In the midst of this cacophony of discordant, often accusatory voices, mothers cannot help but feel accused and confused. Even if a mother, after some difficulty, manages to locate a good preschool for her child, she invariably feels a sense of guilt and dereliction of duty. Conversely, a woman who chooses to stay home with her child is subject to real or imagined criticism from feminists and other employed women. Fathers are not completely immune to these feelings, but balancing parenting and work remains clearly a woman's problem.

Since women have been largely absent from the corridors of legislative and policy-making authority, it is perhaps not surprising that so little has been done to resolve the issue.

Declining Relevance of the Traditional Approach

Returning to the question of child welfare's role in the changing world of working women, divorce, unwed mothers, impoverished lone-parent families, and indifferent government bureaucracies whose priorities are elsewhere, we can see limitations in the traditional approach to child welfare. With its focus on the deficits of parents in meeting their parental role responsibilities, its concern with psychological faults and shortcomings, it is unable to recognize or embrace the new structural realities. However, given the enormous impact poverty has had on the problems that bring children to the attention of the public child welfare system, the realities are becoming increasingly difficult to ignore (Wallerstein and Kelly, 1979). The role of welfare programs such as AFDC in the United States or social assistance in Canada, which attempt to ameliorate poverty, are inextricably entwined with deeply felt political issues, and in their effort to achieve professional status the public child welfare bureaucracy has had to tread softly. By avoiding the issue of poverty, however, the child welfare system has given itself over to treating symptoms and not causes (Pine, 1986).

The result continues to be an ever increasing host of problems laid at the doorstep of the residual child welfare system, which finds itself increasingly incapable of dealing with them. Without the means of addressing the broad structural problems that produce poverty, the residual child welfare system, using the traditional approach, has progressively restricted its focus only to those children experiencing ever more "severe" forms of abuse and neglect. The problem, of course, is that the approach's residual orientation provides too narrow a perspective to achieve the changes required by current social realities. Although the residual perspective was congruent with the traditional casework method, the problems children and their lone-parents face require an expansion of perspective to truly understand the social and structural dimensions within which family problems arise.

While the residual perspective may have been appropriate for an earlier time, it no longer represents an effective approach toward the problems that children and families face in the late twentieth century. For decades it allowed society to provide services "on the cheap," targeting only those "most in need." The residual approach retains its enduring appeal because it promises to do the least and, thus, cost the least. However, it has, over time, proven itself ineffective in dealing with long-term problems brought about by irrevocable social changes. Somehow a new understanding of the limits and possibilities of child welfare must be developed, one that reflects the enriched knowledge base in the field and an understanding of the social conditions within which public child welfare services operate.

In this regard, the needs of children are similar to the needs of business. Business and industry, for example, routinely look to the government for assistance in developing the capacity to compete in the global economy. Indeed, the business community *requires* an economic infrastructure that provides assistance in a variety of forms to all businesses, not just those businesses in difficulty. The business community would certainly not accept anything resembling a residual perspective in developing policies and programs that regulate commerce and industry. Likewise, families and children, which represent the country's future, require a broad based infrastructure to support their development and economic opportunity.

Yet Another Challenge

While it may seem, after this catalog of such vast social changes, that the traditional approach had little opportunity to continue, it nevertheless continued to hold sway throughout the field of child welfare, but with very little practical effect—a tree eaten hollow by termites. As we shall see, a social phenomenon was building that would eclipse all efforts for child welfare reform, that would, within a few years, remove any pretense of maintaining the traditional approach to child welfare delineated by Kadushin (1967). It would everywhere redirect the mandate of child welfare agencies in their delivery of services. The phenomenon was child abuse. Overnight, almost out of nowhere, the beating and killing of children would command headlines, mobilize legislators, and transform child welfare agencies. Within less than a decade child welfare agencies across North America would be foundering in a flood of child abuse reports, which rising statistics would show had little possibility of being resolved. Besides stymying all reform of the traditional approach to child welfare, child abuse would begin revealing, as nothing else had ever done, the inherent futility of reforming the residual perspective that has guided child welfare for 150 years.

Summary and Conclusion

Starting in the 1950s changes began altering the social landscape in which the traditional approach to child welfare operated. Women began entering the work force in record numbers. Divorce rates rose, as did the number of unwed mothers. The result was a dramatic increase in the number of impoverished lone-parent families. The traditional portrait of the family began to fracture. At the same time, child welfare policies and programs failed to respond to the needs created by these changes. Government programs and policies that would address the problems these changes produced failed to materialize. Although public school education provides for the care of children between six and eighteen during the day, mothers with children under six were left to their own resources. The need for publicly supported child care was left unmet. The traditional approach to child welfare was no longer able to cope with the problems produced by these changes using a casework method that focused on the parent/child relationship.

The two-parent family has always been viewed as the ideal setting for children. Two parents are much better situated to raise children. They have greater earning capacity. The average lone-parent in the United States earns about one quarter of what the average two-parent family earns. More importantly, the two-parent family is able to share in the labor-intensive effort required to nurture and discipline their children. Further, as David Archard (1993, 120-21) points out, "We feel, somehow instinctively, that a child should have parents of both sexes in order to make those identifications and form those attachments which are a prerequisite of healthy development. Again much of this may be self-confirming ideological prejudice, especially when what is understood as 'mother' and 'father' are, in fact, specific and stereotypical gender roles."

Lone-parents are at an enormous disadvantage. Lone-parents must carry responsibility for child rearing while maintaining the home and earning an income. Most lone-parents are unable to satisfactorily balance and carry these responsibilities. Certainly in comparison to the their two-parent counterparts, the lone-parents will almost always be found wanting.

Further, the children of lone-parents may become victims of stereotyped expectations that children from "broken" homes are more troublesome and difficult to manage. As Archard (1993) observes, "If a child is brought up to believe that it is less well-off and abnormal for having only one parent, then that belief can only too easily be self-confirming" (p. 120).

Should public policy aim at assisting lone-parents who are disadvantaged? To do so could be viewed as either disfavoring the two-parent family or favoring the lone-parent. Should public policy discourage the formation of lone-parent families? It would appear that lone-parent families suffer too much already. Rather, lone-parent families need support to insure their children have opportunity.

Unfortunately, the child welfare system had failed to understand and adequately respond to the dynamic changes affecting the family. Holding to a view of the family that was becoming less tenable for the children in poverty, who formed the essential client base of the public child system, the residual approach continued to guide policies and programs for children into the era of the rediscovery of child abuse.

Somehow the need for universal child care was missed. The focus remained on those parents who failed to properly care for their children. As the numbers mounted, the staff simply increased. Yet no progress toward solving the root causes was made. To borrow an analogy from Marshall McLuhan, the child welfare profession continued to drive forward with eyes fixed on the rear view mirror. We drove based on our knowledge of the roads behind, instead of seeing the road ahead and the changing conditions of the family. The residual approach of the past continued to shape and guide policies and programs despite its apparent deficiencies and inadequacies in the new era.

5

The Transformation of Child Welfare into Children's Protective Services

There I was confronted by a startling finding. An examination of the *Reader's Guide to Periodical Literature* and the *Social Science and Humanities Index* showed that absolutely no articles on "child abuse" (regardless of what term one used) had been published before 1962. Later research in other indexes proved me slightly wrong.[37]

Barbara Nelson, *Making an Issue of Child Abuse*

In 1946, a distinguished radiologist, John Caffey, exploring the use of X-rays with infants and young children, reported puzzling symptoms in children who had been admitted to the hospital for treatment of subdural hematoma (pooling of blood under the skull). Caffey's X-rays revealed that, in addition to the subdural hematoma, the children had multiple long-bone fractures in their arms and legs. Altogether in the six children studied he found twenty-three long bone fractures and four contusions (injuries to subsurface tissues where the skin is not broken). It was a puzzling phenomenon. What had caused such fractures and tissue injury? By this time, rickets and bone syphilis had become rare diseases. The most likely explanation was trauma of some sort (i.e., an externally caused injury), resulting perhaps from an accident or fall. Caffey knew that trauma did indeed produce such skeletal changes in infants and young children (Caffey and Silverman, 1945). Being a radiologist who did not have direct contact with the patient or the family, Caffey had no reason to suspect trauma from assault. Were the fractures related somehow to the subdural hematoma? Might the two be symptoms of some new children's disease? Caffey (1946) duly reported the symptoms in the *American Journal of Roentgenology*, the professional journal for research on the medical applications of X-ray technology.

---

37. Nelson (1984, 63) counted 1,235 articles in *Index Medicus* from 1950 to 1980 on child abuse, only one of which was published prior to 1962.

Table 5.1 The Emergence of Medical Evidence of Physical Child Abuse

Year	Author	Title / Journal	Summary
1945	Caffey and Silverman	Infantile Cortical Hyperostos *American Journal of Roentgenology**	Use of X-ray to examine injuries to children
1946	Caffey	Multiple Fractures in Long Bones of Infants Suffering from Subdural Hematoma *American Journal of Roentgenology*	Identified 6 children with skull injuries also had fresh, healing multiple fractures without adequate explanation
1950	Lis and Frauenberger	Multiple Fractures Associated with Subdural Hematoma in Infancy *Pediatrics*	Additional case similar to Caffey's findings, no etiology established
1950	Smith	Subdural Hematoma with Multiple Fractures *American Journal of Roentgenology*	Case report similar to Caffey's but no explanation of origin
1951	Barmeyer and others	Traumatic Peristitis in Young Children *Journal of Pediatrics*	Finding of increased metaphysical fragility in infants, no etiology
1952	Marquezy and others	Hematome sousdural et fractures multiplas des os longs chez un nourrisson de N. mois *Arch. franc. pediat.*	An additional case similar to Caffey's
1953	Silverman	Roentgen Manifestations of Unrecognized Skeletal Trauma in Infants *American Journal of Roentgenology*	Reported 3 cases similar to Caffey's and urged the need to obtain reliable histories of patients
1954	Marie and others	Hematome sousdural du nourrisson associe a des fractures des membres *Semaine hop. Paris*	An additional case similar to Caffey's
1955	Woolley and Evans	Significance of Skeletal Lesions in Infants Resembling those of Traumatic Origin *Journal of American Medical Association*	Study finds multiple injuries to 12 infants are associated with unstable households
1956	Bakwin	Roentgenographic Changes in Homes following Trauma *Journal of Pediatrics*	Examines 3 case studies of children with multiple injuries
1958	Fisher	Skeletal Manifestations of Parent-induced Trauma in Infants and Children *8th Medical Journal*	Indicates importance of parental history in underst 'ling injury to children
1959	Kempe and Silver	The Problem of Parental Criminal Neglect and Severe Abuse in Children *Journal of Diseases of Children*	Suggests injuries to children need to be brought to the attention of legal authorities
1959	Miller	Fractures among Children-1, Parental Assault as Causative Agent *Minnesota Medicine*	Suggests that multiple injuries are often result of parental assault
1961	Adelson	Slaughter of the Innocents: A Study of 46 homicides in which Victims were Children *New England Journal of Medicine*	Retrospective study of 46 child homicides, 37 were killed by their parents
1961	Gwinn and others	Roentgenographic Manifestations of Trauma in Infancy: A Problem of Medical, Social, and Legal Importance *Journal of American Medical Association*	Examines 25 cases of children with multiple injuries and stresses need to remove child from dangerous environment else death may occur
1962	Kempe and others	The Battered Child Syndrome *Journal of American Medical Association*	Evidence of the "battered child syndrome"

*Roentgenology is a medical specialty concerned with the use of X rays for diagnosis and treatment of bonefractures and disease.

During the decade following Caffey's report, other radiologists and physicians reported similar findings. Lis and Frauenberger (1950) in the United States, Smith (1950) in Canada, Marquezy, Bach, and Blondeau (1952), and Marie (1954) in France all reported cases similar to that reported by Caffey (see Table 5.1). In 1953, Silverman reported three cases of infants with symptoms similar to those observed by Caffey. Silverman, however, concluded that the bone changes observed with X-rays were obviously the result of traumatic injuries accumulated over time. He urged physicians to obtain reliable patient histories so that the etiology of these injuries might be better understood. However, Silverman cautioned that physicians not alarm parents with feelings of guilt by asking too many questions or appearing too suspicious about the parents' actions and intents.[38]

Such cases continued to accumulate. In 1955, Woolley and Evans published a review of reports of infants coming into medical facilities with serious physical injuries that were "unaccompanied by readily volunteered and adequate account of injury." Woolley and Evans identified two syndromes of serious physical injury of unknown origin in infants: (1) subdural hematoma with multiple long bone fractures, and (2) traumatic periostitis (inflammation of bone tissue). Little evidence existed to suggest that these syndromes were due either to a disease process or to an unusual bone fragility in the affected infants. In their search for an explanation, the researchers examined the infants' family backgrounds for explanations. Their study of twelve infants "presenting multiple areas of bone damage which appeared to have accrued over an extended period of time and for which no easily elicited story of injury was available," revealed that the infants "came invariably from unstable households with a high incidence of neurotic or frankly psychotic behavior on the part of at least one adult" (Woolley and Evans, 1955, 542-543).

Woolley and Evans published their work in the *Journal of the American Medical Association* where "it reached the radio, television, and press and electrified the public" (Radbill, 1974, 18). The study contributed to the emerging concern of the U.S. Children's Bureau with child abuse reporting legislation. It laid the foundation for the understanding of "battered children" developed by Kempe and his colleagues, six years later. Summarizing

---

38. Scott (1978) suggests that the early reports of the radiologists (Caffey, Lis, and Frauenberger, Smith, Silverman, and others) failed to understand the role of parents in the traumatic injury to infants because they had limited contact with parents (Cameron, 1978; Churchill, 1974). Radiologists do most of their work "in a darkened and silent room, far from the crying babies and weeping or sullen parents" (Scott, 1978, 175).

the work of the radiologists Costin (1992, 194) wrote, "The long dormancy of child abuse as a major professional and public issue might have continued had it not been interrupted by new knowledge and the skills of radiologists."

The Battered Child Syndrome

In 1962, C. Henry Kempe and his colleagues surveyed eighty-eight hospitals in which they identified 302 children who had been "battered." Kempe sharpened the focus on what was clearly emerging as "child abuse" by defining the "battered child syndrome," as an infant or child less than three years old who presented the physician with unusual injuries, broken bones, or cranial injuries that were inadequately or inconsistently explained. When published, this survey, which graphically catalogued brutality to young children, many of whom suffered multiple injuries, ignited a broad-based national effort to find ways to protect children (Gil, 1970; Nagi, 1977). Specifically, it led to calls for implementation of mandated child abuse reporting systems, to ensure that whenever a "battered child" was even suspected, the case would be reported and measures taken to protect the child. Reporting was viewed as the first step in providing protection to the suspected "battered child."

During this period (early 1960s) the Children's Bureau, responding to physicians' concerns, began developing a model reporting law that mandated that physicians report cases of suspected child battering. By 1963 thirteen states had adopted mandatory reporting laws. Bagley and King (1990, 33) report, that "by 1966 all fifty American states had passed new legislation regulating child abuse." Shortly after, every state had developed much broader definitions of abuse than the "battered child syndrome," all of which mandated reporting. In 1986, every state but one required reporting of neglect, and forty-one states made explicit reference to reporting of emotional or psychological abuse (Hutchison, 1993). Parallel developments occurred in Canada and the United Kingdom (Bagley and King, 1990, 33).

The early intent had been to limit mandated reporting to physicians only. However, the American Medical Association, which objected to being singled out, urged that mandated reporting be required of other professionals as well. As a result, no state mandatory reporting laws limits reporters solely to medical professionals and must include teachers, nurses, counselors, and the general public.

Table 5.2 Reports of Child Abuse

	Abuse Reports	Rate per 1,000 Children	Proportion Substantiated (%)	Child Abuse Fatalities
1967	9,563	0.1		
1968	11,000	0.2		
1975	294,796	4.5	60	
1976	669,000	10	65	
1977	838,000	13		
1978	836,000	13		
1979	988,000	15		
1980	1,154,000	18		
1981	1,211,323	19		
1982	1,262,000	19		
1983	1,477,000	23		
1984	1,727,000	27	42	
1985	1,919,000	30		805
1986	2,086,000	33	40	1,014
1987	2,157,000	34	40	1,074
1988	2,265,000	35		1,093
1989	2,435,000	38		1,103
1990	2,557,000	40		1,143
1991	2,723,000	42		1,255
1992	2,936,000	45		1,261

Source: McCurdy and Daro (1993).

The Avalanche of Child Abuse Reports

The state mandated reporting laws resulted in an immediate and meteoric rise in child abuse reports across the United States. Florida, for example, saw the number of abuse reports increase in one year from 17 (1970) to 19,120 (1971).[39] In 1962, when Kempe and his colleagues published their report, "The Battered Child Syndrome," there had been about 10,000 child abuse reports (see Table 5.2). By 1976, the number or child abuse reports

---

39. Florida installed an (800) toll-free twenty-four-hour child abuse report hotline and combined it with a public information campaign mounted through the mass media (Sussman and Cohen, 1975, 125). Between 1971 and 1975 the number of reports leveled off at twenty-five to thirty thousand a year. In 1981, Florida received 68,446 reports. This number increased to 130,393 by 1985. Between 1987 and 1988, the number of reports in Florida increased 14 percent (Select Committee on Children, Youth and Families, 1989a, 109-111).

had risen to more than 669,000, and by 1978, to 836,000. By 1992, according to the National Committee for the Prevention of Child Abuse (McCurdy and Daro, 1993), there were almost three million reports of child abuse nationwide, including 1,261 child-abuse-related fatalities. A proportional increase occurred in Canada (Johnson and Chisholm, 1989).[40]

Historical Precedents for Protective Services

To understand the impact of child abuse reports on child welfare agencies, it is important to understand the perceived mission of child welfare agencies prior to this time. Public child welfare agencies' responsibility to protect children from harm and cruelty began well before the turn of the century (Antler and Antler, 1979). When, in 1874, eight-year-old Mary Ellen was brought before a New York court wrapped in a blanket, the judge turned his head away rather than view the child's tortured body. The judge removed the child from her guardian and placed her in the custody of the American Society for the Protection of Animals, there being no organization at the time to protect children. The case led to the founding that year of the New York Society for the Prevention of Cruelty to Children.

Organized efforts to protect children from cruelty spread rapidly. In 1887, Kelso helped found the Toronto Humane Society to prevent cruelty to both children and animals (Bellamy and Irving, 1986). Four years later, following the example of the Children's Aid Society established in New York by Charles Loring Brace, Kelso expanded the scope of child welfare by setting up the Toronto Children's Aid Society. In 1893 an Act for the Prevention of Cruelty to and Better Protection of Children was passed in Ontario. Although child protection in North America began with a narrow focus on cases of physical cruelty, it soon broadened its focus to include physical neglect, abandonment, and child welfare in general (Antler, 1981; Lynch, 1985). Gradually child abuse became only one of many concerns of the public child welfare system.

Although cases of severe physical abuse continued to arouse public outrage and so provide substantial support for the efforts of the children's aid societies, the main focus of the societies was, in fact, the thousands of abandoned and orphaned children. By the early twentieth century, severe physi-

---

40. Martyn Kendrick (1990, 94) has observed, "Over the past decade, all provinces have reported a 500 to 1,000 percent increase in the number of abuse allegations and a concomitant rise in the number of investigations."

cal abuse had become a small part of the agencies' concern, because it represented such a small part of the problems that came to their attention (Costin, 1992). As Kadushin observed, the absorption of protective services into public child welfare resulted in a "decline of interest [in protective services] between 1920 and the 1960s. Child maltreatment as a social concern dropped out of the public agenda" (Kadushin and Martin, 1988, 222-223). Thus, while child abuse and the child protective movement was "discovered" in 1874 and spread rapidly, it just as quickly receded. Costin (1992, 177) observed, "By 1910, more than 200 societies [to prevent child cruelty] existed in the United States. Twenty years later, however, the anticruelty movement had lost momentum, changed in purpose, and become much less visible. The social work literature of the early 1900s through the 1950s reflects a sharply diminished discussion of child abuse as a condition requiring intervention by community agents."

Indeed, the child welfare studies by Brace (1880), Theis (1924), and Trotzkey (1930) focused on the relative merits of foster care and institutional care. No major studies on child abuse appeared during this period. As for the calls for research in the 1950s, little mention was made of child abuse (Dybwad, 1949; Kahn, 1956; Norris and Wallace, 1965).

Part of the problem had to do with proving that children's injuries had been inflicted by the parents, who often could provide a variety of plausible explanations for an injury. The only person who could contradict them were the children, who were generally regarded as neither credible or reliable. As well, even in the face of the most severe brutality, the child would often cling to whatever love and bond existed with the parent (Elmer, 1967). Social workers lacked the tools to determine when the bruises and severe injuries were accidental and when they were intentionally inflicted by an angry parent.

Thus, by the time the Social Security Act was passed in 1935, the child welfare system had been defined as being for the "protection and care of homeless, dependent and neglected children and children in danger of becoming delinquent." Concern with the issue of physical child abuse had receded. For the next thirty years child welfare services went about providing foster care services along with an assortment of other services (including diminishing institutional care) to needy children and families.

The decades from 1950 to 1970, which saw the rapid growth of the public child welfare system, were characterized by an effort to construct an empirical knowledge base that would guide and inform the child welfare system. Alfred Kadushin synthesized the results of the emerging research into a theoretical framework that firmly established the field. The child welfare system, according to Kadushin, was to help parents meet their child-rearing responsibilities through the provision of supportive and supplementary services or, when that was not possible, to remove the children from their parents and provide substitute care. Child abuse was not central to the perspective, but regarded as an "interaction event" that derived from problems in the parent-child relationship (Kadushin and Martin, 1988). Kadushin's definition was illustrative of how psychological theories that had been evolving steadily since the 1920s were being integrated into social welfare practice. With the emergence of mandated child abuse reporting, however, the perspective changed, and the goals of the agencies were abruptly redirected toward a whole new set of problems. The view developed by Kadushin, which may have been appropriate for an earlier time, was swept aside by the tide of child abuse reports. As Besharov reported (1983, 155), "the great bulk of reports now received by child protective agencies would not have been made but for the passage of mandatory child abuse reporting laws and the media campaigns that accompanied them."

Impact of Child Abuse Reporting on the Child Welfare System

In 1990 Kamerman and Kahn reported on their comprehensive study of child welfare programs in a range of localities throughout the United States. Although they found major differences between the locations they studied, one over-arching theme emerged: Child welfare agencies within the decade of the 80s had been changed from foster care agencies into protective service agencies whose function was to investigate the ever-increasing avalanche of child abuse reports. Kamerman and Kahn (1990) write:

> Child Protective Services (CPS) (covering physical abuse, sexual abuse, and neglect reports, investigations, assessments, and resultant actions) have emerged as the dominant public child and family service, in effect "driving" the public agency and often taking over child welfare entirely... Child protective services today constitute the core public child and family service, the fulcrum and sometimes, in some places, the totality of the system. Depending on the terms used, public social service agency administrators state either that "Child protection is child welfare", or that "The increased demand for child protection has driven out all other child welfare services." (Pp. 7-8)

> For the most part these protective services are child rather than family-focused. They are organized around investigation and risk assessment rather than treatment, and as a result the large proportion of cases where the allegations are not substantiated receive no help regardless of how troubled the children and families may be... Child protective staff fear errors—especially the failure to take endangered children into care—and the subsequent public response to deaths or severe abuse and neglect. (P. 8)

Child welfare resources were, as a result of mandatory reporting laws, redirected from providing services to needy children and families toward investigating and intervening in the increasing number of child abuse reports. For every report that was received, a child welfare agency worker was sent to investigate. The worker interviewed parents, neighbors, teachers—anyone who might have evidence to substantiate or deny the allegations brought forth in the complaint. The investigation might take a week, two weeks, a month, or longer, before sufficient data was collected that would permit a decision on what action should be taken. The process was difficult and expensive.[41]

Throughout the seventies and eighties, as public awareness campaigns alerted the public to the prevalence of child abuse, the number of reports escalated, which, in turn increased the need for more investigators and resources in child welfare agencies. At the same time the mood in society and government was turning increasingly skeptical toward social programs. Throughout the decade of the eighties, expenditures for social services were repeatedly cut. Paradoxically, while the public continued to demand greater efforts be made to curb child abuse, it was increasingly unwilling to fund those efforts. Thus, child welfare was having to confront a steadily growing problem with steadily diminishing resources (Faller, 1985). Even for a field that from the beginning had been required to accomplish more with less, the task was impossible. The result was a continual narrowing of focus regarding who should receive child welfare services (Garbarino, Carson, and Flood, 1983; Weston, 1974).

The residual approach had always necessitated a "means test"—poverty, neglect, abandonment, being orphaned—before the child would be

---

41. There have been other concerns with the reporting laws. For example, Besharov has suggested that increased reporting has often led to higher numbers of unfounded reports (Besharov, 1990a; Eckenrode, et al., 1988: Giovannoni, 1989). However, Finkelhor (1990) has criticized this view. Also see Daro (1991) and Besharov's response (1991).

granted services. Child abuse now became the litmus test for conferring eligibility for services. Moreover, how severe was the abuse? Was the child being beaten, sexually molested, starved, tortured? Was the situation life-threatening? The millions of children living in destitute families, whose hopes and dreams were daily obliterated by poverty, and whom the agencies had previously attempted to aid, now, because they did not qualify, began dropping through the holes of the protective services safety net.

To make matters worse, family supportive services that might have alleviated the demand for child welfare services were often cut to finance the new protective service investigations. In Virginia, for example, "increases in CPS budgets for investigation... were matched by decreases in AFDC service budgets" (Dattalo, 1991, 13).

From the outset, the approach taken by agencies in investigating child abuse reports was accusatory. That is, the caseworker's responsibility was to collect information that might eventually be used to build a case against the accused parent in order to protect the affected child. Whereas previously the welfare worker might have been viewed as coming forward to help a troubled family, the worker now was unmistakably cast in the role of inquisitor prying into and judging the affairs of the family, with predictably adverse effects on the family. Elizabeth Hutchison (1993, 60) notes:

> Investigation of a report of child maltreatment is not an innocuous intrusion into family life. By the time an investigation is complete, the family has had to cope with anxieties in both their formal and informal support systems alerted to state suspicion of their parenting. Even if the report is expunged from the central registry due to lack of substantiation, it is seldom expunged from the mind of the family—or from the memories of persons in the support system.

Pelton (1989, 123) offers a perspective on the predicament of parents who are reported for alleged child abuse:

> The parent-agency interaction represents a particular type of conflict, one in which—far from the two parties having more or less equal power—one party is vastly more powerful than the other. The agency has on its side the police, the law, and public opinion. The caseworker has emergency legal power to remove a child from his home on the spot. When the agency goes to court, it has an abundance of reports containing interpretations according to its own lights, the product of vast investigatory resources. The case record is embellished with reports in sophisticated language with opinion freely

expressed, from school officials, psychologists, and representatives of other agencies. It contains the results of psychological tests and medical examinations, not to mention the allegations of neighbors. Confronted with this array of power, the parent may see little means at her disposal, except to "clam up," become secretive, pull her shades down, avoid the social worker and neighbors, prevent her children from talking with anyone, lie, and "say what the caseworker wants to hear."

While protective services seeks to protect the child, the parent, who may be innocent of the charge, is without protection.[42] Pelton (1989, 123) continues:

> No one is advocate for the allegedly abusive or neglectful parent. No one investigates and collects evidence on her behalf, presents her side of the story, presents results of psychological tests commissioned by her rather than the government, nor bears witness on her behalf. Pathologized by psychiatrists and victimized through her interaction with the agency, she stands isolated and alone. As cruel as her actions toward her children might appear, she deserves an advocate. Her hostility, which has often been observed within the context of her interaction with the agency, may stem at least in part from her utter powerlessness within the situation, having no advocate.

While impoverished parents may often experience the situation Pelton describes, the more affluent parents have other options. Attorney Douglas Besharov (1990b, 220) offers the following sage advice to accused parents with adequate financial resources:

> The problem is knowing whether you need a lawyer during the investigation. Early representation by a lawyer can be crucial to preventing a court action. It is much easier to convince investigators and prosecutors not to seek an indictment than it is to have them dismiss one. Many court actions are filed because of a simple breakdown in communication. A lawyer may be able to convince investigators that you are innocent or that the case is better resolved informally. No jurisdiction, however, will provide a lawyer

---

42. Kendrick (1990) observes that in situations where there is disagreement between the child welfare social worker and the parent about an alleged abuse, the cards are stacked against the parent. "In such situations, the [Children's Aids] Society's ability to assemble a case against a parent dwarfs the ability of a parent to mount a defense against the state, especially when the agency has the ability to almost reshape the historical events that form the basis for the termination" (p. 111).

before the initiation of a court case against you. Hence, if you want legal representation during the investigation, you will have to pay for it yourself. Legal fees are expensive: Expect hourly charges of $75 to $200, with a required retainer of $1,000 to $5,000.

You should consider hiring a lawyer whenever you are unhappy with the direction the investigation is taking. (Italics in original)

Besharov and Pelton are not examining different phenomenon. They are simply writing to different audiences. Pelton is concerned with understanding the existential condition of the many single mothers accused and investigated for child abuse (who constitute the majority of those who have their children removed) and how they come to perceive the child protection services provided. For Pelton it is not possible to separate child welfare services from an understanding of the poverty and economic despair most clients of public child welfare endure. Besharov, as a lawyer, is providing a practical word on how the system works to the nonpoor parents who can afford legal advise in the rare instances when they might be accused. These vastly different accounts, with one resembling an image from Kafka's *Trial* and the other a *Better Homes and Gardens* coffee table chat with the expert, point out the inherent injustice of the current system. Those who can afford counsel are less likely to be accused. In the rare instance whey they are accused, they are able to effectively protect themselves against an unfair or unsubstantiated allegation. Unfortunately, the same cannot be said of the lone-mother mired in poverty who is accused of abuse or neglect. She will be unable to afford independent legal counsel. She is at the mercy of the court and, to an ever greater extent, the child welfare caseworker.

Has Mandated Child Abuse Reporting Reduced Child Abuse?

From the beginning, mandatory reporting was perceived as leading to a decline in child abuse, especially fatalities. Besharov (1990b, 10-11), the first director of the National Center on Child Abuse and Neglect, argues the case for increased reporting:

Child protective services still have major problems...Nevertheless, one must be impressed with the results of this twenty-year effort to upgrade them. Specialized "child protective agencies" have been established to receive reports (usually via highly publicized hotlines) and then to investigate them.

And treatment services for maltreated children and their parents have been expanded substantially.

As a result, many thousands of children have been saved from death and serious injury. The best estimate is that over the past twenty years, *deaths from child abuse and neglect have fallen from over 3,000 a year (and perhaps as many as 5,000) to about 1,000 a year.* In New York State, for example, within five years of the passage of a comprehensive reporting law that also created specialized investigative staffs, there was a 50 percent reduction in child fatalities, from about 200 a year to under 100. Similarly, Drs. Ruth and C. Henry Kempe, well-known leaders in the field, reported that "in Denver, the number of hospitalized abused children who die from their injuries has dropped from 20 a year (between 1960 and 1975) to less than one a year." (Italics added)

According to this assessment increased reporting not only saved thousands of childrens' lives but probably also spared even larger numbers of children from physical and sexual abuse that did not end in death. This view holds that child abuse fatalities are just the tip of the iceberg. Underneath the fatality counts are thousands of children who suffer severe pain and injury at the hands of their parents, yet continue to cling to life.

There is considerable debate about the nature and seriousness of various forms of emotional abuse or sexual abuse and even physical abuse (Giovannoni and Becerra, 1979; Ringwalt and Caye, 1989; Select Committee on Children, Youth, and Families, 1989a, 225). By selecting child abuse fatalities Besharov has selected the ultimate dependent variable. Death, unlike other forms of abuse, is difficult to cover up. It calls for an involvement of the police and the courts as well as the social worker. Most of the time an autopsy is required, especially if there are any unusual circumstances (Greenland, 1987; Schloesser, Pierpont, and Poertner, 1992).[43] Although disagreements may arise over whether the fatality was due to child abuse, there is usually agreement that a nonaccidental death occurred. The death might be ruled suspicious or homicide, but the death is recorded. Conse-

---

43. Citing data from the National Center for Health Statistics, Sharpe and Lundstrom (1991) report that autopsies are performed by states on any child under nine years of age from 30 to 60 percent of the time. However, for children who die of Sudden Infant Death Syndrome (SIDS), autopsies are performed between 70 to 100 percent of the time (with the exception of Arkansas). Approximately 5,000 infants die each year in the United States from SIDS, making it the most common cause of death for infants one week to one year old. Sharpe and Lundstrom (1991, 2) speculate that "while the vast majority of suspected SIDS cases are legitimate, some murders are discovered only by chance."

quently, if it can be demonstrated that increased reporting has led to a reduction in child abuse fatalities generally, measured as either homicide or homicide plus deaths caused by "injury undetermined whether accidentally or purposefully inflicted," the argument that increased reporting has decreased child abuse is significantly strengthened. This would mean that child abuse fatalities are perhaps the most reliable and valid indicator of child abuse currently available. Unfortunately, Besharov's assertion of a decline in child abuse fatalities "from over 3,000 a year (and perhaps as many as 5,000) to about 1,000 a year" after mandatory reporting laws were enacted is contradicted by data from several important sources (Sedlak, 1991).[44]

Data from the National Center for Health Statistics

According to the National Center for Health Statistics the homicide rates for both infants (zero to one) and children one to four have not declined over the last twenty years, but have increased. In 1975, approximately 720 children died as a result of homicide or "injury undetermined whether accidentally or purposefully inflicted" (Select Committee on Children, Youth, and Families, 1989b, 174-175). By 1986, this number had increased to about 770. Not all of these "undetermined injury" deaths were the result of child abuse. Yet, the number of child homicides also increased from 1970 to 1987 (see Figure 5.1). Meanwhile, between 1975 and 1986 there had been a several fold increase in the number of official child abuse reports.

Data from the National Committee for the Prevention of Child Abuse

The National Committee for the Prevention of Child Abuse (NCPCA) data corresponds closely with the data reported by the National Center for Health Statistics (Figure 5.2). According to NCPCA data (McCurdy and Daro, 1993), the number of child abuse fatalities reported each year has risen only slightly over the last decade. Since the passage and implementation of mandated reporting the NCPCA has observed no decline in child abuse fatalities.

---

44. Howitt (1992, 196) observes, "If accurate, this is a remarkable figure. But, of course, one needs to know precisely what such statistics refer to." To date, Besharov has not provided a source.

Figure 5.1 Deaths of Infants and Children in the United States, 1960-1987

Rate of homicides per 100,000 children both with and without deaths from undetermined injury

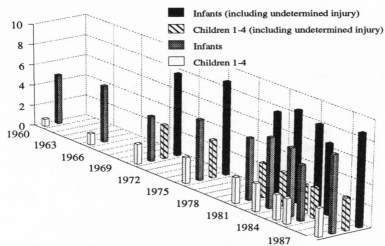

Source: Select Committee on Children, Youth, and Families (1989b).

Figure 5.2 Trends in Child Abuse Reporting and Child Fatalities, 1975-1991

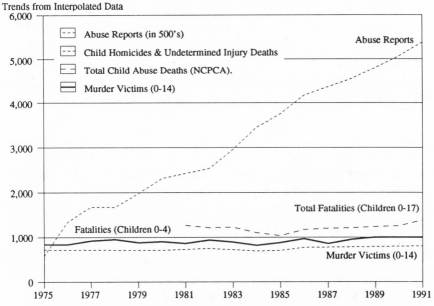

Source: Select Committee on Children, Youth, and Families (1989b, 174). American Association for Protecting Children, *Highlights of Official Child Neglect and Abuse Reporting*, various years. National Committee for the Prevention of Child Abuse (McCurdy and Daro, 1993).

Figure 5.3 Child Murder Victims by Year of Age, 1962-1991

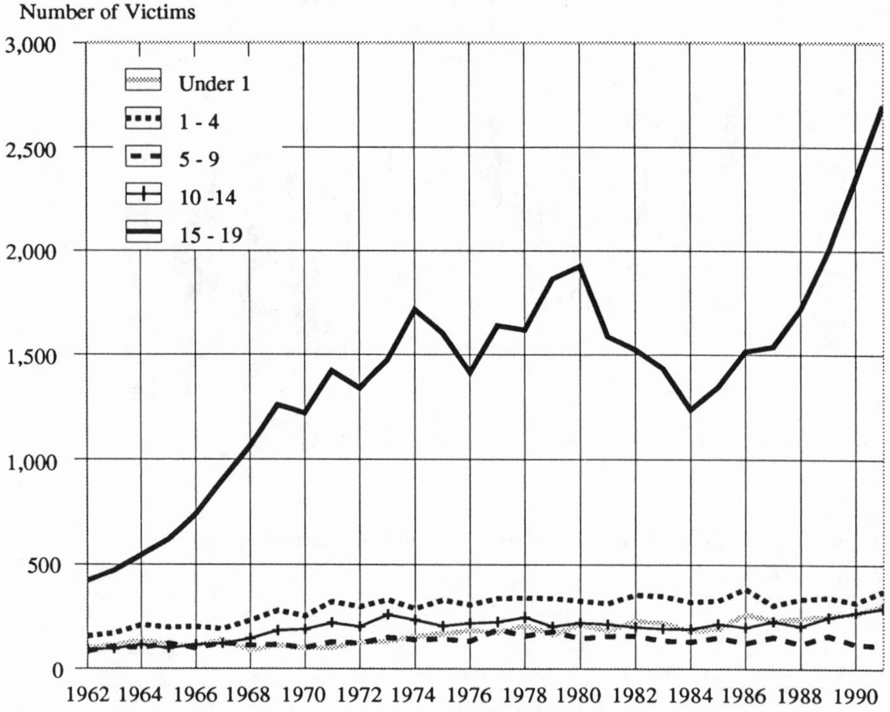

Number of Victims

Source: *Uniform Crime Reports for the United States,* Federal Bureau of Investigation (Various Years).

Data From Uniform Crime Reports: According to the Federal Bureau of Investigation (FBI) data in Figure 5.3, the number of children reported murdered each year has risen only slightly over the last three decades. Since the implementation of mandated reporting no discernible decline in the number of children murdered each year has been reported by the FBI. Most of the child murders reported by the FBI occur among juveniles aged fifteen to nineteen, which appears to be the most vulnerable age for children.

As can be seen in the Figure 5.4, children become more vulnerable as they grow older. Black males ages 15 to 19 and 20 to 24 are particularly vulnerable, with a risk of homicide more than eight times that for whites.[45]

---

45. From 1984 to 1990 the number of children under 18 arrested on murder charges increased from less than 1,000 to 2,555. Viewed in light of the increase in homicides among young males, it would appear that many young males are killing themselves.

Figure 5.4 Child Homicide Rates in the United States by Race, Sex, and Age, 1989

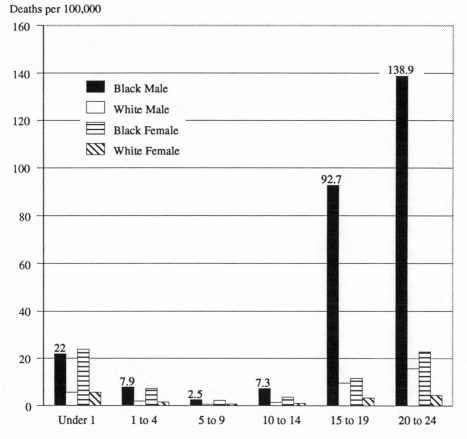

Deaths per 100,000

Legend:
- ■ Black Male
- □ White Male
- ▤ Black Female
- ▨ White Female

Values shown: Under 1: 22; 1 to 4: 7.9; 5 to 9: 2.5; 10 to 14: 7.3; 15 to 19: 92.7; 20 to 24: 138.9

Source: National Center for Health Statistics, Trend C, (1991, table 292A).

Efforts to protect children from violence must begin with threats they face at this age. If the interest is to reduce homicide for those most vulnerable, efforts will focus on the great risk which young Black males face.

Clearly, the data reported by the National Center for Health Statistics, the FBI, the National Incidence Studies, and the National Committee for the Prevention of Child Abuse fail to confirm Besharov's assertion that mandatory reporting has led to a reduction in child abuse fatalities.

Comparison of Child Abuse Reporting and Fatality Rates between States

If increased reporting did indeed reduce child abuse fatalities, we would expect to find a relation between rates of child abuse fatalities and rates of child abuse reporting among the states (that is, those states with higher reporting rates would be expected to have had fewer fatalities than those with lower reporting rates). However, the data comparing rates of child abuse reports and fatalities by state do not support this hypothesis (see Figure 5.5).

States with higher reporting have not had fewer fatalities when compared with states with low reporting rates. For example, the rate of child abuse reports in Missouri is more than five times greater than the rate in Pennsylvania. Yet the rate of child fatalities is about the same in both states. The same comparison can be made for Rhode Island and Colorado, or South Dakota and Minnesota. Louisiana and New Jersey have about the same reporting rate, and yet Louisiana's rate of child fatalities is six times greater than New Jersey's.[46]

Other Discrepancies in Besharov's Data

Besharov (1990b) indicated that child abuse fatalities in New York had declined from about 200 to under 100 within five years of the passage of a comprehensive reporting law. Evidently, the effect of the law was short lived because about five years later (1986) New York reported 181 child fatalities. In 1988 the state reported 198 child fatalities (Select Committee on Children, Youth, and Families, 1989a, 113-114), and in 1990, 212 child abuse fatalities (Pryor, 1991, table 12).

Further, Besharov indicated that in Colorado, the number of child abuse deaths had declined from about twenty a year to only one after the mandatory reporting laws were implemented. In fact, Colorado reported twenty-six child abuse fatalities in 1988, indicating that the decline from about twenty a year reported in Denver hospitals to less than one a year was not sustained by the progress in child abuse reporting (Select Committee on Children, Youth and Families, 1989a, 113).

---

46. I computed a least squares regression analysis of the rates of child fatalities in 1986 with the rate of child abuse reports (1986) by state (Select Committee on Children, Youth, and Families, 1989a, 111-114). The results indicated no relationship between child abuse reports and fatalities ($R^2 = .008$).

Figure 5.5 Child Abuse Reports and Fatalities by State (1986)

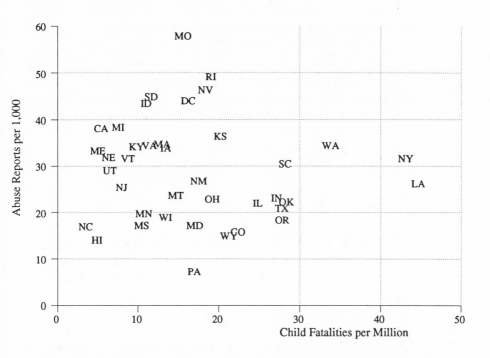

Source: Select Committee on Children, Youth, and Families (1987; 1989b, table7).

Counting child abuse fatalities has always proven a controversial issue. Since child protection advocates are concerned that the full measure of the problem be understood, national estimates are viewed as being unable to detect alleged "hidden" child abuse fatalities that are covered up or made to appear as accidents. Nevertheless, it is surprising to find that four major national studies of the incidence of child abuse fatalities arrive at similar numbers. According to the National Center for Health Statistics, the National Committee for the Prevention of Child Abuse, the National Incidence Studies of Child Abuse and Neglect by the United States Department of Health and Human Services (Sedlak, 1989, 1991), and the FBI's *Uniform Crime Reports*, the total number of child abuse fatalities in the United States has remained roughly stable at 1,000 per year for the last thirty years.

Given this, we are inclined to conclude that, contrary to Besharov, increased reporting has not affected the rate of child abuse fatalities.

Would Fatalities Have Been Greater without Reporting?

It may be that without the increase in reporting since 1962 many more child fatalities would have occurred, and that increased reporting held down the increase in fatalities. We can examine this issue by (1) analyzing data on nationwide trends in violence in the family, (2) examining the relative change in child homicides compared to the rates of homicide for other age groups and, (3) comparing rates of abuse reports and fatalities between states.

Nationwide Trends in Domestic Violence

In 1975, Straus, Gelles, and Steinmetz (1980) conducted a study of violence in the family, entitled *Behind Closed Doors,* in which they estimated that between 3.1 million and 4 million children were kicked, bitten, or punched by their parents at some point during childhood. According to the data they collected, approximately 2 million children were seriously beaten by a parent or threatened with a gun or knife. Further, they estimated that 46,000 children were actually shot or stabbed by a parent and that more than 1,000 died as a result of these attacks. Straus and Gelles (1986) replicated this study ten years later and found a 47 percent decrease in the level of serious violence against children.[47] They found that about 1 million children were subjected to serious physical child abuse in 1985. The data from these studies suggest the level of violence in families did not increase during the period 1975 to 1985, but rather declined.

Even though the level of violence toward children which the surveys by Straus and his colleagues revealed had declined, the number of child abuse reports rose sharply. Their data would seem to indicate that rather than a nationwide increase in violence toward children, there has been a decline in violence toward children. If their data were correct we would expect a decline in the number of child abuse reports. However, during the period

---

47. Gelles and Straus (1987) provide a number of explanations for the decrease in violence. Both their original study and its replication involved two-parent families and, thus, may not be representative of all children who are abused. They also suggest that the increased public concern with child abuse may have made parents more reluctant to self report abuse in 1985.

when the Straus surveys indicated violence toward children had declined, the number of child abuse reports increased six fold. Further, there was no decline in the number of child fatalities even though the overall rate of violence had decreased and surveillance, in the form of mandatory child abuse reporting, had increased.

Child Homicides vs. Adult Homicides

If family violence had increased nationwide, its influence could be seen by examining the relative increase in the rate of homicides for children compared to the increase in the rate of homicides for adults. Yet FBI data indicate that, relative to adults, the homicide rate for children has not declined. In other words, mandated reporting has not had a consistent measurable impact on the relative risk of homicide for infants and children. What is most alarming in the data in Figure 5.3 is the increase in child fatalities among adolescents. The most vulnerable children are not young children, but adolescents.

Declining Rates of "Failure to Safeguard" in Great Britain

The argument for a protective services approach to child welfare has also been made in Europe. After examining child fatality statistics for Britain and Western Europe, Colin Pritchard (1992) reported an encouraging finding quite similar to Besharov. Examining standardized homicide data from the World Health Organization (WHO) between 1973 and 1988 for England, Pritchard (1992, 669) concludes, "There was a 59 percent fall in baby murders in England and Wales between 1973 and 1988...whilst total children's homicide fell by 56 percent for the Anglo-Welsh." The actual number of homicides reported for England are displayed in Table 5.3.[48] Pritchard (1992, 677) postulates "that as the vast majority of child murder is the end product of intra-family violence (Bourget and Bradford, 1990; Somander and Ramner, 1991), major variation in levels of child homicide reflects the effectiveness of a society's child protection service."

---

48. Pritchard (1992) also includes data from Scotland that was analyzed separately. However, the number of fatalities are too small to permit meaningful analysis. Thus, we have not included them here.

Table 5.3 Annual Child Homicides in England, 1973-1988

		Ages		
	<1	1-4	5-14	Total
1973	40	34	28	102
1974	35	40	31	106
1975	33	30	23	86
1976	36	26	23	85
1977	18	33	27	78
1978	29	38	25	92
1979	38	28	28	94
1980	13	17	17	47
1981	10	6	14	30
1982	13	19	18	50
1983	15	22	8	45
1984	9	23	18	50
1985	11	28	20	59
1986	15	9	19	43
1987	10	15	13	38
1988	21	19	14	54

Source: Pritchard (1992).

According to Pritchard (1992) there are other extraneous influences that affect child homicide rates.[49] "Nonetheless, what is beyond doubt is that there has been a substantial reduction in children's homicide in Scotland and in England and Wales greater than the rest of Europe" (p. 677). Why the decline? Pritchard (1992) points out that external factors would seem to have suggested homicides would increase. During the period when homicides, according to Pritchard, declined, "British poverty and unemployment were amongst the worst in Europe... leading to more client problems associated with poverty" (p. 678). These problems were reflected in a substantial

---

49. Although some of the improvement might be explained by homicides disguised as accidents, Pritchard (1992, 675-76) reports, "when child mortality improvements were correlated with the accident rates there was no significant correlation, which suggests that whatever factors influenced the improvements in child homicide, they were not statistically linked to the accident death rate."

increase in "children at risk" registrations during the period covered and "reflects a real rise in child neglect and abuse." Thus, even as child neglect and abuse increased, child protection efforts were, according to Pritchard, able to safeguard children at risk.

Pritchard (1992, 680) asks,

> What is the main implication from this analysis of aggregated data? In spite of the socio-economic pressures affecting the majority of Western Europe, six countries had reductions in children's homicide, which is an encouraging finding for the child protection services of Denmark, West Germany, Italy, Norway, and England and Wales and Scotland. It is important to note, however, that the substantial decline in children's deaths occurred during a time of deteriorating socio-economic conditions when rises might have been expected, and the fact that England and Wales and Scotland had the greatest decline gives cause for satisfaction.

Yet, careful review of the *disaggregated* (or annual) data in Figure 5.6 indicate wide yearly fluctuation in rates for the countries Pritchard points to as experiencing a reduction in child homicides. There have been few child homicides in Denmark and very few in Norway. Yet, even these small numbers have fluctuated widely. Denmark had a high of 10 in 1981 and a low of 5 in 1974, 1975, 1978, 1986, and 1987. Norway had a high of 7 in 1986 and a low of 1 in 1974, 1978, 1984, and 1988. Likewise, homicides in Italy have gone down, then up, then down, then up again and again. Germany has trended down but with wide fluctuations, recording a high of 125 in 1976 and a low of 70 in 1973 and 1987. England and Wales experienced a high of 106 in 1974 and a low of 30 in 1981. By 1988 the number of homicides had increased to 54. Overall it is difficult to draw the same conclusion as Pritchard when the data are disaggregated and examined over time.

Effectiveness of Child Protection Efforts

Rarely has social work been able to report success, especially so marked a success as Pritchard was able to report in this study published in the *British Journal of Social Work*. In his closing Pritchard (1992, 60) writes:

> It is argued that as the reduction in children's fatalities is so marked, this is a real improvement in British child protection services, led by social work. Such an assertion may appear controversial because it runs against the long-

Figure 5.6 International Comparison of Child Homicides

Child Homicides (Ages 0 to 14)

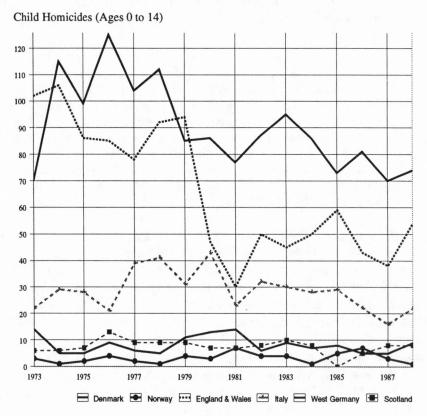

Denmark ⊟ Norway ◉ England & Wales ⋯ Italy ◭ West Germany ⊟ Scotland ▣

Source: World Health Organization, 1973 to 1988.

standing negative image which appears to permeate into the profession's 'consciousness', leading to a relative collective pessimism (Aldridge, 1990). There may be different explanations for the results, and others may make claims for different disciplines, but when disasters occur, the media are quick to remind social workers of their primary statutory responsibilities for children (Brindle, 1991; Noyes, 1991). It seems reasonable, therefore, by virtue of social work's child care responsibilities, and until there is evidence to the contrary, cautiously to claim some credit for British social work as having contributed to a real reduction in the toll of the ultimate abuse of children. (p. 60)

Although Pritchard makes numerous statements asserting "real improvement" and "marked" changes, no statistical tests of these trends were employed.[50]

The study reported by Pritchard provides the data used in the analysis and permits reanalysis. Examining the data in Table 5.3 it is apparent the major change occurring in the number of homicides is between decades. By selecting to compare 1973/74 with 1987/88 Pritchard is able to maximize the difference observed. However, the major change occurred between 1979, 1980, and 1981. In 1979 there were ninety-four homicides. This number declined to forty-seven in 1980, a rather dramatic drop and for no reason provided by Pritchard. Then in 1981 the number of homicides declined to a low of thirty. Since 1981 the number of homicides has been substantially higher than thirty.

What is puzzling about this data is the sharp drop during this three year period. It appears to be the result of a different method for counting homicides since it goes down sharply in 1980 and then comes back up again in 1982. Data from the British office of Population, Censuses, and Surveys Mortality Statistics reported by Corby (1987) indicate that, indeed, this may be the explanation. The child homicide data reported by this office is reported separately by "child deaths in suspicious circumstances" ("injury undetermined whether accidentally or purposefully inflicted") and "child deaths as a result of inflicted violence" ("homicide and injury purposefully inflicted by other persons"). The data for 1979 to 1982 are displayed in Table 5.4 below. It is important to note that there is a discrepancy between the homicide data reported by the World Health Organization (and used by

---

50. Peter Huxley (1986) examined the first fourteen volumes of the *British Journal of Social Work* (1971-1984) and found thirty-eight articles that contained numerical data without statistical analysis. He decried the use of such data without proper analysis. Huxley (1988) later examined these articles in detail to ascertain whether they contained assertions that could be tested statistically. More than half of the articles (twenty-one) contained assertions that could be tested. Sixteen of the twenty-one articles contained assertions that were not warranted by the data presented in the article. Huxley's study underscores the importance of publishing articles that will provide the profession with scientifically tested knowledge (Gambrill, 1990). It is useful for journal articles to record the accomplishments of the profession. Journals must serve to ensure the careful and objective analysis and, when appropriate, statistical analysis of empirical data in the process.

Table 5.4 Child Deaths from Suspicious Circumstances and Homicide

Cause of Death	1979	1980	1981	1982
Suspicious circumstances	64	43	91	62
Homicide	84	47	30	55
Total	148	90	121	117
Homicides as a percent of total deaths	57	52	25	47

Source: Corby (1987).

Pritchard) and the data reported by the Office of Population, Censuses, and Surveys Mortality Statistics (reported by Corby). This discrepancy highlights the problem of obtaining reliable counts of child homicides. This further complicates the interpretation of annual fluctuations of homicide data, especially with regard to assessing the effectiveness of child protection efforts (Creighton, 1984; Peckham and Jobling, 1975).

During the period when child homicides fell sharply there was a shift in the proportion of child deaths classified as *suspicious circumstances* and homicide. During the two year interval between 1979 to 1981 child homicides went from accounting for 57 percent of total deaths (from both suspicious circumstances and homicide) to 25 percent. This was also the period when child homicides reached a low of thirty (in 1981) from which they would increase for the rest of the decade. It does not appear to be a coincidence that when homicides as a percentage of total suspected child abuse deaths reached an all time low (25 percent) was also the time when total child homicides reached their all time low. Rather, the all time low number of homicides seems to be the result of a change in accounting methods classifying homicides and suspicious deaths.

When the data presented by Pritchard (1992) are shown by decade, as in Figure 5.7, it can be observed that there was a slight decline in homicides for the decade of the seventies (beginning in 1973). However, for the most recent decade, from 1980 to 1988, there has been an increasing trend in the number of fatalities, although not at a statistically significant level. Using linear regression permits a cursory test. The downward trend in the number of homicides during the decade of the seventies (1973-79) was not statistically significant ($F = 1.4$, n.s.). Likewise, the upward trend in the number of homicides in the decade of the eighties was not significant ($F = .57$, n.s.).

Figure 5.7 Child Homicide in England, 1973-1988

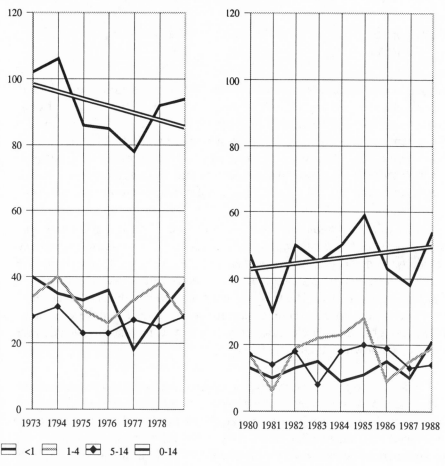

 ◻ <1 ◻ 1-4 ◆ 5-14 ◻ 0-14

Source: Pritchard (1992).

Only the data for the two decades combined were significant ($F = 26.63$, $p. < .01$) and that was due to the large drop that occurred from 1979 to 1981. Rather than a trend, there was a sharp drop in the number of homicides reported by the World Health Organization. When the data including deaths from "suspicious circumstances" are examined for the period 1975 to 1984, there was not a statistically significant trend ($F = 1.5$, n.s.).

According to the available data, the efforts at child protection in England and Wales have not succeeded, as Pritchard claims. Rather, the data suggest that the child protection system has failed to safeguard children to a statistically significant degree during the last nine years.

Explaining the Absence of a Relationship between Increased Reporting and Fatalities

Logically one would assume that increased child protection efforts, including mandatory reporting of child abuse, would reduce the number of child abuse fatalities. Yet the data do not support this conclusion. What explains the absence of a relationship between increased child protection efforts and child homicides? Three possible explanations come to mind: (1) inadequate technology in the areas of risk assessment and child abuse prevention, (2) insufficient funding, and (3) too broad a definition for required reporting.

Inadequate Technology. The transformation of child welfare into protective services has not been the result of scientific breakthroughs in understanding child abuse. The achievements of the radiologists were in the area of identifying that severe physical abuse had occurred and was apparently inflicted by a caretaker. But this was not followed by advances in developing a technology to treat, cure, or prevent child abuse. There were no major breakthroughs in research and theory that led to increased protection for children (Baldwin and Oliver, 1975).

Risk Assessment. Presumably, increased reporting allows more families to be identified and screened in order to prevent future child abuse. However, does the child welfare caseworker know how to adequately assess the risk faced by children after they are reported? Further, even if a child's risk of abuse could be assessed, the agency may not have the knowledge, technology, or skills to provide adequate protection for the child assessed as being at risk (Alfaro, 1988; Anderson et al., 1983; Fein, 1979). In 1990 Daro and Mitchel reported that approximately half of all children identified as child abuse fatalities were active cases known to local protective service agencies at the time of their death.

Protection against child abuse is usually attempted by either increasing surveillance on suspected families or removing the child from the family in which the alleged abuse occurred. Both types of protection have proven difficult to provide. First, although it might be feasible to implement a system of surveillance that would prevent any child from ever being harmed, it is far from clear that, as Dingwall (1989, 49) observes, "a free society would ever tolerate the sort of surveillance that would be necessary to provide such a guarantee. More to the point, we have seen that our tools can never be refined sufficiently to achieve this goal."

Removing a child from the home where abuse has occurred has also proven an illusive goal. Before removing the child the agency must conduct an investigation of the facts and make a determination based on those facts. Studies of children placed in foster care have questioned the reliability of the decision-making process that leads to removal. Further, empirical studies of risk assessment and prevention strategies have consistently reported imprecision and low reliability in predicting abuse (Dingwall, 1989; McDonald and Marks, 1991; Starr, R.H., 1982; Wald and Woolverton, 1990). After reviewing the risk assessment literature Dingwall (1989, 51) concludes, "this paper must come to a bleak conclusion. The amount of scientifically validated research on child abuse and neglect is vanishingly small. The value of any self-styled predictive checklist is negligible."

Neither have efforts to identify potential child abusers in the general population met with great success. In 1981, Garbarino and Stocking reported, "The most detailed and fully developed of these profiles [Helfer, 1978] designated 60 percent of the general population at risk for becoming involved in child abuse" (p. 7). When more than half the population is determined to be at risk of abuse, then questions have to be raised about the adequacy, appropriateness and precision of the risk assessment process.

As Besharov (1987, 306-307) has indicated:

> The unvarnished truth is that there is no way of predicting, with any degree of certainty, whether a particular parent will become abusive or neglectful. Despite years of research, there is no psychological profile that accurately identifies parents who will abuse or neglect their child in the future. At the present time, unless the parent is suffering from a severe mental disability, the only reliable basis for predicting future danger is the parents' past behavior.

Child Abuse Prevention. Related to the issue of risk assessment is prevention. If it were possible to identify those children at greatest risk of serious abuse, prevention strategies could be targeted to these "at risk" populations. However, the development of prevention technology has not been sufficiently successful that we can safely rely on the approaches we have (Hardicker, Exton, and Barker, 1991; Kaplan and Reich, 1976). Kempe and Kempe (1978) examined a sample of 350 children in which they identified 100 mothers as "high-risk" child abusers. As a comparison group they selected a low-risk group of 50 mothers. However, only 8 of the 100 high-risk families were ever reported to the Central Child Abuse Registry. Using this definition of child abuse, Montgomery (1982) suggested that the Kempe and Kempe screening was only 8 percent accurate—or 92 percent wrong.

Kempe and his colleagues then divided the original group of 100 mothers into two groups. Half of the high-risk mothers received routine follow-up services, while the other half received intervention and prevention services especially designed to prevent abuse. The prevention strategy included close monitoring and care by a pediatrician, detailed observation in the hospital, frequent telephone contact, regular health visitor contact, and, when necessary, referral to medical and mental health facilities. However, analysis of the results of these prevention efforts found no statistically significant difference between the two groups on the key measure of Central Child Abuse Registry reports, observed abnormal parenting practices, accidents, or scores on the Denver Development Screening test (Gray et al., 1977).

The largest screening and prevention program subjected to clinical examination was conducted by Lealman and colleagues (1983). These investigators screened 2,802 maternity cases and identified 511 families as "at risk." These families were divided into three treatment and intervention groups. One group of 103 was treated as "high risk intervention" and provided contact with a project social worker. A second group of 209 was regarded as a high risk nonintervention group and given no treatment or intervention. The third group of 199 was assigned to the high risk social work group where families were already receiving social work support. How successful was intervention in reducing child abuse in this British sample? The researchers reported that "we have no statistical evidence to support the view that intervention improved parenting practice"

After reviewing the research studies on prevention, Parton (1985, 144) observes: "Certainly if there are two populations who suffer from the disease and only one is treated you would anticipate the incidence and prevalence of the disease in the treated population to decrease. However, there are very few studies which attempt to evaluate the success of interventions into child abuse. Those that do, cast serious doubt on the efficacy of such efforts."

Child Abuse Treatment. Children who have been abused need care and treatment for the injuries suffered. Yet, Cohn and Daro (1987) argue that waiting until abuse and neglect occur before providing treatment is to wait too long. They reviewed major evaluation studies of child abuse treatment programs that served more than three thousand families in ninety different programs. The findings raised concern about the effectiveness of such treatment. Cohn and Daro (1987) write, "Treatment effects in general are not very successful. Child abuse and neglect continue despite early, thoughtful, and often costly intervention. Treatment programs have been relatively ineffective in initially halting abusive and neglectful behavior or in reducing the future likelihood of maltreatment" (p. 440).

Inadequate Funding. The second explanation for the failure of mandated reporting to reduce child abuse is that our current child protective services agencies are inadequately funded for the tasks presented them. If sufficient funds were provided to handle the large volume of reports, abuse would decline. Anne Cohn Donnelly (1991, 106) President of the National Committee for the Prevention of Child Abuse, argues the point:

> Times have changed a lot for children's protective service agencies in this country [U.S.A.]. Once the agency to whom families were referred for help when problems of child abuse were apparent (and from whom help was provided), children's protective services today largely serve only an investigative function. With increased numbers of reports and no increases in funding have come increased caseload sizes and, most regrettably, fewer and fewer services for families. Once families at risk for abuse were helped by CPS; today, even in the most serious of confirmed child abuse cases, help may not be offered. The result—abuse continues. As long as protective service agencies are not offering help to families, efforts to prevent child abuse will be stymied. During the next decade we must work to restore to children's protective service agencies their original function of helping families, largely by ensuring they receive the increased funding required.

Too Broad a Definition of Abuse

A major concern about the mandatory reporting laws has been that their definition of abuse is too broad (Besharov, 1990a; Hutchison, 1993). Beginning with a limited concern with the severe physical abuse observed by physicians, the definition of child abuse was expanded to include any act that harms a child. Since the mandatory child abuse reporting laws were not accompanied with additional funding, public child welfare agencies have had to shift their focus and reduce their services, with the result that many children receive nothing more than an "investigation." Recent data in California suggest that approximately 9 percent of children who are reported for child abuse and neglect receive any services (Barth, 1991, verbal communication; see Barth, Berrick, and Courtney, 1990). Thus, for more than 90 percent of children their services are limited to investigation.

Hutchison (1993) has suggested that narrowing the definition of child abuse would allow for greater protection of those children most vulnerable to serious injury or death. She urges that serious physical injury to a child, threats of imminent physical harm, or acts of sexual molestation should be the only forms of abuse included in mandated reporting legislation.

Hutchison is not alone in attempting to narrow the definition of abuse. For nearly two decades, legal theorists have been suggesting that the state should intrude into family life only in cases of severe abuse (Goldstein, Freud, and Solnit, 1979; Mnookin, 1973)—that is, when the children have been "severely assaulted," "systematically tortured," "sexually abused," or in a situation "so dangerous that it poses an immediate threat of serious injury." As described earlier, it was the medical evidence of cases of serious physical abuse that led to the mandatory reporting laws. Nevertheless, among the public from whom the reports emerge, the perception of abuse covers a wide range.

In 1991, Pryor reported that in New York state, less than 1 percent of child abuse allegations involved "battered children" (that is, children presenting serious physical injuries including fractures, subdural hematoma/internal injuries or death). The most frequent reason for a child abuse allegation was "lack of supervision" (Pryor, 1991).

The broadening of the definition of child abuse has also limited progress in the search for predictors. Dingwall (1989, 42) has indicated that two methodological fallacies have been responsible for the limited scientific advances made in the field of child abuse: "The definitional fallacy is the confusion of social and scientific problems and the failure to construct persuasive operational definitions of abuse or neglect. The statistical fallacy is the failure to recognize that, when one is dealing with a phenomenon which has a low rate of prevalence, even the best predictors yield a high and probably unacceptable level of errors."

Fatalities Are an Outlier. For various reasons, then, it appears that increased reporting is not a variable affecting the rate of child abuse as indicated by child fatalities. But are fatalities even a reliable indicator of the rate of abuse? Child abuse fatalities are, in fact, a rare event. In 1990, there were fewer than one fatality for every two thousand child abuse reports in the United States. Despite this, for the general public, fatality data are the most important indicator of abuse. Few events mobilize public sentiment more than the death of an innocent child at the hands of the parent(s). The American Humane Association examined the coverage of child abuse in the major newspapers in forty-eight states in the same year that the "Battered Child Syndrome" was published (1962) and identified 662 reports of abuse (DeFrancis, 1966). Of these, 178 led to a child fatality. In other words, one of every four abuse reports covered in the mass media were fatalities, even though fatalities represent only a small segment of abuse reports, less than one per 2,500. In 1985 Corby examined the coverage of child abuse in the British newspaper, *The Guardian*, and found eight cases where children were abused by their parents. In six of these cases the children died. Clearly, it is the dramatic horror of a child fatality which attracts media attention. Unfortunately, this disproportionate reporting of cases of child brutality and fatalities leads to popular misconceptions about the nature and extent of the problem of child abuse (cf. Nunnally, 1961).

Do Children, Once Identified, Get Protection?

It is not clear that even if precise definitions of abuse were available that those children who are reported are eventually provided adequate protection (Zigler, 1979). As mentioned, child welfare agencies have found it difficult to determine whether or not a child should be removed from the home (Franklin, 1975). This has been true even for severe abuse cases (Dingwall, 1989). The literature consistently indicates imprecision and even bias in deciding whether or not to remove a child from his or her family because of abuse (Lindsey, 1991b; Packman, Randall, and Jacques, 1986).

In 1986 Katz and colleagues examined the records of 185 suspected abused or neglected children admitted to Boston's Children's Hospital. The investigators sought to determine how demographic variables and measures of the severity of injury influenced the decision to remove the child. They developed a four-point scale to assess the injuries of children coming to the hospital. Was the injury:

- Life threatening (death imminent without medical intervention)?
- Serious (death unlikely but further deterioration of function highly probable without medical intervention)?
- Moderate (death or deterioration of function unlikely but the condition serious enough to interfere with the usual function and treatment of some type necessary to hasten reversal of the injurious process)?
- Minimal possibility of slight loss of function (injury can resolve with or without medical intervention)?

Most of the children in the sample were treated either through the hospital emergency room (44 %) or through the surgical emergency room (39.2 percent). After assessing cases according to this scale three case outcomes were distinguished: the child was returned home without services, the child was returned home with services, or the child was removed from the home.

To what extent did the severity of the child's injury influence removal from the home? Katz and colleagues (1986, 257, 259) report: "Severity of condition was not significantly associated with [a particular] outcome. [In fact]... The presence of a physical injury decreased the likelihood of a child being placed outside of the home... Specifically, families that were Medicaid-eligible were more likely to have their children removed than were more affluent families in cases of physical injury." Hampton and Newberger (1985) found that social class and race were more important than the degree of severity of abuse. They write: "If the reporting of child abuse is as biased by class and race as these data suggest, there is a need for a critical review of the system as well as the process of reporting. To the extent that we selectively invoke agents of the state to police the lives of the poor and nonwhite families, we may be inappropriately and unfairly condemning these families as evil" (p. 58).

The same weak relationship between severity of abuse and removal of a child from the home has been observed in sexual abuse cases. Using a logistic regression model, Hunter and colleagues (1990) reported "severity of abuse" (i.e., fondling versus penetration) was not predictive of removal of the child in their sample (See table 1, p. 412). Thus, severity of abuse, when it can be reliably determined, is no gauge of whether or not the child will be subsequently protected.

Is this the Right Direction?

It is not a question of acute failure of a single element of the system. Instead, the child protection system is plagued by 'chronic and critical multiple organ failure.' No matter which element of the system that the Board examined—prevention, investigation, treatment, training, or research—the Board found a system in disarray, a societal response ill-suited in form or scope to respond to the profound problem facing it...The system the nation has devised to respond to child abuse and neglect is failing.

U.S. Advisory Board on Child Abuse and Neglect, *A Caring Community*

We have reached a point where it is useful to ask: Is the child welfare system going in the right direction by concentrating resources on child protection? Has the narrowing of focus and purpose achieved by the transformation of child welfare into child protective services led to improvement in the welfare of children? Despite the increased reporting of child abuse, child fatalities have not been reduced. Rather, as a result of the increased reporting, agencies are overburdened and underfunded. Child welfare agencies have been forced to abandon goals of fighting child poverty that had been developed from the field's inception. There is little evidence that this shift of direction or resources has achieved the goal of providing safety for children and a reduction in child abuse. If such evidence existed, we could be satisfied that child welfare in its current manifestation as child protective services, is going in the right direction.

In one sense, mandatory reporting laws have accomplished nothing more than to change the framework of the intake process of the child welfare system. Before the advent of mandatory child abuse reporting laws children were removed and services provided to the biological family in order to restore the children to their home when the parental problems that led to the removal had been addressed. The goal was to achieve "permanency planning," in which children were reunited with their families as soon as possible, while providing services to that family (Emlen et al., 1977; Fein et al., 1983; Pike et al., 1977; Stein et al., 1978).[51]

---

51. The term permanency planning highlighted the concern that foster care didn't provide children with a permanent home. Instead, children were viewed as drifting in foster care for years. Permanency planning allowed that foster care might not be detrimental to a child, even though it didn't provide the type of permanent home the child would have reunited with his or her parent or placed for adoption.

Within the prevailing protective services approach children are removed within a context of accusation and blame (Janko, 1991). Services are allocated not on the basis of a parent failing to adequately provide for the child but from an assessment deriving from alleged abuse, in which the parent is the suspect. The caseworker is not intervening primarily to help the family but to investigate and determine wrong doing.

The crucial question is whether the caseworker is qualified to adequately conduct such an investigation. Is the resulting assessment of risk accurate and reliable, and does it lead to adequate protection? The limited available data suggest that the answer is "no" on all issues. The protective service caseworker does not seem to be able to reliably assess risk nor provide protection when abuse is substantial except in extreme cases.

The question then becomes: Why mandate reporting if correct assessment cannot be reliably made and sufficient protection provided? The only result, as we have seen, is that agencies are forced to shift limited resources to clients who cannot be reliably identified. In the process the child welfare system takes an accusatory tone toward parents, making them a less-than-willing participant in the recovery process. Traditional goals are abandoned. Millions of other needy and deserving children go unserved.

Case Finding

The central problem for child welfare narrows to the question: Who should receive services and why? It is a question that highlights the essential drawbacks of a residual system of service, in which scarce resources cannot be given to all who need them. Child abuse has shaped the process by saying that only those who have been abused get services. But what an odd way to deliver child welfare services, for it means that services are no longer provided before abuse occurs, but only after. Child welfare services are now allocated on the basis of risk instead of need. And services are no longer provided within a noncoercive framework of help rather within a coercive framework that shields the child from the accused parent through protective services. But is it the accused who are abusing their children? In some instances parents do severely physically or sexually assault their children. But these instances are the exception. Most children, as we shall see, are taken into care by the child welfare agencies for other reasons.

The proper foundation for effective child abuse prevention strategies involves the ability of parents to provide the basic needs of food, shelter, clothing, housing, and medical care for their children. In 1975, Sussman and Cohen who were architects of the early mandatory reporting laws, pointed out the need to ensure that parents not be reported for abuse or neglect simply because they lacked the resources to provide for their children. They urged delaying enactment of expanded mandatory reporting laws until programs designed to ensure that affected parents had the resources to provide adequate food, shelter, and housing for their children were in place.

Sussman and Cohen (1975) pointed toward the crux of the problem at the time the mandated reporting laws were being expanded: Without proper provision for the basic necessities of food, shelter, and medical care, mandated reporting may be rendered ineffective. Summarizing a review of the factors that contributed to child abuse fatalities for a sample of 100 children in Canada, Cyril Greenland (1987) concluded, "it should now be obvious that little progress can be made in reducing the incidence of deaths due to child abuse and neglect until the problem of poverty afflicting some 35 million Americans, mostly women and children, is effectively dealt with" (p. 36).

Summary and Conclusion

The public child welfare system has been transformed into a child protective service system designed to protect children from physical and sexual abuse at the hands of their parents. The horror and pain of the circumstances of these young children mobilizes all of us to action. Yet how many children's lives have been saved as a result of the enormous increase in child abuse reporting? It is important that the achievements of improved reporting not be exaggerated. Although it is difficult to determine how much of a difference increased reporting has made for abused children, the data examined here would suggest that the difference is negligible.

There is no evidence that the transformation of the child welfare system into protective services has resulted in reduced child abuse fatalities. Nor is there evidence that children are safer as a result of the transformation. We do know that the transformation reduced the number of children receiving services, while increasing the number of families being investigated for abuse. In the process, the nature of the child welfare agency has changed from one of helping parents to one of "soft" policing of parents.

The laudable effort to increase mandated child abuse reporting must be assessed against evidence demonstrating that children are safer as a result. Without ensuring that the basic needs of all children are met, the potential effectiveness of mandated reporting may go unrealized, just as the drafters of the original mandated child abuse reporting laws cautioned.

In the next chapter we examine the decision-making process as it exists among child welfare caseworkers in the hope that it may point us toward the direction to take in solving the problem.

6

Decision-making in Child Welfare:
Linchpin of the Residual Model

Only one variable other than single motherhood was a better predictor of child removal: poverty...The Society [protective services] was sensitive to allegations that it kidnapped poor people's children, and its stated policy was that it never removed children from their homes for poverty alone. But poverty was never alone. The characteristic signs of child neglect in this period [1880-1920]—dirty clothing, soiled linen, lice and worms, crowded sleeping conditions, lack of attention and supervision, untreated infections and running sores, rickets and other malformations, truancy, malnutrition, overwork—were often the results of poverty.

Linda Gordon, *Heroes of Their Own Lives*

Throughout the twentieth century the main service offered by public child welfare agencies has been foster care. Although major changes have occurred among the families served by public child welfare agencies, the essential service provided—foster care—remains intact. Efforts to reduce the number of children in foster care through "permanency planning" led to temporary reductions. However, with the transformation of child welfare into child protection, the numbers of children in foster care returned to previous levels.

In 1993, 450,000 children were living in foster care in the United States, with the number expected to increase to more than 500,000 by 1994 (Select Committee on Children, Youth and Families, 1989a). In Canada in 1985 more than 75,000 children had been placed out of their own homes (Callahan, 1985, table 1). The vast majority of these children were not orphaned or abandoned but purposely removed from their families by the public child welfare system.

Upon what evidence did child welfare professionals decide to place these children in foster care? What factors influenced the decision? Were the decisions reliable, consistent, fair? In so far as foster care has become the de facto solution to child abuse, which has become the principal concern of child welfare agencies, the answers to such questions are the key to evaluating the direction, fairness, and effectiveness of the child welfare system. Over time, the residual perspective has tended to narrow the scope of the child welfare system in determining who gets what. In the context of shrinking resources, the function of decision-making has been to allocate increasingly limited services to a narrowing group of children, by determining the child's risk of abuse at the hands of alleged abusing parents. Reliable and valid decision thus represent the linchpin of the current child welfare system.

Review of the Literature

Although research studies have examined the decision-making process that leads to foster care, professionals have never fully understood exactly how such decisions are made. In 1963 Scott Briar observed: "Perhaps no decisions in social casework practice pose more awesome responsibilities for the caseworker and are more far-reaching in their potential consequences for the client than those involved in the placement of children in foster care... Systematically, we know next to nothing about how the child-placement worker makes these decisions" (p. 161).

More than twenty years later, Schwab, Bruce, and McRoy (1986) while attempting to build a computer model to assist in the child placement decision-making process, noted that research had found "no consensus among social workers about which placements were best for which children" (p. 360; cf. Schuerman and Vogel, 1986; Allan, 1978). In 1989, Howling and colleagues summarized:

> The extensive body of research on the etiology and effects of child maltreatment is characterized by flawed methodology, marked by inadequate definitions, lack of sound theoretical foundation, cross-sectional design limitations, sampling gaps, inadequate or missing control groups, and unidimensional measures. As a result, far reaching decisions in the field of child welfare have been based on questionable findings. (p. 3)

Deborah Daro (1988) provides a similar assessment of the literature. She writes, "The scholarly and popular literature on child maltreatment since 1962 is, to say the least, abundant...Unfortunately, the results of these research efforts have not been as accessible or as useful to the decision-making process as their authors had hoped. Barriers to effective utilization have included methodological problems such as small, nonrepresentative samples, an uncertainty over which variables to explore and monitor, a very narrow range of intervention strategies to assess, and the absence of control groups" (p. 2-3).

Nevertheless, the child welfare system, which has been transformed into a child protective system, must protect children from dangerous or unacceptable home situations. Providing such protection requires intrusion into the homes of families suspected of improperly caring for their children and deciding whether or not to remove them. From it earliest days the child welfare system has struggled with the potential bias such intrusion into family represents. Examining the early history of child protection in the United States, Gordon (1990, 95) observes:

> The problems of single mothers in child neglect cases defy any clear distinction between agency bias and objective reality. The "bias" of social workers against single mothers might, for example, be described as prediction based on past experience. Furthermore, neither the social workers nor contemporary researchers studying the case records could easily distinguish children's deprivations caused by poverty from those caused by parental indifference and hostility: because parental indifference and hostility were among the most common products of poverty, and because parents' depression was implicated both as a cause and effect of poverty. Further social workers' very standards of what constituted deprivation, and the entire notion of children's rights to a certain standard of treatment, were "biased," the product of specific class and cultural experience.

The decision-making process involved in determining which children are removed from their parents is, thus, central to the operation of the child welfare system. In a secular society, decision-making in child welfare must have a scientific basis to insure that the decision to remove children is not biased or prejudicial. However, there is concern that the decision-making does not have an adequate scientific basis. As Stein, Gambrill and Wiltse (1978) observe, "Children have been removed because the court disapproved of the parents' life style or child rearing practices. Removal has occurred, for example, because the parents were not married, because the mother frequented taverns or had male visitors overnight, because the parents adhered to extreme religious beliefs or lived in a communal setting, because the parent was a lesbian or male homosexual, because the parents' home was filthy or because the woman was the mother of an illegitimate child. In none of these cases was there evidence of harm to the children. In such instances, socially unacceptable behavior of the parents is condemned on the pretext of acting in the child's best interest" (p. 5).

When a moralistic approach takes precedence over a scientific approach, discretionary decision-making based upon personal and subjective value judgments and opinions is encouraged. Such a nonscientific decision-making base undermines the whole purpose of state intervention to protect children, thereby making it difficult to establish accountability for services provided.

Early Approaches to Diagnostic Assessment and Placement

Over the years, attempts have been made to develop guidelines and diagnostic criteria that would aid the caseworker in deciding for or against placement. The first major contributions emphasized the use of the casework method for clients (Charnley, 1955; Gordon, 1956). However, these studies did not address the issue of the foster care placement decision-making process. In 1957 Glickman pioneered the use of psychodynamic theory in child welfare, which emphasized two psychological factors: First, was the level of emotional disturbance severe enough to upset the family balance? Did sufficient compensations exist within the family to offset the imbalance? Second, what was the location of the disturbance (i.e., in the child, mother, father, siblings, mother's boyfriend?), and did it intrude upon the parent-child relationship?

In 1972 Kline and Overstreet, building on the work of Glickman, developed a similar psychodynamic approach, in which they delineated four clinical areas where the diagnostic judgements for decision-making should focus:

- The nature of the crisis and the presenting problems of the child and family.
- The ego functioning of the parents in their major life roles and their capacity to cope with the current family crisis.
- The family's situation, organizational level, and resources.
- The developmental status and condition of the children.

Within the framework proposed by such clinical work the placement decision was based on a quasi-psychiatric diagnosis of both the type and degree of emotional pathology experienced by the parent. For Kadushin

(1965, 28-29) the need for placement was seen as resulting from such factors as:

- parental incapacity to love because the parent himself has not adequately loved,
- parental incapacity in meeting dependency needs since the parent himself is still childishly dependent,
- reactivation by the child of unresolved conflicts relating to the Oedipal situation, sibling rivalry, sexual identification—a reactivation which threatens the precarious emotional equilibrium of the parents,
- parental narcissism manifested in neglect of the child's needs,
- a superego which is not sufficiently controlling to help the parent consistently meet the demands of parenthood, with this superego deficiency a consequence of a lack of stable, affectionate opportunities for identification.

The shorthand characterization of such parents is that they are immature and in their immaturity neglect their children. Personality disturbance, if not the sole cause for separation, is regarded as the principal cause. The practitioner, while recognizing that ego faces id, superego, and the world of outer reality, tends to the ego's relationship to id and the superego in assessing the factors which have resulted in failure to perform adequately.

Thus, early work on the child placement decision focused on the clinical dimensions of the child and the family, gradually narrowing to the psychological problems of the parent (Specht, 1990). The approaches were based on a deficit model, in which lack of personality development and psychological growth in the parent prevented the parent from adequately caring for the child (Stein et al., 1978, 9-11). The social or structural issues that affected these families—such as inadequate income, unemployment, discrimination, lack of decent employment opportunities, deteriorating neighborhood conditions (including such factors as widespread drug addiction and crime)—were outside the concern and intervention of the child welfare caseworker. As Kadushin (1965) explained: "Although the social situation is recognized as a contributing factor, it is given secondary consideration and is always somewhat suspect as the 'true' cause of the problem. Reality stresses tend to be regarded as convenient parental rationalization which permit the parent to defend himself against a recognition of his true rejection of the child" (p. 29).

However, clinical approaches designed to identify the normative model that child welfare workers should use in deciding whether to remove a child from the family had limitations. First, as Mahoney and Mahoney (1974) pointed out, the clinical models provided no empirical support for the diagnostic criteria they identified. The psychodynamic model could not be subjected to scientific examination. Rather, the views derived from clinical case analysis and judgement.[52] Second and more important, one could not assume that child welfare caseworkers responsible for making foster care placement decisions had the professional training in clinical diagnosis that the models required. No evidence suggests that caseworkers involved in this decision-making process were ever trained in these areas.

In the final analysis, the psychodynamic models that the clinicians developed went largely unused since few child welfare caseworkers ever became familiar with them.[53] We can see this by evaluating the decision-making process as it has, in fact, been carried out by caseworkers even to the present day.

Reliability of the Decision-making Process: Three Studies

First Study. In 1963, Briar, in one of the earliest studies on the reliability of foster care placement decision-making, examined caseworker judgement using hypothetical case material. Each worker in the study was asked to prepare diagnostic and prognostic judgments about two hypothetical cases involving either a mildly or severely disturbed child. One group of twenty-one caseworkers received cases involving a mildly disturbed child, while a second group of twenty-two caseworkers received cases involving a severely disturbed child.

Principally, Briar wanted to know whether the child's problem (i.e., mild or severe disturbance) determined the type of placement he or she would

---

52. The one exception was the research by Boehm (1962), which examined the criteria used to decide when a child should be removed. Boehm asked child welfare caseworkers to rate 100 placement and 100 nonplacement families on a checklist of behavioral items. The major difference between the two groups was on the dimension of maternal behavior. Boehm concluded that the decision to remove a child was dependent on the worker's view of the relationship between the parent and child.

53. Goldstein, Freud, and Solnit (1973; 1979) used the psychodynamic model to urge that children be removed from their family only under the most extreme conditions of severe physical or sexual abuse. The bonding between the parent and child, they argued, was essential for healthy development and should be disrupted only to prevent the most extreme harmful conditions.

receive. The study revealed only a limited association between the two. Although Briar found a relationship between the child's problem and type of placement, it was variable and unpredictable. While some agreement on diagnosis existed, predictions regarding the child's probable future varied substantially from caseworker to caseworker. Briar reported a coefficient for prognostic items of only .15. Given that accurate prognosis is the critical factor in determining removal of the child, the study raised doubts about the reliability of the decision-making process. Briar reported that, in fact, the mother's preference largely determined the type of placement the caseworker ultimately selected. In cases where the mother opposed foster care placement, 77 percent of the workers recommended institutional placement. Similarly, when the mother opposed institutional placement, fewer than half of the workers recommended it.[54]

In 1970, Edmund Mech reviewed the literature on decision-making in child welfare and found that, with regard to the decision to return a child home or keep a child in care, no differential factors could be identified (p. 44). He concluded that no framework for decision-making existed, and that developing one was vital. This call led to additional studies.

Second Study. In 1972, Phillips, Haring, and Shyne sought to develop an interview guide that would explicitly define the factors leading to in-home or out-of-home service. They asked workers to make case plans detailing what services were intended for children in foster care and what efforts would be made to restore the children to their families. The caseworkers developed plans for 309 children in need of service, 71 for whom placement had been recommended. The researchers compared the placement and non-placement groups on the nature of the service request, socioeconomic characteristics, behavioral and attitudinal evaluations of mother, father and child, and adequacy of parental care.

Fifty variables were associated with the decision to remove a child from the home, so many that it was difficult to understand which factors influ-

---

54. Local environmental conditions also influenced the caseworkers' recommendations more strongly than did the child's problem. The study revealed a significant association between the workers' placement recommendations and placement patterns of their agencies. For example, foster care was recommended by 63 percent of workers employed in agencies where this form of care predominated. In contrast, institutional placement was recommended by 75 percent of the workers employed in agencies where institutional care predominated. Workers commented that practical realities, such as the availability of resources, strongly influenced their placement decisions.

**Table 6.1 Recommended Dispositions of 127
Foster Care Placement Cases**

	Remove Child	Keep at Home
Judge A	53%	47%
Judge B	17	83
Judge C	72	28
Judge D	43	57
Judge E	34	66
Judge F	49	51
Caseworkers	38	62

Source: Phillips, Haring, and Shyne (1971).

enced placement. Although the research sought to group the variables into meaningful components, considerable overlap between the component groups existed. The researchers therefore sorted the variables into seven groups to improve their predictive capacity. For both two-parent and lone-mother households, background factors and child traits differentiated between children who were removed and children who were not. For lone-mother households, mother traits also differentiated between the two groups, while for two-parent families father traits became the differentiating characteristics. The study found that background factors were by far the best predictors of placement, with socioeconomic status being the major determinant (see Garbarino and Stocking, 1981; Page, 1987).

In developing and refining the interview schedule, the researchers also assessed the *reliability* of experienced child welfare workers and judges in recommending for or against removal. In the disposition decisions made for 127 child placement cases the researchers found considerable disagreement between the judges and caseworkers (See Table 6.1). The overall agreement of the six judges was less than 25 percent (p. 24). The contrast between two judges (B and C) was particularly remarkable: Judge C was four times more likely to recommend in-home services than was Judge B. Moreover, even when judges agreed to remove a child, which was rare, they varied substan-tially on the type of plan and services to be provided.

**Table 6.2 Recommended Dispositions of 45
Foster Care Placement Cases in California**

	Percent Child Removed	Percent Child Keep at Home
San Bernardino	29	71
Riverside	51	49
Alameda	58	42
San Francisco	36	64

Source: Donnelly (1980).

Third Study. In 1980, Donnelly examined foster care placement decisions by asking experienced caseworkers in four California counties to make recommendations on fifteen hypothetical cases. As in the previous studies, the decision to remove a child from the home varied substantially between the caseworkers. Those in Riverside and Alameda counties were more likely to remove a child than were caseworkers in San Bernadino and San Francisco counties, despite the geographic proximities (see Table 6.2)

Part of the low reliability of decision-making found in these studies may be related to the validity of the stimulus materials used. That is, in all three studies the caseworkers used written case materials instead of actually meeting and interviewing the families. The studies by Briar (1963) and Donnelly (1980) used hypothetical case materials, while Philips, Haring and Shyne (1971) used actual case materials. The use of vignettes and case materials presents potential validity problems, since interviewing the families and children directly may have permitted a greater depth of inquiry.

Nevertheless, in the absence of reliability studies with actual cases, these studies represent the best current indicator of reliability in foster care placement. The studies suggest that limited consensus exists on what criteria should be used in removing a child from the home. Further, the reliability of the decision-making process is either not statistically significant (Donnelley, 1980; Gart, 1971; Philips, Haring, and Shyne, 1971) or low (Briar, 1963).

Decision-making as a Stochastic Process

What are the consequences of such a low rate of reliability for the selection of children for placement in foster care? To answer this question, we examined this rate within the context of a hypothetical model that viewed decision-making as a stochastic (random) process (Groenveld and Giovannoni, 1977; Tyler and Brassard, 1984). We considered a hypothetical system involving 100 children serviced by an "ideal" decision-making child welfare system in which the reliability rate was 1.0 (see Table 6.3). That is, every placement decision made by the system was correct. In this system thirty-one children would possess "true need for placement" and be placed in foster care, while the sixty-nine who possessed lesser "true need for placement" would be retained with their families.

When an assumption of a reliability of .25 was applied to the system (a level of reliability that is greater than has been found in previous studies), the model demonstrated the limitations of the current decision-making process with its low reliability. Almost half of the children who, under ideal circumstances, would have been identified as "in need of placement" were instead assessed as not in need of placement and replaced with children of lesser "true need for placement." That is, only sixteen of the thirty-one children who should have been placed in foster care were properly selected, while fifteen of the thirty-one children placed were improperly taken from their biological parent(s). These fifteen children displaced fifteen children who needed placement but did not receive it. In short, the low reliability leads to a system that is unable to discern which child should be removed and which child should be left at home.

The model confirms Pelton's suspicion (1989, 67):

> There are certainly some children of those endangered by severe harm for whom placement in foster care, despite its known deficiencies and attendant harms, would be the relatively least detrimental alternative. But who are these children who cannot be protected in their own homes by less disruptive and relatively harmful means than child removal? It is my belief that not only are there many children in foster care who should not have been placed there, but that there are other children who are being wrongfully left in their natural homes. In short, children are being removed from their homes in the wrong cases and being left at home in the wrong cases. Furthermore, it is my belief that if only those children were placed in foster care who would actually need it, we would have very few children in foster care.

Table 6.3 Disposition of 100 Hypothetical Foster Care Placement Cases under a Model of Assessment Reliability of .25

Model with True Quality in Standard Deviations		Number of Placements Decisions Considered	Expected Midpoint in Standard Deviations	Percent Placed in Foster Home	Model with Reliability of .25	
					Expected Foster Home Placements	Expected Own Home Placements
-3	to -2.5	1	-2.75	1.43	0	1
-2.5	-2	1	-2.25	2.87	0	1
-2	-1.5	5	-1.75	5.37	0	5
-1.5	-1	9	-1.25	9.34	1 -{improperly	8
-1	-.5	15	-.75	15.15	2 I left in	13
-0.5	0	19	-.25	22.96	4 I home}	15
0.0	-.5	19	.25	32.28	6 I	13
				{decision line}		
.5	to 1	15	.75	43.25	6	9
1	1.5	9	1.25	54.78	5 I{properly	4 I{improperly
1.5	2	5	1.75	65.91	3 I placed}	2 I taken from
2	2.5	1	2.25	75.80	1 I	0 parent(s)}
2.5	3	1	2.75	83.89	1 I	0

These results assume that the true "need for placement" and the observed decision have a bivariate normal distribution with a correlation equal to the square root of the reliability. If ρ^2 is the reliability, the probability of placing a child whose true "need for placement" is X is given by:

$$1 - \Phi \, [\, (\, 1 - X \rho \,) \, / \, \text{sqrt}[1 - \rho^2 \,]$$

where Φ (.) is the cumulative normal distribution function.

The most salient feature of the stochastic model is that it does not require assumptions of bias or prejudice on the part of the child welfare caseworker to account for the removal of a great many children not in need of placement or the returning home of a large number of children in true need of placement. Caseworkers in doubt about a child's situation make the safe decision to remove a child. Too often, as Stein, Gambrill and Wiltse (1978) point out, the caseworker is in doubt, thus the caseworker too often places the child in foster care. Kamerman and Kahn (1990, 8) observe, "Child protective staff fear errors, especially the failure to take endangered children into care, and the subsequent public response to deaths or severe abuse and neglect."

It is hard to imagine how the results of the stochastic model could be more distressful, in terms of what it suggests for the outcome of children considered for removal. If the level of reliability were to slip much further than .25, all children, except in the most extreme cases, would have an equal likelihood of being placed in foster homes, meaning that the decision-making process would be roughly equivalent to a lottery!

Explaining Low Reliability

Why is the level of reliability in assessing need for placement so low? Stein and Rzepnicki (1984, 8) identified a number of probable factors:

> While worker's decision-making behavior is constrained by resource deficits, by the fact that some decisions are made by others before a worker receives a case, and by practices within a given agency, failure to identify practice principles that govern the selection of options is distressing... It is not surprising, therefore, that reliability in decision-making is poor and that individual discretion and personal bias have been found to exert a strong influence on the decision-making behavior of child welfare staff.

The studies of the psychodynamic model, which focused on the parent-child relationship, assumed a supporting body of scientific knowledge that, in fact, did not exist. A review of these studies reveals idiosyncratic decision-making within a context of limited scientific knowledge. Caseworkers, even had they known of these models, and had been following them, would likely have achieved little better than random success. But even within an ideal scientific context limits exist on the ability of skilled practitioners to successfully predict client behavior. As Besharov (1987, 307) has observed: "Expecting child protective workers and judges to predict future child maltreatment is completely unrealistic and ultimately counterproductive. Overstating their ability to predict future maltreatment puts them under enormous pressure to remove children from their parents lest they be blamed if a child subsequently suffers serious harm."

Two points must be underscored. First, the child welfare field does not possess an adequate scientific knowledge base for determining which cases are best served in-home and which need out-of-home care (see Stein et al., 1978; Stein and Rzepnicki, 1984). The limited research in this area has often only categorized and documented current casework procedure, forsaking systematic investigation that might identify which indicators in fact do lead to the desired outcome for children. To date, we still do not know with any precision when foster care is appropriate, for how long it should be administered, or what services should be combined with it. Second, environmental factors, funding patterns, and organizational characteristics of social service bureaucracies (i.e., variables external to children and their family) may be more instrumental in influencing the worker's decision about placement (Amacher and Maas, 1985; Hutchison, 1989; Proch and Howard, 1986).

Factors Affecting the Foster Care Placement Decision

At this point we turn from the question of *reliability* of the decision-making process under the psychodynamic and casework models to the *validity* of those models. So far, the studies indicate that the decision-making about foster care lacks consistency and reliability, due perhaps to an absence of a scientific foundation for their decision-making. Now the question becomes, how valid are the models in guiding the decision to remove a child? In other words, are the criteria discussed in theory with respect to the decision-making process the actual criteria used in practice?

To determine what factors actually lead to removal, we used a statistical approach to examine a representative sample of children who had been removed from their homes. Our interest was to determine whether the factors the theoretical models identified a priori as critical and determinative in the decision-making process, actually played a part in the decisions made. And if so, how much?

We employed a discriminant analysis, which included variables that theory and previous research had indicated are commonly used in deciding to place a child in foster care (Jenkins and Sauber, 1966; Palmer, 1971; Phillips et al., 1972; Stein and Rzepnick, 1984). The discriminant analysis sought to determine which variables best differentiated between children who were either: (1) removed from their parent(s) and placed in foster care, or (2) kept in their home and provided supportive services. Only those children whose circumstances were severe enough to require intervention were included. Children in different age groups were analyzed separately (Hornby and Collins, 1981). We thus computed four different discriminant analyses.

The resulting values of this analysis, displayed in Table 6.4, represent the relative weight or emphasis given a variable by the caseworker in deciding whether or not to place a child in foster care. The larger the value, the greater the weight or emphasis. For example, the variable that received

Table 6.4 Variables Predicting Whether a Child Received Family Foster Care Placement or Supportive Services, Controlling for Age

Independent Variables	Preschool (0-5) Foster	Support	Elementary School (6-12) Foster	Support	Early Teens (13-15) Foster	Support	Late Teens (16-18) Foster	Support
Income Source								
Self Support	-1.315	+.578	-.834	+.367	-.698	+.307	-.699	+.307
Government	-1.634	+.719	-1.142	+.502	-1.127	+.496	-.718	+.316
Self & Govt.	-0.909	+.400	-.887	+.390	-.938	+.412	-.786	+.345
Neither Self nor Govt	-0.354	+.156	-.122	+.054	+.010	-.004	-.107	+.047
Referral Source								
Parent	-0.464	+.204	-.341	+.150	-.175	+.077	-.263	+.116
Professional	-0.184	+.081	-.359	+.158	-.051	+.022	-.185	+.081
Agency	-0.147	+.065	-.332	+.146	+.147	-.065	-.808	+.355
Informal	-0.033	+.015	+.039	-.017	+.154	-.068	-.235	+.103
Legal	-0.010	+.004	-.016	+.007	+.426	-.187	-.283	+.124
Referral Reason								
Neglect	+0.439	-.193	+.348	-.153	+.179	-.079	-.072	+.032
Abuse	+0.156	-.069	-.039	+.017	-.004	+.002	-.695	+.306
Parent Problem	+0.265	-.117	+.346	-.152	+.148	-.065	+.190	-.084
Child Behavior	-0.053	+.023	-.018	+.008	-.269	+.118	-.386	+.368
Emergency	+0.506	-.223	+.617	-.271	+.410	-.180	-.006	+.003

Source: Compiled by Author.

greatest weight in the worker's decision to remove a preschool child was "government income support" (-1.634), meaning that if the parent (defined as the principal child caring person) was receiving government income (i.e., public assistance) their children were less likely to be removed. During computation the model dropped variables that presented a value too small to have any discriminative affect.

Even a cursory examination of the data reveals that for preschool children through Early Teens, the economic security of the parents (income source variables) are the most influential variables in discriminating between placement and supportive services, far above referral reason and referral source variables. Those preschool children whose parents were without reliable income were most likely to be removed and placed in foster care, while children whose parents were either self-supporting or received government assistance were likely to remain in the home and receive supportive services. Surprisingly, those with government support were less likely to have their children removed than those with self-support wage income. Clearly, government income support (i.e., welfare) prevents placement.

For elementary school and early teenage children, the pattern was similar: the income source variables were the most important in predicting placement. Those parents without adequate income source were most likely to have their children removed. The provision of government assistance to the parent (1.142) was instrumental in preventing placement.

Services Controlling for Age

Interestingly, the predictive ability of the discriminant function for children in all categories was quite high. When modeled to determine reliability of the placement decision, the function was able to correctly classify between 70 and 80 percent of the cases in each of the four categories, compared to interrater reliability coefficients of less than .25 for the traditional psychodynamic models. While a lack of agreement might have existed within the traditional model on why a child should or shouldn't be removed, when we examined the children who actually had been removed, we found that it was adequacy of family income which best differentiated those who had been removed from those who had not.

Adequacy of Income

Before the data were analyzed we expected to find that referral reason variables (neglect, abuse, etc.) would be the best predictors of placement. The literature, as well as common sense, suggested this. Although the data reflects an influence from such variables, the discriminant analysis revealed that income source variables exerted the predominant influence in the decision process. Unequivocally, the discriminant analysis indicated that children were being removed from their parents and placed in foster care because their parents possessed inadequate income security. As Fanshel and

Shinn (1978) had observed, "Foster children tend to come largely out of the ghettos and poverty areas of our country in what seems to be almost a random process. There is no research in the literature to indicate that entrance into foster care can be predicted."[55] (p. 506).

Child welfare workers can only use the intervention services available to them. Increasingly, they are limited to foster care as the only available method of intervention. If social workers could provide preventive or income support services to families, the number of children placed in foster care would likely decline (Olson, 1970; Stein, Gambrill, and Wiltse, 1978; Torczyner and Pare, 1979).[56]

To account for the emphasis on income, we must look to other factors linked to income. What, for example, is the link between education and income? In this sample, the parents, by and large, lacked education. Emlen (1977, 19) found in his sample of families whose children were in foster care in Oregon that 83 percent of the mothers and 85 percent of the fathers had not gone past the eighth grade, a condition that certainly affected their ability to gain and hold employment.[57] Emlen reported that 92 percent of the mothers and 69 percent of the biological fathers were unable to report having steady employment. Some 76 percent of the mothers and 46 percent of the fathers had always or usually been on public assistance. Marjorie Martin (1985, 53) has observed, "All available evidence from historical sources and recent studies indicates that poor families are disproportionately higher users of public child welfare services in Canada."

---

55. At times it appears that the process of placing children in foster care is almost random. After simply shifting to a family perspective one agency reported that it was able to reduce the number of children removed from their parents by 84 percent. Colon (1981) reported the agency, "used to place twenty to thirty children each year in foster care. After shifting to a family perspective that made them scrutinize the reasons for foster placement, they offered family therapy instead and were able to reduce the number of placements to three to five a year."

56. In part, this is the argument of advocates of family preservation services. Their argument is that provision of preventive and support services would alleviate the need to remove a child and allow preservation of the family (compare with the approach developed in the Nashville-Davidson county Comprehensive Emergency Services program discussed in Chapter 3).

57. Several of the children in the sample lived with their mother and a legal father who was not their biological father (i.e., stepfather). In those cases where it was applicable, 56 percent of the legal fathers were unable to report steady employment.

Table 6.5 Family Composition and Source of Income

	Two Parent	Lone-Parent
Self Support	63%	28%
	(234,467)	(307,233)
Not Self Support	37%	72%
	(148,623)	(765,661)

Lone-Parenthood

A connection can certainly be made to the predicament of lone-parents. Most of the children in foster care come from impoverished lone-parent households. In 1987, the poverty rate for children in lone-mother households was 55 percent, and 12 percent for all others (Select Committee on Children, Youth, and Families, 1989b). Bebbington and Miles (1989) report from a survey of 2,300 children coming into care in Britain that living in lone-parent families was the most significant factor associated with admission into care. Children from lone-parent families were eight times more likely to be taken into care than other children. One of the major reasons many of these families are poor stems from the departure of the income producing parent who seldom contributes to the support of the children left behind (Colon, 1981). Numerous studies have documented that child support payments from the income earning spouse to the child caring spouse are erratic and often nonexistent, especially for low income households (Chambers, 1979; Kamerman and Kahn, 1988a; Stuart, 1986).

The data in Table 6.5 show that two-parent homes are more likely to be self supportive, while lone-parent families are not.

Yet the data in Table 6.6 show that within every category of income source the difference between rates of placement for two-parent versus lone-parent families is small. The overall placement rate for two-parent and lone-parent families was roughly equivalent: 45 percent for two-parent homes, and 43 percent for lone-parent homes. In other words, being a lone-parent per se does not lead to removal of a child. Rather, it is the lack of adequate income that befalls the lone-parent that leads to removal. When

Table 6.6 Family Composition and Foster Care Placement, Controlling for Income Source

		Child Removed	Child Kept at Home	Placement Rate (%)
Self Support	Two parent	33,861	49,589	41
	Lone-parent	68,149	79,250	46
Government	Two parent	11,780	10,596	53
Support	Lone-parent	85,569	173,304	33
Both Self and	Two parent	5,629	8,034	41
Government	Lone-parent	12,469	38,933	24
Neither Self Nor	Two parent	8,446	3,323	72
Government	Lone-parent	65,923	16,916	80
	Total two parent	59,716	71,542	45
	Total lone-parent	232,110	308,403	43

the lone-parent has neither self nor government support, the placement rate is at its highest—80 percent.

Without question, these data, in combination with the discriminant analysis findings, demonstrate that adequacy of income is the crucial determinant in the decision to remove a child. Even though the normative and psychodynamic theories that focus on the parent child relationship may not consider income source variables, they nevertheless have the greatest discriminative accuracy in differentiating children who are removed and placed in foster care, from those who are not. This direct measurable influence has yet to be demonstrated by the other clinical variables.

It may be that the measures employed in the discriminant analysis study did not adequately assess the clinical variables. Perhaps the subjective measures do not lend themselves to objective quantitative analysis. Despite this, the data suggest that no measure of the parent-child relationship was a major determinant in the decision to remove a child.

While the analysis shows that income security may be the major determinant in removing a child, it has usually not been a determinant in returning the child. In 1975 Jenkins and Norman conducted a follow-up study of

Table 6.7 Services to the Biological Family

	Child Removed (%)	Child Retained at Home (%)
Counseling	35.2	42.7
Employment	3.8	7.5
Family planning	5.4	6.8
Financial assistance	17.8	26.2
Health	9.2	16.8
Homemaking	3.8	10.4
Legal	4.2	2.9
Transportation	8.1	16.7

children in foster care. Five years after the sample entered care, 73 percent had been discharged to the care of their biological mothers. The researchers noted that "the chronic conditions that underlay their placement still persisted. Most families were living on the borderline of self-management, in terms of income, health and stability" (pp. 131-132). In fact, the financial situations of the mothers had deteriorated.[58]

Services to the Biological Family

Depending on the problems that led to placement, we would expect that services would be provided to address these problems (Gambrill, 1990). For example, if a child is removed because of a parent's drug and alcohol problem, clinical services would be forthcoming to address this problem. However, the data in Table 6.7 indicate that once the child was removed from the home, the biological parent was less likely to receive services than if the child was kept at home.

That large numbers of parents receive no services once their children are removed challenges fundamental premises on which removal is based,

---

58. At the time of the original placement 48 percent of the mothers were on AFDC, while five years later 71 percent were on AFDC. Little had changed for these families except the return of the child from foster care (Jenkins and Norman, 1972). The return of the child to the biological family did not appear to be related to improvements made in the biological family situation.

implying essentially that little effort is being made to restore the child. Fanshel and Shinn (1978) observed, "This is another indication that service to parents of children in placement is the most manifest and blatant area of failure in service delivery that one can find as one reviews the foster care phenomenon" (p. 486).

Instead of assisting the biological mothers with the immediate demands of child care, the placement worker may inadvertently be increasing their problems and reducing the likelihood of their ever regaining custody and care of their children. Besharov (1988b, 198) has observed:

> Treatment services for the parents of children in foster care are largely non-existent. In fact, the child's placement usually results in a reduction in the level of services parents receive. For example, the parent's public assistance grant will be reduced by the amount attributable to the child, often requiring the parent to move into a smaller, less attractive apartment— from which she will have to move again (to a larger apartment) before she can regain custody of the child. In today's housing market, this is no easy task. In addition, food stamps, homemaker services, and even the intermittent case-worker visits may be suspended during the time the child is in foster care. Only parents who wish to be relieved of the obligations of parenthood gain anything from their child's placement.

Factors Influencing the Foster Care Placement Decision

We turn now to an analysis of the variables involved in the decision to place a child in foster care. Whereas the discriminant analysis identified the variables most critical to the placement decision, it could not measure the relation between the variables, either individually or in combination. In exploring such questions, we are examining what Kadushin (1965, 38) termed the "separation rates" associated with factors that influence the decision-making process. To do this we applied an odds ratio approach[59] that identified the independent influence (or odds) of the variables associated with the sample examined previously by discriminant analysis.[60] Although the odds ratio appears only rarely in child welfare research studies (Hutchison, 1989; Munroe-Blum et al., 1989), it is widely used in chemical,

---

59. In order to determine how strongly two variables are related, it is possible to calculate the odds of a given value for both categories in a two-by-two table (Fienberg, 1981). If the odds for the two categories are sufficiently different then there is a relationship. It is useful to compare the odds more explicitly by calculating their ratio.

genetic, and medical contexts (Agresti, 1984; Anderson and Davidovits, 1975; Goodman, 1985; Kimura, 1965).[61] The odds ratio (quantity α) provides a clear interpretative value,[62] and is ideally suited for analyzing multidimensional tables of the type presented by this study.[63]

The analysis considered all factors generally leading to referral: reason for referral (dependency, neglect, abuse, etc.),[64] source of referral (parent legal, professional), demographic variables (race, sex, family composition), and finally, economic security, including employment of parent and adequacy of family income.[65]

Reasons for Referral

In the sample the major reasons for referral were:

- *Dependency.* Includes parent(s) unable to take care of their child, children without anyone to care for them, and children released for adoption.
- *Child reason.* Includes behavioral problems of the children at home, in the community, or at school, as well as any physical or mental health problems the child may have.

---

60. The large sample limits the use of goodness-of-fit statistics to analyze the data in this sample (Fienberg, 1981). As sample size exceeds several hundred cases, the standard errors diminish and all differences tend to be significant. Further, the goodness-of-fit models do not reveal the strength or form of the relationship. A further confounding factor for this sample is a skewed marginal distribution of the dependent variable (removal and placement of the child). The classification of cases into placement and nonplacement yields disproportionate marginals of removed and not removed. To control for these limitations in the following analysis we adopted an odds ratio approach (Bishop, Fienberg, and Holland, 1975).

61. The odds ratio also provides a number of maximum likelihood estimators for sample data, which permit tests of significance and association. However, with the large sample size, the tests of significance are not as useful as the indication of the relative influence of the independent variables.

62. If the odds are the same in both categories, their ratio will equal one. Thus, a value of one indicates no relationship. Likewise, a value greater or less than one indicates the existence of a relationship. The greater the departure from one the stronger the relationship.

63. If we begin by viewing the row totals as fixed, then $p11/p12$ is simply the odds of being in the first column given that one is in the first row, while $p21/p22$ is the odds of being in the second row. Thus, the relative odds for the two rows, or the odds ratio, is:

$$\frac{p11/p12}{p21/p22} = \frac{p11/p22}{p12/p21} = \alpha.$$

- *Parental condition.* Centers on mental or physical problems of the parent including incarceration.
- *Drug and alcohol problems* of the parents.
- *Neglect.* Includes abandonment and parent unwillingness to care for the child.
- *Abuse.* Includes exploitation and any physical harm that necessitates protective care.
- *Interpersonal problems.* Includes parent and child conflict problems of adjustment on returning home, as well as custody disputes.
- *Environmental.* Evaluates provision of adequate financial and housing needs.

Because just under one-half of all neglect cases (45.4%) received placement, we chose neglect as a base of comparison for examining other reasons for placement. Odds for the various reasons are listed in Table 6.8.

Child Characteristics and Chances of Removal

Race. Although representation by race in these data were disproportionate to the racial proportions of the population nationwide, when children receiving services was taken as the base population, there appeared to be minimal association between race and placement. Whites and blacks were placed equally often, Hispanics having a slightly less chance of placement than whites, .83.

When race was considered together with reason for referral, variations began to emerge. In dependency cases, both blacks and Hispanics were placed twice as often as whites. For drug and alcohol cases, no differences in placement rates were apparent. However, for parental condition, all races

---

64. One of the limitations of these categories is that they lack a reliably defined standard and are often overlapping. For instance, Giovannoni and Billingsley (1970) found that low-income "neglectful" mothers were under greater economic and environmental stress and had fewer social supports to cope with their stress than did the low-income mothers in their study who were coping adequately. Thus, the mother whose child is removed for neglect may just as likely have had "environmental" as the reason for referral. Giovannoni and Billingsley point out that under continued stress of poverty and inadequate shelter the competent low-income mother of today may become the neglectful mother of tomorrow.

65. The combination of variables which could be examined were derived from a time sequence model and restricted to those variables where an influence on outcome emerged.

**Table 6.8 Odds Ratio Analysis of Reason
for Seeking Services and Placement**

Reason for Seeking Service	Odds Ratio for Removal of the Child
Dependency	2.21
Child problem	1.06
Neglect	1.00
Drug-alcohol	.90
Parental condition	.88
Interpersonal	.49
Abuse	.34
Environmental	.28

had lower odds of placement than did whites (1.00), .89 for blacks, and .72 for Hispanics. In neglect cases, blacks received placement equally as often as whites, while Hispanics received it less, .60. Virtual equivalency among races existed in abuse cases, which appeared to be independent of race. Finally, environmental reasons found blacks at higher risk of placement, 1.30, while all other categories had equal odds of placement.

The data examined here are congruent with Giovannoni and Becerra's (1979) finding that races perceive different forms of maltreatment as more serious. Although children may follow similar paths to treatment, irrespective of race, there is evidence that black children remain in care longer. Goerge (1990) examined the length of time a sample of Illinois children spent in foster care. There was wide variation of time in care depending on whether the child was black or non-black and whether the child was residing in Cook County or not (see Figure 6.1). The black children in Cook County were in care for an average of four and one-half years, while the non-black children in Cook county were in care an average of one and one-half years (one third as long). Children outside of Cook County (both black and non-black) were in care an average of less than half a year. Goerge (1990) observes, "These figures suggest that something about residing in Cook County causes children, especially black children, to remain in care in Cook County, which may also explain the longer durations in care" (p. 434). What is this "something about residing in Cook County" that leads to such differences in time in foster care? Apparently Cook County contains the

Figure 6.1 Median Number of Months in Foster Care for Children by Race, Illinois (1990)

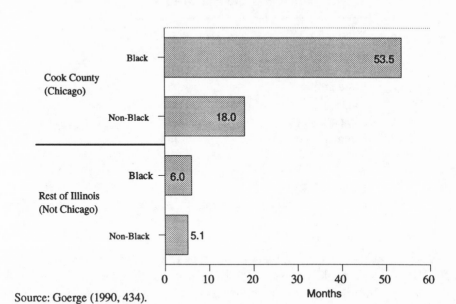

Source: Goerge (1990, 434).

"ghettos and poverty areas" that Fanshel and Shinn (1978, 506) suggest provide the children who come into foster care. According to a 1989 Ohio legislative report black children were four times more likely to be placed in foster care and remained in care longer. Similarly, in California black children were five times more likely to be in foster care in 1990 (Children's Defense Fund, 1993, 43).

Gender. Although the odds for placement for a boy were 1.39 times greater than for a girl, gender exerted limited influence on placement decisions. The odds ratio for source of referral, reason for referral and other variables, when correlated with gender, all showed similar results.

Child's Family Composition. When no parent is present, placement is almost a certainty (99.3%), which is appropriate since, historically, the public child welfare system emerged to serve the needs of just such children, predominantly orphans. When the family consisted solely of the biological or adoptive father, the child was placed 1.80 times as often as when the family consisted solely of the mother. It is not clear whether this reflects a prej-

Table 6.9 Odds Ratio Analysis of Employment Status and Placement

Employment Status	Odds Ratio for Removal of the Child
Full-time	1.00
Part-time	2.78
Unemployed	.54
Not in paid labor-force	1.44

udice against the father or the father's unwillingness to take responsibility for the child as often as the mother does. However, exempting a particular reason for referral, a child from a lone-parent family was no more likely to receive placement than a child from a two-parent family.

However, when dependency and drug-alcohol were the issue, lone-parent families were most subject to having their children removed, facing odds of 5.69 (dependency) and 3.19 (drug-alcohol) to 1 (compared to 2.21 and .90 for all families). In other words, dependency and drug-alcohol problems placed lone-parent families at far greater risk of having their children removed. Other reasons for referral showed only a slightly greater chance for placement when lone-parent families were involved.

Economic Security. The discriminant analysis indicated that the difference between those children placed in foster care and those not was adequacy of parental income. However, the discriminant analysis approach could not examine the influence of the separate variables or the relation between them. It simply indicates that adequacy of income was the factor which best discriminated between those children removed and those left home. If adequacy of income is the crucial factor leading to placement, we would expect that the odds of placement for children in families without an adequate income would be greater than for those children from households with income security. Did the odds ratio analysis confirm this, and what were the odds?

Parental Employment. As the data in Table 6.9 shows, part-time employment increased the odds of removal over "unemployment" or "not in the

**Table 6.10 Odds Ratio Analysis of Major
Source of Income and Placement**

Source of Income	Odds Ratio for Removal of the Child
Self-support	1.00
Government only	1.03
Government and self-support	.67
Family, friends, alimony	121.32

labor force," regardless of whether the family had two parents or a lone-parent—a finding that is difficult to reconcile with policy initiatives designed to encourage part-time employment for lone-parents with major child caring responsibilities (see Haveman, 1988; Kamerman and Kahn, 1988b). Apparently, the income derived from part-time employment was either not enough to reduce the likelihood of referral or affected the ability to provide proper child care sufficient to increase the odds of having the child removed. The data would suggest that low income lone-parents should either find full-time employment or avoid working altogether, since part-time employment leads to a significantly higher likelihood of removal.

Source of Income. Previous studies had suggested that income problems were fundamental to the clients of public child welfare (Fanshel and Shinn, 1978; Jenkins and Norman, 1975; Pelton, 1989). In this sample the client's actual income was not available. Instead, the study had collected data on source of income. Table 6.10 lists the source of income variables and their associated odds for achieving removal and placement of the child.

As can be seen, the vulnerable child was the one whose family received income from neither government nor self-support (cf. Table 6.6 earlier). Presumably their income derived from other sources: family, friends and alimony, all of which have the potential of being less stable and predictable than government or self-support. Such a child was 120 times (!) more likely to be removed and placed in foster care than the child whose family income derived from self-support.

Clearly, an unstable income source represented the highest predictor of removal. This finding, which is consistent with previous research on the impact of income on placement (Fanshel and Shinn, 1978; Lindsey, 1991d; Testa and Goerge, 1988), suggests that programs providing direct income support to the parent would likely prove effective in preventing placement. In 1978, reflecting on the foster care children in their longitudinal sample, Fanshel and Shinn wrote:

> We have no faith in the ability to predict or prevent the entrance of children into foster care. True prevention would require strong support for all families in their child-rearing efforts, particularly the most impoverished. If such support is not forthcoming in our country, more children will inevitably wind up in foster care. Cutting public assistance budgets, ending support for public housing, terminating mental health facilities—all grim phenomena of this recent period—are sure ways to increase the number of families where parental breakdown will occur and children will require foster care. (P. 507)

Summary

In this chapter we have examined the decision-making process from several angles. In every case the results have been disturbing. First, the stochastic model, assuming an optimistic reliability factor of .25, revealed that current decision-making practices possessed little predictive value in accurately assessing who should receive foster care and who should not.

Second, using a discriminant analysis function, we examined the client variables thought to impact, according to placement theories, the decision-making process. The discriminant function revealed that, despite what factors theory suggests "ought" to determine foster care placement, the single most important criterion was source of income.

Finally, we examined the various client variables using an odds ratio approach. While "reason" and "source" variables increased or decreased the odds for placement anywhere from 1.5 to 5 times, inadequacy of income increased the odds for placement by more than 120 times!

Some have concluded that placing children in foster care is a random process (Fanshel and Shinn, 1978), or at least one lacking a codified or standard set of guidelines (Stein, Gambrill, and Wiltse, 1978; Stein and Rzepnicki, 1984). As Sinanoglu (1981, 8) observed, "Standards and statutes for the removal of a child from his or her parents are broad, vague, and inconsistent. There are no clear definitions of 'neglected' children and 'fit' or 'unfit' parents. Hence, parents, children, and foster parents are subject to a rule of wide discretion and subjective determination." Our findings suggest that an underlying guideline does exist, although it may not be stated explicitly in many agencies: adequacy of income.

Decision-making and the Law

Legal theorists have long maintained that child abuse should be the primary reason a child is removed. However, medical studies have reported that "severity of abuse" is not predictive of removal (Hampton and Newberger, 1985; Hunter et al., 1990; Katz et al., 1986). Kienberger, Jaudes and Morris (1990) examined 180 children admitted to a Chicago hospital for sexual abuse to discern which factors predicted removal from parents and placement in foster care. None of the many variables they examined predicted outcome. As we saw earlier, Katz and his colleagues found that among a group of children referred for suspected abuse in the emergency and surgical units of a hospital, the best predictor of removal of the child from the family was not severity of abuse, but Medicaid eligibility, which we might interpret as a proxy variable for the income status of the family. Although abuse occurred, low income was more important in predicting removal of the child than was severity of injury.

In 1973, Mnookin suggested that two principles should govern the decision to remove a child:

- Removal should be a last resort, used only when the child cannot be protected within the home.
- The decision should be based on legal standards that could be applied in a consistent and even-handed way, and not influenced by the values of the deciding judge.

As the analysis presented here suggests, Mnookin's principles have not been widely implemented. Currently child welfare caseworkers may simply be relabeling "inadequate income" as "abuse," "neglect," "child behavior"—all socially and legally acceptable reasons for child removal. A lone-parent without adequate income apparently has little chance of keeping her child once she has come to the attention of the public child protection system. How often is such removal the last resort? In many cases, might not services designed to retain the child in the home be more effective? At what economic cost—and what human anguish over the loss of one's children and the stigma that attaches to both parent and child—are alternatives ignored?

Removing a child from his or her parent is a severe form of state intervention, even if the removal is only temporary. As Fanshel and Shinn (1978) have written: "People should not be penalized because they are poor, because they are mentally ill, or because they are afflicted with drug addiction or alcoholism. They should not be penalized because it is less expensive for society to terminate their (parental) rights and allow others, endowed with better economic means, to replace them as the parents of their children."

Conclusion

With more than half a million children in foster care in North America and the number expected to continue to rise, it is important to recognize how children are selected for removal from their parents. Overall, the data examined in this and other studies clearly demonstrate that child abuse is not the major reason children are removed from their parents. Rather, inadequacy of income, more than any other factor, constitutes the reason that children are removed.

Such conclusions strike at the very heart of the child welfare system. Over time, the residual model has erected a child welfare bureaucracy whose function is to develop and maintain selected residual categories. The model assumes that we can ultimately resolve the problems children face by precisely identifying those residual categories. Unfortunately, the central tenant is flawed. The research has consistently demonstrated that only a limited consensus exists on what children fit what categories. More and more the variables we thought had some bearing in deciding the issue appear a smoke screen masking the real issue, which is poverty. At the very least, we need to be honest about why children are being taken away.

With the transformation into child protection the framework for decision-making in child welfare has shifted from "assessment of the child's needs" to "investigation and substantiation" of an abuse and neglect report.

Within the child protection framework lone-parents and poor families, who form the core of those "investigated," are no longer seen as families-in-need who might merit support services but instead are treated as alleged child abusers who may be deserving of reproach and punishment. Consequently, the new case finding system stigmatizes and publicly reprimands the parents served by the public child welfare system. We need to rethink this approach.

Dealing with Child Abuse,
the Red Herring of Child Welfare

From the outset, the current system is fueled by an inclination to investigate parents to find evidence that they are to blame for the harms and dangers befalling their children, and the balance in the dual role is tipped toward the investigative/coercive/child removal role to the detriment of the helping role. Attention is deflected from the context of poverty in which most families live who are reported to the agency.

LeRoy Pelton, "Beyond Permanency Planning"

Although not originally a concern of the residual model, child abuse is today the principle focus of child welfare agencies, to the exclusion of nearly all other issues. How and why this happened is no mystery, since child abuse represents the extreme, logical focus of the residual approach. If the residual model seeks to help the socially excluded—the outcasts, the abandoned, the less fortunate—the abused child is the perfect client, since he or she is excluded in a way that no one else can be. While others may suffer poverty, neglect, prejudice, racism, the abused child is denied the most precious and necessary qualities human beings require when they awaken upon the earth—love, tenderness, compassion, and nurture from the parent. Child abuse that ends in death becomes the ultimate exclusion: an innocent purposely denied opportunity at life.

Thus, it should come as no surprise that in adhering to the residual perspective the child welfare profession has narrowed its focus almost exclusively on child abuse. Child abuse, especially severe physical and sexual assault, are high valence issues—they draw our attention. All other issues are set aside while focus is riveted to these horrific incidents. The irony is that the more effort, attention, and resources we devote to the problem, the less we achieve. The worse child abuse becomes, the more our obsession with it grows.

A *red herring* is a highly charged issue that draws attention away from the real and more difficult problem.

In untangling the problem of child abuse, we encounter a number of important and interrelated issues. Child abuse is not just a social phenomenon in and of itself but an issue that has affected child welfare practice as nothing else has ever done, transforming child welfare policy in a way that obscures the traditional focus of what child welfare is all about. Further, it has detrimentally affected the legal justice system, corroding and impeding the rights of families and individuals. Preoccupation with child abuse wastes valuable human and monetary resources, and daily deprives agencies of the ability to deliver services to others more appropriately in need of their services. By handing responsibility for dealing with severe physical and sexual assault over to the child welfare system, we deny children the protection the police would otherwise provide and, consequently, expose them to greater harm. By sidestepping the police we allow perpetrators to escape criminal sanction and prosecution, leaving them free to repeat their offense.

Scope of the Problem

The highly charged nature of criminal child abuse makes it difficult to find rational agreement on just how prevalent child abuse fatalities are. Large-scale studies all indicate that child abuse fatalities are relatively rare. The estimate of the National Incidence Study (Sedlak, 1991) that approximately 1,000 children a year die from child abuse corresponds with data reported from the National Center on Health Statistics (Select Committee on Children, Youth, and Families, 1989b) on deaths to children from homicide or "undetermined injury." The figures from these studies closely match data reported by the American Humane Association, the Federal Bureau of Investigation, and the National Committee for the Prevention of Child Abuse (see Figure 5.2).

One of the most comprehensive in-depth reviews of child abuse fatalities was conducted by Cyril Greenland (1987). Working with extensive data from a study of 100 child abuse fatalities in Ontario, Canada, Greenland (1987, 19) observed, "With the passing of the rhetoric about the virtual epidemic of child-abuse deaths, it is reassuring to discover that abuse and neglect severe enough to maim or destroy young children is comparatively rare. However, due to the moral panic associated with child abuse, this conclusion may not be welcomed by the professional community"

Greenland's conclusion is supported by other statistics. Pryor (1991) reported that in 1990 in New York state less than 1 percent of all reports to

Figure 7.1 Allegations Reported by Category, New York (1990)

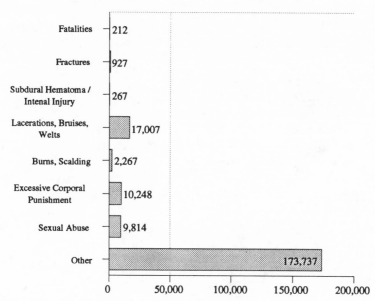

Source: Pryor (1991, table 22).

child welfare agencies involved severe physical abuse. The state of New York implemented a Central Register for all child abuse and neglect reports and classified them as either abuse or maltreatment. For the decade 1981 to 1990 abuse reports accounted for about 10 percent of all reports registered (Pryor, 1991, table 3).[66] In 1990 abuse accounted for 8.7 percent of all reports, while maltreatment accounted for 91.3 percent. The child abuse allegations are displayed by category in Figure 7.1.

---

66. This proportion is similar to data reported in England. In 1964, the National Society for the Prevention of Cruelty to Children (Britain) reported that less than 10 percent of children helped (9,632 of 120,000) were said to be assaulted (Coleman, 1965). Likewise, the latest data reported by Hepworth (1985, 48, table 12) indicates that in 1978 child abuse reports account for 3.2 percent of all reports received by the Child Protection Registry in Alberta. Child neglect reports accounted for the remaining 96.8 percent. In 1980, Ontario reported 18,121 new protection and prevention case during that year (Hepworth, 1985, 48, table 11). During the same year 1,222 cases of child abuse were reported to the Central Registry (Eichler, 1988, 329, table 9.6). Thus, 6.7 percent of all new cases in Ontario were reported for child abuse. In Quebec, 2.3 percent of all cases were for child abuse (Hepworth, 1985, 44, table 8).

Figure 7.2 Circumstances of Children in the United States, 1994

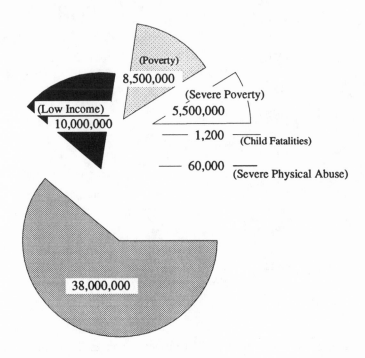

Source: Compiled by Author.

When viewed within the larger scope of child welfare problems, serious physical and sexual assault affects a relatively small portion of children. Of the 3 million child abuse reports received a year, probably about 60,000 involve cases of severe physical child abuse, while approximately 1,000 die from severe physical child abuse. When measured against the total number of children living in poverty (8,500,000) and extreme poverty (5,500,000), severe child abuse represents a small segment (see Figure 7.2).

This data does not mean that criminal child abuse is not a severe and compelling problem, but it does compel us to ask: Are our efforts for the care and protection of children being channeled in the right direction? Is our definition of child abuse broad enough? Should child abuse be confined to the 1,200 children killed each year by their parents or should it include the more than 14,000,000 children living in homes of poverty and despair?

As serious and often horrible as physical and sexual child abuse is, does it warrant the complete transformation of the public child welfare system? For in response to a widespread public reaction to the horrors of child abuse public child welfare has been transformed from a system serving a broad range of disadvantaged children into one designed primarily to protect children from battering and sexual assault. The result is that most children who come to the attention of child welfare agencies and who have not been battered or sexually assaulted, but are the victims of neglect or inadequate care, are, given the new priorities, virtually excluded from receiving assistance.

The abuse reporting laws enacted in the late 1960s and early 1970s that resulted in the meteoric rise in reports did not include additional resources for child welfare agency budgets to meet the increased demand for services these laws produced.[67] To fund the new demand for services, child welfare agencies changed the definition of who they serve. These agencies now rarely respond to requests for service unless an allegation of abuse is involved, and even then the cases are screened over the phone to reduce investigative requirements. Requests for service or aid to families in distress or chronic crisis receive low priority and, in some instances, no response at all (Kamerman and Kahn, 1990).

Commenting on the almost exclusive focus on physical and sexual abuse, Greenland (1987) observed that "many child-protection agencies have little or no interest in the equally pernicious mischief caused to children by poverty and neglect. The challenge for the child welfare field in the next decade must surely be to deploy its resources, moral as well as economic and political, to promote the welfare of all children. Treating emotionally, physically, and sexually abused children who come to public attention is most important—but it is not enough" (p. xiii).

Popular Misconceptions about Threatened Children

Why agencies have a preoccupation with child abuse to the exclusion of almost everything else is not difficult to understand. Public outrage and fear, fanned by media coverage of horrifying incidents, tend to grossly misrepresent the dimensions of the problem (Spector and Kitsuse, 1977). In 1978,

---

67. Only Illinois passed an appropriation with its first reporting law (Nelson, 1984, 132).

then Congressman Paul Simon stated that "50,000 young people disappear each year, because of `stranger kidnapping.' That is the most conservative estimate you will get anywhere." (U.S. House of Representatives, 1981, p. 10). This statement was later embellished by others with such phrases as "there is general agreement among professionals" [that 50,000 children a year are kidnapped by strangers]. Although it was never clear where this figure came from, few questioned it. The more it was quoted, the more alarmed the public became. Pictures of missing children began appearing on milk cartons and grocery bags. In school, public education programs warned children of the perils of talking to strangers. The media, alert for a story that would sell (and often irrespective of its veracity), highlighted the most tragic cases of abducted children.[68] Testifying to Congress (U.S. Senate, 1983), the father of one missing child reported, "This country is littered with mutilated, decapitated, raped, and strangled children" (p. 33). When runaways and children abducted in child custody disputes were included, the number of missing children swelled to 1.5 million. The emotional uproar made it difficult to objectively assess the problem of missing children.[69] Anyone who questioned the facts or figures was suspect of lacking compassion for the plight of threatened children (Best, 1990).

In 1985, a Pulitzer prize-winning story in the *Denver Post* finally debunked the issue, suggesting that the problem of missing children had been blown completely out of proportion (Best, 1990). Using FBI statistics, the newspaper reported that in 1984 the number of child abductions by strangers was not 1,500,000 but 67. Commenting on these numbers Gelles suggested, "The odds of a child being abducted by a stranger are about the same as his chances of being struck by lightning" (cited in Best, 1990). As suddenly as they had begun waving it, the media now dropped and furled

---

68. In 1973, U.S. Congressman Mario Biaggi testified at a U.S. Senate hearing on the Child Abuse and Neglect Prevention and Treatment Act that child abuse was the "number one killer of children in America today" (cited in Pelton, 1989, 30). *The New York Times* reported in November 30, 1975, that, "More than a million American children suffer physical abuse or neglect each year, and at least one in five of the young victims die from their mistreatment, the Government announced today" (cited in Pelton, 1989, 29). This meant that 200,000 children die each year as a result of child abuse. Yet, as we have seen in Chapter 5, the number of child abuse fatalities in 1975 was approximately 1,000. Thus, the number of abuse fatalities reported for one year was the number that would have occurred over two centuries. Pelton reported that this exaggerated number continued to gain nationwide publicity through the news media for several weeks. The number of fatalities was based on an interview with Douglas Besharov, then Director of the National Center on Child Abuse. Besharov claims he said 2,000.

the banner of missing children. As Best (1991) reports: "*US News and World Report* called the concern with missing children a 'faddish hysteria,' *Harper's* referred to it as a 'national myth' (Schneider, 1987, 50); Nicholas von Hoffman in the *New Republic* mocked claims that there ever had been 1.5 million abductions a year: 'In a decade, that means that 15 million children have gone through the doughnut hole into the anti-world.'"

Looking back now, we smile that such inflated statistics received public acceptance. Yet, child abuse represents a nearly identical situation. When even one child dies from abuse, the child welfare system comes under immediate scrutiny. How was this allowed to happen, the public demands? How many other children are being clubbed to death in their cribs? Are we wasting our money on these bungling child welfare bureaucrats? Over the last two decades, such questions have transformed child welfare agencies from benevolent, helping organizations into a quasi-legal investigative, accusatory, protective service systems (Frost and Stein, 1989; Howells, 1975).

---

69. Media has a central role in mediating information and forming public opinion. The media casts an eye on events that few of us directly experience and renders otherwise remote happenings observable and meaningful. Consequently, if an issue is to be established in modern society as a social problem requiring state intervention, the role of the media is crucial (Best, 1991). In this regard, press coverage of an issue that produces such public outrage as the brutal death of a child can be angry and critical of a system that is seen as responsible for preventing the senseless death, yet somehow unable and unwilling to act. Newspaper headlines in Britain in 1973 are illustrative (Parton, 1985, 89-99): "The *Times* headlines include: 'Social Worker Made Error of Judgement' (3 November); 'Social Worker Booed at Brighton Enquiry' (6 November); 'Social Workers Wrong, QC Tells Inquiry Into the Death of Maria Colwell' (8 November); 'Social Worker Accepted Bruises' (13 November); 'Social Worker's Job "Not at Risk" After Took Little Interest in the Child's Death' (14 November). The front page report is head-lined 'Two-Babies Are Battered to Death Each Day.'" A study of 29 men imprisoned in at Brixton for killing their children was reported in the press: "One of the most disturbing findings...is the lack of guaranteed security for abused children once their plight has come to light...Eight men in the Brixton cases were being visited by social agencies because of child abuse when they killed their children" (Scott, 1973). Golding and Middleton (1982) quote additional headlines from 1980, "'Malcolm Died As He Lived. Freezing Cold, Starving And Surrounded by Social Workers' (*Daily Mirror*, 16 January 1980); 'Early Victim of Do-Nothing Welfare Team' (*Daily Mail*, 21 February); 'Welfare Woman in Row over a Dead Baby' (*Daily Mail*, 4 November)." Reviewing these press reports Golding and Middleton (1982, 90) argue, "That such children suffer from ineffectual intervention by incompetent social workers is a common theme in these cases...Social workers represent in human form the excessive intervention of the state in people's lives, and also the naivete of the bureaucratic mind...Thus social workers are too numerous, do not act when they should, and are largely unnecessary."

Investigation and Prevention of Child Abuse

One of the earliest groups organized to combat violence against children emerged in England. In 1889, the various organizations concerned with child abuse were melded into the National Society for the Prevention of Cruelty to Children (NSPCC). In its initial form the NSPCC used investigators who acted in a police inspector role. The NSPCC were, in a sense, soft police. These soft police inspectors even wore uniforms with badges. Over the years the role of the investigator began to change. Instead of prosecuting those who assault children, the NSPCC shifted to a role of prevention through casework services. Eventually, the NSPCC officers gave up their badges and uniforms and acquired training in providing casework services (Parton, 1985, p. 59). This shift reflected the view that "punishment plays no part in curing the problem of preventing recurrences, so investigation by the police... can be dangerously inappropriate. On the other hand, a juvenile court may be of great help, concerned as it is for the welfare of the child in its family as a whole" (Isaacs, 1972, p. 756).

Growth of Discretionary Agency Authority and Power

The shift of responsibilities for investigating child abuse from the police to child welfare agencies has changed the practice of the courts (Donzelot, 1979). During the last decade there has been an increase in the discretionary power of agencies along with an increase in court involvement in child welfare cases.

During the last decade the discretionary power of child welfare agencies has increased, as has court involvement in child welfare cases. With the courts and legal system behind them, child welfare caseworkers now exercise considerable authority to remove children from their biological parents. This power often intimidates the mother whose child is the subject of an abuse allegation, since she knows that the caseworker can call on the courts to enforce any requests the caseworker makes.

The removal of children from parents can occur in two ways. First, the parent may voluntarily release the child to the care of the child welfare social worker and agency, or second, if the parent refuses to cooperate voluntarily, the caseworker may petition the court to order placement.[70] When a court becomes involved it makes both a jurisdictional and a dispositional judgment, decisions that may occur in varying time frames. The court assumes jurisdiction based not on specific harms to the child but on such descriptive criteria as observed parental behavior, apparent neglect or abuse to the child, and so on. Once jurisdiction is established, investigation of specifics commences. The dispositional judgement that follows an investigation, and which rests upon a standard known as "in the child's best interest" (Wald, 1976, 629), decides upon a remedy based upon the specific harms to the child revealed by the investigation.

It is no exaggeration to say that caseworkers often establish jurisdiction through a subtle masquerade of benevolent intent. Knocking on a family's door, they ask to "assess" the family situation, the implication being that services and aid may be forthcoming. It is an innocent request that once granted often backfires on parents who cooperate, for, if accepted, it establishes the caseworker's legal jurisdiction. At any point thereafter "assessment" can turn into "investigation" and benevolent "inquiry" into "accusation."[71] As Giovannoni and Becerra (1979, 69-70) have observed:

> The social workers have brought with them their special orientation to and definitions of the problems and modes of managing them. The nature of the ideal social work intervention is one of therapy and rehabilitation, not one of social control. Social workers' authority rests on professional competence rather than legal authority. Justification for use of the authority is thus not customarily sought on legal grounds but rather on the grounds of the benefits to the clientele.

Given that most children are removed from their families not for abuse, or even severe abuse, but for reasons related to poverty, the upshot may be a dispositional judgement recommended by the caseworker and acceded to by the court, that the family neither expects nor deserves.

The relationship between the child welfare agency and the court should be understood. In many jurisdictions, the court and agency work hand-in-glove in the disposition of abuse and neglect cases. What the agency recom-

---

70. Court involvement is sometimes mandatory as a matter of agency policy, regardless of whether the parent voluntarily relinquishes the child.

71. Theodore Stein (1991b) has observed that, "the courts are beginning to rule that if a social worker is conducting an investigation and has as her/his purpose the possible criminal prosecution of a parent [which due to all the criminal prosecutions of sex abuse reports happens with increasing frequency] she or he may well be responsible for providing a *Miranda* warning to police conducting similar investigations." Other attorneys have suggested they would advise clients not to permit "assessments" or investigations without a court order. Further, they would recommend that clients not discuss their situation with a social worker in an abuse investigation without the presence of counsel (a lawyer).

mends, the court approves with minimal review, becoming, in essence, little more than a rubber stamp to the policies of the child welfare agency. It is not so much cynical indifference or corrupt collusion that promotes this but simple expediency. Because their dockets are full to bursting, the courts find it convenient to relinquish more and more decision-making authority to the child welfare professional. As the National Commission on Children (1991) reported, "Most judges have 35 to 40 cases on their individual calendars [every day], and they have an average of 10 minutes to spend on each case. Five years from now, with double the caseloads, the judges will have not 10 minutes, but five minutes to determine each child's fate and each family's future" (p. 283, citing Paul Blond, Presiding Judge at Los Angeles County Juvenile Court).

The muted objections of impoverished parents, too intimidated by the court process to vociferously defend their rights as parents, are swept aside. "In acting symbiotically with the child welfare agencies, the courts have assumed the 'coloration' of social agencies" (Levine citing Eastman, 1973, 34). By allowing child welfare agencies to intrude into the lives of families where no "criminal" wrong doing exists, and to act on recommendations based on that intrusion, the courts have empowered the child welfare agency to act as their agent. In this regard, they have abandoned their duty to make independent and perhaps conflicting judgments apart from the agency. By invoking the courts in neglect and maltreatment situations, child welfare agencies have used the court to sanctify their actions. In the context of expediency, the court has failed to provide conventional safeguards. As a result, court involvement has become a corrosion of the legal system that is slowly undermining the rights of poor families and threatening traditional due process.

The Court as Independent Agent

The value of the court rests in its role as an independent and impartial party to determine if "criminal abuse" has occurred. The decision to remove a child from the home is not a technical question subject to the expertise of the child welfare social worker but rather a moral and legal determination belonging to the court, with the child welfare social worker providing expert testimony and advice. The proper role of the court is to protect the rights of children and parents, in which expert testimony in defense of the parents is also provided. With the involvement of child welfare caseworkers, whose primary efforts have been in the "best interests of the child," the courts have too often proven more responsive to the recommendations of the case-worker than to the rights of the parent.[72]

Because the combination of benevolent and intrusive power held by the caseworker so confounds the caseworker's relationship to the parents in abuse and neglect situations, Levine (1973) has argued that the worker should intervene only without application of legal authority, that is, only without the authority to take any jurisdictional or dispositional action. Although due process safeguards have been implemented at the hearing level in abuse and neglect cases, this still leaves open what may occur prior to entering the courtroom. Levine (1973, 37) argues that withholding proce-dural safeguards for families until the dispositional hearing occurs is too late (c.f. Besharov, 1990b). In establishing jurisdiction should caseworkers follow strict procedures that safeguard the parent? Until such procedures and safeguards are recognized, some legal theorists argue that the parent should not answer the door when the caseworker comes knocking.[73]

Blurring Abuse and Neglect

One of the most serious problems in the decision-making process is the merging of child abuse with child neglect. Child abuse and child neglect are two qualitatively different issues that should be treated in fundamentally different ways. Too often the boundary between child abuse, for which there should be clear legal grounds for criminal investigation and intervention, is blurred with child neglect, where issues of poverty and public policy arise. As a result, fuzzy decision-making often characterizes the actions of child protective services workers in child abuse cases.

---

72. An additional explanation of the rubber-stamp behavior of the court has been that child welfare caseworkers and other professionals shape their recommendations to conform to what they think a particular judge will want to decide (Mnookin, 1973, 628). For example, child welfare caseworkers seeking to terminate parental rights in the Oregon Project assumed an active role in obtaining evidence and researching statutes, yet upon entering the court the caseworker had to conform to the district attorney's recommendations based on available legal resources (Burt, 1971; Regional Research Institute for Human Services, 1978, 35).

73. The same concern with legal safeguards applies to the police. In the District of Columbia the police have been responsible for investigating all child abuse reports. As long as the police treat the investigation as a civil, rather than a criminal matter, [and most abuse cases have been treated as *civil*] the procedural safeguards provided in criminal investigations do not apply (Stein, 1991b). In order to provide these safeguards legislation is needed to ensure that child abuse investigations be treated as criminal investigations.

Child abuse involves the intentional physical harm a parent inflicts upon a child.[74] According to the residual view, the etiology of child abuse is found in the psychodynamic relationship between parent and child (Kadushin and Martin, 1981). Central issues include such things as family stress, inadequate understanding of child rearing approaches, an inability to properly manage the child, a proclivity toward or tolerance of violence, and so on.

Neglect involves improper care of children, which derives for the most part from the parent's inability to provide properly for the child. The parents do not have sufficient economic means to furnish adequate food, medical care, clothing, shelter, and the like. In the United States, de facto neglect exists for at least 5 million children whose families have income less than one-half the poverty line.

Historically, child welfare agencies have operated from the principle that no child should be removed "for reasons of poverty,"[75] which means that if at all possible children suffering neglect should be aided in their homes. The approach is not only less expensive but may be less harmful to the child than removal, since the psychological damage that may occur when a child is removed from his or her biological parents is potentially great.[76] When a child is being severely physically or sexually abused, however, the question of removal is fundamentally different. Although it may be less expensive to retain the child in the home, the potential danger to the child is the greater issue, and removal is warranted.

In the last two decades child abuse and child neglect problems have converged into a combined category of "child abuse and neglect" or "child maltreatment." This approach has led to conceptual confusion. By blending these two fundamentally different problems, we have diminished our ability to deal effectively with either. Caseworkers examining abuse and neglect

---

74. The "battered child syndrome" discovered by C. Henry Kempe and colleagues (1962) was defined as a child under three years old who suffered severe physical abuse.

75. Since 1909 there has been an historic principle that children should not be removed from their home for "reasons of poverty" (Bremner,1971; Pelton, 1989). To remove a child from his or her parent(s) for reasons of poverty would be "cruel and unusual punishment" or severely harsh punishment for conditions which the parent(s) may be unable, at least temporarily, to change. Instead, the child welfare social worker has been mandated to provide services and resources to the family so that removal of the child for reasons of poverty would not be necessary (Barth & Berry,1987).

76. The study of filial deprivation by Jenkins and Norman (1972) indicates an intensive and long-lasting pain and anguish associated with removal.

allegations are increasingly unable to distinguish one from the other. As seen in the previous chapter, determinations on identical cases vary from caseworker to caseworker, from judge to judge. What predominates is not agreement but lack of consensus. In some cases children are removed from their families for poverty and neglect, while in others they are left in obviously abusive situations to face increasing violence and danger to their lives. As a result, abuse deaths continue unabated, while neglected, deprived, and dependent children are left without services.

If current approaches had proven successful in reducing child fatalities, we might have reason to be satisfied with the transformation of the child welfare system. However, as we saw in Chapter 5, the rate of child fatalities has continued to rise. Further, approximately half of the deaths from child abuse involve children known to the child protective service system. The failure to make progress in reducing harm to children requires us to question the current approach of reporting child abuse, especially severe child abuse, to public child welfare agencies.

What is required is a separation and clarification of the two issues of criminal abuse and neglect, accompanied by interventions tailored to the unique requirements of each (Pelton, 1992). Severe child abuse, which is a criminal act, should be reported to the police and prosecuted in the courts. It demands strict legal efforts to punish the abuser and provide protection to the abused. In contrast, child neglect requires the compassionate ear and helpful hand of the social worker, with the court playing only a minor role to resolve concerns about cases of abandonment or endangerment of the child, and then only after the parent's rights have been safeguarded.

Currently, the decision to remove a child from the home remains a loosely negotiated one between the parent(s), the caseworker, and the court, in which the decision-making criteria is altogether too fuzzy. A more formalized and rule-oriented procedure is required, preceded by conceptual clarification, from which more reliable judgements and greater consensus between parties can emerge. Further, before we can begin to deal effectively with severe physical and sexual child abuse, we should begin regarding it for what it is. It is not over-zealous discipline, nor uncontrolled aggressiveness, nor careless rough housing, nor hot-temperedness, nor impatience, nor inappropriate sexual attention, nor any of the other psychological labels that are used to excuse it. Child abuse, in whatever degree, is *criminal assault* and needs to be recognized as such. It requires firm investigation and prosecution by the police, backed by the courts.

Wife Battering

> Assault by a male social partner accounts for more injury to women than
> auto accidents, mugging, and rape combined. Even more far reaching than
> injury and death are the psychosocial consequences of abuse. We also found
> that woman abuse is a factor in almost half of all child abuse and in more
> than a third of all divorces and is a major cause of attempted suicide, alco-
> holism, and mental illness among women.
>
>   Evan Stark, "Framing and Reframing Battered Women"

Until a few years ago, a woman entering a police station seeking protection
from a battering husband received little more than sympathy. Hers was a
"domestic," "marital" problem not within police jurisdiction. The police
would take action only if he severely hurt or killed her. After the woman
was treated at the hospital, and if it was a slow night, an officer might escort
her home and attempt to negotiate a reconciliation. If this could not be
achieved, the woman was advised to stay with a relative or friend, later to
see a counselor, or perhaps a minister. Now, of course, we would think it
foolish that a woman being assaulted by her husband would call a social
worker for help. Rather, the advise is to, "Call the police!" They will intervene immediately, using force if necessary to subdue the assailant, who will
be led away in handcuffs, the details to be sorted out later by a judge.

What has changed? Wife-battering is no longer regarded as a private
domestic affair. Instead it is *criminal assault*, plain and simple, requiring
decisive police intervention. In several jurisdictions in the United States
police are mandated to make an arrest if there is evidence the woman has
been battered, even if the victim does not wish to press charges. In cases of
wife battering the responsibilities of the police and social worker are clear.
The role of the police is to investigate and prosecute criminal wrongdoing,
while the social worker's role is to provide the battered woman with support
and other casework services. The social worker is not expected to conduct a
criminal investigation.

Studies of wife abuse have suggested the variable that has the greatest
impact on reducing subsequent abuse is police involvement (Berk et al.,
1992; Pate and Hamilton, 1992; Sherman and Berk, 1984). Unfortunately,
even with police involvement, the assailant is still likely to continue with
some level of abuse. This underscores the importance of police involvement
to provide the best available protection. Even though police involvement

will not assure an end to abuse, it provides the best approach to protection from future abuse.

How Physical Abuse of Children Differs

Currently, if a child is beaten senseless by a parent, with multiple broken limbs, perhaps a concussion, there is no guarantee that the child will be removed and provided any protection whatsoever from the abusive parent. Indeed, as we have seen, the child is more likely to be removed from the home for reasons of poverty than abuse. Nor is the parent likely to be arrested, unless, of course, the child dies. Instead, if the residual perspective is followed, which emphasizes the psychodynamic child-parent relationship and the parent's personal and psychological "deficits," the parent will likely receive nothing more than "therapy," or "counselling," with the caseworker stopping by from time to time to monitor progress.

The whole routine would be laughably ridiculous were it not so tragic. While counselling and therapy may eventually constitute a partial solution to whatever psychological malfunction has led the parent to abuse the child, the fact remains that another human being has been assaulted, and the assailant is subject to prosecution under the law, which should be applied vigorously and equally to everyone irrespective of race, income, or sex. While the perpetrator should be afforded full legal safeguards, he or she must realize that physical or sexual assault against a child is illegal and will be prosecuted to the full extent of the law.

An effective child abuse protection system administered by the police could *mandate* arrest if there is evidence of severe physical abuse. The arrest should be required even if the child or nonabusing parent wishes otherwise.

At what age does striking an individual with a fist or club, with the purposeful intent to inflict bodily harm, change from child abuse (treatable by counseling or therapy) to criminal assault (punishable by imprisonment, fine, or both)? Presumably, a person twenty-one years of age could legally press criminal charges against a parent for assault. Why then cannot a teenager, a child, an infant do the same? At what age does a child cease to be the ward of quasi-legal protective service workers and gain the full protection of the law? In fact, the teenager, child or infant should not have to press charges. Rather, arrest should be *mandated* if there is evidence of severe physical abuse.

Child abuse, like other physical assault, is not an action that falls within the purview of child welfare agencies. Child abuse is not a clinical syndrome or a psychological disorder requiring specialized therapeutic intervention, support, and care. Child abuse is, first and foremost, a *criminal act*, requiring decisive coercive control, and is therefore a police matter. The sooner it is treated as such, the sooner children will be protected to the fullest extent possible. This does not mean that the perpetrator shouldn't be provided with treatment and counseling, rather, it means that the child abuse needs first to be prosecuted as a criminal act and then, when advisable, to provide treatment to the perpetrator with the best available therapeutic services.

There are significant advantages to adopting this view, aside from the improved protection it will afford children.

First, redefining child abuse as criminal assault would clarify the roles of all parties—parent, police, courts, and social worker. Currently, child abuse allegations are resolved in a shifting ambiguous jurisdiction where almost no one is arrested unless a child dies or is permanently disabled; where the law bends to fit bureaucratic rules and regulations, and where defendants' rights may not always apply; where the prosecutor and the judge too often form a darkly suspicious alliance that serves expedience more than justice, and where the charge itself (abuse) is only vaguely defined, ranging from homicide to leaving children unattended, with the penalty often not fitting the crime.

With child abuse recognized as criminal assault, the police would have clear jurisdiction and responsibility to act decisively, where now, out of apprehension, often they do not. Any allegation would be clearly stated, and the parent assured proper defense. Civil rights, due process, and other legal procedures and safeguards would be clarified and upheld. The court, disentangled at last from its unhealthy relationship with child welfare agencies, would be able to make a just determination.

Second, with abuse properly defined, and the roles of the participants clarified, the ability to prevent child abuse and provide police protection for abused children would increase. Even an angry parent, knowing that he or she is breaking the law and subject to arrest, prosecution, and conviction, would think twice before bruising their child, who might subsequently be observed and reported to the police by a neighbor or teacher.

Finally, child welfare social workers would be freed to return to the duties for which they are most qualified—providing effective and needful services to impoverished and disadvantaged families. Child welfare caseworkers are not police, nor were they intended to be. If they find themselves acting as investigators now, it is only because the role has been mandated for them to investigate the avalanche of child abuse and neglect reports. They have neither the training, the authority, nor perhaps the disposition to effectively investigate criminal activities. Since child abuse, like all other acts of assault, is a criminal act, its investigation and prosecution should be transferred to the police, who have the training and resources to appropriately respond.

Gaping Holes in the Child Welfare System

The current child protective service system staffed by child welfare social workers too often fails to protect children because it has gaping holes. Child protection agencies do not have the investigative technology, training, and resources that are available to the police. They do not have crime laboratories, finger print identification equipment, highly trained and skilled criminal investigators who are familiar with the latest advances in forensic science. Child welfare social workers do not have the legal training, knowledge of court procedures and rules of evidence and other education that would enable them to effectively investigate and prosecute criminal behavior. Schools of social work do not offer courses in these areas.

The emphasis in social work education is on helping—it is, after all, a helping profession. When responsibility for investigating child abuse reports is shifted to child welfare agencies, or even child protection units within these agencies, the affected children are denied adequate protection. The problem of child abuse comes to be seen as one amenable to therapeutic and professional help rather than criminal investigation.

Nevertheless, child abuse reports have historically been reported to child welfare agencies. There is a nugget of truth that has led to this approach. Social workers have interviewing and assessment skills that are useful in determining whether abuse has occurred (Cooper, 1993). The child welfare social worker may be able to establish a better rapport with the abused child and even the abusing parent. This entree into the abusive situation provides a perspective that is often denied the police. From this vantage point, the child welfare social worker may be in the best situation to determine if abuse has occurred. In this regard, child welfare social workers could be hired by police departments for this role. In this setting social workers would function much as they do in hospitals or in schools by providing their particular services to assist the agency in achieving its objectives. The child welfare social worker would be "deputized" to investigate and thus would provide the child with the strongest possible protection and the "alleged" abusive parent with legal safeguards (that is, providing proper *Miranda* warning to the parent).

The child welfare social workers in the community, realizing they are now strictly an accessory to the legal apparatus that prosecutes child abuse, would be more likely to aggressively identify for police those families in which criminal child abuse is occurring. Currently, caseworkers are often reluctant to accuse parents of abuse, preferring to view it in terms that match their therapeutic interventions (Dingwall, Eekelaar, and Murray, 1983).[77] The child's broken arm, bruised face, or scalded leg are due to the parent's "impulsivity," "alienation," "depression," "ego-centricity," "over-aggressiveness," "lack of self-esteem," and the like, all of which are regarded as treatable through therapy or counselling (Margolin, 1992). Yet, there is precious little evidence to support the effectiveness of these optimistic interpretations of severe abuse. Sadly, on the hope of such unproven optimism for rehabilitation of criminal child abusers are sacrificed the lives of countless children.

Too, caseworkers sense their lack of experience and authority to investigate and prove allegations of abuse. Even if they could prove abuse, they have no technology to correct it. Like most people they want to get along, to promote harmony and cooperation with the parent, whose goodwill they view as essential to restoring the family to health. The result is that too many severe abuse situations are politely swept under the rug, leaving the endangered child virtually defenseless.

With abuse cases being investigated and prosecuted by police and justice departments, the child welfare agency's principal responsibility in abuse cases would become one of providing a "place of safety" for the assaulted

---

77. One of the unique qualities of the child welfare social worker, derived from professional training, is that he or she often focuses on the strengths of the parents even in severe abuse cases. Dingwall, Eekelaar, and Murray (1983) found that caseworkers operate under a "rule of optimism." They suggest that at each stage of the decision-making process caseworkers tend to favor the least stigmatizing interpretation of available information and the least coercive disposition. Their research indicated that the only situation that provoked coercive intervention involved "parental incorrigibility" (when parents failed to cooperate and appreciate the contribution of the child welfare caseworker) and a "failure of containment" (when concern that action be taken moved outside the sphere of influence and control of the child welfare caseworker and the family to involve other family members or other agencies).

child. Although the agency might also assist in the investigation, the responsibility of pursuing the assailant would properly belong with the police. To leave this responsibility with child welfare transforms the traditional helping function of the child welfare agency into a police function, which it is incapable of performing effectively. The child welfare social workers become, at most, soft police unable to effectuate an arrest or conduct a thorough criminal investigation. When children have been criminally assaulted and abused they are entitled to more than soft police. They are entitled to the same protection afforded all citizens. They are entitled to full police protection.

Establishing Rule-oriented Standards

Concomitant with a new understanding of child abuse should come revised rule-oriented standards for the removal of children in abuse and neglect cases. The wide discretion currently permitted enforcers of child abuse laws has failed to protect children, and left both parents and the public unclear regarding what the rules governing abuse and neglect are.

Professionals have long wrestled with the problem of developing a rule-oriented standard for child removal. Mnookin, Wald, and others have argued for a standard that would retain the child at home unless a clear and present danger exists to the child's well-being. Mnookin holds that before removal occurs, evidence of physical harm must be demonstrated by an explanation of why intervention with the child remaining at home would not be possible (Mnookin, 1973, 631). Wald (1976) has proposed that state intervention is legitimate in cases where the child has suffered either serious physical harm, serious and specifically defined emotional damage, or sexual abuse, or where the child is in imminent physical danger (p. 642). He would require the level of proof to vary depending upon the harm in question (i.e., physical abuse would require less proof than emotional damage).

Goldstein, Freud, and Solnit (1979) advocate limiting the coercive arm of the state to those cases where the child faces an "imminent risk of death or serious bodily harm." Advocates of strict legal standards suggest that removal is justified only if the parents' past behavior was itself sufficiently harmful—that is, if it caused or was capable of causing "serious harm." Legal scholars have proposed specific guidelines to determine if a child should be removed (Besharov, 1987, 312-313). The framework shown in the appendix at the end of the chapter is illustrative of the "rule oriented" approach.

When possible, the length of placement should be specified before placement occurs. Placement decisions should be based on a common set of principles with the same criteria applied equally to all. Even if the parent(s) desire placement, they should know that the child will return home after a specific time—either that or the state will arrange for another permanent home including, if necessary, court action to terminate parental rights (Mnookin, 1973, 637). The Oregon Project's effort to terminate parental rights in certain cases of long term foster care "drift" provides examples of how the court can take decisive action in this regard (Hewitt, 1983; Mlyniec, 1983). Of course, before placements occur, the state should offer, when appropriate, alternative services that would enable a child to remain at home.

The most disturbing aspect of the wide discretionary power that child welfare authorities currently wield in removing children is that the results are unfair and discriminatory. Too often, child removal has been limited to poor families. Less than one fourth of the children removed from their families and placed in foster care are from financially self-supporting families. Rein, Nutt, and Weiss (1974) point out that while many children are in out of home placements such as boarding schools, military schools, and living with friends and relatives, it is poor children, by and large, who are placed in foster care. The research by Hampton and Newberger (1985) suggested that income status and race were the most important variables that distinguished reported from unreported cases of abuse.

Developing a Child Abuse Legislation Model

In addition to rule-oriented standards for removal, child abuse legislation is needed that would outline specific guidelines to regulate the investigation and decision-making process in abuse and neglect cases (Duquette, 1980; Falconer and Swift, 1983). Such legislation would provide criteria to follow at each stage of an investigation (along the lines of the appendix at the end of the chapter).

For example, if a child were abused severely enough to require medical treatment, the criteria might specify that the child be placed in a "safe house" for seventy-two hours during which the police investigated the alleged or suspected abuse. If abuse were substantiated, the police would file charges against the perpetrator while seeking protective service supervision (e.g., foster care arranged by a child welfare worker) for a specified period of time (e.g., three months). If the physical abuse were repeated severely enough to require medical attention, the police would seek "termination of parental rights."

Likewise, if a child were sexually abused, the police would remove the child from the home environment where the abuse occurred, investigate, and, if the allegations were substantiated, prosecute the perpetrator. If the abuse were repeated, further prosecution would follow along with an effort to terminate parental rights. The parent would not be held harmless solely because he or she did not actually engage in the abuse. The only permissible excuse would be that the parent was unaware of the sexual abuse and exercised reasonable care to protect the child from it.

In such a way, legislation would articulate the specifics of criminal physical and sexual assault, detailing the steps to be taken and penalties to be imposed, should the specific allegations be substantiated (Turner and Shields, 1985). The law would be applied as firmly and consistently as feasible. If parents knew that child abuse law was clearly defined, and violations prosecuted vigorously, physical and sexual assault of children would likely decline.

Again, we note that the investigating officer would not be a child welfare caseworker but a law enforcement official specifically trained to investigate such criminal matters. The child welfare worker would provide appropriate casework services, such as counselling the abusing parent if the court so ordered it, and arranging foster care services for the child. Beyond this, the child welfare agency might assist in public relations efforts to prevent and combat child abuse.

Summary and Conclusion

Severe physical or sexual assault of a child is a crime and should be treated as such by authorities charged with investigating and prosecuting criminal behavior. Preoccupation with this narrow aspect of child welfare has displaced the child welfare system's obligation to a much larger population of children. By dealing decisively with the problem of child abuse, by defining it in a proper social and legal framework, by clarifying the roles that the courts, the police, the social worker, and the parent play in the phenomenon of child abuse, we can make progress in stemming the growing tide of abuse while freeing the child welfare system to return to its true mandate.

In North America more than 15 million children live in poverty. More than 5 million children in the United States live in households with income less than "half the poverty line"—a phrase that does not adequately reveal the depths of hopelessness these children daily experience. They are the poorest of the poor, subject not only to severe physical and sexual assault, but to hunger, disease, despair, and death. Their concerns have been lost in our frantic effort to cope only with the dramatic horror of physical abuse against the youngest and most vulnerable among us.

The mission of the child welfare system is not to protect children from criminal abuse but to aid impoverished children. Should it ever hope to do this, it must shift responsibility for protecting criminally abused children back to the police and the courts, where it can best be handled. Only then can the child welfare system concentrate on providing an infrastructure of social programs that will ensure the economic security and well-being of disadvantaged and impoverished children. The system should be judged by its success in reducing poverty among children, in providing them the means to break the cycle of poverty to become productive citizens, not by its effectiveness in controlling the incidence of criminal physical and sexual assaults, in which it will continue to fail, since criminal activity is not now, nor ever will be, predictable.

Appendix
Framework for Intervention in Allegations of Child Abuse

Death

Immediate action: If police have any suspicion a child's death was not accidental, then a homicide investigation would be conducted. A coroner's examination should be mandated in all child fatalities.

Aggravated Assaults

- Fractures
- Subdural hematoma / internal injury
- Severe physical injury
- Brain damage
- Poisoning
- Torture

Requirements for establishing jurisdiction: If police have reason to believe these injuries are not accidental.

Immediate action: Temporary removal for 2 weeks.

Care of child: The child will be cared for in a "place of safety" home and receive needed medical and psychological treatment.

Police action: During this period the police will be responsible for conducting a criminal investigation of the alleged assault and reporting to the court, with a copy to the child welfare agency.

Child welfare agency action: The child welfare agency will obtain a medical evaluation and police report. Based on these reports the agency will prepare a recommendation to the court on "behalf of the child." If the agency believes the child was intentionally assaulted then it should prepare a recommendation that the parental rights be terminated and the child freed for adoption depending on the outcome of the criminal trial against the assailant.

Court action: Within two weeks the court will decide if the child should remain in a "place of safety" pending the outcome of a criminal investigation and trial of the alleged perpetrator. The child would be returned home only after a court hearing approves the return of the child.

Severe Abuse

- Burns, scalding
- Lacerations, bruises, welts, sprains
- Contusions
- Sexual abuse involving genital contact

Requirements for establishing jurisdiction: If police have reason to believe the injuries are not accidental or abuse occurred.

Immediate action: Temporary removal for seventy-two hours.

Care of child: as above.

Police action: as above.

Child welfare agency action: as above. If the child welfare agency believes that the child was intentionally assaulted then it should prepare a recommendation that the parents behavior be censored and ask the court to warn the parents that subsequent abuse will result in the termination of parental rights.

Court action: as above. Specify the length of time the child will remain in a "place of safety."

Mistreatment

· Excessive corporal punishment

· Tying / confinement

· Sexual abuse, not involving genital contact

Requirements for establishing jurisdiction: If police have reason to believe the alleged mistreatment is not accidental, likely to continue, and that the child's safety is in danger.

Immediate action: On-site investigation and, if deemed necessary, seventy-two hour removal.

Care of child: If required, as above.

Police action: If the child is removed, the police will be responsible for conducting a criminal investigation of the alleged assault and reporting to the court.

Child welfare agency action: as above. If the agency believes the child was intentionally mistreated, then it should prepare a recommendation that the parents behavior be censored and ask the court to warn the parents that continued mistreatment may result in the termination of parental rights.

Court action: The child may be returned as soon as either the police or the court approves.

Severe Neglect

· Abandonment

· Failure to provide medical care

Requirements for establishing jurisdiction: If the police have reason to believe that the child has been abandoned or that the denial of medical treatment is likely to continue and that the child's health is at great risk.

Immediate action: On-site investigation and, if necessary, placement until claimed by parent.

Care of child: If required, as above.

Police action: If the child is taken into custody, the police will be responsible for searching for the parent and conducting a criminal investigation of the alleged abandonment and reporting to the court.

Child welfare agency action: as above. If the child welfare agency believes that the child was abandoned, then it should prepare a recommendation that the parental rights be terminated. If the child is returned home, it should occur under court supervision. The agency should make sure that the "best interests of the child" are protected, while also offering needed services to the biological parent.

Court action: The child may be returned as soon as either the police or the courts approve. If the parent is located then efforts should be made to return the child, if the parent so wishes. The parent should be advised that if the child remains in long-term foster care for more than six months, then the court will initiate proceedings to terminate parental rights.

Chronic Neglect

· Leaving the child unattended

· Lock-out

· Emotional neglect

· Educational neglect

Requirements for establishing jurisdiction: If the police have reason to believe that the child's health is at great risk.

Immediate action: On-site investigation and, if deemed necessary, seventy-two hour removal.

Care of child: If required, as above.

Police action: If the child is removed, the police will be responsible for conducting a criminal investigation of the alleged neglect and reporting to the court.

Child welfare agency action: as above. If the agency believes that the neglect endangered the health and safety of the child then it should recommend that the parents behavior be censored and ask the court to warn the parents that continued neglect may result in the termination of parental rights.

Court action: The child may be returned as soon as either the police, child welfare agency or the court approves.

Endangerment

· Parental use of illicit drugs

· Parental involvement in criminal behavior

· Parental drug addiction

· Parental alcohol addiction

Requirements for establishing jurisdiction: If the police have reason to believe that the parent's behavior places the child's health at great risk.

Immediate action: On-site investigation and, if deemed necessary, seventy-two hour removal.

Care of child: If required, as above.

Police action: If the child is removed, the police will be responsible for conducting a criminal investigation of the alleged endangerment and reporting to the court.

Child welfare agency action: as above. The agency should provide the parent with services for their particular problems. If the child welfare agency believes the endangerment places the child at great risk, then it should prepare a recommendation that the parents behavior be censored and ask the court to warn the parents that continued endangerment may result in the termination of parental rights. Parents should be urged to seek treatment.

Court action: The child should be returned as soon as either the police, child welfare agency or the court approves.

Inability to Care for the Child

· Parent permanently and totally disabled by mental or physical illness
· Parent incarcerated for an extended period

Requirements for establishing jurisdiction: If police have reason to believe the parent is unable to properly care for the child and that continued and serious neglect will result unless the child is taken into custody.

Immediate action: On-site investigation and, if deemed necessary, seventy-two hour removal.

Care of child: If required, as above.

Police action: If the child is removed, the police will be responsible for conducting a criminal investigation of the alleged endangerment and reporting to the court.

Child welfare agency action: as above. The agency should work with the parent to develop a case plan for the child. The parent and agency should develop a contract specifying when return of the child will occur and provide for parental visiting. The plan should include a provision for parental contribution to the cost of maintaining the child in state custody. The agency should involve the biological parent in the selection of a foster home and development of a case plan. Parents should be prepared to have the child returned home as soon as possible, and should demonstrate reasonable efforts to achieve restoration. If the parent fails to make reasonable efforts at restoration, then the agency should prepare a recommendation that the parents behavior be censored and ask the court to warn the parents that failure to make reasonable efforts will result in the termination of parental rights. Parents should be urged to seek treatment.

Court action: The child should be returned as soon as either the police, child welfare agency, or the court approves.

Impoverishment
- Lack of food, clothing
- Inadequate shelter / homelessness
- Disorganized and chaotic household
- Unsanitary living conditions

The child welfare agency will assign a caseworker to the parents and provide the services necessary to address the impoverishment and prevent placement.

Part II

Ending Child Poverty

The Great Depression stimulated the development of income support policy in the 1930s. The Social Security Act, unemployment compensation, and welfare programs were passed in response to massive unemployment, bread lines, and families being evicted from their homes. They established the principle that the resources of the government are required to deal with those aspects of poverty and insecurity that are not due to personal inadequacies or indolence.

Robert Haveman, *Starting Even*

One by one, with astonishing rapidity, the Communist regimes of Eastern Europe and the Soviet Union crumbled before the assertion of people's power, whose common watchword was the realization of a genuinely representative and responsible democratic form of government. In the last decade of the twentieth century democracy rediscovered its optimism and universality.

Neil Harding, "The Marxist-Leninist Detour"

Instead of understanding the broad social problems of the poor as the product of the dysfunctional behaviors of individuals, social reformers during the Great Depression struggled to alter dysfunctional social arrangements. The great strength of the free market economic system was found in its link to the democratic political system. When broad economic problems arose, the democratic political system provided the flexibility needed for adjustments and reform. The recent collapse of the socialist economies was as much a failure of political structure, as it was the crumbling of stale economic ideas.

When economic calamity struck in the 1930s a deep and wide despair spread across North America. Faith in fundamental social, political, and economic institutions began to give way. Bold and imaginative leadership was called for. In the United States Franklin Roosevelt initiated sweeping social programs and policies that helped, along with the advent of World War II, to lead the country to economic recovery. Following World War II, the United States emerged as the most powerful economy in the world.

185

Once again, calamity has struck, only this time it is confined to a narrow segment of society—children. In 1994 more the 14 million children live in poverty in the United States and another one million in Canada. Current programs that deal with child poverty were developed decades ago and are hopelessly outdated. What is needed are innovative and imaginative solutions that will address the problems poor children face in a post industrial economy.

The major barrier to progress against child poverty has been the limited view of our collective responsibility. Social policies and programs have been guided by a perspective that requires we wait until disaster strikes before we act. However, when millions of children live in poverty, with no end in sight, we must begin looking to structural explanations and solutions that will prevent disaster from ever striking.

To the extent that the problems which children in poverty face are structural (i.e., induced by external socioeconomic forces and circumstances), they must be approached at that level. Until now the approach in child welfare has predominantly been a residual one in which limited resources are allocated to society's less fortunate when they can be identified. While the residual approach may have been sufficient in the nineteenth and early twentieth centuries, it is not suited to the social conditions to which our society has evolved.

The child welfare system must confront the problem of child poverty head-on. If there is to be any hope of developing workable solutions to child poverty, the child welfare system must begin looking to the wider social and economic problems which families face.

In the following chapters, I attempt to identify those child welfare problems that are best treated through a structural approach, while redefining and clarifying those services that must continue to be addressed through a residual approach. I begin in Chapter 8 by examining the distribution of economic resources in North America and other industrialized market economies. What economic and social assumptions drive our free market system? How much wealth and income is produced and distributed? How is wealth and income allocated? How much goes to children, especially children in poverty? With what consequences? Poverty has two dimensions— income and wealth. Both dimensions of child poverty are examined in detail. This chapter aims at providing a perspective on the scope of the problem and how it must be addressed through public programs and policies.

Chapter 9 examines social policy and program initiatives designed to alter the current structural arrangements responsible for the condition of poor children. If the families served by child welfare agencies suffer from severe economic hardship, and this hardship is a factor that contributes to the problems child welfare is attempting to solve, social and economic policy changes to address this hardship need to be pursued. Further, solutions to these problems do not necessarily require more money as much as a rethinking and redesign of policies and programs that have proven ineffective and out of date. Children suffer because of an ineffective and obsolete court-administered child support collection system. They also suffer because of inequities and inefficiencies in the publicly funded income support programs for children. I review these programs and suggest needed reforms.

Chapter 10 examines the root causes of many child welfare problems. When young people start a family before they have the resources and maturity to be self-supporting they are forced to rely on public assistance. For most of these young people the consequence will be a life of poverty and despair. For many this is part of a larger cycle of poverty stemming from the lack of opportunity for poor children. In this chapter I challenge common myths which only serve to divide and antagonize. I focus on developing innovative approaches that would lead us out of the woods of the stale welfare debate.[78]

Chapter 11 offers a "social savings" approach that would break the continuing "cycle of poverty" among children. This is the same approach that was used to effectively end poverty among the elderly. No doubt the proposal has limitations, but it suggests the kinds of approaches and strategies, within a broader structural understanding of child welfare, that might solve the problems children face. Child poverty is a phenomenon that can be eradicated. Not all developed countries have child poverty, certainly not to the extent it is found in the United States. To end child poverty will take more

---

78. On a personal note I should add that I am disheartened by much of the current welfare debate. Too often it fails to recognize the plight of the children involved. I share these concerns not to stifle criticism or proffer some form of a "politically correct" debate. Rather, it is to suggest that during the debate we need to respect the dignity and humanity of the subjects of our inquiry, lest we further exacerbate the problems we wish to redress. Those who are suspicious of the morals and values of lone-mothers who struggle to raise their children might do well to spend time with these mothers who endure poverty with fortitude and sacrifice against insurmountable odds to provide and care for their children in the face of a frequently mean-spirited and dehumanizing welfare system (Berrick, 1993; Polakow, 1993).

than programs that provide income assistance for immediate relief of hardship. Long-term solutions designed to break the cycle of poverty are required.

The closing chapter brings the arguments together and presents a summary of the analysis and a discussion of future directions.

8

The Economic Condition of Children

In the game that determines how our national income is distributed, there are winners, there are losers, and there are those who aren't even in the game.

Robert Haveman, *Starting Even*

The social welfare system enacted in this century has all but eliminated poverty among the aged, but has had much less effect on children, leaving high rates of poverty at any one time, and horrendous rates over time.

Daniel Patrick Moynihan, "Towards a Post-Industrial Social Policy"

By 1950, not only were the modern postindustrial societies of North America the showcase of democracy and the standard of egalitarian achievement for the world, they were also among the wealthiest nations in the world. During the 1950s and 1960s, the United States economy led the world, producing an extraordinary 40 percent of the world's wealth (Hewlett, 1991, 271). The free enterprise market economies of the United States and Canada had produced such affluence that their citizens were enjoying a level of material abundance unparalleled in the history of civilization.[79] Disease was receding, hunger and want were disappearing, and thanks to technology and free enterprise, which appeared capable of accomplishing almost anything, life was getting better (Keynes, 1964). Except for a few nagging social problems, which would, within a few years, probably work themselves out, society was approaching what looked like utopia.

Things have not worked out quite the way we envisioned. While many things have indeed improved, many others have gotten worse. Despite our fabulous wealth, poverty has gotten worse, poverty among families, espe-

---

79. World War II had destroyed the economies of Europe and Asia. It would be almost two decades before these economies were restored. After World War II the per capita GNP of the United States was four times greater than West Germany and fifteen times greater than Japan. According to Lester Thurow (1992, 28), "The 1990s start from a very different place. In broad terms, there are now three relatively equal contenders—Japan; the European community, centered around its most powerful country, Germany; and the United States."

cially lone-parent families, among people of color, and of particular concern, among children (Bush, 1987; Sarri and Finn, 1992a, b).

In examining this poverty, it is useful to pull back and review the economic circumstances of the United States and Canada as examples of how free enterprise market economies create income and wealth. My interest is to examine how well modern economies have provided and continue to provide for children. A nation's collective economic and social future is shaped by the manner in which it provides for its children. We behold our future in the faces of our children, not only as a species, but as a nation and society. If many of our children are despairing, suffering from poverty and disease, especially in the midst of plenty, not only are we as guardians called to question, a warning is sounded for our society as well.

Examined within a broader sociological and economic prism, society is seen as an organization that allows for the production and distribution of resources among its members. The social order established plays a major role in determining what kind of opportunities children have and the type of life they will be able to achieve for themselves. If there is a system in place that allows every child to have an equal or at least a fair start, then opportunity will be assured. However, if there is substantial inequality and no measures are taken to ensure a fair start for all children, then the life prospects of many children will be significantly diminished. A society concerned with equity, fairness and opportunity for all children pursues strategies and policies to ensure all children, regardless of the socioeconomic status they were born into, a fair start and real opportunity.

The problem with the residual view of child welfare is that it assumes that child abuse is something that can only happen within the family—that it is centered around the parent/child relationship. This may be true of severe cases of child abuse that involve the brutal and horrible assault of children. But child abuse and neglect can also happen at a broader societal level (Gil, 1970, 1975). Children living in poverty in a nation of great material abundance suffer from abuse. It may be a less acute form of abuse; rather, it is a form of chronic abuse. Yet, it is the corrosive and indifferent character of this chronic abuse which makes it so difficult to endure. The brutality of severe physical abuse and the horror and betrayal of sexual assault of children are easily recognized, but too often we acquiesce to the inequity and unfairness of a situation where children, because of the life of poverty they were born into, are denied the basic economic resources for a decent life and as a result have little chance for achieving personal success in a market economy. As David Archard (1993, 156-157) points out, "More children suffer significantly reduced life opportunities as a result of their socioeconomic circumstances than are injured as a result of parental behavior...there is a general political unwillingness to see that the elimination of child abuse requires a major egalitarian programme of social and economic reform." Yet, it is the broad and extensive child poverty that is the fundamental problem which confronts child welfare. To understand child poverty requires viewing it within a broader economic perspective.

The Broader Purpose of Child Welfare

Economic growth in modern market economies require the development and continual nourishment of an affluent middle class. In advanced market economies governments provide the infrastructure for the development of an affluent middle class by ensuring equality of opportunity and providing a safety net of income protection for all citizens. In this regard, child welfare programs are responsible for both providing avenues of opportunity for all children and ensuring that children from families that have been least successful also have fair opportunities.[80]

Economic theorists have developed understandings of the economic order to explain poverty in post industrial society. In his study, *The New Industrial State*, John Kenneth Galbraith (1967) has argued that in the new industrial order knowledge and technology emerge as the primary ingredients for economic growth and success. Poverty in the new industrial order is not the result of the exploitation of the lower classes. Rather, most of those who live in poverty are outside the new industrial order. In private free enterprise economies many of the poor are essentially on the outside of the economic system looking in. They are denied or lack productive roles in the new high technology and global economies, and are attached through a parsimonious and increasingly reluctant welfare state apparatus. Oddly, the poor are not exploited for their surplus labor. Because of modern technology and offshore manufacturing much of the unskilled and low skilled labor the poor can provide is not required. Yet, not all societies have dealt with these economic changes in the same way. In North America those in the unskilled and low skilled work force have received different treatment than in Japan and Western Europe (Thurow, 1992).

---

80. Ensuring fair opportunity, as we shall see later, is a difficult balance between assisting children from low income families and encouraging independence and personal responsibility among the parents of these children that income support for children might undermine.

Another key feature characterizing advanced market economies in recent years is "stagflation," a period of low inflation, low interest rates and low levels of economic growth. Economists find this situation perplexing. However, the period is also characterized by low levels of growth in personal earnings (which have not grown since the 70s), an increase in low paying service jobs and overall decline in the average wage rate increase.

The reduction in growth raises the question of how the economic energies of a nation can be released? During the early emergence of industrial society in Great Britain, Adam Smith (1776) examined just this question. His inquiry focused on what was required to allow the newly emerging industrial society and market economy to prosper and produce the "wealth of a nation." Smith identified the major elements of the modern market economy and the importance of the division of labor. Key among these elements was private ownership and management of the economy. Private ownership of the "means of production" provided greater initiative and creative adaptation to changing market needs.

Adam Smith also emphasized the importance of allowing private individuals to accumulate wealth and invest their savings. He argued that the actions of these private individuals within a market economy were guided by an "invisible hand" that assured the wise deployment of resources. Although much has changed since the observations of Adam Smith, his essential analysis remains in force.

Nations with advanced market economies have been able to produce substantial material affluence for most of their citizens. These economies have generated wealth for a broad middle class as well as produced substantial and even enormous affluence for the upper income and wealth holding families. Governments have played a key role in allowing for the distribution of income and wealth based on the contributions, skills and fortune of its citizenry. The most successful advanced market economies with a strong industrial base have also achieved the broadest social participation in the wealth of the nation. For example, in Japan there is a broad middle class with a substantial wealthy class, but the *concentration* of income and wealth among those at the top has been far less than in European and North American countries.

As occurred during Smith's time, the concentration of wealth has also led to the emergence of a substantial underclass in urban areas. During the last several decades the United States has developed a large underclass of individuals and families characterized by severe poverty and diminished opportunity and hope (Wilson, 1987).

By definition, poverty in the United States derives from the unequal distribution of wealth and income. Part of the unequal distribution of wealth is a result of the variation in effort and reward which is central to the free enterprise market economy. However, when the distribution leaves millions of children in poverty, obviously through no action of their own, then the rules, policies and programs governing the distribution need to be reexamined. As Michael Katz (1989, 7) observes, when we talk about poverty "some things remain unsaid. Mainstream discourse about poverty, whether liberal or conservative, largely stays silent about politics, power and equality. But poverty, after all, is about distribution; it results because some people receive a great deal less than others...Poverty no longer is natural; it is a social product. As nations emerge from the tyranny of subsistence, gain control over the production of wealth, develop the ability to feed their citizens and generate surpluses, poverty becomes not the product of scarcity, but of political economy."

Poverty among a large portion of the population in the United States is not a natural product, but an expensive by-product of a highly skewed (or unequal) distribution of wealth. In the coming years it will be difficult for countries like the United States to compete in the global economy while carrying the burden of a large underclass of families in poverty. Other developed free market economies with democratic forms of government have, according to Polakow (1993, 173) "succeeded in alleviating the 'social asphyxia' of poverty. There are workable models, plausible and practical proposals, that speak to mixed economies."

Other nations who do not have to carry a similar burden of poverty as the United States will be at a substantial economic advantage. The economic expense of providing support for a large portion of the able population who are outside the economic mainstream places too great a marginal strain on the productive work force through higher taxes and reduced internal markets. To effectively compete in the global economy will require efforts designed to quickly reduce the number of children and families who are outside the mainstream of the productive workforce and to ensure participation of all.

In this task the child welfare system should play a major role. The child welfare system in modern market economies is responsible for *ensuring opportunity for all children*. When the child welfare system fails to protect children's economic futures, the long term consequences for the nation are the burden of supporting a large welfare class, increased need for "residual services" for such problems as drug and alcohol abuse, delinquency, and teenage pregnancy. The failure to protect children's economic futures results in the denial of opportunity and equity which is at the heart of child welfare concerns in North America as it enters the third millennium. It is this denial of opportunity which must be at the forefront of child welfare reform. To understand this issue requires examining the current economic situation of children and families within the context of the broader social and economic order.

Wealth: Who Has It and Who Doesn't?

In 1990, total privately owned assets in the United States were estimated to exceed 25 trillion dollars (Phillips, 1990, 118; Thurow, 1992, 235), which, if it were divided equally among the country's roughly 250 million population, would amount to $100,000 for each man, woman, and child, or, for a typical family of four, more than $400,000.[81]

It is difficult to argue against an economic system that has produced such great wealth. The free enterprise system with its commitment to market mechanisms and individual ownership of "the means of production" has released enormous productive energies. The imagination of the entrepreneur combined with the efficient regulation of the free market has proven an optimal economic arrangement (Gilder, 1984).

Distribution of Assets. A closer examination, however, reveals inequities. If the $25 trillion worth of privately owned assets were viewed as a giant pie, most families in the United States would own a very small slice, disproportionate to their share. In 1983, the United States Federal Reserve Board surveyed a representative sample of 40,000 families and found that the typical family had total financial assets of roughly $2,300 (Avery, Elliehausen, and Canner, 1984a, b; Chawla, 1990).[82] When total net worth was calculated—including all financial assets, home and real estate equity, minus financial liabilities, such as mortgage and other debt—fewer than one family in fifty had a net worth greater than $250,000. According to Rose

---

81. Canada's net wealth was estimated by Statistics Canada to be $2.2 trillion at the end of 1992 (Canadian Press, 1993, B12).

82. Total financial assets includes saving, checking, and money market accounts, certificates of deposit, IRA and Keogh accounts, bonds, stocks, and trusts.

Table 8.1 Distribution of Wealth in the United States

Personal Assets	Percent of Population	Group Wealth ($)	
Negative to $10,000	Bottom 25	-75	billion (owe)
$10,000 to $100,000	Middle 50	5	trillion (own)
$100,000 or more	Top 25	20	trillion
$500,000 or more	Top 3	7	trillion

Source: Rose (1992, 22).

(1992), the bottom 25 percent, rather than owning wealth, ended up, as a group, owing a total of 75 billion dollars (see Table 8.1). The middle 50 percent of the population own about a fifth of the wealth, while the top 25 percent own the remaining four-fifths. The top 3 percent own more than the bottom 75 percent.[83]

Clearly, wealth in the United States is concentrated in a small percentage of households. This concentration is most easily discerned by examining the ownership of corporate assets—stocks and bonds. As Figure 8.1 shows, the top 10 percent of the families in the United States own twice as much wealth as the remaining 90 percent.

Stocks. Virtually all businesses and corporations in the free enterprise economies, which are responsible for the country's industrial production, are privately owned. Among the available corporate assets (stocks, corporate bonds, and tax-free bonds) stocks are the most widely held, and represent the "title" of corporate ownership. Only about 20 percent of all families in the United States own stock. Of these, fewer than 7 percent are active shareholders trading regularly in stock (Avery, et al., 1984a, b). Further, more than half of all corporate stock in the United States is owned by less than 1 percent of the families (Phillips, 1993, 112-113).

Bonds. Besides stocks, corporate bonds are the other major way of participating in the productive capacity of the nation. Whereas stocks represent

83. Raj Chawla (1990) compared the distribution of wealth in the United States and Canada and found them quite similar (the Gini coefficient for total wealth was .65 for Canada and .69 for the United States). The poor in Canada generally lack assets as in the United States. However, in terms of income, the poorest 10 percent of the population in Canada are not nearly as destitute as the poor in the United States (Love and Poulin, 1991).

Figure 8.1 Distribution of Wealth in the United States, 1983

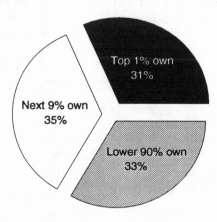

Source: Avery, Elliehausen, and Canner (1984 a, b).

outright ownership of a company, bonds represent money owed to an individual by the company. In 1984, businesses owed more than $2.1 trillion (*Wall Street Journal*, May 9, 1985, page 1), most of which took the form of corporate bonds. Again, less than 3 percent of all families in the United States own corporate bonds. Furthermore, about 40 percent of all corporate bonds are held by the same 2 percent of families which own more than fifty percent of the corporations. The wealthiest 10 percent of families own 70 percent of all bonds.

Tax-free Bonds. Tax-free bonds are issued by state or local municipalities in the United States to raise money for capital projects (dams, power generating stations, highways, schools). The interest paid on these bonds is tax free to encourage individuals to invest in projects that benefit the society at large. Most tax-free bonds provide income free of both federal and state income taxes. Who invests in such bonds? Again, less than 3 percent of all families in the United States. About 70 percent of the approximately one trillion outstanding tax-free bonds are owned by the top 2 percent of the wealthiest families in the United States. The wealthiest 10 percent own 86 percent of all tax-free bonds.

Impact of Economic Policy on the Accumulation of Wealth

During the 1980s federal economic and social policies in North America and Britain were aimed at stimulating the accumulation of wealth needed for capital investment and economic expansion.[84] While there is some question whether these goals were accomplished (Thurow, 1991), the policies did significantly enhance the economic position of the upper income groups (Phillips, 1990; Sherraden, 1990), so that there is now an increased concentration of wealth. One indicator of this is the increased number of millionaires in the United States. In 1964, fewer than 100,000 millionaires were recorded in the United States. By 1988, this figure had grown to more than 1,300,000. Even after adjusting for inflation, the number of millionaires grew at an extraordinarily high rate. According to Stanley (1988) the population of millionaires has increased at a rate almost 15 times faster than the rest of the population. Along with the number of millionaires, there was also a dramatic increase in the number of individuals with million-dollar annual incomes (from 1978 to 1988 the number increased from 2,041 to 65,303). Thus, we are observing a trend, already quite advanced, in which a relatively small percentage of families has been able to acquire ownership of the vast majority of wealth created in the North America.

Distribution of Income

A family's income normally derives from a variety of sources: labor force participation (wages), financial assets (dividends and interest), and real estate holdings (rent). Not all families receive an equal share of income, in large part because not all families have equal assets. In 1989, the median yearly household income for a family in the United States was $30,853, which is to say that half of all families reported an income greater than this amount, and half reported less.[85] While this median figure gives a general idea of where the typical family is financially, a more revealing picture is gained by examining the distribution of income across society.

Figure 8.2 divides all people in the United States in 1990 into 5 equal groups ranging from lowest income to highest income. The wealthiest 20

---

84. Similar economic policies were pursued in Great Britain by the Thatcher and Major governments and in Canada by the Mulroney administration.

85. In statistical terms, the average family income is usually defined as the median. In Canada the median income was $47,742 in Canadian dollars.

Figure 8.2 Distribution of Household Income in the U.S., by Quartile, 1990

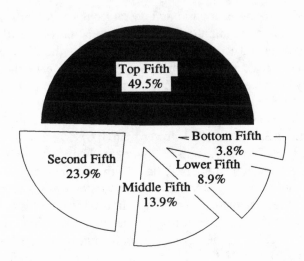

Source: Center on Budget and Policy Priorities (1991).

percent received almost half of all recorded income (51.1 percent), while the poorest 20 percent received less than one-twelfth of that (3.6 percent). It is the bottom fifth (the poor) who receive such a small share of income who make up the client base served by the public child welfare system.

Narrowed further, the wealthiest 1 percent of the population in the United States received an average annual income of $463,800, while the bottom 10 percent received an average annual income of less than $3,805, or less than 1 percent as much. Viewed another way, the combined income of the wealthiest 1 percent of the American population nearly equals the combined income of the poorest 40 percent of all Americans (Labor Trends, August 1990; Nasar, 1992). The shape of the distribution of wealth, where a few have so much and so many have so little, is not a naturally occurring phenomenon in wealthy, highly developed industrial democracies. Rather, it is shaped by tax policies and social programs that shift wealth upwards and withdraws the floor of social support for the poor (Katz, 1989).

There is also a major difference in income by race. As can be seen in Table 8.2, the poorest of the poor are Black. More than 20 percent of Black families live in household with income less than $8,000 per year. This is less than half the income of the poorest fifth of white families.

Figure 8.3 International Comparison of the Distribution of Income

Ratio Between the Highest and Lowest 20% of Household Income

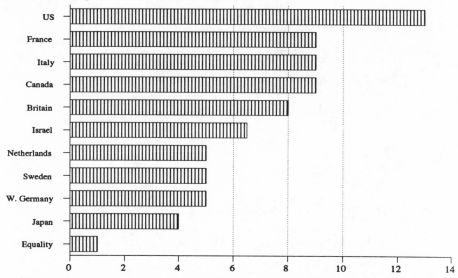

Note: Definitions of "household income" vary among countries. Figures are for various years in the late 1970s and early 1980s, with U.S. data for 1990.
Source: Los Angeles Times, October 21, 1984; Nasar (1992); Statistics Canada (1987); and Wilson (1985).

Table 8.2 Distribution of Income by Race (1991)

	Bottom	Lower	Middle	Upper	Top 5%
White	$18,922	$31,000	$44,874	$64,950	$106,119
Black	7,780	16,000	27,530	43,900	72,800

Source: U.S. Bureau of the Census.
Note: These figure represent the upper limit in each quintile. The top quintile is the lower limit of the top 5 percent.

Comparison with Other Countries

Although most industrialized market economies are characterized by an unequal distribution of wealth and income, the discrepancy between rich and poor is substantially greater in the United States than any other industrialized economy. Of all the industrial nations Japan has achieved the most egalitarian distribution of income (See Figure 8.3). Recent economic research suggests, in fact, that there is a positive correlation between equitable distribution of wealth and rates of economic growth (Nasar, 1994).

Figure 8.4 International Comparison of Gross Domestic Product Per Person

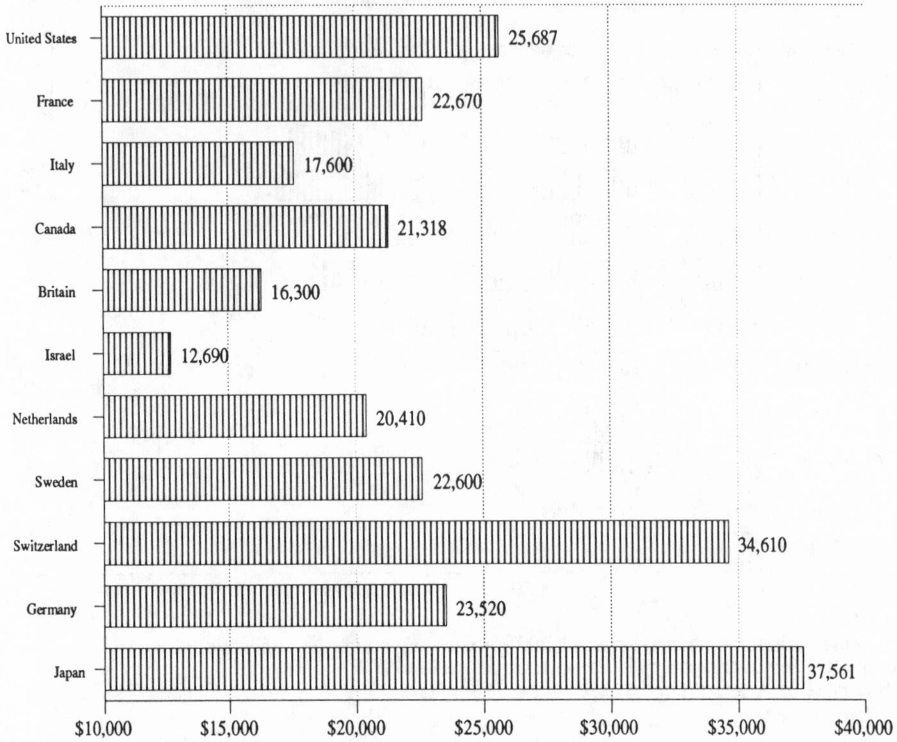

Source: *Globe and Mail* (1994).

The difference between the portions of income going to the top fifth of the population and to the bottom fifth varies sharply by country.[86] Those countries with the most egalitarian distribution have also proven most effective in producing the greatest amount of overall income per person. The standard indicator of the economic productivity of a society is to measure the Gross Domestic Product (GDP). The data in Figure 8.4 indicate the GDP of selected industrial countries. The country with the most equitable distribution of wealth, Japan, also has achieved the highest levels of GDP.[87]

---

86. The concern is not to produce an equal distribution of wealth, but to achieve a distribution of wealth that does not result in crippling poverty for large segments of the population (Sawyer, 1976). If the poverty experienced on the poor end of the distribution is so severe as to cripple, then policies and programs are needed to ensure opportunity and participation for all. Industrialized nations such as the former Soviet Union, East Germany and other socialist countries may have achieved a more equal distribution of wealth than the United States, but the failure of their economic arrangements to tap the imagination, creativity and energies of their citizens resulted in substantially less for all.

Figure 8.5 Change in United States Family Income from 1977 to 1990

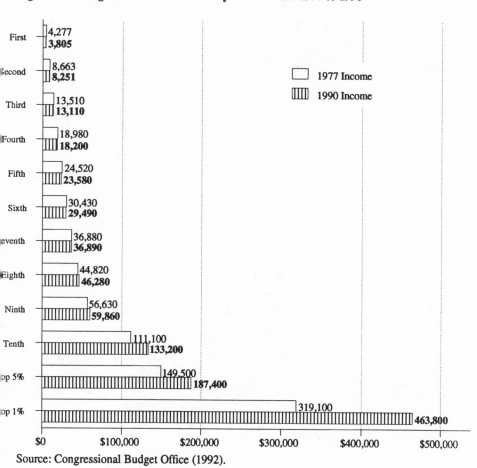

Source: Congressional Budget Office (1992).

When and How Changes in Income Occur

Although poverty has always existed in the United States, it was during the 1980s that the poorest families experienced the most precipitous decline in their earning power. From 1977 to 1990 income of the poorest 10 percent of families declined 11 percent, from $4,277 to $3,805 (See Figures 8.5 and

---

87. Among developing countries the disparity between the top and bottom 20 percent can be even greater. For Brazil, for example, the ratio is 26 to 1.

Figure 8.6 Percent Change in United States Family Income from 1977 to 1990

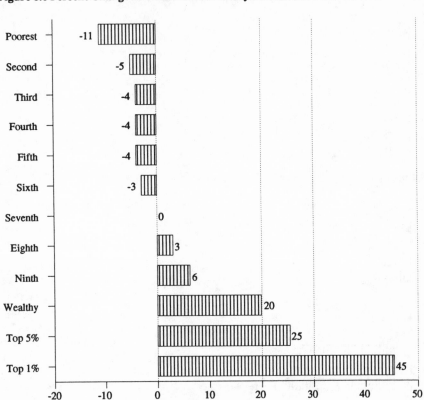

Source: Congressional Budget Office (1992).

8.6). During this period the wealthiest 10 percent of families increased their income almost 20 percent from $111,100 to $133,200, while the top 1 percent increased more than 45 percent, from $319,100 to $463,800. Clearly, the 1980s produced substantial gains for the wealthiest families in America, while the situation of the poor deteriorated. The income of the middle class remained almost constant during this period, the median family income increased from $30,668 in 1973 (in constant 1987 dollars) to $30,853 in 1987 (U.S. Bureau of the Census, 1987).

Even before the 1980s, the wealthy had made substantial income gains. From 1969 to 1982 the income share of the top 10 percent of wealthy Americans climbed from 29 percent to 33 percent, a gain of 4 percentage points. Lester Thurow (1987, 6) observed, "That's a real earthquake if the top 10

Figure 8.7 Distribution of After-Tax Income Gains in the United States, 1977-1989

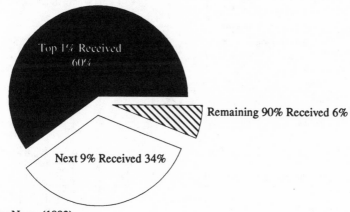

Source: Nasar (1992).

percent of the population can add 4 percentage points to their total share of income. The 4 percentage points are a big fraction of somebody's income lower down the spectrum." In fact, this increase alone was greater than the total income of the bottom 10 percent. According to Phillips (1990), in 1981 the top 1 percent of Americans had 8.1 percent of all reported income. By 1986, with the help of rising stock markets, that share had increased to an unprecedented 14.7 percent. In short, in less than two decades the top one percent had almost doubled their share of total income.[88]

Research by Paul Krugman (1992) of the Massachusetts Institute of Technology indicates that the decade of the 1980s produced substantial gains for high income groups. During the 1980s the top 1 percent of families in the United States got 60 percent of the after tax income gain achieved during the decade. Overall, the portion of the income gain going to the top 10 percent of the population was 94 percent, while the other 90 percent of the population shared the remaining 6 percent of the gain (see Figure 8.7). As the economy grew from 1977 to 1990, the income of the top 10 percent grew by 25 percent, while the income of the bottom fifth of families actually

88. After the election of the conservative federal government of Mulroney in Canada the income taxes paid by the working poor and middle class increased while they decreased for upper income families (National Council of Welfare, 1989; Philp, 1994a). Under Thatcher the top tax rate in Britain was cut in half from 83 to 40 percent. During the last fifteen years of conservative government "the richest fifth of the British population is 50 percent better off while the real incomes of the poorest fifth have dropped by 3 percent" (Koring, 1994, A1).

Figure 8.8 Effective Tax Rate for the Average Family Compared to the Top 1%

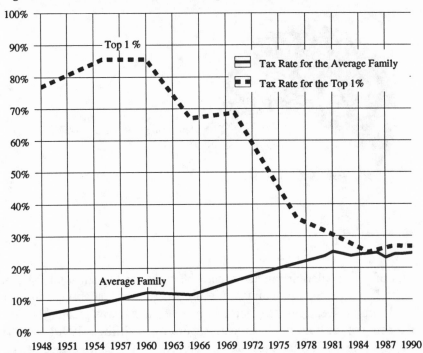

Source: Phillips (1993, 110).

fell by 11 percent. Economic policies of the eighties produced substantial gains for the wealthy, while the poor were left out (LaRoe and Pool, 1988).

The Impact of Tax Policy

How did the shift of wealth upward during the decade of the eighties come about? The increased concentration of wealth and income in the United States during the last decade was largely the product of conservative economic policies that led to a quiet but massive redistribution of wealth through tax cuts that shifted income and wealth upwards (see Figure 8.8).[89] The argument was that by cutting taxes on the wealthy, more wealth would be accumulated and concentrated and thus made available for the nation

---

89. The data in Figure 8.8 come from Kevin Phillips (1993). The top 1 percent are defined as the top income group earning more than a million dollars a year.

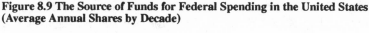

Figure 8.9 The Source of Funds for Federal Spending in the United States (Average Annual Shares by Decade)

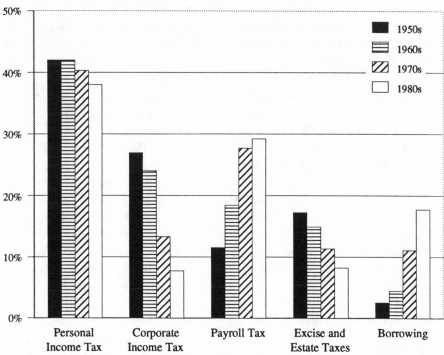

Source: Phillips (1993, 111).

through capital reinvestment, and all members of society would benefit. During the last several decades the top 1 percent of families were, in fact, able to accumulate a greater share of the wealth, but not so much through the production of new wealth as through a redistribution of existing wealth through a program of substantial tax reductions for high income earners. As seen in Figure 8.8, the *effective* tax rate on the wealthiest families has declined during the last three decades from about 85 percent to about 27 percent. With the passage of the tax code revisions in 1993, the maximum rate was increased to 39 percent.

These tax cuts were not financed through a reduction in federal spending. In the eighties the federal government reduced spending on domestic programs that were more than matched with increased spending on military defense. Rather, as seen in Figure 8.9, over the years the source of taxation has shifted from a reliance on corporate income tax, excise and estate taxes, which primarily affect the wealthy, to increased borrowing and reliance on payroll tax for funding Social Security. Over the last several decades the portion of federal revenue collected from personal income tax remained relatively stable. However, the corporate income tax rate was cut sharply. The United States now has one of the lowest corporate income tax rates in the world. The corporate income tax rate in Japan is roughly equivalent to the rate in the United States in the fifties. Likewise in Canada, the total income taxes paid by individuals almost doubled from 4.7 percent of GDP in 1966 to 8.9 percent in 1990 as the total taxes paid by corporations fell one third from 2.7 percent in 1966 to 1.8 percent in 1990 (Philp, 1994a, A4).

Payroll taxes collected to pay for Social Security has risen steadily over the last four decades. Payroll tax is regressive because it is used to fund a "social savings" program (Social Security) but allows wealthy individuals to stop paying tax on their income once it exceeds $61,000 (in 1994). In other words, all families pay about 15 percent of their income to Social Security (combined employee and employer contribution) up to a limit of about $60,000, after which their income is no longer taxed. Taxes that were carried primarily by the wealthy, such as estate taxes, have also been cut over the last several decades. Observing the net result of these tax policies in recent decades Phillips (1993, 123) concludes, "the progressivity of the U.S. income tax system had been largely lost."

One of the major sources of revenue tapped to pay for the large tax cuts, and that have primarily benefited high income and wealthy families, has been increased federal borrowing. This has resulted in an even greater shift of wealth upward. After all, it is the wealthy who purchase the government bonds that finance the debt. For many wealthy families the tax cuts, rather than producing substantial investment capital, instead produced funds to finance the debt. The net result is that the unequal distribution of wealth has been further increased. As Phillips (1993, xxiii) points out, "In the United States, merely to service the $4 trillion national debt of 1992—up fourfold from $1 trillion in 1980—required some $235 billion a year in net interest payments, most of which went to high-income bondholders (and some went abroad) while the money to make the payments was raised from broad-based taxes."[90] However, Phillips argues, since the poor have so little the tax burden is primarily shouldered by a shrinking and increasingly overburdened middle class.

As can be seen in Figure 8.10, tax cuts enacted on the argument that they would encourage increased accumulation of capital were substantial. The tax cuts resulting from the Tax Reform Act of 1986 alone amounted to more than $18 billion a year for the wealthiest 65,000 families (less that 1/30th of

Figure 8.10 Tax Cut Resulting from the Tax Reform Act of 1986, by Income (1989)

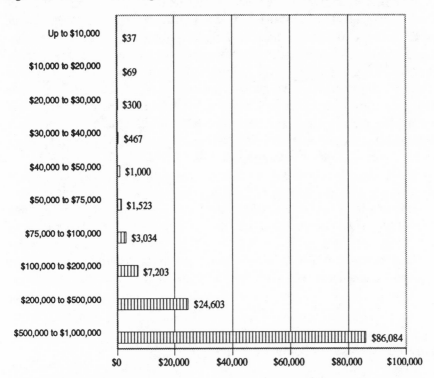

Source: Phillips (1993, figure 4).

one percent of all families). For the top 10 percent the tax cuts were close to 100 billion dollars a year (in 1989). Likewise in Canada, tax cuts have primarily benefited the wealthy. A study by economists at Statistics Canada indicated, "These changes, including cuts to corporate and sales taxes and heftier write offs for business, cost $14.2 billion in foregone revenue in 1979—a year when the deficit had reached 11.6 billion. By 1991, federal interest charges accounted for 32 percent of Canadian tax dollars, three times as much as the mid-1970s" (Philp, 1994, A4).

---

90. To pay the interest on the accumulated federal debt requires half of all personal income taxes collected. The accumulation of this federal debt thus further compounds the shift of wealth upwards. Columnist George Will (1988) writes, "This represents, as Senator Pat Moynihan has said, a transfer of wealth from labor to capital unprecedented in American history. Tax revenues are being collected from average Americans and given to the buyers of U.S. government bonds—buyers in Beverly Hills, Lake Forest, Shaker Heights, and Grosse Pointe, and Tokyo and Riyadh."

In the eighties it was argued that tax cuts on the wealthy would stimulate them to accumulate capital that they would use for investments that would produce economic growth and, in the end, produce even more taxes than was temporarily lost through the tax cuts. This approach didn't work.[91] Rather, the federal deficit in the United States increased from about $1 trillion at the beginning of the eighties to more than $4 trillion at the beginning of the nineties. The deficit problem was compounded because the increase in ongoing interest payments must be financed with continued borrowing. The tax policies of the eighties left the wealthy even wealthier and the rest of the nation in collective debt to the debt holders. As Thurow (1992, 129) observes, "Domestic saving is at an all time low, and the trade deficit is at an all-time high. By saving very little and selling off existing American assets to finance a trade deficit that allows them to consume more than they produce, today's Americans gain consumption privileges at the expense of tomorrow's Americans." What is sacrificed by these tax policies is not current consumption and well-being, but the prosperity passed on to the next generation. In a sense, what is being sacrificed is our children's future.[92]

The Growing Abyss of Poverty: Creating Poor Families Through Social and Economic Policy

As we have seen, the growth of poverty in the United States during the last decade, along with the growth of wealth, was largely the product of eco-

---

91. When taxes on higher income groups were cut in the early 1980s it was predicted, Thurow observed (1991, 264), "that high-income Americans would save more if they were taxed less. Their income taxes were cut, but the American taxpayer spent his or her extra after-tax income on a consumption binge. Private-savings rates fell to all-time lows in the aftermath of the Reagan tax cuts (2.9 percent of disposable income in 1987). On the expenditure side of the budget, defense spending rose sharply, from $131 billion in 1980 to $314 billion in 1990." In 1990 the top 1 percent of income earners paid 27 percent of all income taxes collected (up from 18 percent a decade earlier). This change indicates the degree to which wealth and income have been shifted upward. The top pay such a large share because they have been able to accumulate such a large share of the wealth and income. They pay a larger share even though they pay a lower rate. This is another inidicator of the enormous shift of wealth and income upward.

92. For instance, in the five-year period between 1985 to 1990 foreigners purchased ownership of corporations in the United States, as represented by stock ownership, of almost 10 percent of the total stock market capitalization, whereas foreigners purchased less than 1 percent of stock market capitalization in Japan (Thurow, 1992, 131-132). To the extent that the competition in the current era is economic, Japan is ascending.

nomic and taxation policies. Although conservative economic theorists have developed arguments which blame poverty on the poor because of indolence and avoidance of work, the facts point elsewhere. Kevin Phillips (1993) has argued that the tax policies of the 80s led to a squeeze on the middle class. He observes,

> The victories of Thatcher and Reagan in 1979-80 in the West's two leading financial centers launched what conservatives excitedly called "revolutions"—transformations that were supposed to unleash capitalist energies and market economies on a grand scale. By 1986-87 the Group of Seven leading economic nations had undergone startling political alignments: aggressive free-market conservatism was in style, more so than at any other time since World War I. The ensuing policy changes, ranging from tax reductions to financial deregulation, regulatory permissiveness, strict treatment of labor and glorification of the rich, proved to be an elixir for global stock markets, property values and business opportunities, just as supply-side economists had predicted. The drawback in the United States, however, was that as the 1980s boom crested, rising taxes and other costs were gobbling up much of the nominal income gain of the middle class, while public services and the government safety net were starting to deteriorate. (P. xx)

In the absence of similar policies and programs to improve opportunities for the poor, the economic situation of the poor has markedly declined. The shift of income and wealth from the poor and middle class to the wealthy created what Phillips (1990, 14) termed an extraordinary pyramid of affluence in the United States:

> A record number of billionaires, three thousand to four thousand families each worth over $50 million, almost one hundred thousand with assets over $10 million, and at least one and a quarter million households with a net worth exceeding $1 million...The caveat was that if two to three million Americans were in clover—and another thirty to thirty-five million were justifiably pleased with their circumstances in the late 1980s—a larger number were facing deteriorating personal or family incomes or a vague but troubling sense of harder times ahead.

To measure the number of persons lacking sufficient economic resources to meet basic needs (food, clothing, and shelter), the federal government uses an index of poverty developed by Orshansky for the Social Security Administration in 1964 and revised in 1969 (Orshansky, 1965, 1967).

According to this formula, the poverty line is calculated at three times what the Department of Agriculture estimates a given family spends on food. [93] Thus, if a family of four needs $300 a month for food, a monthly income of less than $900 means the family is living below the poverty line. In this calculation, income includes cash payments from Aid to Families with Dependent Children (AFDC), Supplemental Security Income (SSI), General Assistance, and other income assistance programs.[94] In 1991, the poverty line was approximately $10,400 annually for a three-person family and $13,924 for a family of four. Thus a lone-mother and two children with annual income below $10,860 would be defined as "poor."

Some observers have suggested that by not counting "in-kind" benefits (i.e., food stamps, subsidized housing), along with alleged under-reporting of income, the poverty line may overstate the number of people actually living in poverty. Levitan (1990) estimates that if both cash and in-kind income, which in the past went a long way toward helping many poor families, were counted in measuring poverty, the percent of the population living below the poverty line in 1988 would have declined from the official report of 13.1 percent to 10 percent.

Overall, however, the actual number of poor families is probably larger than official estimates. The major problem for an increasing number of poor is housing (Massey and Denton, 1993). During the last decade funding for public housing in the United States has been reduced by 80 percent (Polakow, 1993, 163-164). Nonetheless, housing has become the major financial expense for the poor. In 39 states the fair market rent is greater than the full amount of financial support provided by AFDC. In fact, in several states and metropolitan areas the fair market rent is several times the maximum grant provided by AFDC (Polakow, 1993). In 1987, according to the Children's Defense Fund, half of all renter households in poverty were spending more than 70 percent of their income on housing (Polakow, 1993, 164).

While the government's measure of poverty is a function of a family's ability to purchase the necessities of life, poverty can also be measured relative to the income of others (Frank, 1985). Even here, the relative position

---

93. Although the poverty line is adjusted for family size, there is no adjustment for local and regional differences. With the great variation in the cost of housing among the different regions, this is a major limitation. The poverty line measure takes into account such variables as family size, commissions, tips, other cash benefits before deductions for taxes and pensions.

94. Income does not include the cash value of medical assistance, social services, food stamps, subsidized housing, child care, and other in-kind benefits.

of the poor has declined over the years. In 1960 the poverty line was roughly equivalent to half the median income for a family of four, but by 1988 it had declined to less than a third of the median family income (Levitan, 1990). This change reflects the dramatic shift in the distribution of wealth upwards. If poverty were defined in relative terms, such as one half the median family income proposed by some economists and widely used by European economists, a much greater number of families would have slipped into poverty than the currently defined poverty line suggests.

Who the Poor Are—Past and Present

The Elderly

In the early part of this century, the poor consisted primarily of the elderly. Fortunate was the man or woman who, in his or her seventies and eighties, was sheltered in the family of a child now grown.

In the United States it was only with the enactment of the Social Security Act in 1935 that the elderly began emerging from poverty. Adopted during the New Deal, the Social Security Act provided: (1) a federal "social savings" program to make sure people have income in their later years (Old Age and Survivors Insurance) and (2) federal welfare programs for the elderly (Old Age Assistance), for widows and orphans (Aid to Dependent Children), and for the disabled (Aid to the Permanently and Totally Disabled) (Bell, 1965). The "social savings"[95] provision for the elderly has emerged as the major program of the Social Security Act.

As a mandatory "social savings" program Social Security requires employees (and their employers) to make provision for the employee's retirement by paying premiums to a Social Security fund through automatic payroll tax deductions during the employee's working years. When the individuals retire, or are no longer able to work, they are entitled to receive ben-

---

95. Social Security is often referred to as a "social insurance" program because it collectively sets aside money to "insure" that the elderly have a basic income during their retirement years. However, the term "insurance" usually refers to the pooling of funds by the collective to protect individuals from personal peril. Thus, unemployment insurance is a form of social insurance that protects workers when, through misfortune, they are unemployed. Crop insurance is another example. However, Social Security is more concerned with "saving" funds for an event that it is known all will experience. The term "social savings" thus highlights the savings aspect of Social Security.

efits from the fund based, in part, on the amount of their contribution. With only a few exceptions for government workers, Social Security is mandatory and provides universal coverage for all U.S. citizens.

As the main program of aid to the elderly, Social Security can only be regarded as a resounding success. As Pechman (1989, 160) observes, "There is no question that the Social Security system has successfully redistributed a large and growing amount of income from younger to older people, so that their spending power (relative to their needs) is now equal to or greater than that for most other groups in the society—including families with children."

Still, despite Social Security, the economic situation of the elderly continued to be characterized by high rates of poverty well into mid-century. By 1959, more than one third of the elderly in the United States still lived in households with income below the poverty line. The War on Poverty and the Great Society programs of the 1960s and early 1970s, which were targeted at the problems of racial discrimination and unskilled and untrained workers who were unemployable, did little for the elderly. Only with the passage of the SSI in 1972 did the economic situation of the elderly poor begin to change substantially (Lindsey and Ozawa, 1979). In 1966, 40 percent of persons sixty-five or older lived in households below the poverty line (Orshansky, 1967). By 1979 this had been reduced to 16 percent—a more than 60 percent decline in poverty among the elderly. From 1979 to 1989 the number had dropped to 9 percent. Moreover, this decline occurred during the last two decades, at a time when the elderly population increased 50 percent. Haveman (1988, 82-83) observes, "One of the biggest success stories chalked up to the nation's redistribution system is its role in pulling up the average standard of living of the nation's older population. As a group, the elderly are no longer poor—no longer a source of equity or fairness concerns."

The elimination of poverty among the elderly is largely the result of government income transfers. Taking inflation into account, the average cash transfer received by the poor elderly between 1967 and 1984 increased from less than $5,000 a year to more than $7,000 (Danziger and Gottschalk, 1986). Combined spending for the elderly has steadily risen during the last three decades (Figure 8.11). From 1960 to 1990 total federal spending on Social Security and Medicare increased 150 percent, after controlling for inflation. Without question, the federal government has played a major role in providing income support of the elderly.

Figure 8.11 Federal Spending on Social Security and Medicare for the Elderly, 1960-1990

(in 1988 dollars)

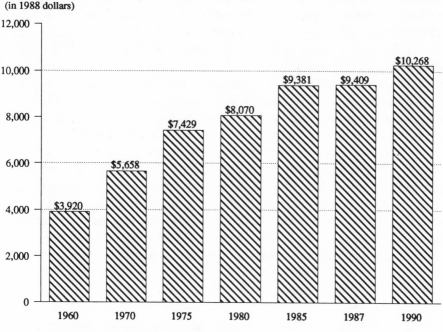

Source: Levitan (1990, 30); Ozawa (1993, 521).

In 1990 the federal government spent $11,350 per aged person compared to $1,020 per child under 18 (Ozawa, 1993, 521-522). In short, on a per person basis the federal government spent 10 times more on seniors than on children, a differential in spending that is perplexing.

Programs to Protect the Economic Security of the Elderly in Canada. To protect the incomes of its senior citizens, Canada provides a flat rate universal Old Age Security benefit combined with two income tested supplements, the Guaranteed Income Supplement and the Spouse's Allowance (OAS/GIS/SA).[96] In addition, Canada provides the Canada and Quebec Pension Plans (C/QPP), a compulsory social savings program for practically all individuals in the labor market. These programs, along with private pensions and individual retirement accounts (called RRSPs), ensure that the elderly in Canada will have sufficient income in their retirement years to keep them from falling into poverty (Guest, 1985). In 1965 half of the elderly in Canada lived in poverty. The above programs ended this poverty. In the fiscal year ending March 31, 1994, the federal government in Canada "mailed out 8.8 million pension cheques and spent close to $39 billion on public retirement programs—almost three times as much as in the mid-1970s" (Philp, 1994a, A4). This amounts to almost $13,000 per aged person. As in the United States, this figure dwarfs spending on children (Canadian Council on Social Development, 1988). Relative to other groups in Canadian society, the economic situation of the elderly has been protected by the "social savings" programs. Ross and Shillington (1989, 53) have observed that between 1973 and 1986 the depth of poverty, as measured by the poverty gap (the amount needed to end poverty), fell a half billion dollars for the elderly, while it rose $2.2 billion for working-age families.[97]

Not only has the poverty gap for the elderly fallen substantially while it has increased for others, the incidence of poverty among the elderly has dropped. Ross and Shillington (1989, 43) point out, "By age, the highest incidence [of poverty] among families was registered by the under-25 age group. Its rate almost doubled between 1973 and 1986. On the other hand, the rate of poverty among elderly families in 1986 was less than a third of what it had been in 1973." The "social savings" approach for ending poverty among the elderly in Canada succeeded almost as dramatically as it did in the United States.

Although the elderly have seen their economic circumstances improve during the last three decades, not all groups have been as fortunate (Ryan, 1972). Who are the poor in the United States and Canada that share so little in their nation's wealth?

Children

> Why, we might ask, is it so difficult to see that children do not catch poverty
> but are made poor by state neglect; that single mothers need not be destined

---

96. Both Canada and the United States use a "social savings" approach to protecting the incomes of citizens in their retirement years. It is remarkable how similar the programs in Canada and the United States are. Both countries offer a compulsory universal social savings program: Old Age Security and Canada/Quebec Pension Plans in Canada and Social Security in the United States. Guaranteed Income Supplement and Spouse's Allowance in Canada and Supplemental Security Income in the United States provide an "income-tested" benefit to insure that no elderly live in poverty. Registered Retirement Savings Plans in Canada and Individual Retirement Accounts in the United States provide for individual savings through tax sheltered savings plans administered through stock brokers and securities dealers.

97. The poverty gap is defined as the amount of money required to eliminate poverty. It is a useful indicator because it assesses both the rate and depth of poverty.

to fall into poverty but are made poor by a state-constructed policy? A different set of policies and a different kind of discourse can change lives.

Valarie Polakow, *Lives on the Edge*

The largest group of poor are, and have been for some time, children. In 1959, almost two-thirds of all nonwhite children in the United States were living in families with incomes below the poverty line. At the same time almost one fifth of all white children were living in families with incomes below the poverty line.

As Table 8.3 indicates, from 1959 to 1969, during the years of the War on Poverty and a period of economic growth, the number of children in poverty declined from more than 17 million to 10.5 million, even though the child population was increasing. The number of white children in poverty fell almost by half, while the percentage of nonwhite children living in poverty fell from 65 percent to 42 percent. Clearly, the War on Poverty had an impact on reducing poverty among children.

Since 1969, however, the economic situation of children has been deteriorating. From 1969 to 1979 the percentage of white children living below the poverty line increased more than 25 percent (from 10.5 percent to 13.4 percent), while the percentage of nonwhite children living in poverty increased from 41.5 percent to 42.1 percent. In contrast, the situation for the elderly continued to improve. From 1969 to 1979 the percentage of elderly living in poverty declined from 24.6 percent to 16 percent.

By the seventies children had replaced the elderly as the poorest age group in the United States (O'Higgins, 1988; Schorr, 1989). During the next two decades poverty among children actually increased one third, from 15 percent to 20 percent, while the percentage of elderly living in poverty continued to decline, falling from 16.2 percent in 1979 to 12.2 percent in 1987. By 1980, the poverty rate among preschool children was more than twice the poverty rate of the elderly.

Thus, while the elderly in the United States were lifted out of poverty through a "social savings" scheme (Social Security and SSI programs), children continued a steady slide into poverty.

The elderly in Canada also exited poverty through compulsory "social savings" programs (OAS/GIS/SA and C/QPP). Between 1973 and 1986 the percent of elderly in Canada living in poverty declined from 24.2 to 9.5 percent. While poverty among the elderly was reduced by two-thirds between 1973 and 1986, the poverty rate for children remained roughly the same. Ross and Shillington (1989, 43) observe: "The poverty rate for families

Table 8.3 Children and Elderly in Poverty, 1959-1987

	1959	1969	1979	1987
White children	11,433,000	6,285,500	7,035,000	7,680,000
	(20.6)	(10.5)	(13.4)	(15.0)
Nonwhite	5,681,100	4,399,000	4,715,200	5,366,900
	(65.3)	(41.5)	(42.1)	(45.1)
All Children	64,200,000	69,600,000	62,500,000	63,100,000
	(26.9)	(14.9)	(17.9)	(20.0)
	17,114,100	10,604,500	11,543,000	13,016,000
Elderly	5,481,000	4,778,700	3,028,510	3,184,733
	(35.2)	(24.6)	(16.0)	(12.2)
	15,571,023	18,888,142	24,622,034	27,219,943

Note: Percentages in parentheses.
Source: U.S. Census Bureau (various years).

headed by women is as persistent as it is high—58 percent in 1973, about 56 percent in 1979 and 1986—it has not drawn much attention from policy makers." In 1991, the poverty rate for single parent mothers increased to 62 percent (National Council of Welfare, 1993, Graph N).

Children in Lone-parent Families. As we saw in Chapter 4, beginning in the 1960s, the traditional two-parent family began to experience increasing social and economic pressures. More mothers began working outside the home (see Figure 4.1) and the divorce rate rose sharply (see Figure 4.2). As a consequence, the number of lone-parent families began increasing dramatically. During the last fifteen years the proportion of lone-parent families with children under the age of eighteen has almost doubled, increasing from 10 percent in 1970 to 19 percent in 1985 to more than 20 percent in 1990. Not surprisingly, children of lone-parent families have become the focus of poverty. Frank Levy (1987) observes:

Some of the disparity [in income between rich and poor households] was the inequity between investment bankers and high school dropouts. But a more direct cause was the increasing division of American families into two extremes: female-headed families on the one hand and two-paycheck families on the other... The division has implications for the future because the poorest twenty percent of families (many headed by single women) now contain almost one-quarter of all the nation's children. (P. vi)

The lone-parent raising a child is confronted by a social and economic situation that has proven difficult, and often, impossible to change. Polakow (1993) has argued that women have been relegated to the secondary labor market. The primary labor market offers higher wages, steady employment, substantial fringe benefits, and unemployment compensation. For women trying to raise children on their own, opportunities for employment in the primary labor market has been severely restricted. Polakow (1993) observes, "Women often become casual, secondary-sector workers, ineligible for unemployment and health insurance benefits by virtue of their low wages and part-time work." Pearce (1990) indicates that 87 percent of recipients of primary benefits are in white families headed by men or married couples; only 3 percent are headed by black single mothers.

With reduced economic resources, increased child-rearing responsibilities and limited earning power, the lone-parent is severely restricted in choices and opportunities. The odds are high that such a parent will remain in poverty for an extended period of time. Children of such lone-parents have virtually no way of altering or escaping the economic circumstances in which they find themselves. The fate of children is entwined with that of their mothers'. Through no fault of their own children are deprived of a host of developmental opportunities available to children of wealthier, two-parent families. The data in Figure 8.12 indicate the length of time children in lone-parent families are likely to live in poverty. Most (60 percent) are likely to spend more than seven of their first ten years in poverty compared to less than 2 percent for those children who live with both parents.

Minorities and Lone-Parents

During the last decade the economic situation of Afro-American and Hispanic families with members under thirty has deteriorated markedly relative to the situation of white families in the United States (Figure 8.13). The median income of Afro-American families declined almost 30 percent from 1973 to 1986 and the median income for Hispanic families declined 16 percent while the median income of white families declined less than 8 percent. In addition, the economic situation of lone-parent families also declined.

Figure 8.12 Duration of Poverty During the First Ten Years of Childhood by Family Type in the United States

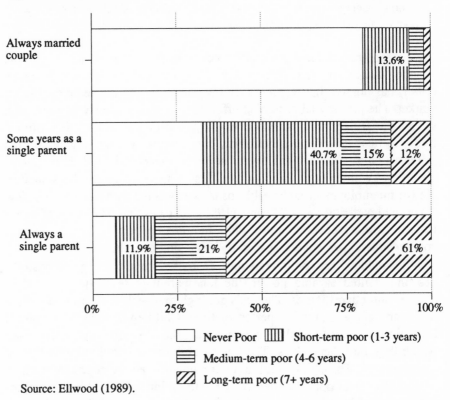

Source: Ellwood (1989).

While the median income of married couples declined less than 4 percent, the median income of mother-only families declined more than 25 percent.

Lone-mothers and their children thus represent the most vulnerable group in North America. Much of their economic circumstances result from inequalities of opportunity. Because they earn substantially less than men even when performing equivalent tasks and because they carry enormous child-care demands, neither they, nor their children, are ever likely to escape poverty. Women with a college education and professional training may be able to establish a viable independent economic household, but most unskilled and semiskilled women will not.

Poverty continues to be viewed as a private affair. When lone-mothers are unable to adequately provide for their children they are blamed for circumstances that are often well beyond their control. Because of their pov-

Figure 8.13 Median Income of U.S. Families Headed by Persons Under 30 (1973 1986)

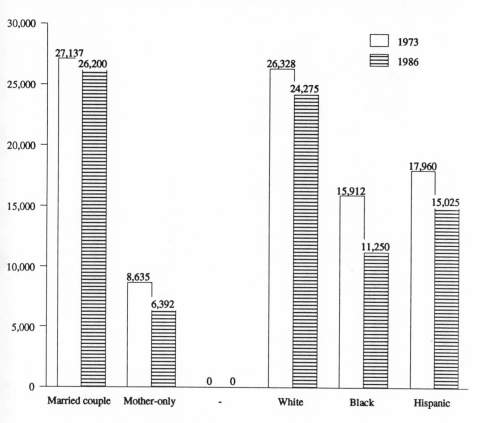

Source: Johnson, Sum, and Weill (1988, appendix: table 3, 76).

erty they find their values and judgment questioned. Consequently, lone-mothers are reluctantly provided income assistance reasoning that there is no guarantee the funds provided will be spent on the children. Will lone-mothers spend it on nutritious food or just on cigarettes and alcohol? Yet to ask the question is to answer it. The behavior of lone mothers is scrutinized in a manner others, like the elderly, would find objectionable—an insult to their integrity and dignity. "This discourse," argues Polakow (1993, 47) "serves to conceal the continuing mean-spirited treatment of poor people and legitimates the minimalist and degrading support policies for single mothers and their children, who suffer the snowball effects of class and race as well as gender discrimination."

Figure 8.14 Percentage in Poverty in the United States by Age, 1987

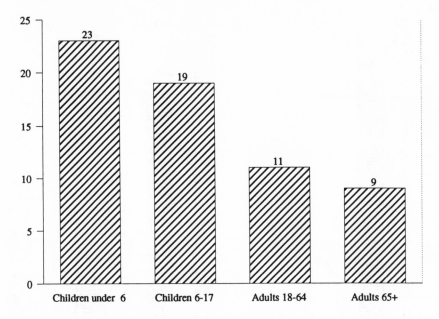

Source: National Center for Children in Poverty (1990).

Children under Age Six

We can narrow the focus of poverty even further. The economic situation of children under six, of lone-parents, especially lone-mothers, is the most severe of any group (Norman and Glick, 1986). According to the National Center for Children in Poverty (1990) at Columbia University, the number of poor children under six increased by 35 percent between 1968 and 1987, even though the population of children under six remained relatively stable. In contrast, the poverty rate of the elderly fell substantially, while the elderly population increased from 18.5 million to more than 27 million. The data in Figure 8.14 indicates the poverty rate by various age groups. Clearly the highest rates of poverty in the United States are to be found among children, with children under six at the bottom.[98]

---

98. Only lone-parents with children under age three have a higher incidence of poverty.

Figure 8.15 Poverty Rates for U.S. Children Under Age Six by Race and Family Type (1987)

Percent Living in Poverty

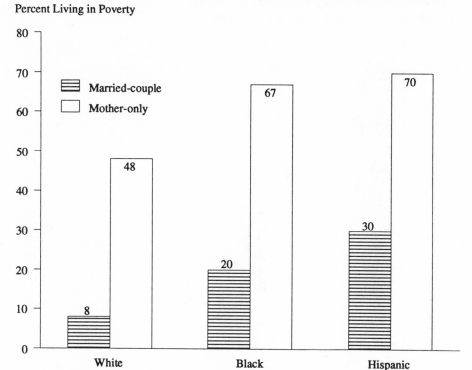

Source: National Center for Children in Poverty (1990, figure 9, 28).

Minority children under six are especially vulnerable to poverty. As Figure 8.15 shows, when lone-parenthood is combined with minority status, the probability of the child living in poverty in the United States greatly increases. Thus, Hispanic children under six living with only their mother have a 70 percent chance of being in poverty. For similar Afro-American children the poverty rate is 67 percent. For whites, the rate is 48 percent.

Why is the poverty rate highest for children under six? After all, this is a group whom are the most vulnerable and certainly the least "deserving" of their fate. The explanation is obvious. Child care, especially for lone-mothers, is too great a burden (see Chapter 4). The absence of universal child care, as found in other countries that do not have these high rates of child poverty, is what drives this perplexing and unsettling phenomenon. Even when lone-mothers work full time at minimum wage all year long, child

Figure 8.16 International Child Poverty Rates

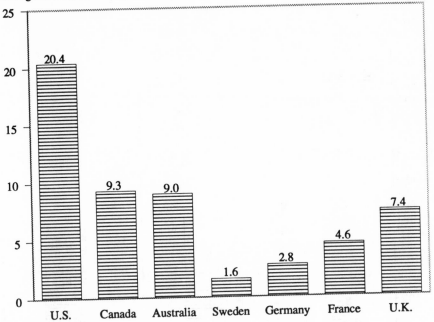

Percentage of Children Living in Poverty

Source: Smeeding (1992, table 2, 14).

care costs require between 45 percent to 77 percent of income, depending on local costs (Polakow, 1993, 167). Universal public education provides essentially free child care for children between the ages of six and eighteen (up to age twenty if low cost community colleges are counted). Yet from zero to five, when the need for child care is greatest, nothing is universally provided. For lone-mothers this burden too often leads to poverty. Without subsidized child care, a lone-mother's ability to properly care for her children is severely restricted, especially in light of the barriers she faces in the labor market.[99]

International Comparisons

Rates of poverty among children in other developed countries are often less than half the rate observed in the United States (see Figure 8.16). Most of the developed nations of Western Europe and Asia have essentially ended

Figure 8.17 Economic Condition of Children in Single- and Two-Parent Families in Various Parts of the World

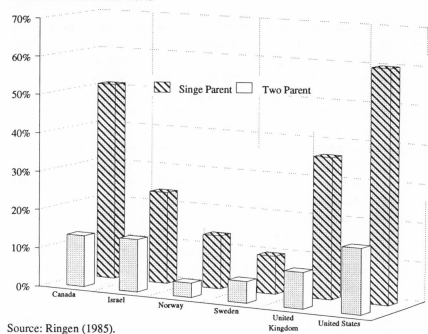

Source: Ringen (1985).

poverty among children and lone-parent families (Polakow, 1993). As seen in Figure 8.16, the poverty rate for children in European countries is less than one-fourth the rate found in the United States.

Worldwide, the situation of lone-mothers is characterized by higher rates of poverty than is found in two-parent families. As the data in Figure 8.17 indicate, the discrepancy between lone- and two- parent families is greatest in the United States and Canada and, to a lesser extent in, Britain (O'Higgins, Schmaus, and Stephenson, 1985; Lefaucher and Martin, 1993).

---

99. The conservative approach to lone-mothers is paradoxical. Mothers are advised that the early years of a child's life are essential to the development of character and values and that it is more important for the mother to focus on child rearing than developing a career. As a result, conservative politicians have opposed public support for early child care. Yet, lone-mothers are urged to be self supporting, even if it means placing their children in child care. However, the absence of subsidized child care is perhaps the major barrier most lone-mothers face in their effort to become self supporting.

Summary

During the last three decades major public policies and programs in North America have virtually ended poverty among the elderly. In the early 1960s close to 40 percent of the elderly in the United States were living in households below the poverty line, restricted from materially altering their condition by physical constraints (old age) and labor market constraints.This has changed. As a result of the Social Security program, less than 10 percent of the elderly live in households below the poverty line.

Children have not been so fortunate. While the period after World War II began with great hope and expectation of ending poverty among children, this hope has not been realized. During the War on Poverty in the 1960s, the percentage of children in poverty in the United States began dropping, indicating that federal social programs could have an impact. During the seventies, however, the trend reversed. During the last two decades children replaced the elderly as the group having the greatest percentage of poor in both the United States and Canada. The last decade in North America has not only witnessed an increase in the number of children in poverty, but the poverty they must endure has become more severe.

The current scale of poverty prompts several conclusions. First, to permit the continuance of such poverty among the most helpless and innocent of our population without taking any action is reprehensible. No child should be abandoned to poverty. As Miriam Wright Edelman (1987, 22) implores, "For God's sake and our children's future, let us seize the opportunities and avoid the dangers that we know are lurking. Let us focus on what unites us, on the overwhelming majority of poverty that we can do something about now, and on preventing another generation of Afro-American babies from becoming the poor Afro-American mothers and fathers that we so begrudgingly try to help today through our social policies." To ignore this call will be to ignore one of the principal obligations our time.

Second, as child welfare professionals, we must acknowledge that impoverished children represent our client base. Poverty directly affects efforts to aid these clients. In confronting such increasing levels of poverty the child welfare social worker is not unlike the child holding a finger in the dike. At some point the flood becomes too great and threatens to sweep all efforts aside. We have reached that point. With almost a half million children in foster care in North America, most for reasons of poverty, we have reached the point where the dike is breaking. All of the counselling, the casework, the means testing—all the tools in the bag of "residual" tricks, which have been the major tools thus far—are no longer sufficient. Something qualitatively different is required.

Third, our understanding of poverty has focused on the personal deficits of the poor. As a consequence, we have seen poverty as a private affair. Doing so has allowed us to collectively shirk responsibility for the impact of poverty on children. Yet poverty is a public responsibility. In affluent societies poverty is a result of policies that govern the distribution of wealth and income and that preserve the status quo of poverty among lone-mothers and their children. Our usual understanding of the boundary of child welfare must extend to policies that address structural unemployment, gender and racial inequality, discrimination in housing (Massey and Denton, 1993), a lack of publicly subsidized child care, inadequate health care coverage, and more. As Polakow (1993, 172) observes, "all these changes and reforms have been proposed by leading critics and social and public policy analysts...But until private interests give way to public responsibility and to a notion of civic entitlements rather than undeserving poor benefits, poor people will remain poor in a land of affluence."

Finally, from a larger sociopolitical perspective, the continuation of poverty among youth imperils the future of both the United States and Canada. Since 1776, when Adam Smith wrote his treatise, *The Wealth of Nations*, outlining the "natural laws" that govern a democratic free enterprise system, economists have recognized the need for the accumulation and concentration of wealth among the people, wealth that is reinvested as capital in the economic machinery of society. Whereas Adam Smith saw this accumulation accruing largely through profits to a few industrialists, it has now come to be recognized that such accumulation must occur within the broadest base of the population.

In North America and most modern market economies with limited public sector involvement, a very small percentage of families have accumulated ownership of the vast majority of the country's wealth. Why this has happened is subject to debate. Some argue that selective laws of nature are at work. Poor individuals simply do not have the skill, intelligence, enterprise, or gumption to effectively maximize the economic system for their financial benefit. Others feel that the poor are denied opportunity to fully participate through discriminatory social practices. Still others argue that such unequal distribution of wealth reflects an artificial construction of reality in which powerful political groups, aided by the collective approbation (or acquiescence) of citizens, have, through legislative processes vulnerable to leveraged financial contributions, shaped and controlled economic opportunities to the advantage of the wealthy at the expense of the poor.

It is not our intent to argue one view over another but to emphasize that regardless the reason for the unequal and inequitable distribution of wealth, to permit its continued massive negative impact on large numbers of children within a country is unwise in the extreme. For what has distinguished the democratic free enterprise market economies of the United States, Canada, and other modern industrial nations has been their ability to promote the development of a prosperous middle class, in which populations of extremely poor and extremely rich are minimized. A financially healthy middle class not only provides the purchasing power needed to sustain economic growth, it ensures a socially stable population. When large segments of society are excluded from the economic mainstream to the extent we have documented in this chapter, increasingly they begin to affect the society in negative ways—the growth of crime, racial and ethnic hatred, gang violence, child abuse, homicides among children, drug abuse and dependency. Instead of adding to the wealth of the nation through their productivity and consumption, the impoverished children become an ever increasing social burden. In the child welfare field, with a half million children removed from their parents and placed in foster care, we see only the tip of a subterranean mountain that extends everywhere beneath the facade of our society, like a great underworld populated by increasing numbers of welfare programs, police forces, courts, juvenile detention facilities, prisons, and drug rehabilitation programs, and more.

If poverty among large segments of children continues unabated, the wealth of the nation, as it is embodied in the children, will certainly be depleted and destroyed. As we have provided substantial income protection for the elderly, we must not leave children to suffer in poverty. To make children endure poverty during the crucial years when their character and outlook are being formed is not sound social policy. For the sake of the nation as well as these children, we must begin developing policies and programs that promote wider participation in the benefits of our free enterprise market economy. Welfare programs that only provide income assistance to the poor are not sufficient. What is needed is a means of investing in children, of providing opportunity, thereby ensuring a broader participation in the nation's economic enterprise. This will require economic and social policies that fit with and benefit from the distinctive features of the free market economy. In this sense, programs that provide a hand up, not a handout are required. In the next chapters I explore options that might accomplish this.

Yet we must always remember that children are more than economic units. They reflect the heart and soul of a nation. As Polakow (1993, 101) cautions, "Poor children, it seems, are deserving of public money only if investment in their early lives has demonstrable economic payoffs. They matter instrumentally, not existentially. Born as they are to the undeserving poor, many to single mothers, they, like young Oliver Twist, are badged and ticketed." Progress for children will involve "changing the discourse, reframing the 'problem' of poverty in a way that does not vitiate the existential character of destitution and that places responsibility for destitution on an impaired society in which its most vulnerable citizens, poor single mothers and their children, are at risk every day of their lives" (p. 164).

Conclusion

The advanced free market economies of Europe, North America, and Asia have produced a substantial material affluence for most of their citizens. All of these economies have generated wealth for a broad middle class as well as produced substantial and even enormous affluence for the upper income and wealth holding class. It is the growth of a broad middle class that has sustained and fostered the development of these modern economies. Governments play a key role in allowing for the distribution of income and wealth based on the contributions, skills, and fortune of its citizenry. The most successful advanced market economies with a strong industrial base have also achieved the broadest participation in the wealth of the nation.

The child welfare system in modern market economies must play a vital role in promoting and ensuring the economic opportunity for all children. In this sense, public concern with the welfare of children, expressed through the child welfare system, allows these economies to tap the energies and possibilities of the most important resource for their future—and that is their children. When the child welfare system fails to protect children's economic futures, the long-term consequences for the nation are support of a large welfare class along with increased need for "residual services" for such problems as drug and alcohol abuse, delinquency, child abuse, teenage pregnancy, and so on.

It is a paradox that those nations with the largest and most expensive public child welfare systems in the industrialized world (the United States and Canada) also have the highest rate of children in poverty. Further, the country that pioneered in the development of protective services for children has, by far, the highest rate and actual numbers of child abuse reports. How could this be? Part of the problem is how public child welfare services have been organized. If a country fails to provide income protection for children, there is inevitably going to be a large number of children who are harmed by the consequences of poverty. It may seem appropriate to rescue only those selected children who are most harmed by the consequences of policies and programs that permit widespread child poverty. In fact, it would be unforgivable not to do *something*. That *something* has primarily involved removing the children from the ravages of the impoverished family, leaving the remaining members of the family to do the best they can. In this effort public child welfare has acted in "the best interests of the children" as it is narrowly defined. Unfortunately, the removed children have too often been placed in temporary holding places—foster care—where they lingered for years. Meanwhile, we have failed to address the root of the problem and that is the causes of poverty and neglect that lead to placement. No doubt there will always be need for some children to be placed in foster care. It is the number of children in care in the United States—more than 500,000—that is of such concern. After all, Japan, with half the population of the United States, has fewer than 3,000 children in foster care (Ozawa, 1991a).

The greatest problem our society faces is the neglect and impoverishment which blights the lives of large numbers of children. However, because they are still children, it is not too late to organize collective efforts and provide children with opportunity. If we make a commitment and develop programs to ensure all children economic and social justice and the opportunity to live productive lives, we will—perhaps more than anything else we can do—be making major advances toward building not only a more productive but a better society.

9

Programs and Policies for Achieving Income Equity for Children

In the U.S. today, there are nearly 9 million mothers with children whose fathers do not live with them. Only about 2 million of these families received their full child support payments in 1985. Another 1 million families received partial payments and almost 6 million received nothing. We can and should do better.

Former U.S. Representative Thomas Downey

One returns, therefore, to the central theme of this discussion. AFDC is not an appropriate response to the problem of childhood poverty. What is needed is a consistent and coherent social policy for all children, a component of which would be a scheme of income guarantees that does not differentiate between poor and nonpoor children and provides the means for poor families to escape poverty. By implication this means a "universal" approach, one in which benefits are provided to all children without regard to their financial status.

George Hoshino, "AFDC as Child Welfare"

The difficulties faced by the families who come to the attention of the public child welfare system pose problems that have not been adequately addressed in recent years. The problems include inequalities in income, failed child support collection mechanisms, vast unmet child care demands, and insufficient opportunities to acquire skills and training to improve their situation. The program and policies designed to address these social problems are sorely out of date. During the 1980s there was little federal interest in social policies to address these problems. During the sixties and seventies social policy was designed for a different set of inequalities and problems. The War on Poverty initiatives focused on overcoming barriers to employment by providing training and fighting discrimination. Most income assistance programs were designed simply to relieve income poverty through income transfer. Aid to Families with Dependent Children (AFDC) was developed in 1935 as a program primarily for widows. During this period most mothers did not work outside the home. Further, there were few lone-parent families. Yet time and circumstances have changed dramatically. Today AFDC is simply a public assistance (or welfare) program. It does little or nothing to address the needs of lone-parent families or provide mechanisms for establishing independence. It also does little to increase human capital or improve skills (education and training) and assure equal opportunities (Haveman, 1988). The program designed more than half a century ago is simply obsolete—it has failed to adapt to the needs of the clients it is intended to serve. The needs of children, especially, have been overlooked by this program.[100]

Adopting a Structural Approach

Expressed in economic terms, child welfare has been concerned principally with the "supply" side of welfare services—that is, supplying services such as foster care to children in need. The approach, dictated by the residual perspective, was successful, or at least adequate, as long as the "demand" for these residual services remained within feasible limits. Today, social and economic forces are creating a demand for child welfare services that far exceeds anything the system is capable of supplying. In the face of such demand, the answer has been to reduce and narrow services, to redefine the service mission, and to restrict access.

The permanency planning demonstration projects of the 1970s, as well as the more recent family preservation projects, have attempted to find ways in which the number of children in foster care could be reduced by reforming the supply side of services. The suspicion was that we were removing children from families when they did not need to be removed and keeping them in foster care much longer than we should. If we could make the system more efficient, more streamlined, more accountable, we could provide better service to fewer people. The need for reform these projects demonstrated might have been effectively implemented had not the changing social conditions of families, particularly the ballooning phenomenon of child abuse, altered the entire equation, transforming child welfare into something it was never intended to be—child protective services. Confronted by a demand for services beyond its capacity, the child welfare sys-

---

100. Provisions in the 1988 JOBS legislation allowed for training and day care services for AFDC recipients but the states have generally failed to take advantage of the federal matching funds to increase participation (about 7 percent).

tem must begin implementing broad institutional programs and policies that will allow it to reduce the demand for services in the long run.

During the last two decades the research has repeatedly and consistently indicated that the children served by child welfare services come from circumstances characterized by the twin features of poverty and lone-parenthood. While these circumstances have never been central to child welfare's traditional psychological and clinical focus, the sheer magnitude of their presence demands that they be understood as relevant and decisive factors in any solutions we examine and propose.

In the United States the difficulties faced by lone-parent families in poverty are not adequately addressed by current social programs or policy. Current public assistance programs, designed for a different set of problems than are faced by lone-parent families today, are outdated and ineffective and require fundamental change. Likewise in Canada, as Guest (1985, 239) has suggested, the "welfare state is beginning to suffer from obsolescence. Social and economic changes are overtaking a social security system whose major assumptions were formulated in the latter part of the nineteenth and the first half of the twentieth century."

What is needed to address the problem of widespread poverty among children and lone-parents are new policies and programs that, as Haveman (1988, 23) has suggested, "enable recipients to become more self-sufficient, to assure their independence through their own efforts. Long-term and permanent progress against poverty and inequality is possible only through programs that make it possible for individuals to acquire sufficient skills and training to become economically independent, and give them the incentives and hope to make the effort." Likewise, Thurow (1992, 36) has added, "Social welfare policies are seen as a necessary part of a market economy. Unfettered capitalism is believed to generate levels of income inequality that are unacceptable." The poor, especially poor children, cannot be expected to escape their circumstances without adequate and effective social policies and programs.

In this chapter I propose two programs that could ensure adequate income support for children of lone-parent families—neither of which would require major new government funding. The first addresses the problems of the current mechanisms for collecting child support, the second proposes a solution to fair child income transfers through a guaranteed child's exemption. Both focus on reducing "income poverty" among children but without the drawbacks of residual programs that encourage dependency or chip away at one's sense of personal dignity (Danziger and Stern, 1990).

Child Support—Collecting What's Due

When a two-parent family breaks apart, the income-earning parent usually goes off and starts afresh becoming, as it were, a free person—free of any labor-intensive child-care responsibilities. The remaining parent is left with increased child-care demands, limited employment opportunity, and reduced earning capacity.[101] In most instances, the lone-parent with the children rarely receives, through the current court administered mechanisms of child support collection, adequate or equitable financial support for the children from the free, noncustodial parent.

In 1973, for example, Ross and Sawhill found that only 22 percent of court-ordered support payments to AFDC families were made in full, and for half of the cases no payment was made at all. In 1976, Sewell reported that less than half of the absent fathers in Travis County, Texas, had paid more than 10 percent of their court-ordered child support payments. Further, 19 percent had never paid any of the court-ordered support. Using the data from the 5,000 families included in the *Panel Study on Family Income Dynamics* collected by the Institute for Social Research at the University of Michigan, Cassetty (1978) determined that less than 30 percent of absent fathers had paid any support at all.

Less Than 56 Cents a Day

Haskins, Burnett, and Dobelstein (1983) estimated that in 1978 roughly $10 billion in child support payments went uncollected in the United States, or approximately 69 percent of what was due to the support of dependent children by parents following divorce or separation. This is a figure substantially higher than the "8.6 billion federal dollars we spent on AFDC in 1985" (Edelman, 1987, 68). Irwin Garfinkel (1992, 63) estimates, "If there were child support awards in all cases, all the awards were reasonable, and all that was owed were paid, child support payments in the United States would increase by $25.6 billion." According to the Clinton administration (1994, 25), "Recent analyses suggest that the potential for child support col-

---

101. I use the term "free parent" instead of the conventional term noncustodial parent to indicate that this particular parent is "free" of child caring responsibilities. I use the term "child-caring parent" to identify the parent who has the principle child- caring responsibilities.

lection exceeds $47 billion." In 1988 only $7 billion was collected in child support, or less than one quarter of what was due. The $7 billion was not distributed equally to all who were owed. The poorest children, those who could least afford to lose support, received the least. The record of children in welfare (or AFDC) families is particularly striking. In 1988 about $1.5 billion in child support payments were collected for the 7.3 children in AFDC families or about 56 cents a day per child.

In the United States only 61 percent of children who live with their lone-mothers are covered by any court-determined child award. Of this 61 percent, less than half ever receive the full amount, while 30 percent get nothing at all (Garfinkel and McLanahan, 1988). As a result, only 40 percent of white fathers and 19 percent of African-American fathers pay any child support (Haveman, 1988, 218; McLanahan and Garfinkel, 1993, 22). For those lone-mothers who do receive child support, the average monthly payments are $104 for whites and $27 for African Americans (McLanahan and Garfinkel, 1993, 21 [derived from table 2.1]). Thus, child support payments and alimony amount to less than 10 percent of family income for white lone-mother families and less than 4 percent for black lone-mother families (McLanahan and Garfinkel, 1993, 21 [derived from table 2.1]; Garfinkel, Meyer, and Sandefur, 1992).

In Canada, Burtch, Pitcher-LaPrairie, and Wachtel (1980) found similar low rates of payment. In 1978, two-thirds of active child support cases were in arrears. In Calgary, 85 percent of the cases were in default, while in Ontario 70 percent of cases were in default at some point during the year. In 1987, only about 15 percent of court-ordered support payments were complied with in Ontario. In an effort to improve enforcement Ontario's attorney general spent $14 million a year to collect child support from 62,000 court-ordered payments. Yet only about 26 percent of these cases were complied with (Conway, 1990, 125), leading to more than $650 million in child support payments in arrears.

Viewing Child Support Collection as the Mother's Responsibility

In North America, collection of child support has historically been viewed as a civil matter requiring that the child-caring parent, usually the mother, collect child support from the free parent, usually the father. This is the fundamental problem of the child support system. Let us examine the steps the mother will likely be required to follow in attempting to get any child support from a father unwilling to pay it. First, she must acquire the services of an attorney. Since competent attorneys are expensive, this may require considerable outlay of her already limited financial resources, something she will have to weigh against the possible amount of child support it may produce. Second, she will have to meet with the attorney. While this may seem trivial, it can amount to a considerable burden to a woman already over-burdened with a job, child-care responsibilities, and maintaining a house-hold. Third, she will have to provide all necessary documentation proving nonpayment, taking care to observe any technical requirements of the court designed to safeguard the rights of the father. Fourth, she may have to assist in locating the father who may have gone off to another state, a task that may require the services of a private investigator. Fifth, and not of least import-ance, the mother will find herself having to assume an adversarial stance toward the father, which could well aggravate an already tense and difficult relationship, thereby significantly undermining any hope of reconciliation and accord.

Even should she finally get the father into court, and the court order him to pay child support, there is no assurance he will ever do so. Should this happen, the mother can, if she wishes, turn to local civil authorities for help in forcing free or noncustodial parents to pay court ordered child support. The amount of manpower and resources devoted to this endeavor is signifi-cant. On any given day in many large metropolitan area, such as Los Ange-les County, half or more of the district attorneys are working to collect money from absent parents in child support cases (Sisman, 1990). But even with this enormous legal effort, the results are discouraging, because such legal enforcement frequently costs more than paying child support directly to lone-mothers and their children. To be cost effective, child support enforcement programs must select only cases where a reasonable probabil-ity of obtaining support payments exists. Such a policy is, of course, unfair and counter to the legal doctrine that requires the law be applied equally to everyone. Further, it is children from poor families that most need assis-tance in child support collections but who are the least likely to represent cases that would prove cost-effective for collection efforts.

Faced with such an exhausting and costly legal gauntlet which, after all is said and done, may not lead anywhere anyway, many lone-mothers conclude that it is easier to make ends meet without child support than it is to fight to collect it, thereby avoiding (at least) an even greater measure of anger and bitterness. The only mothers who are assured that their collection efforts will be cost-effective (i.e., their efforts will generate money more than they cost) are welfare mothers, whose legal fees are guaranteed by the state, but even here, most of what money is collected goes not to the mother, but to the attorney and welfare bureaucracy to reduce welfare costs.

Reasons for Not Paying Child Support

Much speculation has focused upon why free parents do not pay child support (Chambers, 1979). The most obvious answer is: Why should they? Aside from any moral obligation, which thus far has not proved sufficient, most fathers sense they have little to fear if they stubbornly refuse to pay. The mother, after all, lacks the traditional reciprocity arrangements available to other creditors in civil court. Unlike a bank out to collect an automobile loan, she cannot obtain a court order to repossess anything resembling a valued commodity. In fact, many fathers angrily believe she already possesses everything of value. The mother cannot even register delinquent payments with credit bureaus, something that might constitute a very effective means of forcing payment.

Beyond this, it is reasoned that free parents with low income simply lack sufficient funds to assist with support payments, while more affluent free parents are forestalled by continuing acrimony and bitterness (Sisman, 1990). Yet most free or noncustodial parents have adequate income. In 1983 the average income of free parents was $19,346, compared to $22,482 for all men between 25 and 64 years old (Garfinkel, 1992, 130-131).[102]

Determining the Amount of the Monthly Child Support Payment: One crucial problem has always been determining an equitable method of assessing the free parent's ability to make support payments to the child caring parent. Customarily, such decisions have been made by the courts and have involved a great deal of judicial discretion, in which it has not been easy to discern any objective standards, systematic theory, or procedure used in determining the free parent's ability to pay. In Florida a study of judicial decision-making indicated that while judges appeared to use a con-

---

102. One problem is that there are wide variations in the earnings of noncustodial fathers. Garfinkel (1992, 130-131) indicates that the incomes of fathers of children born out of wedlock are low (about $6,000 to $10,000 a year) compared to divorced fathers (about $11,000 to $20,000 a year). This explains, in part, why a marriage does not take place for many women in this context; the father would be unable to adequately provide for the family. In fact, welfare, even with all its failings, may be viewed as a more reliable provider. This problem highlights how important insuring employment opportunity is to efforts at welfare reform.

sistent standard for determining a free parent's ability to pay (White, 1976), no consistency *between* judges could be discerned—consistency that, it should be pointed out, was the objective of the Florida statute under which the judges operated.

Even when support payments are secured by the courts, the payments are frequently unreliable and tend to diminish over time (Cassetty, 1978, 39). When payments stop, the lone child caring parent, usually the mother, must wait several months before beginning legal action. Lacking financial resources, the impoverished lone-mother depends on the welfare office to pursue enforcement. Yet when, and if, the payments are reestablished, much of the money goes to the welfare office to reimburse legal costs and whatever payments have been made to the client in the interim. Knowing this, many fathers view child support less as money directed to their children as money for the welfare system.

Ability to Pay: The Cassetty Research

One of the more popular and detrimental myths about child support is that most free parents (fathers) do not pay child support because they simply do not have the money. After leaving their former spouse and children, it is argued, they incur new expenses and demands that prevent them from making adequate child support payments. This issue was carefully examined by Cassetty (1978) using data from a longitudinal study of family income for 5,000 families.

To measure how much the free parent was able to contribute, Cassetty developed an "ability to pay" measure that involved two principles: First, payment of child support should never reduce the free parent's income below the poverty line (as defined for his or her current family). Second, the free parent should not be forced to pay support if the child-caring parent's position, relative to the poverty line, was better than the free parent's. Following these two principles, Cassetty calculated the free parent's ability to pay by subtracting an amount equal to the parent's poverty level from his or her total income. Using the subsample of family divorces and separations in the longitudinal *Panel Study of Income Dynamics*, Cassetty examined the relative position of the free parent and the lone child caring parent relative to the poverty line. She found that 80 percent of the free parents' households were better off financially after leaving their former families and far better off than the families they left behind. Could some of the free-parent surplus,

Table 9.1 Findings of the Cassetty Research

Class	Number	Y/PL of Female-Headed Household	Actual Monthly Child Support Received (1974)	Expected Monthly Child Support if Y/PL Were Equalized	Expected Child Support Paid (%)
Poor	86	0 - .99	$24.12	$338.58	7.2
At Risk	40	1 - 2.0	43.10	188.50	22.8
Nonpoor	67	2.01 +	72.31	308.81	23.4
Overall	193		$44.90 (mean)	$297.15 (mean)	15.1%

Note: Y/PL indicates income (Y) relative to the poverty line (PL) for the particular case.
Source: Cassetty, J. *Child Support and public policy.* Lexington, Mass.: D.C. Heath, 1978 [from table 4.4, 73].

which derived in part from the lifting of child-care expenses, be used to off-set the declining financial condition of the lone-parent's family?

To examine this question Cassetty applied the AAP index to the sample of family splits in the Michigan data. Her findings revealed the great disparity between what a free parent might be able to contribute, in a context of equity, and what the average free parent does in fact contribute. As the data in Table 9.1 indicate, the disparity was greatest among the poor, where payments by free parents amounted to only 7 percent of what they might equitably have been expected to pay (a $24 monthly payment compared to an AAP calculation of $338). The more affluent parents, however, did not contribute much more. The affluent paid only 23 percent of what they might equitably have been expected to pay ($72 vs. $308).

The Cassetty data suggest that, overall, only 15 percent of expected child support payments are actually paid. That is, free spouses keep for themselves 85 percent of what they might otherwise be expected to pay.

Poor children are especially affected by this. Data from the National Center for Children in Poverty (1990, 45) indicate that nearly 80 percent of all poor mothers receive no child support whatsoever. For poor mothers who were never married, the figure rises to 90 percent, while only 56 percent of nonpoor mothers *ever* receive any child support.

Children are being denied child support, not because the funds are unavailable, but because the court-administered collection mechanism has proven ineffective. Using the Census Bureau and the Center for Children in Poverty data, we estimate that the average monthly child support payment that could be paid because the fathers have the money, would be approximately $200 per child. Based on Cassetty's findings on payment patterns and updated with recent reports from the Census Bureau, we estimated the "expected monthly payments" received by poor children is about $16. In short, the current court-administered collection mechanism takes in less than ten percent of what is available.

Proponents of the current system may continue to argue that child support enforcement policies—if efficiently tightened, automated, and streamlined—might eventually reduce the current failure of the court administered child support collection system. However, as Cassetty concluded (1978): "The court administered child support system in the United States has largely failed in its responsibility to secure the well-being of children confined to mother-only family life by nonmarriage or broken marriages. (p. 74)... For the most part... the legal-judicial enforcement system is ineffective in its well-intentioned, but limited, ability to enforce the parental child support obligation" (p. 106). Not only are millions of children being deprived of the financial support due them but the public is being forced to intervene at great cost and with little overall effectiveness in order to preserve a cumbersome and inefficient court administered system. Because of the enormous increase in divorces, the court administered system places too great a burden on an already overcrowded and overburdened court system. The time is right to consider a fundamental change from a court administered system to one operated through the conventional income redistribution mechanisms available through social programs and the tax system. The courts should be viewed as an avenue of last resort. Efforts should be made to reduce or obviate the need for court involvement.

As we have seen, free parents can pay substantially more child support than they currently do. The available evidence suggests that the reason so little is paid in child support results not from the absent parents inability to pay, but from a court-administered child support system that allows most absent fathers to avoid their financial responsibility for their children when those children no longer live with them. There are many situations where a "court administered system" is appropriate but the collection of child support is not one of them. In terms of efficiently collecting child support from the absent parent and transferring it to the child caring parent, the "court administered system" has proven too cumbersome and slow. Further, it requires that the animus driving the system be the parent who fails to collect child support due for children in her custody. But placing this burden on the child caring parent only serves to antagonize relationships between separated parents, when the effort should be on smoothing and rebuilding that relationship. What is needed is a child support collection system that uses a different collection mechanism than the current "court administered system" and that no longer avails free (or noncustodial) parents a means of cleverly escaping responsibility.

Universal Child Support Collection Program (UCSC)

The financial needs of children in lone-parent families cannot simply be ignored. Because they are unable to protect their own social and economic interests, their well-being must be safeguarded by formal measures that will force noncustodial parents to fulfill their financial child support responsibilities. Children should not have to rely on (or impose on) their custodial parent to collect the payments due them from the noncustodial parent. Too many suffer in simply trying to maintain a relationship with their absent parents. Furstenberg and Cherlin (1991) report that fewer than "one child in six saw his or her father as often as once a week on average. Close to half had not visited with their fathers" in a year. What is needed is an easy and reliable means of collecting child support payments from free parents that doesn't directly intrude on the relationship between the noncustodial parent and the child. Such a program would lift many children out of poverty, and thereby reduce the demand for child welfare services.

Using the Current Tax Collection System

The collection of child support payments is—like bank deposit insurance, defense, road building, and public education—too important to society to leave outside the federal tax system. The mechanism by which child support could be efficiently and effectively collected and redistributed through taxation is not complicated. Basically, noncustodial parents would be shifted to a "child support" tax table at the time of separation or divorce, thereby subjecting them to a higher tax rate based on their gross earnings and the number of children concerned. Their employer would withhold the additional money for child support along with other withholding taxes. The additional withholding for child support would then go, indirectly, to the absent parent's children or custodian, through a central collection system.

Noncustodial parents would pay, say, an additional 12 percent in federal income tax.[103] Benefits to custodial parents or guardians would be set according to a fixed national schedule. The lone-parent might receive, for example, $200 for the first child, $100 for the second and for each additional child a month.[104] The child support payment would be provided to every custodial parent regardless of income. The mandatory payroll deduction could only be disregarded if the free parent obtained a waiver from the court because other appropriate payment arrangements had been made. In the case of wealthy free parents, the deduction would not prevent the child-caring spouse from obtaining additional support through civil litigation. While the support assured in this manner would perhaps not amount to a great deal for wealthy parents, it would ensure that every lone-parent received the minimal child support to meet the financial needs of the children in their custody.[105]

The UCSC program would be based upon several axioms: First, the free parent should not be allowed to abandon responsibility for the economic well-being of their children. Second, the enforcement of child support payments should not severely affect the free parent's economic situation. Support payments should not prove a severe financial burden on the free parent or discourage their participation in the labor force. In brief, a child support policy should not greatly diminish the free parent's motivation to engage in gainful employment. Third, ensuring child support collection should not constitute a burden carried solely by the custodial parent or, failing such collection, shift to become, indirectly through the AFDC program, a burden carried by the general public. As a United States Congressional Report of the Subcommittee on Fiscal Policy (1974, 95) observed two decades ago: "Until effective child support measures are enacted and enforced, the burden of supporting children in the rising number of fatherless families will

---

103. Jones, Gordon, and Sawhill (1976) found that the income of most single noncustodial fathers rises an average of 12 percent while the income of their related custodial spouses declines.

104. Irwin Garfinkel (1992, 47) proposes a child support assurance system that would guarantee each child between $2,000 to $2,500 per year for the first child and $1,000 for each additional child.

105. If the noncustodial parent moves out of state, the custodial parent would not be required to use the collection mechanisms of the state where the noncustodial parent moved to because the federal tax system would automatically collect the necessary funds regardless of locality.

continue to fall disproportionately on mothers raising children alone and on taxpayers financing income maintenance programs."

The UCSC program suggested here assumes that responsibility for collecting child support rests with society at large, whose future depends ultimately upon the health and well-being of its children. The mechanisms used to accomplish this transfer of income must be elevated in significance so that noncompliance is removed as the central issue. The role of the government must become one of facilitating and enforcing an important and necessary obligation in as efficient a manner as possible.[106] Such a collection program does not involve new public tax dollars to provide income support. It merely represents a reform mechanism for more effective collection and distribution of income.[107]

Initially, the UCSC program would cause some disruption in current child support arrangements. Many free spouses presently paying child support might ask for a reduction in their payment level to reflect the tax that would be levied against them. This could be achieved by a consent order signed and agreed to by the child caring parent. The program would not abolish the right of child caring parents to take legal action to obtain standards of child support compatible with the free spouse's earning capacity. Rather, the program would provide a floor of support which could, through the courts, be augmented. Should two parents work out a mutually acceptable agreement for child support payments, such evidence could be used to release the free spouse from the incremental tax rate.

Finally, the UCSC program would also help eliminate an aggravating problem that exists at every socioeconomic level of society: love that has somehow twisted into hate; two people trapped in unrelenting bitterness and acrimony, husbands unwilling to pay "the least dime to that [expletive deleted]," wives angry about the "dead beat [expletive deleted] who ran out on his family." In the middle are the children, growing more disillusioned and despairing at what the future holds for them. In their eyes can be seen the pain of a heartless and brutal policy that has failed to protect those least able to protect themselves.

---

106. This is how the obligation is administered in other countries such as New Zealand (Kamerman and Kahn, 1983; Stuart, 1986).

107. Garfinkel (1992) provides detailed estimates of the Child Support Assurance system that indicate the cost would be less than one billion dollars a year in the short term but would within two years produce a net cost savings.

Developing equitable and effective child support collection can be achieved at little or no public expense. It simply requires the political will to demand that those who have brought children into this world be required to shoulder the costs of raising those children even when they no longer reside with them. Payment of child support should not be linked to other issues such as visitation rights. Establishing a universal child support collection program would reduce the expense of child support collections by replacing the current inefficient court administered mechanism with a simple modification of the federal income tax collection system. Just as the federal government is entitled to collect its taxes when income is earned, so must children be entitled to collect their child support from income as it is earned. Implementing such a program would shift a substantial burden of income support for children in lone-parent families from the general public to nonpaying free parents and produce considerable tax savings.

Alternative Approach: Child Support Assurance

Recently Garfinkel (1992) proposed a Child Support Assurance System (CSAS) that would accomplish much the same goal as the UCSC program proposed above. The CSAS program is based on the same principal of federally insured child support collection proposed by Schorr (1965) several decades earlier. The program would require that all "free parents" (Garfinkel uses the term "nonresident parents") provide a share of their income for the care and support of their children. The sharing rate would be a proportion of the free parent's gross income and would be determined by legislation. The predetermined amount would be withheld from income. A variant of this approach has been implemented in Wisconsin and proven successful. Under the new approach proposed by Garfinkel (1992) the child would receive the full amount owed, as determined by legislation, directly from the government. As such, the CSAS is quite similar to the program suggested here.

Welfare: Conundrum or Solvable Problem?

Two decades ago one of the most ambitious attempts at reforming the public welfare system was launched in the United States when the Nixon Administration proposed the Family Assistance Plan as an alternative to the current welfare program (including AFDC). It was, as Daniel Patrick Moynihan acknowledged, one of the most fundamental reforms of a public institution in the United States since the New Deal (Moynihan, 1973). Viewing the welfare system as wasteful and inefficient, the Nixon Administration devised the Family Assistance Plan to provide, in lieu of welfare, a guaranteed income to lone-mothers and their children. The program would have provided an income floor below which no one would fall. "Means-tested" categorical public assistance would have been replaced by universal guaranteed income for all families, including the aged, permanently disabled, blind, and mentally ill. Since all families would have been guaranteed a minimal income, there would be no need for welfare.

The guaranteed minimal income approach would have gotten rid of the need for a "means-tested" welfare or income support program. Some argued that such an approach would lead to greater labor force participation among the poor, since working would not result in the loss of welfare or other income assistance. Earned income would always be on top off the guaranteed income. The poor would not have to perform a complicated calculus to determine the profitability of working, taking into account lost welfare assistance and other "means-tested" benefits such as housing assistance, food stamps, medicare, etcetera. However, the guaranteed income approach was opposed by a coalition of conservative southern Democrats, who thought it too wasteful (a dole for the undeserving), and liberal Democrats who saw it as too stingy (not enough to do any good). The proposal was defeated.

Nevertheless, following the rancorous debate over welfare reform, Congress quickly passed the Supplemental Security Income (SSI) program, which transferred categorical aid programs for the elderly, the mentally ill, and the permanently disabled from the welfare system to the Social Security system, thereby providing them with a guaranteed income (Lindsey and Ozawa, 1979).[108] This simple transfer eliminated a great deal of bureaucratic waste. It meant that these groups no longer had to continually prove their eligibility to receive assistance payments (Pechman, 1989). The only category left out was children. Commenting on this irony, Moynihan (1986,

---

108. At the time of its passage, the SSI program was viewed as a set of technical amendments to the Social Security program (Lindsey and Ozawa, 1977). In fact, the SSI program represented major reform of public welfare for the elderly and the totally disabled. The unanticipated consequence was to leave children as the only group in the conventional low paying means tested welfare program.

14) observed, "The Family Assistance Plan had been devised first and foremost to provide a guaranteed income for children and for families with children. In the end, the only persons left out were children and families with
children."

Children's Allowance and Family Allowance Programs

While Congress was considering Nixon's Family Assistance Plan, attention
was briefly given to a "Children's Allowance" program similar to what
sixty-seven nations including all of Western Europe and North America
(Canada, England, France, Mexico, Belgium, etc.) now provide their children (Burns, 1967; Kamerman and Kahn, 1983; McLanahan and Garfinkel,
1993, 28).[109] A children's allowance, which recognizes the financial burden
that parents have in raising children, takes the form of direct payments to
every family for their children, and is applied universally, from the poorest
families to the wealthiest (Brazer, 1967; Garfinkel and Uhr, 1987).[110]
Underlying the children's allowance approach is the assumption that children are the bedrock of a society's future. To ensure their care and well-
being is to ensure the future of the society (Rejda, 1970).

Canada's Family Allowance. In 1944, the Canadian government intro-
duced the Family Allowances Act to provide a monthly grant payable to all
children up to the age of sixteen. The Act, which was promoted as a bill
designed to protect the upcoming generation and to ensure the basic needs
of all children, was described as "one of the most progressive and worth-
while pieces of legislation ever enacted by the Canadian government" (Stapleford and Lea, 1949). At the time it was implemented the program's price
tag represented an amount "exceeding all welfare expenditures by all units
of government in Canada, including public health and unemployment aid, in
any typical year from 1936 to 1939" (Guest, 1985, 130). Nevertheless, the
legislation passed unanimously. In 1973, a new Family Allowances Act was

---

109. The first consideration of children's allowances in the United States was by former
United States Senators John F. Kennedy (Massachusetts) and Richard Neuberger (Oregon).
However, nothing came of the proposal (Moynihan, 1986, 5).

110. An example is the children's allowance program in West Germany, which provides
$450 a month during the first six months of a child's life and $166 a month thereafter
(Haanes-Olson, 1972; Wilson, 1990). In addition, the standard tax deduction is $4,500 per
child.

passed that nearly tripled the amount provided each child. The Act retained strong popular support, in large measure, because of its universal coverage (Banting, 1987). Nevertheless, in the 1980s the conservative administration of Brian Mulroney began gutting the program through a strategy called "claw-back" that simply let high inflation reduce the value of the allowance (Mendelson, 1987). In 1993, with little fanfare, the historic Family Allowance program was replaced by a so-called "child benefits" program that conditions part of the benefits received to the parent's labor-force participation.

Providing the Children's Allowance through a Tax Exemption. In the United States, the children's allowance takes the form of a tax exemption, which excludes more than $2,000 from federal, state, and local income for each child living as a dependent in a household. For families with an average or higher income, this exemption represents a substantial benefit—in 1990, for example, as much as $677 in actual cash savings from federal taxes alone.[111] However, for low-income families the benefit is negligible, and for children in families below the poverty line it is essentially zero. Administering a child's allowance in this tax deduction fashion has regressive consequences. It has the drawback of conditioning receipt of the "children's allowance" to income earning activities that are beyond the control of the child for whom the benefit is intended. It results in a situation where the children most in need receive the least, while the children least in need receive the most. As seen in Figure 9.1, the net value of the exemption for children from low income families is substantially less than the value of the exemption for high income families.

The regressive distributive effect of the tax exemption for children has also been a problem in Canada. The value in 1990 of the child tax exemption for a Canadian family with income below $10,000 a year was zero, while for a family with income greater than $80,000 a year the value was more than $1,000. To correct for this limitation, Canada provides a "Child Tax Credit" that levels the distributive effect and eliminates the penalty children from low income and poor families would otherwise suffer.

---

111. In Germany the federal government, in addition to providing the usual child allowance, provides $1,000 a year per child (under age eight) to a parent who stays at home to take care of a child.

Figure 9.1 The Net Value of One Child's Exemption for a Family (1991)

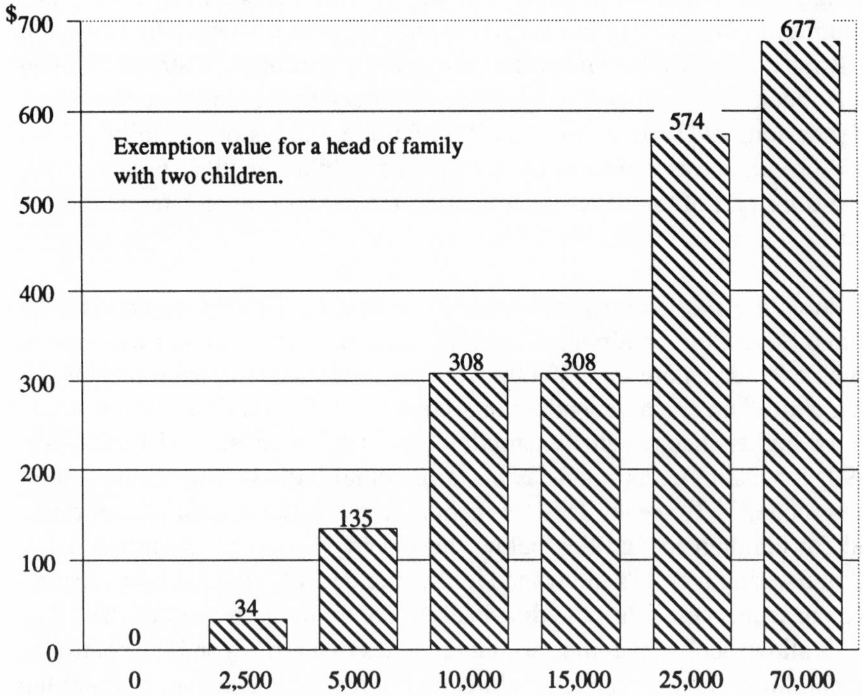

Source: Data compiled by author.

Guaranteeing the Child's Exemption

The problem of inequity with the child's exemption in the United States can be remedied by simply *guaranteeing* the exemption for all children, thus ensuring that poor children, as well as wealthy children, receive an equal "allowance." This is the approach followed in Canada. Implementing a program to do this would be a simple matter. When parents secure employment, they would declare the number of dependent children in their household. Based on this declaration, the parent, whether working full or part time, would be paid the value of the exemption through reduced payroll deductions (which is what happens now). Those parents who were unemployed or not in the labor market would receive regular (monthly) cash payments up to the value of the exemption. All children could thus be *guaranteed* their child's exemption of $50 a month. Thus, an unemployed parent with two children would receive a monthly cash payment of $100.[112] This payment would be separate and independent of AFDC or other income transfer programs designed to help the lone-parent in need. Further, if a child were ever placed in foster care or other substitute care arrangement, the guaranteed benefit would go with the child and be paid directly to the child's caretaker.[113]

The first report of the National Commission on Children (1991) in the United States proposed a $1,000 children's tax credit for all children. However, the tax credit would not have taken into account the substantial tax advantage currently enjoyed by children in high-income families. The advantage of the guaranteed child's exemption is that it would seek to achieve equity by making benefits available to those who are denied them under current tax law. The National Commission's proposed child tax credit was estimated to cost approximately $29 billion a year. In contrast, we estimate the guaranteed child's exemption would have a net cost of approximately $3 to $4 billion a year since most of the benefits would accrue to the 14 million children now living in poverty who are effectively denied the benefit of the tax deduction.[114] It would promote equity and fairness for all children by ensuring that low income or poverty families receive the benefits that wealthier families do.

Additional Features

One of the main tax advantages denied poor families with children in the United States is the benefit derived from the mortgage deduction. This can be quite substantial. For example, for a family with an income of $15,000 a year and a $75,000 mortgage, the mortgage deduction amounts to about $1,000 a year (see Figure 9.2).[115] For a family with an annual income of

---

112. Over the years the value of the child's exemption has decreasing substantially. The 1990 exemption of $2,150 was one-third the value of the child's exemption in 1948 (Taylor, 1991; National Commission on Children, 1991). Consequently, many have suggested doubling the exemption for children. The Progressive Policy Institute has recommended that the child exemption be increased from $2,300 to $6,000 or $7,000 per child in order to restore the exemption to the value it had in 1948 (Browning and Evison, 1993, 716)

113. This assumes the benefit has an annual value of $600 to the average family (or $50 a month).

114. Since the children who benefit are primarily from families receiving AFDC, the additional income received by these families would reduce the required AFDC benefit and thus produce substantial offsetting costs (cf Schorr, 1987).

Figure 9.2 The Value of the Mortgage Deduction for Families Based on Income (1990)

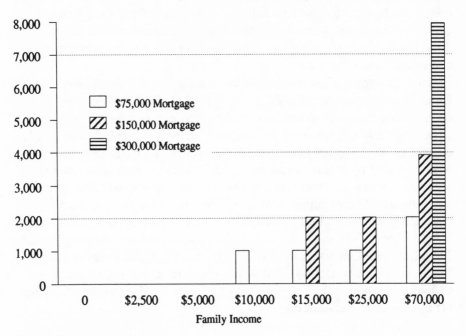

Source: Data compiled by author.

more than $25,000 a year and a home mortgage of $150,000, the deduction is more than $2,000 a year. A family with an annual income of more than $75,000 and a home mortgage of $300,000 receives an annual federal benefit of almost $8,000. Clearly, for families with high-cost housing and mortgage payments, the benefit of the mortgage deduction is considerably more than the average annual welfare benefit received by an AFDC family with two children.[116] Further, since the deduction is often permitted against state and local income tax, it can be worth even more. As Jonathan Kozol (1991, 55) observes, "In 1984, for instance, property-tax deductions granted [to

---

115. These calculations are based on an 8 percent mortgage with a 30 year term.

116. This allowance could be used to supplement current board and care payments for foster care and help alleviate the crisis in recruiting foster care parents. The allowance would also reduce the financial barriers to adoption that many children in the child welfare system confront by providing a form of subsidy to adoptive parents.

homeowners] by the federal government were $9 billion. An additional $23 billion in mortgage-interest deductions were provided to homeowners: a total of some $32 billion. Federal grants to local schools, in contrast, totaled only $7 billion, and only part of this was earmarked for low income districts. Federal policy, in this respect, increases the existing gulf between the richest and poorest schools."

Since poor families are usually unable to benefit from mortgage deductions, the deduction has had an unintended disequalizing effect among the population.[117] To a poor family struggling to provide for its children and unable to buy a house, the tax advantage is effectively denied. Even if the poor family were able to purchase a house and acquire a mortgage, the benefit would be limited compared to the high-income family. The guaranteed child's exemption could be used to balance this disadvantage. If the custodial parent did not claim a mortgage deduction, the family would be entitled to a double guaranteed child's exemption.[118] Permitting a double exemption would serve to more effectively equalize the distribution of tax benefits to all families.[119]

---

117. Recently the Federal Reserve Board has reported a pattern of discrimination in mortgage lending in the United States. Banks throughout the country have been found to deny mortgages to African-Americans twice as often as to white people (Jackson, 1993, p. 75). The Federal Reserve Board found that people of color were 60 percent more likely to have their mortgage loan applications rejected even when the applications were nearly identical. In New York, a major bank, Manufacturers Hanover, was found to reject 45 percent of high income Latino and 43 percent of high income African-Americans, compared with 18 percent of high income white applicants. The same pattern was reported in Houston, San Francisco, Milwaukee, and Washington, D.C.. In Houston, NCNB Texas rejected 59 percent of low income African-Americans compared with 19 percent of low income whites. Massey and Denton (1993) provide further support of these patterns of discrimination in mortgages and examine the issue within the broader perspective of racial segregation.

118. What little borrowing low-income families can do is usually limited to credit cards and other nonsecured loans that are not tax deductible. Consequently, the poor pay high interest rates and receive no tax benefits.

119. The mortgage deduction was placed in the tax code to stimulate and encourage home ownership. This deduction has been very successful, since today the wealth of most U.S. families is represented by home ownership. Avery, Elliehausen, and Canner (1984a, b) observed that the average family net worth of homeowners was $50,125, compared to $15 for the average renter. Housing is where most families have built their savings. In 1988, 43 percent of total net worth in the United States derived from home ownership (*Wall Street Journal*, 1991). Phillips (1993, 180) observes, "Right up to the 95th percentile, the solid middle class was home-dependent because only the top 1 percent or 2 percent of U.S. households had most of their net worth in financial assets like stocks and bonds."

Advantages of a Guaranteed Child Exemption

Unlike income transfers through AFDC, the guaranteed child's exemption, because it would be universally applied, would not carry the stigma of a "welfare" or public assistance. As well, it would not discourage independent efforts to earn other income. If the custodial parent worked, he or she would continue to receive the benefit through decreased payroll deductions. Further, the program would be efficient and inexpensive to administer, since it would involve no means-test or complex eligibility requirements. Finally, it would prove an efficient distribution mechanism in terms of targeting needed benefits to poor children, benefits the wealthy already receive.

Limitations.

It might be argued that the guaranteed exemption might, as does AFDC, serve as a disincentive for labor-force participation, since the exemption is specifically designed to eliminate any "conditioning" of the children's allowance on the work effort of the parent. Yet, children should not be denied adequate support because of their parent's actions, especially through such arbitrary mechanisms as the mortgage tax deduction or the "dependency" tax deduction.[120] Better ways exist to encourage labor force participation than conditioning a child benefit to it. Conditioning child benefits to parent's actions has the net effect of trying to motivate the parent by threatening to punish his or her child. Empirical studies suggest that the best way to encourage labor force participation is (1) to provide child care services, (2) establish benefits that specifically reward labor force participation (such as the earned income tax credit program now in effect), and (3) to pursue policies that increase the demand in the labor market for employment of lone-parents (Ellwood, 1989; Levitan, 1990).

While the deduction mechanism has been widely used to achieve a variety of "socially desirable" purposes, its main limitation as applied to children is that it denies benefits to poor children for actions over which they have no control. For example, the federal government provides a dependent care tax credit that allows parents to deduct between 20 to 30 percent of their child care expenses up to a maximum of $480 per child. The net effect

---

120. Ozawa (1991b) has pointed out that the current AFDC program already treats children unfairly by allowing wide variations in benefits, and thus federal contribution, among states, with some southern states having very low benefit levels.

of this approach to providing child care support is to limit benefits for children from low-income families. In 1986, most of the $3.5 billion allocated with this approach went to middle- and upper-middle-income families. The tax exemption approach conditions benefits to children on the employment behavior of their parents. Since children are unable to control their parent's employment behavior, this approach seems both unfair and inequitable. If it is to be maintained, it should, at the very least, be modified to guarantee universal coverage.

It is important to note that, as outlined here, the guaranteed child's exemption scheme is not viewed as a replacement for the AFDC program but is simply intended to ensure that poor children receive the same benefits already provided to wealthier children.[121] The provision of income support to low income mothers is a separate issue and needs to be separated from the provision of the child's exemption. The net effect of the guaranteed child's exemption is to no longer *deny* benefits directed to children and meant for children because of the actions of others, namely their parents, over whom they have no control. The guaranteed exemption is a universal approach that requires all children be treated equally and fairly and without the stigmatization of welfare.

Barriers to a Universal Approach in Child Welfare

Both the Universal Child Support Collection (UCSC) system and the Guaranteed Child Exemption (GCE) approaches suggested here are built on the premise of a universal approach. There are several barriers to adopting a universal approach to child welfare. Some, such as racism, are latent but powerful influences, while others reflect the level of commitment we are collectively willing to make to solve the problem of child poverty (Huston, 1991). We begin with the latent problem of racism.

The powerful public concern with child abuse as a children's issue, even though it is dwarfed by the widespread despair and pain of poverty among millions of children, is difficult to reconcile. From the beginning child abuse

---

121. Gilbert (1986) has pointed out that the growth of the welfare state in the United States occurred without fundamental principles guiding its development. Consequently, it often lacks purpose and direction. The welfare state, according to Sherraden (1991, 73), "consists mostly of a conglomeration of transfers to the nonpoor that do little to help the poor."

has been viewed as a problem that affects all children regardless of income or race. Child abuse has taken on a white face. Whereas child abuse is seen as a problem that effects all children, poverty has come to be viewed as a problem of African American and Hispanic children. Failing to understand the pernicious influence of discrimination and racism on child welfare issues has been a major barrier to developing solutions. Racism is a poison that prevents us from grappling with the real problem of child poverty.

Principally, what stands in the way of the universal approach is a legacy of institutional and personal racism. To many whites, any structural program that might aid poor families is seen as a handout for African Americans and other minorities, because to many whites, these groups constitute the poor.

In the past tension between the races was fueled by a contest for limited resources. Efforts to advance the interests of the poor were restricted because they were viewed as coming at the expense of other groups. That has led to a situation of despair and a sense of futility for minorities. Although African Americans represent 13 percent of the population in the United States, they own less than 1 percent of the privately held wealth. The likelihood of an African American person serving time in prison is almost ten times greater than for a white. An African American child is several times more likely to be born into poverty than a white child. An African American child is many more times likely to be born to an unwed mother than a white child. African American children start out with the odds stacked against them (Children's Defense Fund, 1993). To even the odds requires developing programs targeted at ameliorating the effects of more than two centuries of discrimination.

Economic advancement is not a zero sum game. The size of the economic pie is not fixed. Rather, it is determined by the collective efforts of everyone. Policies and programs are required that release the energy, creativity, and potential in everyone. The result would be a collective advance in not only mind and spirit but material abundance as well, benefiting everyone. Because of its homogenous population, Japan, as it moves to compete in the global economy, has a decided advantage. Multicultural societies like the United States and Canada can little afford hostility and friction among races. Multicultural societies have to tap the best in all of their citizenry by ensuring universal access to opportunity and advancement.

The Federal Debt: Cloud over Child Welfare Reform

In the United States infrastructure investments are running at less than half the rates of the 1960s. Keeping its bridges from falling down is all that America can manage.

Lester Thurow, *Head to Head*

When former President Reagan implemented his fundamental economic reforms he included massive tax cuts for wealthy families that were not combined with reduced federal spending. The theory behind the tax cuts was that reduced taxes would free capital that could then be reinvested in the economy and lead to even greater earnings and subsequent tax collected on those increased earnings. Unfortunately, the theory didn't work. Instead, the reduced taxes meant that the federal government had to incur ballooning debt to pay for government spending that continued to rise. Although social programs were repeatedly cut and reduced, the build up of the military during the mid-eighties more than offset the spending cuts on social programs.[122]

During the last decade large federal budget deficits have led to a Federal debt in 1993 that exceeds $4.5 trillion. When Reagan took office the federal debt was less than one fourth that amount. The cost of servicing the federal debt during the last ten years has consumed all new and available revenue, and then some. Perhaps one of the greatest impediments to bringing about a universal approach in child welfare is the belief that we just don't have the money or resources required—that the federal government is too deep in debt to do anything right now. All that can be done, so it is argued, is to cut federal spending in order to reduce the crippling federal debt amassed during the last dozen years.

When the savings and loan institutions ran into serious financial trouble the federal government understood the seriousness of the issue and provided

---

122. The cut in federal taxes meant the U.S. government accumulated massive debt, most of which is now held by the wealthy families who had their taxes cut. The net result of the tax policies of the eighties was to shift wealth upward and to improve the economic situation of those with substantial wealth. As Phillips (1993, xxiii) observes, "In the United States, merely to service the $4 trillion national debt of 1992—up fourfold from $1 trillion in 1980—required some $235 billion a year in net interest payments, most of which went to high-income bondholders (and some went abroad) while the money to make the payments was raised from broad-based taxes."

a "bail-out" for insolvent institutions. Economist Lester Thurow (1992, 18) observed,

> If government had not come to the rescue, financial capitalism, as it is prac-
> ticed in the United States, would now be collapsing. Most of America's sav-
> ings and loan banks (S & Ls) are in government receivership. Large
> numbers of commercial banks have not yet gone broke but are broke in the
> sense that they could not be liquidated to pay off their depositors if that
> should have to be done° The ultimate cost may not end up being as big as
> that for S & Ls, but it is going to require a lot of taxpayer money.

Using a computer model the Congressional Budget Office estimates the cost of rescuing the savings and loan institutions between the period 1980 and 2000 at approximately $484 billion (Passell, 1992). This currently amounts to about $40 billion a year (Phillips, 1993, 187), several times what the federal government spends on AFDC. The cost of the federal bail-out of the savings and loan industry will be more than the federal government has spent on welfare (AFDC) during its entire history (since 1935). If it is possi-ble to bail out the savings and loan industry, why isn't it possible to bail out the futures of our children?

Resistance to child welfare reform will focus on the money involved. However, the program approaches suggested in this chapter would likely require less than $4 billion a year for the United States in the short-term, but would within several years become cost neutral. The Child's Future Secu-rity account discussed in Chapter 11 would involve enacting a "social sav-ings" program modeled after Social Security for the elderly. Although the cost of that type of program is substantial, it is conceived as self-support-ing.[123]

In a free enterprise marketplace, the emphasis must be on programs that remove the premium placed on eligibility, that build individual initiative, encourage independence and allow beneficiaries to excel on their own. Uni-versal programs allow all to be eligible, to have the resources required to make the most of their individual abilities and opportunities in a free enter-prise market economy. Emphasis shifts to individual initiative, which, after

---

123. Social Security costs more than $320 billion a year but is paid for through Social Secu-rity contributions (or payroll taxes). Likewise, the Child Future Security account would be financed through the contribution of the beneficiaries at a rate less the one fifteenth of the current cost of the Social Security program for the elderly (assuming a parental contribu-tion).

all, is what has allowed the economies of the wealthy industrialized nations to flourish.

The two programs suggested here are similar to the proposals offered by David Ellwood (1988). The proposals create an environment that rewards the poor for working rather than frustrating their efforts at work with large effective tax rates. The programs are designed to achieve equity and fairness in family income protection.

Conclusion

In this chapter I have outlined two approaches to reducing poverty among children—the Universal Child Support Collection program (UCSC), and the Guaranteed Child's Exemption (GCE). The principal advantages of the UCSC and the GCE are several. First, they would ensure families and children a measure of financial security under circumstances that would not simultaneously diminish their sense of self-worth, or make them targets of social resentment, as do many of the current public assistance programs. Existing programs, instead of giving people a handup, provide only a handout, coupled with a bureaucratic imposition on their lives that not only encourages dependency and lassitude but fosters resentment through a continual affront to individual dignity, pride, and self-esteem. Second, these approaches would eliminate much costly bureaucratic inefficiency and waste, thereby saving as much or more than their implementation would cost. Third, in combination the programs would provide a much needed economic safety net for children and their families.

Summarizing his proposals for welfare reform, Ellwood (1988, 185) suggests,

> The core support will come from a child support system and the tax system—systems that affect people of all incomes. Thus, the programs will integrate poor people rather than isolate them. Poor people will have a genuine chance to make it on their own. There will be no welfare dumping ground. There will be transitional support and jobs. More will be expected of people, but many more options will be available. People will have a chance to achieve real independence.

While the two programs would guarantee a minimum economic floor for millions of children now living in poverty, they would still do little to break the continuing cycle of poverty that continues from generation to genera-tion. An approach is still needed that would constitute an "engine of eco-nomic opportunity," allowing every child, regardless of economic back-ground, a positive and substantial boost to launch them into lives that are productive, fulfilling, and of value to society. George Will (1991) under-scores this point, "Physicists refer to the '*escape velocity*' of particles cir-cling in an orbit. Some particles spin, or outside intervention causes them to spin, free from the prison of orbit onto their own long trajectory. Society's challenge is to give poor children outward velocity from the orbit that imprisons them."

Chapter 11 explores a program to provide children just such an outward velocity. First, let us examine the problem that entraps so many.

10

The Underlying Problem of Child Welfare: Families that are Not Economically Self-Supporting

The lack of family-sustaining jobs denies many young men the possibility of forming an economically self-reliant family, the traditional American mark of manhood. Partially in response, the young men's peer groups emphasize sexual prowess as a sign of manhood, with babies as evidence. A sexual game emerges as girls are lured by the (usually older) boys' vague but convincing promises of love and marriage. When the girls submit, they often end up pregnant and abandoned.

These new mothers become eligible for a limited but steady welfare income that may allow them to establish their own household and at times attract other men who need money. But it is simplistic and wrong headed to suggest that if you stop welfare, you will stop this behavior. A fundamental question is: Why do people behave in the ways I have described?

Elijah Anderson, *Streetwise*

When the history of the second half of the twentieth century is written, the most important event in U.S. domestic affairs will be the dissolution of the two-parent African American family. The change happened slowly and perhaps imperceptibly at first but now the consequences are unmistakable. In 1960 more than three quarters of all African American children lived in two-parent families. By 1992 less than one third of these children lived in two parent families with no sign the trend would reverse itself. In 1993 more than two thirds of all African American children were born to unwed mothers. As we have seen in Chapter 8, these young families embark on a life of severe poverty. The prospects of changing this situation are nowhere in sight.

To a large extent the roots of child poverty in the United States stem from the historical treatment of African American families and the institutional racism which still continues (Myrdal, 1944; Clark, 1965). Shortly after passage of the Civil Rights Act of 1964 concerns about the condition of the African American family were raised in a publication entitled, *The*

Negro Family: The Case for National Action, and referred to as the *Moynihan Report* (Moynihan, 1965). Written by former Harvard sociologist and then Assistant Secretary of Labor Daniel Patrick Moynihan, the prophetic Report detailed the increase in male unemployment and the rise of fatherless families in the African American community resulting in widespread poverty. Moynihan argued that the key to the deterioration of the African American community was to be found in the demise of the African American family. Moynihan (1965, 30) stated, "at the center of the tangle of pathology is the weakness of the family structure. Once or twice removed, it will be found to be the principal source of most of the aberrant, inadequate or antisocial behavior that did not establish, but now serves to perpetuate the cycle of poverty."

Even though the *Moynihan Report* was sponsored by then President Lyndon Johnson and included contributions by such distinguished scholars as James Wilson, Kenneth Clark, Erik Erickson, Robert Coles, and Talcott Parsons, there were some who challenged the findings as being prejudicial and possibly contributing to a negative view of the African American family (Rainwater and Yancey, 1967).

In October 1965 Reverend Martin Luther King, Jr. endorsed the *Moynihan Report's* disturbing findings. However, he expressed concern that the *Report* might be misinterpreted. He also prophetically observed (1968, 109), "As public awareness of the predicament of the Negro family increases, there will be danger and opportunity. The opportunity will be to deal fully rather than haphazardly with the problem as a whole—to see it as a social catastrophe...brought on by long years of brutality and oppression—and to meet it as other disasters are met, with an adequacy of resources. The danger will be that the problem will be attributed to innate Negro weaknesses and used to justify further neglect and to rationalize continued oppression."

A number of reasons have been suggested to explain the transformation of the African American family from a two-parent to a lone-parent family unit, and hence the continuation of child poverty. However, the problem of child poverty affects not only the African American family but all poor families. The problem is more concentrated and severe in the African American community but its greatest impact is on children of lone parent families. In the remainder of this chapter I examine this issue by first examining the problem of early childbearing. Then I look at Charles Murray's explanation that welfare is itself the primary cause. This is followed by a review of William Julius Wilson's research that indicates a lack of job opportunities for

African American men and thus their "unmarriageability" is the major cause. Finally, I examine problems related to exiting welfare and becoming self-sufficient.

Examining Out-of-Wedlock Births

If substantial progress against child poverty is ever to be achieved, an essential first step must be to find ways of preventing young people, particularly young women, from starting families they cannot support. To do this we must examine why so many young, unwed women have children to begin with. It is a contested issue on which people hold strongly opposing views. My intention is to explore the issues with a view to making sense of what reasonable direction the scientific evidence suggests we take in solving the problem.

Sexual Experimentation. One immediate fact that presents itself is that increasing numbers of teenagers are experimenting with sex before marriage (Moore, Nord, and Peterson, 1989). Approximately 75 percent of all girls now experience sex during their teenage years (Select Committee on Children, Youth, and Families, 1989b, 241). The proportion of teenage boys aged seventeen to nineteen having sex before marriage increased from two-thirds in 1979 to three-quarters in 1990. The result of this increased sexual activity has naturally been an increase in the number of teen pregnancies (Forrest and Singh, 1990; Henshaw and Van Vort, 1989). Indeed, the teen pregnancy rate in the United States is the highest in the postindustrial world.

Currently, almost one of five black teenagers and one in ten white teenagers between the ages of fifteen and seventeen become pregnant each year. Compared to other developed nations, this pregnancy rate is very high. In Canada the rate is less than one in twenty, in the Netherlands less than one in fifty, and in Japan less than one in a hundred (Smith and Poertner, 1993).

In 1991 there were more than 1.1 million teenage pregnancies that led to 520,000 births (Children's Defense Fund, 1994). Contrary to popular perception, however, there has been a decline in the number of births to teenagers during the last several decades. In 1970 there were more than 656,000 births to teenagers. What has changed, however, is the percentage of teenage mothers who are unmarried. As seen in Figure 10.1, in 1960 less than 14 percent of all teenage mothers were unmarried. By 1990 this percentage had increased to almost 70 percent. The increasing percentage of teenage parents who are unmarried has been largely responsible for the increasing

Figure 10.1 The Percentage of Teenage Mothers Who Are Unmarried, 1950-1990

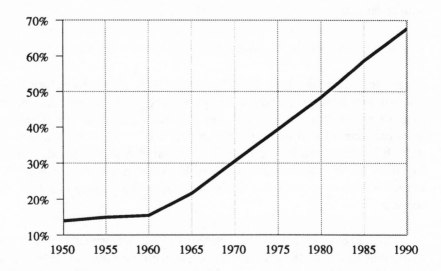

Source: Children's Defense Fund, 1994.

proportion of children born out of wedlock, especially among black families.[124]

Teenage Child-Bearing. Within one year after the birth of their first child
half of all teen mothers are receiving AFDC benefits.[125] Within five years
the percentage grows to more than 75 percent (Besharov, 1993, 51). Of all
mothers under thirty who receive public assistance (AFDC), 71 percent
began their child bearing as teenagers. Once a teenager has a child, the

---

124. Over the last several decades the cultural stigma associated with out-of-wedlock childbearing has receded. In addition, the mechanisms to require responsibility and child support
among fathers have been largely ineffective. Combined with AFDC's requirement of lone-
parent status (with a few exceptions through AFDC-UP), these factors have led to a decline
in marriage rates for teenage mothers.

125. Teenage mothers are a small part of the AFDC caseload. In 1992 they comprised 8.2
percent of the caseload. Most mothers were in their twenties (47.2 percent) or thirties (32.6
percent), while mothers in their forties comprised about 12 percent (Clinton Administration,
1994, 49).

mother and society embark on an eighteen year association that is both difficult in itself and difficult to end. Social programs provide, at best, meager
assistance to the young mother confronted by difficult economic and personal circumstances. The major program available is Aid to Families with
Dependent Children (AFDC). However, the amount of financial support
provided by AFDC is minimal, roughly one-seventh of the average family
income in the United States (Hacker, 1992, 86), or about $388 per month,
per family in 1992 (Clinton Administration, 1994, 49).

Mixed Messages. Young women who get pregnant out-of-wedlock
receive mixed messages. Although more than 40 percent of unwed teens
have abortions, abortions are, in many quarters, discouraged. Advocates for
the unborn argue on moral grounds that abortion is tantamount to taking of
a life. Once the child is born, they say, solutions will be forthcoming.

The unwed mother, however, quickly learns that the society which so
strongly encouraged her not to have an abortion has little interest in supporting her and her child after the birth, and for several reasons. First, many
would like to see the unwed mother give the child up for adoption, which
would not only free the mother to enter the work force but provide the child
a convenient escape from poverty. Adoption, however, is the least-selected
option. Baker (1985) interviewed a sample of adolescent girls across Canada and asked them how they would handle an unplanned pregnancy.
Almost half indicated they would keep their baby and raise it as best they
could, with or without the help of the father. About a third said they would
seek an abortion. Less than 5 percent said they would give their babies up
for adoption. In 1986, Bachrach reported that the release of babies for adoption was something done mostly by white mothers. According to Bachrach,
approximately 12 percent of white unmarried mothers gave their babies up
for adoption, while fewer than 1 black mother in 100 did so.[126]

That so many young women refuse to give their baby up for adoption is
often viewed as evidence of their wish to continue in a state of dependency.

---

126. See Bachrach (1986, 250-251). These data need to be viewed with caution. The data
used by Bachrach came from the National Survey of Family Growth conducted by the
National Center for Health Statistics in 1982. Interviews were completed with 7,969 women
between 15 and 44 years of age. Only 60 women in the sample had placed one or more
babies for adoption (p. 244). Thus, the rates of placement may not be reliable estimates of
national rates. In Ontario, a Provincial government report indicated that 30.1 percent of
unwed mothers kept their children in 1968, but that ten years later the number had increased
to 88.3 percent (Ontario, 1979, 19, table 2).

Yet, for most mothers, young or old, surrendering an infant is almost impossible: the maternal bond is too strong.

Another reason for not supporting the unwed mother is that society is interested in discouraging other young women from taking the same path. The meager public assistance to unwed mothers is essentially a warning to others not to become unwed mothers themselves (Jencks, 1993). In this sense, it constitutes little more than punitive "blame" for the circumstances the mother finds herself in, and as such becomes a reproach suffered not only by the woman, but her children as well. As the weight of research indicates, this approach has failed in discouraging the formation of lone-parent families (Jencks, 1993, 228).

The Condition of Teenage Mothers

Empirical studies have indicated that teenage mothers quickly descend into deep and abject poverty and suffer from "quashed hopes" and profound disillusionment (Butler, 1992; Edelman, 1987; Ellwood, 1988). Baker (1985, 113-114) describes the situation of these young unmarried mothers:

> [They] usually had about Grade 10 education and generally came from lower SES [socioeconomic status] families, spent much of their time watching television or reading romantic novels when they were not caring for their child. Their child-rearing took so much of their time and energy that most had little desire or opportunity to look for work outside the home or to improve their educational qualifications... They saw their lives improving when their children grew older and they could get out more often.

With limited education, few job skills, and the enormous demands of a new infant, most mothers are unable to obtain and hold gainful employment. Further, even when they are able to secure child care and obtain employment, their income is low. Given average annual incomes of less than $7,000 a year, the lone-mothers confront a depressing economic plight, with their children suffering as much as they (Levy, 1987, 151).[127]

Not surprisingly, most unmarried mothers who end up on AFDC find themselves, in a sense, trapped in dependency. Although the program is difficult, degrading, and in many ways inadequate, the lone-mother somehow adapts to the minimal support provided (Segalman and Basu, 1981). In doing so she becomes a victim of the very program designed to assist her. Over time, she loses her pride and sense of self-worth and is viewed with disrespect by the larger society that is now burdened with providing for her and her children. Without child care and adequate benefits, she rarely gains the resources to achieve self-sufficiency (American Public Welfare Association, 1994).

Children in lone-parent families have less provision and opportunity in virtually all areas of life (Boyle, et al., 1987; Offord, et al., 1987). Butler (1992, 5) observes, "Children born to teenage mothers have been found to be at greater risk for health problems, poor cognitive functioning, and poverty." They have a significantly higher likelihood of dropping out of school and will themselves be more likely to give birth out-of-wedlock (McLanahan, 1988).

In the face of the poverty and despair which awaits young people who begin families too early, how is it that so many young people find themselves in this predicament? That is the question Charles Murray addresses.

Murray and the Conservative View

Conservative social theorist Charles Murray (1984) of the American Enterprise Institute has become the principal proponent of the view that while AFDC was designed to alleviate child poverty, it has, in fact, become the primary cause of poverty. The result of providing income support through AFDC has led, Murray (1984, 166) argues, to a dramatic increase in the percentage of lone-mothers and their children relying on welfare (see Figure 10.2). Child bearing becomes a relative advantage for poor and low income women, Murray argues, in that by having a child the women become eligible to receive public assistance that would otherwise be unavailable. Thus, it is argued that many young women intentionally have children in order to receive AFDC benefits (Gilder, 1981, 123; Hazlitt, 1973). Conservative theorists are not alone in this view. Rather, they are tapping into a suspicion held by almost half of all Americans who believe that poor women have children in order to get AFDC (Goodwin, 1972; Lewis and Schneider,

---

127. With an average annual income of less than $7,000 a year, an unintended consequence of current social and economic policy is to impose severe economic hardship on unwed teenagers who *elect to keep their children* and try to raise them as best they can. Those who are opposed to abortion would be wise to focus on improving the circumstances of the lone-mothers who elect to keep their child. For many who carry their child to term, the consequence is a life in poverty for both the mother and the child extending for many years (see Figure 8.10).

Figure 10.2 AFDC Families as a Percent of All Families, 1950-1980

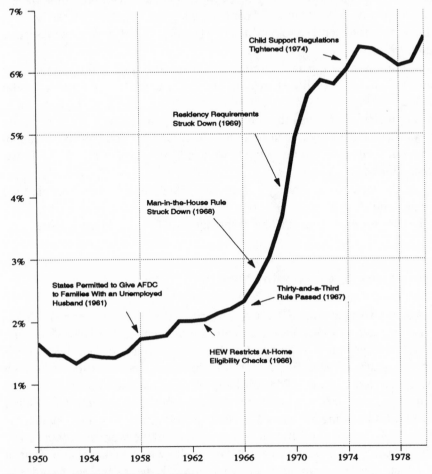

Source: Murray (1984, 165, figure 12.1).

1985).[128] The view is held even more widely among the poor who benefit from AFDC (Ellwood, 1988, 22). Murray (1984, 204) argues that:

> It is impossible to examine the statistics on a topic such as single teenage mothers without admitting that we are witnessing a tragedy. If it had been

---

128. In April 1994 a CNN/Gallup poll found that 68 percent of respondents "say welfare recipients are taking advantage of the system" (Welch, 1994, 7A).

inevitable, if there had been nothing we could have done to avoid it, then we could retain the same policies, trying to do more of the same and hoping for improvement. But once we must entertain the possibility that we are bringing it on ourselves, as I am arguing that both the logic and evidence compel us to do, then it is time to reconsider a social policy that salves our consciences ("Look how compassionate I am") at the expense of those whom we wished to help.

The problem of child poverty—which is essentially poverty among lone-parents and their children—is the core problem Murray addresses. His views have been central to the public discussion in the United States and Britain. Essentially Murray argues that the program designed to relieve child poverty, AFDC, has caused the problem and continues to perpetuate it. This view makes it difficult to solve the problem because it suggests that what we currently do in an effort to help simply exacerbates the problem. The more we do to help the worse the problem seems to get. As a consequence, Murray concludes we would do better doing nothing. Because of the prominence achieved by his views it is important to examine Murray's arguments in detail. While correct on a number of important points, several of his main arguments are incorrect and his fundamental analysis is flawed.

AFDC and Child Poverty. Murray suggests that AFDC and other anti-poverty efforts have led to greater poverty. The empirical data fail to sustain this proposition (Levitan, 1990; Olson, 1970; Schram, 1991). The number of children living in households with income below the poverty line, which is the key measure of poverty, decreased substantially during the years of the Kennedy and Johnson administrations (See Figure 10.2; Schram and Wilken, 1989; Wilson, 1987). In 1959, more than two-thirds of children in black families lived in households with income below the poverty line (see Table 8.3). During the next decade, which witnessed the War on Poverty, the number of black children living in poverty was reduced by more than one third (from 65 percent to 41 percent). This was a period of great progress in reducing child poverty. From 1969 to 1979, however, the percentage of black children living in poverty stopped declining, leveled off, and began to increase slightly to 42 percent. By 1990, the reduction of poverty among children begun in the 1960s had long since ended.

Murray's data, rather than supporting his view, can, in fact, be interpreted as providing evidence contradicting it. Under conservative federal government administrations, which pursued more restrictive welfare poli-

Figure 10.3 The Number of Children on Welfare in the United States, 1954-1990

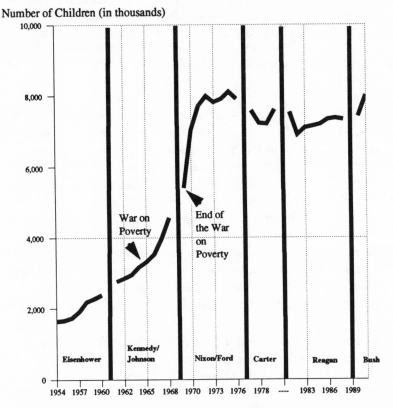

Number of Children (in thousands)

Source: Murray (1984, 244, table 4); Social Security Bulletin (1991).

cies, reliance on AFDC increased. Figure 10.3 examines the same data used by Murray but draws a different conclusion. The number of AFDC recipients increased most dramatically after the election of President Nixon and the end of the War on Poverty. It would be difficult to suggest that this growth in AFDC recipients was a result of the War on Poverty. While the number children receiving AFDC payments did increase during the War on Poverty (by 30 percent), the largest rise in AFDC recipients occurred during the first term of the Nixon Administration when the number of AFDC recipients increased by almost 43 percent.[129] Later, during the Carter administration, the number of children in AFDC families declined more than 4 percent.

AFDC has been in effect since 1935. For the first thirty years the program was used by less than 3.5 million children. Most of the growth in AFDC occurred in the five years between 1967 and 1972 when the number of children receiving benefits doubled from 4 to 8 million (see Figure 10.3). During the next two decades the number of children receiving AFDC benefits fluctuated between 7 and 9 million. If AFDC caused an increase in families unable to support themselves, why wasn't the problem observed decades earlier?[130] Further, why hasn't the exponential growth observed between 1967 and 1972 continued?

Changes in AFDC Caseload are Best Explained by the Increase in Divorce Rates. The thrust of Murray's (1984) work has been to explain the increase in the number of children receiving AFDC. In this regard, one is struck by the remarkable similarity between changes in the number of children receiving AFDC benefits and the increase in the number of children involved in divorce (see Figure 4.2 [page 71]). Figure 10.4 examines these trends in combination including the number of: (1) children receiving AFDC benefits, (2) children involved in divorce, (3) children born out-of-wedlock, and (4) children living in poverty.[131] The change in the number of

---

129. Murray (1984) chooses to place the War on Poverty in the period 1965 to 1970. Yet, the presidential administration responsible for the War on Poverty was defeated in 1968 by Nixon. The greatest increase in the number of AFDC recipients occurred between 1968 and 1972. In Figure 10.2, the data are examined by periods of federal leadership and fail to support the view that the War on Poverty was the cause of the increase in welfare recipients.

130. Murray (1984, 5) observes, "In 1950, social welfare spending for the general public (excluding programs for veterans, and railroad and government personnel) cost a little over three billion dollars; about eleven billion in 1980 dollars." Murray laments, "Overall, civilian social welfare costs increased by twenty times from 1950 to 1980, in constant dollars. During the same period, the United States population increased by half" (p. 14). Murray (1984, 242) reports in his Appendix (table 2) that federal spending on social welfare costs in 1980 exceeded 250 billion dollars. Income assistance to lone-mothers (AFDC) was an insignificant part of this increased spending. Federal spending for entitlement programs for the elderly (Social Security and Medicaid), which form the core of this expenditure (almost 180 billion dollars), dwarfed AFDC costs (less than 8 billion dollars) by a factor of twenty or more. Yet Murray (1984, 1993) focuses almost exclusively on income support programs provided to single mothers and children, a group with relatively limited political power, while leaving untouched income support programs for senior citizens, a group which yields substantial political power. The concern for Murray is not so much the direct costs associated with AFDC as it with the effects of the AFDC program—namely dependency and idleness—on those whom it is intended to help. The task, then, is to reform AFDC so that it provides temporary assistance while not discouraging either labor force participation or marriage for program beneficiaries. The limitation of AFDC is measured by its long-term affects on the life course trajectory of recipients. And here the costs have been too great.

Figure 10.4 Trends in Children on AFDC, Involved in Divorce, Living in Poverty, and Born Out-of-Wedlock, 1954-1992

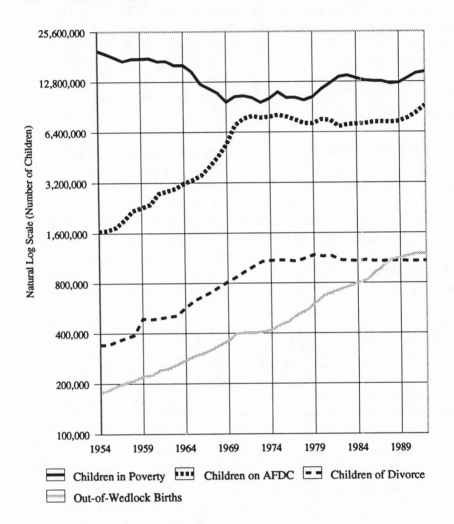

Children in Poverty   Children on AFDC   Children of Divorce

Out-of-Wedlock Births

131. The data for figure 10.4 derive from Figures 4.2, 4.3, 10.3 and Table 8.3. In order to permit a comparison across time for these variables taking into account the different scale measures (that is, "children in poverty" ranging from 10 million to 20 million and "children born out-of-wedlock" ranging from 200,000 to less than 1.5 million) I used a log scale. Data for the early years (1954 to 1959) of "children in poverty" and "children of divorce" are estimated.

Table 10.1 Determinants of Children on AFDC from 1954 to 1992

	Beta Coefficient		Zero-Order Correlation
Children of Divorce	.939	p < .001	.970
Out-of-wedlock Births	.119	n.s.	.741
Children in Poverty	-.122	n.s.	.774

$N = 39$, $R^2 = .945$

children on AFDC closely mirrors the change in the number of children involved in divorce but is relatively independent of other changes such as the number of children born out-of-wedlock. A regression analysis examining the relative impact of divorce and out-of-wedlock births on the number of children on AFDC over the period from 1954 to 1992 revealed that it was the increase in "children involved in divorce" that most influenced the increase in AFDC usage, accounting for more than 94 percent of the variation (see Table 10.1). Evidently when women with children divorced during the period from 1954 to 1992 many of them looked to AFDC for income assistance until they could stand on their own.

AFDC and the Increasing Failure to Form Two-Parent African American Families. The number of African American children living with two parents decreased from 58 percent in 1970 to 35 percent in 1992. If, as Murray suggests, AFDC was the lure that prompted this calamity, we would expect to see a concomitant rise in the numbers of black families enrolling on AFDC. However, during this period, the percentage of black children on the AFDC caseload actually declined, from 34 percent in 1970 to 30 percent in 1988 (see Table 10.2). The failure to build two-parent families did not lead to a concomitant rise in AFDC recipients (See also Darity and Myers, 1983; Levy, 1987; Schram, Turbett, and Wilken, 1988; Schram and Wilken, 1989). From 1972 to 1992 the number of black children living in lone mother families increased from three million to five million. Yet, the number of black children on AFDC remained about the same. Evidently, these lone mothers were not having children in order to obtain AFDC.

Murray also suggests that black women left work to go on AFDC (also see Mead, 1985). In fact, during this period, the number of black, unmarried women entering the labor force increased slightly, from 56.3 percent to 61.2 percent (Ellwood and Crane, 1990). In other words, as the number of two-

Table 10.2 AFDC Benefits and the Changing Family Situation for Black Children, 1960-1988

	AFDC and Food Stamps for a Family of 4	Percent of Black Children Not Living with 2 Parents	Percent of Black Children in AFDC Families
1960	$7,324	33.0%	10.4%
1970	9,900	41.5	33.6
1980	8,325	57.8	34.9
1990	7,741	61.4	30.1

Source: Ellwood and Crane (1990)

parent black families were declining, many more black women were entering the labor force than enrolling on AFDC.

AFDC Benefits and the Rise in Lone-Parent Families. As for the hypothesis that improved AFDC benefits encouraged the growth of lone-parent families, studies of variations in state AFDC payment levels fail to provide support. If high benefits led to growth in the number of AFDC recipients, we would expect to find relatively more recipients in high-benefit states versus low-benefit states. However, empirical studies indicate that the number of lone-parent families found in low-benefit and high-benefit states are similar (Ellwood, 1988, 62, figure 3.8).

Japan has one of the most generous welfare programs in the industrial world. The average welfare payment equals 62 percent of the average family consumption or about $1,121 per month, per family (Ozawa, 1991a). This is almost three times the amount provided in the United States. Nevertheless, Japan has one-fifth as many families on welfare. A similar pattern is found in other industrialized democracies in Western Europe.

Murray contends that the improvement in foods stamps and AFDC benefits also had a negative impact on work incentives and family formation for black families. Although the benefits of these two programs increased between 1960 and 1972, since that period more that two decades ago, the real value of the combined benefits declined. Further, as Table 10.2 shows, while the average AFDC benefit declined, the percentage of black children in lone-parent families increased. Ellwood (1988, 60) observes:

If AFDC was allowing women to become single parents, the number of recipients would have grown along with the number of single parents. But the number did not increase; it fell. The pattern holds for black children as well as white children. The number of black children in female-headed families grew by over 25 percent between 1972 and 1984 while the number on AFDC fell by 15 percent.

In short, as the percentage of children in lone-parent families increased, the percentage of these children receiving AFDC decreased. AFDC can hardly be viewed as being the cause of an *increase* in AFDC use when its use actually *declined*.

Murray argues that it was the improvement of benefits during the sixties that set the stage for the increased participation and sustained involvement with AFDC. In this regard, the empirical data would seem to bear him out. The number of children receiving AFDC benefits reached 8 million in 1971 and remained at about that level for the next two decades. He is probably right that it was not beneficial in the long term to improve AFDC solely by increasing benefits, because it insulated poor mothers and their children from the requirements of self-supporting labor-force participation. Over the years poor mothers may have learned to rely on AFDC benefits, a situation that led to the view that long term reliance on welfare was acceptable in a free market economy, even though such acceptance ran counter to deep-seated values toward parental responsibility and work. What was needed in the sixties (and is still needed now) was reform that incorporated strategies designed to integrate and involve poor mothers and their children into self-sufficient roles and participation in the economic system. As Danziger and Weinberg (1986) point out, the antipoverty efforts of the sixties focused on income transfer programs to the poor but failed to promote greater self-sufficiency by addressing problems of structural unemployment and declining opportunities.

Yet, as we shall see later, simply providing cash assistance has always been the least costly approach to child poverty. No proven cost-effective job creation or welfare-to-work strategy has yet been developed, even though considerable effort and research has been extended in this area. In short, it has proven more expensive to provide a hand up than a hand out. Consequently, AFDC has been limited to providing income assistance to the poor.

AFDC and Out-of-Wedlock Births. Murray (1984, 18) and others have suggested that AFDC encourages out-of-wedlock births and that once mothers are eligible they continue to have additional children to get more benefits (Gilder, 1981; Hazlitt, 1973). He writes (1984, 18), "Many of them had not even been married. Worst of all, they didn't stop having babies after the first lapse. They kept having more...The most flagrantly unrepentant seemed to be mostly black, too." Yet, again, the empirical data fail to support the thesis. During the last decade the average size of the AFDC family has actually decreased (Butler, 1992; DeParle, 1992).[132] Further, little evidence exists that women have children in order to gain AFDC benefits (Ellwood and Bane, 1985; Ellwood, 1988, 58-62). Edelman (1987, 64) points out that teenage "pregnancy rates are higher in states with the lowest welfare benefits and lowest in the states with higher welfare benefits."

Declining Economic Opportunity

As Wilson (1987), Hacker (1992), Edelman (1987) and others have documented, what explains the decline in two-parent black families is the steady erosion of economic opportunities open to young black and Hispanic men and women. Butler (1992, 12) observes:

> The structure of the urban economy has shifted from manufacturing to service industries, and this has particularly hurt low-skilled workers. Cities have lost thousands of manufacturing and blue-collar service jobs over the last several decades, while gaining jobs in white-collar service occupations (e.g., information processing), which generally require higher education. ...The proportion of young men who work in manufacturing dropped by one-quarter between 1974 and 1984 and dropped by almost one half for young men who had not graduated from high school as companies curtailed their hiring and laid off workers with the least seniority. This change has had a particularly devastating effect on the earnings of young men with low education because blue-collar work in manufacturing industries pays considerably better than most other jobs available to low-skilled workers.

---

132. Butler (1992, p. 14) reports that between 1968 and 1987 the average AFDC payment *per family* declined from $676 to $470 per month (in 1988 dollars). There is limited evidence that declining AFDC payments reduced program participation. Although it is clear that the children, who are the majority of recipients, experienced the pain of the reductions. As Jencks (1993, 266) observed, "An unskilled single mother cannot expect to support herself and her children in today's labor market *either* by working *or* by collecting welfare" (italics in original).

In an earlier generation the breakthroughs and advances in agriculture revolutionized farming and vastly reduced the number of employees needed in the agricultural sector. Likewise, the global economy and offshore assembly has systematically reduced the demand for unskilled and semi-skilled manufacturing employment in recent decades. As a result, the individuals and communities that have relied on these manufacturing jobs have encouraged increased unemployment and little hope of new opportunities.

Realistic Hope and Opportunity

Ellwood and Crane (1990, 81) add that "a long and potent literature in social psychology and sociology, strongly supported by various intervention programs, suggests that out-of-wedlock childbearing is lowest among women with the best 'options,' including good employment prospects." They further note that unwed motherhood is a reflection of helplessness and despair. Duncan and Hoffman (1989) report that even though welfare has had little influence on birth rates, the economic 'options' among black teenagers are the crucial determinants. Golden (1992, 5) observes "girls who were persistently poor were 10 times as likely to bear a child before age 18 as girls who were never poor—34 percent of persistently poor young women, compared to 3.5 percent of those who were never poor."

What is most important is that young women believe they have real opportunity that would be *threatened* by an out of wedlock birth. However, many poor young women have little realistic prospects of making it into the middle class and they know it. As Furstenberg (1991, 136) observers:

> Persistent inequality and growing isolation among the poor, blacks especially, set the terms for calculating the costs of an ill-timed birth. As I have said, relatively few teenagers set out to become pregnant when they do. However, I have also noted that while the timing of parenthood is inopportune, having a child confers certain immediate benefits for women whose future prospects are bleak. If this is true for a substantial number of those who enter parenthood prematurely, it suggests that many will not take extraordinary measures to prevent pregnancy from occurring. Given the difficulty of using contraception and the moral dilemmas of abortion, many women will drift into parenthood before they are ready.

Programs designed to promote contraception have produced relatively modest effects in reducing out of wedlock births. The problem is that providing contraception is not enough. Young people have to believe they have opportunity to achieve a good life. Without a sense of hope and opportunity young people will continue to drift in parenthood even when contraception is provided at no cost. Furstenberg (1991, 136) continues:

> I am not assuming, however, that any one couple makes these calculations when they have sex. It is probably more accurate to see these calculations as embedded in a social and cultural context that is familiar to the teens. In part, then, the task of policymakers involves not only widening opportunities for young adults in disadvantaged communities and the institutions which shape the views of children and youth: neighborhoods, schools, churches, volunteer organizations, and, of course, the family. Cultural redefinitions are likely to take root only when communities and local institutions are remoralized—when they come to see that there is more justice and opportunity for themselves and their children. The current pattern of disintegration of marriage and parenthood probably will not be reversed, if it can be reversed at all, without revising the reality of life at the bottom of American society.

Murray's Radical Proposal: Revoke Public Charity

The primary motive supporting public welfare for poor mothers, as Murray (1984) argues, is not any empirical evidence of its effectiveness but rather a notion of charity and compassion (Titmuss, 1968). It is, according to Murray (1984, 236), this charitable orientation that prevents the necessary radical reform of terminating welfare assistance: "A solution that would have us pay less and acknowledge that some would go unhelped is unacceptable. To this extent, the barrier to radical reform of social policy is not the pain it would cause the intended beneficiaries of the present system, but the pain it would cause the donors."

To Murray, continuing to provide assistance to lone-mothers simply compounds the problem, and he recommends (1993, A24), "The AFDC payment should go to zero. Single mothers are not eligible for subsidized housing or for food stamps... From society's perspective, to have a baby that you cannot care for yourself is profoundly irresponsible, and the government will no longer subsidize it." He urges (1993, A24) that "the state stop interfering with the natural forces that have done the job quite effectively for millennia." Murray (1993) proposes that the naive program of charity—that is, welfare—be revoked in order to restore economic hardship: "Restoring economic penalties translates into the first and central policy prescription: to end all economic support for single mothers" (p. A24).[133]

Murray advises that if a lone-parent is unable to adequately care for her child when welfare is revoked, the child could be removed and placed in an orphanage. He observes (1993, A24) that "there are laws already on the books about the right of the state to take a child from a neglectful parent. We have some 360,000 children in foster care because of them." We may, he says, need to consider building orphanages for the many children that will be removed from mothers who are unable to properly care for them—not the cold stark orphanages of the past, but new modern facilities that would provide first rate care.

From within the residual perspective Murray's prescription of restoring severe economic penalties on those unable to provide for themselves would probably work. However, it is a solution that compassionate and civilized society has long since abandoned. We can only assume that the "natural forces" he refers to that would take care of the problem are the same as those described by the late British economist Thomas Malthus who argued that mass death from war, pestilence, and starvation were nature's way of controlling population growth. In a sense, Murray's approach represents a modern day version of the Malthusian approach with a twist which says that trying to solve the problem only aggravates it.[134] He argues that while sympathy and compassion motivate helping, they prevent the needed bitter medicine of ending relief. Yet, equating the suffering, hunger, fear, stress and despair that mothers and children on welfare would experience upon the termination of welfare, with the dubious anguish the alleged "donor" might suffer upon being denied the opportunity to help, as Murray (1984, 236) does, stretches credibility.

Murray's solution is attractive to many because it suggests the problem of poverty can be solved at little or no public expense by simply pulling the plug, as it were, on the economic life support system that now sustains most of the mothers and children living in poverty. This action would, Murray

---

133. The appeal of Murray's arguments can be seen in much of the current efforts at welfare reform that are designed to restore economic penalties to those who start families too early or that are not self-supporting. There is discussion of requiring teenagers who have children out of wedlock to live with their parent(s) in order to receive welfare benefits. Some states now provide reduced assistance or none at all after the first child is born to a young woman on welfare.

134. Murray (1984, 218) writes, "My conclusion is that social programs in a democratic society tend to produce net harm in dealing with the most difficult problems. They will inherently tend to have enough of an inducement to produce bad behavior and not enough of a solution to stimulate good behavior; and the more difficult the problem, the more likely it is that this relationship will prevail."

argues, be so personally devastating to those affected that it would end the behavior which caused the problem—children born out-of-wedlock. But doing this would likely drive people to even more extreme and desperate measures in their scramble for survival. Anderson (1994, F1) observes, "The nihilism that you now see among inner-city people would only increase and spread further beyond the bounds of ghetto communities. Cities would become almost unlivable. Blacks would continue to be the primary victims, though; illegitimacy rates would rise, not diminish."

In a sense, a variant of Murray's recommendation for ending welfare has been tried. In Mississippi the maximum monthly AFDC payment for a lone mother with two children and no other income is $120 a month (Clinton Administration, 1994, 49). In a number of the southern states very low AFDC payment levels have been in effect for decades. Yet, this approach has not led to lower rates of children born out-of-wedlock in these states. Nor has it led to reduced poverty, especially among children. Quite the opposite has, in fact, been the case. The most severe poverty is found in these states which come closest to meeting the reforms urged by Murray.

Murray's (1984) work correctly points out the limitations of a welfare system that provides only cash assistance to the impoverished while ignoring the broader context of available opportunities and possibilities. As Franklin Roosevelt emphasized during development of AFDC and the New Deal work relief programs sixty years earlier, providing the poor with cash assistance alone can be a "dangerous narcotic" (Garfinkel, 1992, 21). It is not sufficient for welfare to provide only a safety net of minimal or subsistence income. Efforts must be made to prepare young mothers for productive and self-reliant roles in a free enterprise economy—even though such efforts are expensive. Without such efforts AFDC will only sustain those in poverty and not allow them to exit their plight.

Essentially Murray's view fails to take into account how the economic policies of the eighties shifted wealth upwards while further *disconnecting* those at the bottom. Virtually no social policies or programs of significance were developed in the eighties to bring those living in poverty into the economic mainstream (Haveman, 1988; Lemov, 1989). Economic and social policy was directed toward improving the situation of asset holders possessing substantial wealth, with the view that their success would trickle down to those below. Murray's recommendation would simply cut the only remaining connection (lifeline) many poor lone mothers and their children have to the economy.

Murray's Approach: Science or Atheoretical Advocacy Research?

The interest of social science is to examine theoretical problems with objective research methods in order to empirically test their validity (Cournand and Meyer, 1976). What is the theory which guides Murray's research? There is no fundamental theory which provides a comprehensive understanding and connects essential concepts together. Instead, there is an hypothesis that states that the AFDC program has aggravated the problem of child poverty and only made it worse. Murray has not taken an objective approach to testing the validity of this hypothesis. Rather, he has systematically collected data which support his hypothesis and argued passionately for its correctness.

What is missing from Murray's analysis is a discussion of the limitation of his hypothesis. Why is it, for instance, that Murray fails to discuss the higher poverty rates for black and Hispanic children? In 1991, more than 40 percent of black and Hispanic children lived in poverty, compared to less than 17 percent for white children. What explanation does Murray's view offer to explain this? Why is it that AFDC, which is available to all children regardless of race, seemingly concentrate its impact on black and Hispanic children? Almost 75 percent of black children live in lone parent families. How does Murray's view explain this differential impact? Murray does not argue that black and Hispanic children are somehow deserving of their plight. Nor does he proffer biological explanations. What then accounts for the fact that child poverty is so highly concentrated among black and Hispanic children? The silence of his views on these central problems highlights the *atheoretical* nature of his views. Murray interest is not in contributing to science as much as it is in advocating for a particular view sponsored by, among others, conservative think tanks of which he is a member. There may well be some validity to Murray's work but it is important to recognize that it is more accurately understood as "advocacy research" than the dispassionate search for truth (Gilbert, 1994).

Policy Analysis. What is needed to address the problem of child poverty are social policies and programs that equip lone-mothers for meaningful and productive involvement in the economic system and allow responsible economic behavior. If the intent is to reduce or end poverty, it is not enough to simply provide a charitable income support payment. A balance between charity and a strategy to ensure responsible behavior must be devised. In this sense, the current welfare reform proposals of the Clinton administration are, insofar as they are premised on the ethic of parental responsibility, a step in this direction. According to an early draft of the Clinton administration's welfare reform options (December 13, 1993): "No one should bring a child into the world until he or she is prepared to support and nurture that child. We need to implement approaches that both require parental responsibility and help individuals to exercise it."

The focus of the Clinton Administration reforms center on lone-mothers after their child is born. The residual perspective requires this focus. In contrast, a structural perspective examines the situation of lone mothers before the birth of their first child and considers the opportunity structure which leads to the choice of early child bearing outside of marriage. How can the opportunity structure for young women be changed to prevent early child bearing. Within the residual perspective prevention efforts are directed toward discouraging the sexual interests of adolescents. Yet, as Marian Wright Edelman (1987, 55) observed, "hope and opportunity and a sense of usefulness are the primary contraceptives [a] nation must provide for all its young." One of the major barriers young women from poor and low income communities face in the formation of economically viable two-parent households is the problem of male joblessness.

Wilson and Male Joblessness

William Julius Wilson presents a view of welfare that is in sharp contrast to Murray's. Wilson (1987, 90) observes that, "Contrary to popular opinion, there is little evidence to provide a strong case for welfare as the primary cause of family breakups, female headed households, and out-of-wedlock births." For Wilson, the growth of lone-parent families can be attributed, as we have mentioned already, to declining economic opportunities for uneducated young men, especially young black men. "The weight of existing evidence," writes Wilson, "suggests that the problem of male joblessness could be the single most important factor underlying the rise in unwed mothers among poor black women" (Wilson, 1987, 73). Wilson has demonstrated that there has been a structural transformation of the urban inner city communities, where uneducated black men are often unable to earn more than $5 an hour. At this wage, even if they worked full-time the entire year, they would be unable to earn more than poverty-line income for a family of four. Further, many are unable to find full-time work. As a consequence, there has been a decline in the pool of "marriageable" men (Wilson, 1987; Wilson

Figure 10.5 The Percentage of Men (25-54) with Poor Earnings by Race and Educational Attainment, 1949-1986

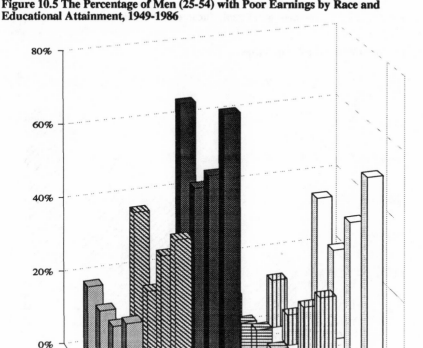

Note: Poor earnings is defined as earnings below the poverty line for a family of four.
Source: Danziger and Stern (1990, 9, table 2).

and Neckerman, 1987). Young women, it is argued, find they can obtain more reliable support from public assistance. Figure 10.5 shows the percentage of young men in the United States with earned income below the poverty line for a family of four.

Young men with less than an eighth-grade education are the least likely individuals to get married. In 1986, almost three-fourths of young black men and more than half of young white men with an eighth-grade education were unable to earn income above the poverty line. With the decline and departure of jobs in the manufacturing sector and growth in the last decade of high technology and knowledge-based industries, family wage job

Figure 10.6 College Enrollment and Family Income in the United States (1988)

Families with Children Enrolled in College

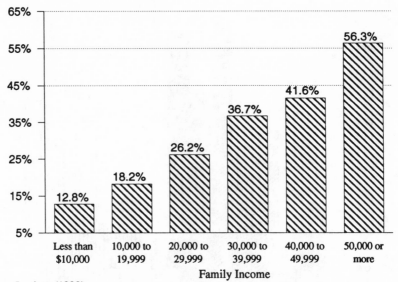

Source: Levitan (1990).

opportunities for young men without a high school education have disappeared. For young black men, even a high school education provides little assurance that they will be able to earn an income above the poverty line.

The best assurance of earning an income that will support a family above the poverty line has traditionally been a high school education (Furstenberg, Brooks-Gunn, and Morgan, 1987). Among the college educated, almost 90 percent of young white men and 75 percent of young black men are able to earn an income above the poverty line for a family of four. Yet, attending college is an expensive proposition beyond the reach of many young black men from low-income families (see Figure 10.6).[135]

Despite the reasoning that education should make a difference, it appears that during the last several decades having a better education has not necessarily increased the likelihood of marriage for blacks. As seen in Table 10.3, marriage rates for black men and women have been declining regardless of education, although they have declined substantially more for those without a high school education.

Table 10.3 Relationship Between Marriage and Education Among African Americans, 1960-1988

	1960	1970	1980	1988
Married black males, age 25-34				
Less than 12 years of school	62.9	60.6	39.1	29.7
High school graduate	64.0	67.5	48.9	42.1
More than 12 years	61.1	66.6	50.1	44.3
Married black females, age 25-34				
Less than 12 years of school	63.4	52.6	34.4	23.3
High school graduate	65.1	60.8	44.8	37.1
More than 12 years	62.5	60.3	45.0	38.6

Source: Ellwood and Crane (1990, 77, table 4 and 80, table 5).

Despite the common sense explanation that black male joblessness is the primary factor explaining the decrease in two-parent family formation and the rise in births to unwed mothers, empirical support for the view has been equivocal. Robert Lerman (1989) reviewed the link between male job opportunities and family formation and failed to find a consistent and significant relationship. Lerman found that the unemployment rate in a community was not correlated with marriage rates and seemed to be independent. Lerman (1989, 66) observes that:

> We are left without a persuasive explanation of family formation trends of recent decades. While it might seem obvious that declines in the earnings of young men were of central importance, a look at family formation patterns early this century should have cast doubt on this assertion. In 1930, when black men earned far less relative to whites than they do today, black men in

---

135. Public higher education represents a form of public investment in young people that, averages more than $17,000 per student (Thurow, 1992). As can be seen in Figure 10.6, the benefit has gone mostly to children from higher income families. Historically, the prevailing ideology suggested that access to higher education should be assured to all irrespective of income. Recently, however, substantial tuition increases at public higher education institutions have resulted in further restriction of access for children from low income families. This trend restricts access, converting higher education into a regressive welfare program that accelerates the advantages of children from high income families at the public expense of all families.

Table 10.4 Relation Between Marriage and Employment Among African Americans

	1960	1970	1980	1988
Married black males, age 25-34				
Currently employed	70.3	71.2	55.1	48.1
Currently not employed	32.0	30.0	26.7	22.9
Married black females, age 25-34				
Currently employed	53.5	52.7	44.5	39.5
Currently not employed	72.1	60.2	38.2	28.3

Source: Ellwood, (1990, 77 and 80)

their twenties were more likely to be married than white men. Further, less educated men who have the lowest earnings, have tended to marry at younger ages than the more educated.

Other data also fail to support the theory of male joblessness. As can be seen in Table 10.4, the percentage of black males who were married, regardless of employment, has fallen steadily since 1960. These data suggest that it was more than male joblessness that led to an increase in the number of black unwed mothers (Ellwood and Crane, 1990). Nonetheless, the data show that the marriage rate for employed black males is more than double the rate for the unemployed and is, therefore, congruent with Wilson's theory.

If male joblessness does not fully explain declining marriage rates, out-of-wedlock births, and the rise of lone parent black families, what does? As it turns out, employment status may be as important for black women as it is for men. As the data in Table 10.4 show, beginning in 1980 there was a crossover with the marriage rates for employed black women exceeding that for the unemployed. In 1970 the marriage rates for employed black women was lower than for those not employed. However, by 1980 this had reversed. By 1988 the marriage rate was substantially higher for employed women.

Unfortunately, the data do not tell us which comes first, getting married or getting a job. In any event, in recent years the responsibility of employment has increased the likelihood of marriage. Since a major concern has been the increasing proportion of children born to unmarried black women, these data would suggest that strategies designed to improve their employment prospects would also have a major influence on reducing the likelihood of out-of-wedlock births.

Murray's argument presumes that there are reasonable employment opportunities for lone parents but that they turn away from these in favor of collecting welfare without having to work. Yet, Murray (1984 and 1993) fails to provide empirical evidence in support of this proposition. The evidence examined above contradicts this proposition.

Explaining the High Percentage of Black Children Born Out-of-Wedlock

When Ellwood and Crane (1990, 68) examined the birth rates of black women aged fifteen to forty-four they found that "the change in the percentage of black children born out-of-wedlock is not a reflection of an increase in the birth rates to unmarried women at all. Rather, it results from dramatic declines in marriage and in the childbearing of married women." As can be seen in Figure 10.7, the birth rates of black unmarried women actually declined from 98 per 1,000 in 1960 to 85 per 1,000 in 1988. What led to the increase in the overall percentage of black children born to unmarried women was the fall in the percentage of black women who married (from 51 percent in 1960 to 29 percent in 1988) combined with a drop in their birth rate (from 187 per 1,000 in 1960 to 82 per 1,000 in 1988). While the birth rate for black married women fell, the birth rate for unmarried black women remained unchanged.[136]

In addition, the proportion of African American women between the ages of 20 to 24 who were married fell from half in 1960 to one-sixth in

---

136. The percentage of children born out-of-wedlock is determined by dividing the number of children born out-of-wedlock [the numerator] by the total number of children born [the denominator]. The denominator includes both those born in and out-of-wedlock. While the birth rate for unmarried black women fell slightly during the last three decades, the birth rate for married women fell sharply. In addition, the marriage rate for black women fell from 51 percent in 1960 to 29 percent in 1988. Thus, there are three-fifths as many black married women having half as many births, resulting in black married women having less than one third the number of children they had three decades earlier. Meanwhile, the number of unmarried black women has increased while their birth rate has only slightly declined. In summary, what has produced the change in the percentage of black children born out-of-wedlock is the decline in the number of black married women having children combined with the declining marriage rate for teenage mothers.

Figure 10.7 Birth Rates for Women (Age 15-44) by Marital Status and Race, 1960-1988

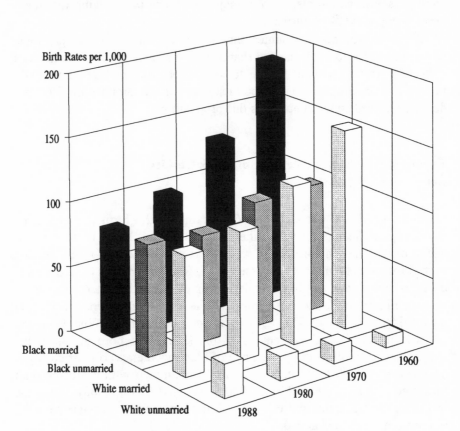

Source: Ellwood and Crane (1990, tables 1 and 2).

1988. For African American women between the ages of 25 to 34 the percent who were married fell from two-thirds in 1960 to one-third in 1988
(Ellwood and Crane, 1990, table 5). Further, as demonstrated earlier, there
has been a sharp decline in the percentage of teenage mothers who are married. In the past, child birth among teenagers was accompanied by marriage,
but that has fallen sharply during the last several decades.

To briefly describe what happened: during the last thirty years the
marriage rates for all black women have been declining. This has reduced the
number of married women and added to the numbers of unmarried women.
While the birth rate for the increasing numbers of unmarried black women

has remained almost the same (declining only slightly), the birth rate for the far fewer married black women has declined sharply. It is this growing differential in the fewer number of married black women having fewer children, compared to the greater number of unmarried black women continuing to have essentially the same number of children, that accounts for the rise in the overall percentage of black children born out-of-wedlock.

Thus, contrary to the widely held view that the AFDC program was instrumental in increasing the percentage of black children born out-of-wedlock, the data suggest that the increase was due to behavioral changes occurring among individuals—i.e., black married women—who were outside the reach of AFDC altogether.[137] Although this view lacks the political appeal of either Murray's or Wilson's propositions, it seems to be the essential explanation. To reverse this trend, which has been building for several decades, will require reversing the declining marriage rate for black women—which Wilson points to—or prohibiting black women from having children outside of marriage—which is the focus of Murray's proposals.

As we saw earlier (in Chapter 4), the rise of the percentage of children born out-of-wedlock has been steady over the last several decades. To reverse this trend will require more than prohibition and punishment for having children out-of-wedlock. After all, young women have been socialized from their earliest years to want to raise and care for children. Unable to build an economically self-sufficient household has not prevented young women from having children in the past and is unlikely to do so in the future (Kunzel, 1993). Efforts to penalize and stigmatize this behavior have been in effect during the last several decades and may have dampened but certainly have not reversed the continuing increase.[138] Perhaps renewed attention to efforts designed to discourage this behavior can have some effect, but it is unlikely that increasing the penalties and stigma will sub-

---

137. It could be argued that AFDC has contributed to a decline in the percentage of teenage mothers who marry since AFDC is essentially limited to lone mothers. Perhaps if AFDC would have been equally available to two parent families, there would not have been the continuous erosion in the percentage of teenage mothers who are married (see Figure 10.1)..

138. One of the great strengths of Social Security is that it does not stigmatize beneficiaries. Before the Old Age Assistance (OAA) (or means-tested welfare for the aged poor) was replaced by the Supplemental Security Income (SSI) program, the elderly poor were viewed as responsible for their fate. It was argued that had they saved and set aside money for their retirement, they would not find themselves in their current predicament. Now the elderly poor receive Social Security benefits, whether they contributed or not, and are protected from poverty and from the sense of personal failure which comes from receiving "welfare". The only group that receives "welfare" are poor children and their parents.

stantially affect this behavior. Summarizing the research, Jencks (1993, 228) concludes, "If the goal of the "make 'em suffer" strategy is to discourage single motherhood, it must be judged a failure."

While Wilson's (1987) work is open to challenge, it nevertheless puts forth valuable suggestions for changes needed to end the rising trend of children born outside of marriage, namely the need for assuring the opportunity for gainful employment. The responsibility employment demands has a stabilizing affect on families. Women who are employed are more likely to be married and less likely to have children they cannot support. Policies and programs intended to reduce the rise of children born out-of-wedlock or to reverse these trends will need to include efforts to *increase the likelihood of employment* for both young men and women.

Function and Goals of AFDC

The logic behind welfare is to provide income support to mothers and children who are currently unable to meet their basic needs for food and shelter. In this regard welfare has been reasonably satisfactory. The public dissatisfaction derives from the number of mothers who continue to receive benefits for extended periods of time. Consequently, the focus should be to *facilitate exit*. Relying on welfare can be personally destructive to a recipient's attitudes and outlook, especially after extended periods of use. In this regard, the problem with welfare is not what it does, for what it does is to provide relief against poverty and this it does reasonably well. *The problem with welfare is that it does not provide opportunities for achieving self sufficiency in a market economy* (Clinton Administration, 1994). In short, the focus of concern with AFDC should shift to strategies that facilitate the exit of mothers from the program (Pavetti, 1993).

Difficulties in Exiting Welfare

AFDC is not intended as a permanent base of support for poor mothers. Rather it is meant to provide *temporary* assistance and income protection for women and children during a time of economic crisis. Applying a content analysis to a sample of AFDC mothers, Rein and Rainwater (1978) found that more than half the sample were women in transition, using AFDC to cushion the transition from married to lone parent life. They found that less than 10 percent of women receiving AFDC remained on the program more than ten years. The majority of women participated only for a short transitional period after separating from a spouse. In this sense, welfare represented for women what unemployment benefits represent for men in similar income disruption situations. For the majority of women in this group, emancipation from welfare was achieved through remarriage and only rarely through employment.

However, the composition of AFDC families, with respect to length of stay, has apparently changed in recent decades. Ellwood (1986) observed that beginning in the 1980s families began receiving AFDC for longer periods. Today, long-term recipients comprise about 65 percent of all current recipients. This would suggest that it is getting more difficult to leave. [139] Nevertheless, the data on welfare recipients indicate that half exit within the first year and more than 70 percent by the second year. Yet, within a year after they leave, 45 percent return. Within three years almost two-thirds are back on (Clinton Administration, 1994, 50).

Disincentives to Remarriage

The principal way lone-mothers exit AFDC is through marriage. Research has found, however, that AFDC provides strong disincentives to remarriage. Ross and Sawhill (1975, 162) report that "the remarriage rates of women on AFDC are much lower than the remarriage rates of other women in similar circumstances, including other poor women." When a lone-mother on welfare meets a potential spouse who is employed, the decision to marry will depend, in part, on the consequences to the combined family income (Becker, 1981).[140] Table 10.5 illustrates the impact on income for a lone-mother marrying an employed spouse with a minimum-wage job ($8,500 a year), and a low income job ($15,000 a year). For both minimum wage and

---

139. Recent data collected by LaDonna Pavetti (1993) suggests that due to frequent on/off cycling, 70 percent of recipients who leave welfare are back on again within five years. Thus, it appears that the cumulative time spent on AFDC seems to have been underestimated in previous studies (Ellwood, 1986). Between 1968 and 1989 the average amount of time spent on welfare per recipient was 6.2 years (Clinton Administration, 1994, 50).

140. Andrea Beller and John Graham (1993, 222) found that the child support awards, for instance, improve remarriage rates. After examining the impact child support awards on the remarriage rates of AFDC mothers, they write, "A priori, child support might raise or lower a women's chances of remarrying. Single mothers remarry for many reasons, but certainly financial considerations play some role, as economic analyses of marriage have shown."

Table 10.5 Determining the Penalty for Marriage Paid by Welfare Recipients

	Minimum Wage Job	Low Income Wage Job
Before Marriage		
Welfare (AFDC and food stamps)	$7,170	$7,170
Potential husband's earnings	8,500	15,000
Work expenses	-1,000	-1,000
Taxes on potential spouses income	-1,090	-2,570
Total income before marriage	13,580	18,600
After Marriage		
Welfare benefits lost	-4,220	-5,780
Change in taxes	1,680	2,090
Total income after marriage	11,040	14,910
Marriage penalty as a percentage of initial combined income	19%	20%

Source: U.S. National Commission on Children (1991, 91)

low income earners the welfare benefits lost through marriage are substantial, ranging between four and six thousand dollars. Under current welfare regulations, the combined family income will be reduced about 20 percent when the lone-mother marries (as opposed to no reduction from living with a partner outside of marriage). Because a twenty percent drop in income is difficult for an impoverished family to absorb, it is not surprising that so many lone-mothers are reluctant to leave welfare by way of marriage.[141] Instead of a penalty, wise public policy should instead provide an advantage in order to encourage marriage as a route to exit welfare. Further, current AFDC eligibility requirements discourage marriage. In most states only

---

141. Women have traditionally faced limited opportunities in the labor market. In 1990, more than 80 percent of women in the United States made less than $20,000 a year, compared to 40 percent of men (Innis, 1991). Education seems to make little difference: the average female high school graduate earns less than the average male high school dropout. Further, the average female college graduate earns less than a male with a high school diploma.

lone parents are eligible. No doubt this policy has contributed to the increase in unmarried teenage mothers (see Figure 10.1). It would seem far wiser to encourage marriage and to provide two-parent families with at least equal treatment. Such an approach would overtime likely reverse the trend of children born out-of-wedlock because it would remove the major barrier to marriage for low income and poor teenage mothers.

Disincentives to Employment

The other way lone mothers attempt to exit welfare is through employment. However, for many women the employment exit has proven even more difficult than marriage (Jencks, 1992, 223-225). Table 10.6 shows the impact on the income of a lone-mother who works at either a minimum-wage job ($8,500 a year), or a low-income wage job ($15,000 a year). Figuring in loss of welfare benefits, the lone-mother working full-time at a minimum wage job sees her net annual income drop to less than $3,000. This provides small incentive to work full-time at a job that probably provides minimal personal satisfaction and reduces the amount of time she can spend with her children.[142]

The message of welfare is—if you go to work you lose the benefit. This is not a message which encourages work. In the face of this high effective tax rate (no one pays higher), it is surprising that so many AFDC mothers work at all, since it makes so little economic sense. As Jencks (1993, 225) observes:

> The calculations...make it quite easy to see why so many unskilled single mothers spend so much of their adult lives on welfare. The essence of the 'welfare trap' is not that welfare warps women's personalities or makes them pathologically dependent, though that may occasionally happen. The essence of the trap is that, although welfare pays badly, low-wage jobs pay even worse. Most welfare mothers are quite willing to work if they end up with significantly more disposable income as a result. But they are not will-

---

142. The same barriers to labor force participation that lone-mothers on welfare face in the United States have been erected in Canada. Evans and McIntyre (1987) examined how much of $250 in monthly earnings lone-mothers with one child would retain by living in different provinces. The amount ranged from $50 to $60 in Quebec and the Yukon, to $250 in Saskatchewan. According to estimates from the Caledon Institute for Social Policy a Canadian who raised her income from $1,000 to $13,000 would "pocket only $2,500 after welfare and Revenue Canada took their shares" (Philp, 1994b, A8).

Table 10.6 Effective Income Tax Rate for Welfare Recipients

	Moving from Welfare to Minimum Wage Job	Moving from Welfare to Low Income Wage Job
Before Working		
Welfare (AFDC and Food Stamps)	$7,170	$7,170
After Working		
Potential earnings	8,500	15,000
Work expenses	-1,250	-1,250
Welfare benefits lost	-5,120	-7,170
Change in taxes	590	-910
Total income after working	9,890	12,840
Actual Benefit from Full-time work		
Full-time annual earnings	8,500	15,000
Annual earnings able to keep (wages less welfare benefits lost)	2,720	5,670
Effective tax rate on wages	68%	62%

Source: U.S. National Commission on Children (1991, 90)

ing to work if working will leave them as poor as they were when they stayed home.

Thus while remarrying often makes little economic sense to a lone-mother on AFDC, working full-time for minimum wage makes even less sense, when the effective net salary amounts to less than what most adolescents are paid for baby-sitting. As Besharov (1993, C3) observes, "should she be lucky enough to get the kind of job held by others of her educational attainment, she'd be working for a net wage of only about $1.50 an hour...Even with the expanded Employment Income Tax Credit, after deducting the costs of benefits and going to work, the net hourly wage would be only about $2.30 or less. If a young parent were to go to work under these circumstances, it still wouldn't be for the money." The motivating reason for those who do work is almost certainly a moral imperative to maintain self-worth.

The Problems of AFDC

AFDC is a residual income assistance program, whose eligibility requirement is to be poor and to have a child. To qualify, applicants must demonstrate they lack sufficient income to care for their children. Once they have proven this, AFDC processes them through a welfare bureaucracy that essentially stigmatizes them, labeling them as unworthy and dependent (Friedman and Friedman, 1979, 107). By itself, AFDC does little to encourage employment, since the more a recipient works, the more the benefits are reduced.

The Two Conflicting Purposes of AFDC

Providing income protection for children is a qualitatively different objective than encouraging labor-force reentry for lone-mothers. Consequently, AFDC has two principle purposes which are incongruent. On the one hand, AFDC is designed to provide income support to children living in poverty, with the intent to be as generous as is reasonable to protect their well-being. On the other hand, AFDC seeks to discourage dependency among women who might otherwise be self-supporting, and to deter other young women who may be thinking of having children they cannot support. To do this, AFDC is not only conditioned on job search requirements, but provides as little support as possible to discourage young single women from starting non-self-supporting families.

The fundamental problem with AFDC is that it combines and thus blurs these different objectives. By conditioning income protection for children on the mother's participation in the labor-force, AFDC punishes children for the economic shortcomings of their parents. Income protection should be provided to the child regardless of the parent's labor-force participation (see Chapter 9). Further, when a lone-mother either marries or finds work she should not lose benefits intended for the child. In this regard, the two objectives must be separated, a task that will, no doubt, take considerable time and effort, and require the development of programs that encourage and facilitate employment in the labor market, and provide job skills training and job development.[143]

Welfare-to-work programs are one possible solution. Unfortunately, an extensive literature on the effectiveness of government administered welfare-to-work and job development programs (Danziger, Jakubson, Schwartz, and Smolensky, 1982; Dickinson, 1986; Levitan, 1990; Morris and Williamson, 1987; Reimer, 1988) indicates only mixed success for such programs (Gideonse and Meyers, 1988). Besharov (1993, C3) observes:

> Even richly funded demonstration programs have found it exceedingly difficult to improve the ability of these mothers to care for their children, let alone become economically self-sufficient... Why don't job training programs cut welfare rolls? Although many suffer from design flaws and administrative weaknesses, the main problem is that—for poorly educated young mothers—such programs cannot break the financial mathematics of life on welfare.

In Canada where similar welfare-to-work approaches have been tried the results have also been disappointing. One study of an ambitious federal-provincial welfare-to-work program found that "training simply lifted people from social assistance onto unemployment insurance, costing the taxpayers more than if they had stayed on welfare" (Philp, 1994a, A4).

Limited evidence exists showing that it is possible to eliminate cash assistance for lone-mothers without creating severe hardship (Dear, 1989; Mason, Wodarski, and Parham, 1985; Schram, 1991). Earning income from gainful employment is always preferable to receiving "unearned" assistance from a social program. Every effort needs to be made to ensure employment opportunity and to promote habits of working. Nevertheless, with millions of individuals already unemployed and looking for work, it is not clear that adding several million low or unskilled individuals into the pool of job seekers is practical, which suggests it may be unrealistic to hope that AFDC can be eliminated altogether through welfare-to-work programs in the short term and without fundamental changes in the labor market. Strategies designed to create jobs for the long-term unemployed also face difficult cost

---

143. The issue of encouraging labor force participation requires comprehensive treatment in its own right. It relates directly to creating opportunities for young people through such approaches as job training, apprenticeship programs, and job corps. It includes an examination of labor market conditions, the demand for the labor market services lone-mothers might provide, and the impact of such policies on current unemployment levels.

questions. According to Congressional Budget Office estimates, the cost of creating even community service jobs would be greater than the cost of simply providing cash assistance through AFDC (Besharov, 1993, C3). Even though welfare-to-work approaches may cost more in the short term, they have the benefit of encouraging habits and a self-concept that will serve participants in the long run—and are cost effective in this broader view.

Separating Child Welfare from Public Welfare

No social program has more affect on children than AFDC which provides direct income support to more than nine million of the poorest children in the United States. Yet, the child welfare field has too often sought to distance itself from AFDC (Steiner, 1976) preferring, instead, to promote residual approaches—such as intensive casework services (family preservation)—that are staffed and administered by child welfare social workers[144] even in the absence of evidence that these approaches have any meaningful impact on the lives of children (Rossi, 1992a,b; Yuan et al., 1980).

Disillusionment with welfare has separated concern with income support programs for children, such as AFDC, from the mainstream issues of public child welfare.[145] This separation has been greeted favorably by child welfare professionals because it has disassociated the child welfare system,

---

144. During recent debates over funding for intensive casework services (called family preservation services a frustrated Senator Moynihan made the wry observation that, in the absence of demonstrated effectiveness of this approach, its net effect seems primarily to be the provision of jobs for social workers. This is one of the great attractions of the residual approach—it provides caseworkers greater opportunities to provide professional services. Yet history and the scientific method fails to provide testimony to the effectiveness of these efforts (see Chapter 2). Moynihan's skeptical view of the success of social programs to achieve personal reformation may seem similar to that expressed by Murray. Yet there is a fundamental difference. Moynihan (1990) believes social programs and policies can make a difference for the poor. For example, Social Security has made a significant difference in poverty among the elderly—it dramatically reduced it. Likewise, social programs and policies in the eighties significantly reduced the tax liabilities of the wealthy and led to substantial income gains for this group. As suggested in Chapter 9, social programs and policies that achieve equity and efficiency and are matched to the inherent nature of the free market could significantly reduce poverty among children. In Chapter 11 I propose an approach for children that is similar to that taken by Social Security for the elderly. The program doesn't seek to reform or rehabilitate but to provide an "engine of opportunity" that requires individual initiative and responsibility. The tension identified here revolves around the role of residual services. There will undoubtedly always be a need for residual services (such as AFDC and casework). The need, however, is minimized by social and economic policies that ensure fairness and economic opportunity to all members of society.

which has always enjoyed broad public support, from the welfare system in general, which has enjoyed limited public support and is often the target of public anger (Steiner, 1976, 147). However, in separating itself from the issue of income support, child welfare may well have sawn off the limb it sits on, since the welfare of children cannot be ensured without programs that provide sufficient income to protect their well-being. Since AFDC is the primary program of income support for children, it has done more to alleviate the suffering among poor children than any other child welfare program (Beeghley, 1983; Steiner, 1976).

According to the Children's Defense Fund, the cost of lifting every child in the United States to the poverty line would be about $28 billion a year (Johnson, Miranda, Sherman, and Weill, 1991, 3), or less than one-half of 1 percent of the Gross National Product (GNP). In Canada, the cost of lifting every child out of poverty in 1986 would have been approximately $3.5 billion. If the cost of ending poverty for children is so affordable, why isn't the money forthcoming? One reason is that it is not that easy to distribute money. Any program designed to end poverty by transferring income to those who have not earned it must consider the impact of that transfer on those who are employed and not receiving any of the transfer themselves. North Americans share deeply held values regarding work and responsibility (Weber, 1958). Providing income to those who have not 'earned' it through employment is counter to powerful public sentiment (Lewis and Schneider, 1985). As Hacker (1992, 91) has written: "While people often mention money, the concern over welfare is not mainly financial. Most Americans find the presence of a supported class unseemly; it runs counter to the way we are supposed to organize our lives."

Finding solutions designed to end child poverty while promoting the responsibility that comes with employment will thus be a complex task. Policies will need to take into account Americans' distaste for welfare (Golding and Middleton, 1982; Handler and Hasenfeld, 1991).[146] If provid-

---

145. As we have seen, income protection programs originally had a central place in the child welfare field. In the early editions of his child welfare textbook, Kadushin (1967) devoted substantial attention to this issue. Concern with the AFDC became a political liability which, when the opportunity arose, the child welfare system quickly jettisoned (Steiner, 1976).

146. It has been suggested that one of the major problems for lone mothers is that they are not working enough (Mead, 1986). As Mead and others (see Kamerman & Kahn, 1987) point out, married mothers are active in the labor market, therefore single mothers should also be expected to work. Yet, most married mothers work part time. Further, single mothers carry full responsibility for child care.

ing increased income transfer payments was the sole issue in solving child poverty, the problem would have been solved long ago.

Some have suggested that a major reason for the hostility toward AFDC in the United States is racism. In Britain only a small percentage of lone-parents are black, whereas in the United States, more than half the lone-parents receiving public assistance are black or Hispanic. In Britain, there has been no similar history of public consternation regarding the problem of "welfare dependency" (Evans, 1992). Debates about the declining condition of the poor have rarely focused on strategies to make mothers work, especially those with young children (Zill, Moore, and Steif, 1989). Rather, the focus has been on developing strategies to encourage and develop employment opportunities for unemployed young men. If lone-mothers in the United States were viewed without reference to race, there might be less resistance to efforts to assist them and their children.

Yet, again, it is probably not racism which leads to disdain for welfare. In the beginning of *Poor Support*, David Ellwood (1988) recounts his dismay on learning of the widespread antipathy for welfare. His research with Mary Jo Bane had indicated that welfare had done much to protect poor children and their families with only modest unintended negative effects. When he reported these findings, however, Ellwood (1988, ix-x) met with consternation and rebuke: "People hated welfare no matter what the evidence. It wasn't just conservatives; liberals also expressed deep mistrust of the system, and the recipients themselves despised it...Yet it was obvious that the vast majority of people I spoke with also believed that society ought to help the poor."

AFDC contrasts sharply with the universal child support and guaranteed child exemption proposals outlined in Chapter 9 which provide income protection to children without regard to the mother's labor force participation. These proposals would reduce the disincentive to work by providing resources not contingent on poverty, and which would not be withdrawn when the mother works. As universal entitlements, they would not force lone-mothers to surrender their benefits at a rate of more than 60 cents for each dollar earned as they must now do when they move from AFDC to work (Table 10.6). These programs would fundamentally alter the mathematics of welfare dependency. With the benefits for their children guaranteed, mothers who now find themselves trapped in a residual welfare system would be able to earn enough to free themselves from AFDC eligibility. In the process they would be able to integrate their families into mainstream society. They would gain self-esteem and self-confidence, while their children would gain increased pride and hope. Further, the programs would permit greater flexibility for experimentation with welfare-to-work programs without putting children at undue risk (American Public Welfare Association, 1994).

Discussion

It is clear that AFDC, as currently structured and funded, has been unable to break the cycle of poverty among children (Duncan and Rodgers, 1991). Despite decades of tinkering, adjusting, and experimenting, poverty persists among children and seems even to have gotten worse. Current efforts to address the problem of young, unmarried women beginning families that are not self-supporting have followed the residual approach. That is, the programs have waited until lone-mothers have started families which they cannot support before invoking strategies that, to a great extent, provide meager support in a situation the public wished they had avoided.

Despite periodic efforts at reform, the number of families receiving public assistance remains high and continues to increase. Why? For one thing, limited market demand exists for the skills and services lone-mothers have to offer. In Canada more than 58 percent of those on welfare are without a high school diploma (Philp, 1994b). For another, the child care needs of lone-mothers, especially those with young children, have gone unmet by public social policy and continue to present a major barrier to employment.[147] The extension of child care to mothers of children under six is pivotal to the success of any effort to end the exclusion of women with young children from the labor market (and thus reliance on welfare), especially lone mothers.[148]

AFDC is a residual approach and, as such, cannot produce a substantial reduction in child poverty. This is because AFDC is designed only to allevi-

147. A study of AFDC recipients in Oregon (1994) indicated that more than 40 percent have children two or less, while more than 60 percent have children five or less. Nationwide almost half of all children on AFDC were under six years of age and thus requiring child care. One-fourth of all children were under three (Clinton Administration, 1994, 50).

148. As discussed in Chapter 4, the labor intensive demands of child care required by an infant present an enormous burden on the young mother trying to enter the labor market. In the absence of publicly funded child care it is unrealistic to expect most young mothers to be able find work that covers the costs of child care, work related requirements (i.e., transportation, clothes, etc.), and lost welfare benefits.

Figure 10.8 Impact of Income Security Programs on the Reduction of Poverty (1989)

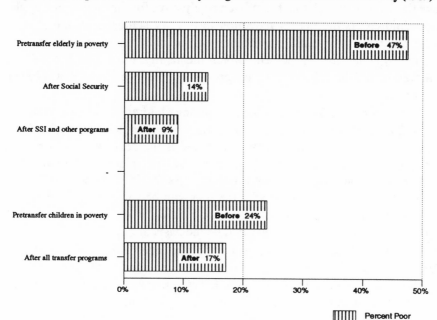

Source: Moynihan (1990).

ate a crisis, not prevent it. In this respect, social policies and programs that wait until the young person is in crisis intervenes too late. Once a young woman begins a family that she is unable to support, efforts within a residual framework designed to make her self-supporting become very difficult. She has the responsibility to raise, provide, and care for the child for the next eighteen years, and society is obliged to help her. Further, it is not at all clear that forcing her to leave her children to pursue wage earning work when the child is very young ought to be the goal. Social policies and programs that wait until the young person is in crisis come too late.

The answer lies outside the residual approach. Again, the solution is not radical, but one that has been successfully applied to other groups that at an earlier time were impoverished, such as the elderly. In 1989 federal programs for the elderly reduced their rate of poverty by more than 81 percent, while programs for children reduced their rate of poverty by less than 29 percent (see Figure 10.8). This rate of child poverty reduction is the lowest in the industrial world—with rates in Britain, France, Netherlands, Sweden and Germany ranging from 67 to 80 percent (Smeeding, 1991). Why not take the same approach that has proven so effective for the elderly and apply it to children? If the rate of reduction in poverty achieved for the elderly were duplicated for children, the number of children in poverty would decline by more than 75 percent, which means that more than ten million children would be lifted out of poverty. AFDC as we know it would no longer exist.

The failure of AFDC to end poverty among children is a classic example of the failure of the residual approach, which requires that nothing be done until a crisis occurs. Rather, what is required is the development of strategies to prevent crises from occurring in the first place, and to do this requires a broader vision of what is possible. As David Ellwood (1988, 243) writes, "Our system of support for the poor can be something more than a holding ground for people who are not making it on their own. It can address the real causes of poverty and be the basis of hope."

＊ Young people strive to make the most of the choices they have available. When those choices are limited by years of poverty and deprivation and the resulting lack of adequate preparation for effective participation in the post industrial labor market, then AFDC may represent the last and best hope. When labor market constraints effectively exclude young people from productive roles in society, they will necessarily become more dependent on welfare. Most of these young people want productive roles in society. The answer to this problem is found by examining solutions to these labor market constraints and in finding ways to prepare disadvantaged young people for productive roles in our postindustrial economy.

Enabling Lone Parents

> While the welfare state is organized around the goal of income maintenance, the enabling state should be organized around the goals of work and individual empowerment. Above all, it should help poor Americans develop the capacities they need to liberate themselves from poverty and dependence. And it should do so directly, bypassing whenever possible public bureaucracies and service providers, and placing responsibility and resources directly into the hands of the people we are trying to help. An enabling strategy should see the poor as the prime agents of their own development, rather than as passive clients of the welfare system.
>
> Will Marshall and Elaine Ciulla Kamarck, *Replacing Welfare with Work*

In its efforts to promote self-sufficiency, the child and public welfare systems need to take into account the inherent nature and essence of the free enterprise economic system. The strengths of the free market system need to be interwoven into the fabric of social policies and programs. In a market economy it is useful to remember, as Blinder (1982, 30) urges, "the wondrous efficiency of the marketplace, and how foolish it is to squander this efficiency without good reason." The keys to unlock the puzzle of persistent and debilitating child poverty are straightforward. Individuals need to be provided with real opportunity. When individuals are unable to find work in the current labor market a social safety net needs to be in place to ensure their basic needs are met until they are able to find work. The safety net should not become a trap net. Exits must be provided through retraining, job development, and apprenticeship opportunities. Work effort needs to be decisively rewarded—which means that the effective tax rate on working should not be prohibitive. The role of government should be on the side of retraining and investment in job development with as little intrusion into the operation of the free market as possible.

Conclusion

The birth control pill was developed and widely adapted in the early sixties. Between 1965 and 1975 there was a sharp rise in divorces and in the number of children involved in divorce. This led to a rapid increase in the number of children on AFDC. Since 1975 the number of divorces and children on AFDC has remained about the same. What has increased is the proportion of children born to unmarried mothers. This increased proportion is caused by two interrelated factors—(1) the declining proportion of teenage parents who marry and (2) the sharp decline in marriage rates among black women.

During the last several decades child poverty has remained stable and has gradually increased. This is disturbing because poverty could have been eliminated. Poverty among the elderly has essentially been eliminated. Yet, among those who are just beginning their life virtually nothing has been done to eliminate poverty.

If our interest is to end poverty we would be wise to study how poverty was eliminated among the elderly and to follow that example for children. In the next chapter that is what we do.

The answer to child poverty will not fully derive from new social programs that intrude into the lives of individuals in need. In this respect, conservative theorists are right when they argue that government cannot solve individual problems. Government programs and policies are best when they focus on building and maintaining an infrastructure that taps and unleashes individual effort. Government must ensure the foundation and then wisely step to the side and encourage creative and responsible individual effort.[149] Young people themselves will need to engineer and orchestrate change. In this regard the most successful programs will invest in the responsibility and decision-making of the individuals themselves, placing resources directly under their control and management (Gilbert and Gilbert, 1989).

As I argue in the next chapter, the cycle of poverty and the problem of the welfare trap derives, in large part, from the absence of opportunities for impoverished children during their transition from childhood to adulthood. Instead of continuing with strategies that attempt to castigate young unmarried women with children, it would be more productive to ask how we might encourage young people to pursue other opportunities before having children and ensure that they have the resources to do so.

In the next chapter, I examine a means by which children growing up in poverty can be guaranteed, during their crucial transition period from childhood to adulthood, the opportunity to achieve a productive, responsible, and self-reliant adult career, thus effectively ending the dual problems of "welfare dependency" and child poverty.

---

149. Effective social programs that ensure opportunity in a market economy place responsibility squarely with the individual. Such programs also make sure the individual has the resources required to succeed in a competitive economy. When social programs understand and abide by the central tenets of the free enterprise system they contribute to economic growth.

Clearly, providing sufficient resources to ensure an opportunity to succeed will not guarantee that all young people will succeed. No doubt, many young people will fail to capitalize on the opportunities afforded them. Yet, such programs will have started young people out on the right track, and this may be the most important objective. For, as child development research demonstrates, as the twig bends so goes the tree and it is much easier to bend a twig than a tree.

11

Developing a Child's Future
Security Account Program

Freedom is not enough. You do not wipe away the scars of centuries by saying: Now you are free to go where you want, do as you desire, choose the
leaders you please.

You do not take a person who for years has been hobbled by chains and
liberate him, bring him up to the starting line of a race and then say, "You
are free to compete with all the others," and still justly believe that you have
been completely fair.

Thus it is not enough just to open the gates of opportunity. All our citizens must have the ability to walk through the gates.

Former President Lyndon B. Johnson

In 1991 the National Commission on Children in the United States, a blue
ribbon panel of distinguished experts and leaders, issued a report proposing
major new funding for a child tax credit, costing more than $40 billion a
year. The report also proposed several other programs, such as full funding
of Head Start and child health proposals that would have totalled some-
where between $52 and $56 billion dollars a year. In a time of massive federal deficits, the proposals were treated as essentially "dead on arrival" by
Bush administration domestic policy advisors. The report caught public and
press attention for about a week and then vanished from the scene.

Essentially, the proposals were viewed as more money to be used in
more or less conventional ways. Yet even with their enormous price tag, the
proposals would have produced only marginal changes.[150] They failed to
inspire sufficient confidence that they would lead to substantial progress
against child poverty.

Without confronting the underlying values and norms of our society that
marginalize children, and especially African American children, no reform

---

150. Likewise, Alvin Schorr (1987) proposed a refundable tax credit that would have spread
benefits among so many that its individual net affects on children would have been limited.
The cost of the program was estimated to be more than fifty billion dollars annually.

can hope to resolve the crisis of child poverty. Certainly, awareness of the problem has increased over the last several decades, but much of that has been in response to pressure from nonpartisan children's advocacy groups, such as the Children's Defense Fund.

Although the child support collection and child income assistance reforms proposed in Chapter 9 are important recommendations that would reduce poverty and result in immediate and substantial tax savings, they will not get at the root causes of child poverty. If there is indeed a long-term structural problem that causes child poverty, we need a new bold approach that implements fundamental reform—a Marshall Plan directed at child poverty.

The Origins of the Problem

At the very earliest years, perhaps less than one, children know whether or not they have hope and opportunity. This knowledge and understanding shapes their development and outlook (Seigal, 1985). When children begin school they usually start, as Jonathan Kozol (1991, 57) observes, "with a degree of faith and optimism, and they often seem to thrive during the first few years. It is sometimes not until the third grade that their teachers start to see the warning signs of failure. By the fourth grade many children see it too...By fifth or sixth grade, many children demonstrate their loss of faith by staying out of school." Policies and programs are required that will stem this process of disillusionment and let every child know that they, indeed, have opportunity in life.

To be effective, any program must continue from childhood through later adolescence, which, too often, is considered beyond the focus of child welfare. Programs to provide opportunity during the child's transition to adult life, their emancipation from the family and embarkation into adult responsibilities, are essential ingredients for any comprehensive child welfare reform. Unless imaginative programmatic efforts to break the cycle of poverty are undertaken that will provide children the escape velocity to break out of patterns established over years, even generations, we have no chance of ending poverty among children.

So what can be done? As we have seen, society does not want to encourage the formation of non-self-supporting households, since once these have been created little can be done to eliminate them. Current social programs provide few positive incentives that discourage early child bearing. Instead, public assistance programs approach the problem using disincentives; that is, offering only the most meagre of income supports to lone-mothers and their children. In recent years, in the face of increased budget deficits, public assistance programs have become even more meagre. The logic is that the less attractive life on AFDC appears, the greater the likelihood that young women will avoid it.

However, efforts to provide income protection for children confront this essential dilemma: how to target money that will effectively shield children from poverty and abuse without encouraging their lone-mothers, who will receive the money, to have more children? Murray (1984, 203-204) poses this question:

> In deciding upon my stance in support or opposition of a policy that automatically provides an adequate living allowance for all single women with children, I am informed that one consequence of this policy is that large numbers of the children get better nutrition and medical care than they would otherwise obtain. Using this known fact and no others, I support the program. Now let us assume two more known facts, that the program induces births by women who otherwise would have had fewer children (or had them under different circumstances), and that child abuse and neglect among these children runs at twice the national average. Does this alter my judgment about whether the allowance is a net good?° What if the incidence of abuse and neglect is three times as high? Five times? Ten times? A hundred times? The crossover point will be different for different people. But a crossover point will occur. At some point, I will say that the benefits of better nutrition and medical care are outweighed by the suffering of abused and neglected children° The first conclusion is that transfers are inherently treacherous. They can be useful; they can be needed; they can be justified. But we should approach them as a good physician uses a dangerous drug— not at all if possible, and no more than absolutely necessary otherwise."

The current meager public assistance benefits attempt to balance the need to provide minimal income protection for children with the need to discourage further childbearing by lone-mothers. Unfortunately, the balance usually neither provides adequate income protection for the children nor discourages disillusioned and alienated young women from having children they cannot adequately provide for.

A way out does exist. To understand what it is, we must appreciate what resources and choices young people require in making the critical and difficult transition from childhood to adulthood

Preparing Young People for the Transition to Self-Supporting Adult Life

Before they are even born, children require proper health care. This need is recognized in the provision of prenatal care and counseling offered pregnant women. After children are born, adequate nutrition, health care (including immunizations), and nurturing by the mother are essential (Siegal, 1985). In the second year of life the list of the child's needs expands to include such services as day care and Head Start, which not only enable the parent to return to the work force, but provide essential mental and physical stimulation for the child's proper growth and development (Kamerman and Kahn, 1988b; Tobin, Wu, and Davidson, 1989).

When they reach school age, children require quality educational opportunities, not only for their own sake, but for society's as well. Free public education is provided in most parts of the world and often begins at three years of age.[151] In the United States this education is provided at a cost of approximately $5,000 a year for every child, from age six to eighteen (Lindsey, 1991c).[152] Public education is regarded as an essential investment that prepares the child for responsible, self-reliant, and productive participation in our free, market-based society.[153]

High school begins the young person's transition to adult life. At this stage adolescents undergo major psychological and physiological growth and change. They develop a sense of personal identity (Erikson, 1959), and begin to consider the career options and opportunities open to them when they leave home: college, vocational training, job apprenticeships. For a few, adolescence is a time of experimentation with deviant behavior (Matza, 1964), as witnessed by the high rates of delinquency during this age.

When young people graduate from high school they begin the most important and difficult transition in their lives. They embark on their adult career, which, ideally, should be characterized by independence and self-sufficiency. If they have prepared for this transition, they will likely become

---

151. While most European countries provide publicly funded child care for 3- to 5- year old children, the United States provides the least (Kamerman and Kahn, 1988).

152. Kozol (1991) points out that great inequalities in education begin at entry into school. Some wealthy school districts spend more than $15,000 per student, while other poor districts spend less than $4,000 per student.

153. Although a lone-parent on AFDC with three children will likely receive less than $5,000 a year in welfare assistance to provide for shelter, clothing, electricity, phone, heating, transportation and other living expenses, the public school system will likely spend more than $15,000 a year for educating her three children.

productive and contributing adults. If not, they will be vulnerable to dependency and failure in a society that demands independence and self-reliance. In a free market economy, the passage from adolescence to adulthood requires more than years of physical, intellectual, and emotional development. It requires that young people have the financial resources that will permit emancipation from nearly two decades of dependence on their family, that will enable them to sever ties with home and family and to embark successfully on an independent life.

Currently, only children from upper middle class and wealthy families have such resources. For children from poor and low income families, the resources, and hence opportunities, are too often absent. In many ways, the social and economic situation that poor youth face at this stage in their lives can be compared to a Monopoly board game. In Monopoly all players begin the game having $1500, which, according to the game's logic, ensures that everyone has an equal opportunity of winning. One can imagine the effect if the rules allowed only selected players to start with any money, while others started with nothing. Those players who must roll the dice and move their token, knowing that they had no money to buy property or even pay rent, would soon regard the game as not much fun and begin "dropping out."

So it is with the "real life" economic game in which young people in a market economy find themselves. Too many children, realizing as they grow up that they will not have the resources and opportunities to move into productive adulthood, turn to early child bearing and public assistance, or worse, to drugs and crime. The Children's Defense Fund (1986) examined this issue with data from the *National Longitudinal Survey of Young Americans*. They compared teenagers from poor families who lacked basic academic skills with those from affluent families and more skilled peers. They found that the poor teenagers were nearly six times more likely to become pregnant. With little confidence in their future, teenagers living in poverty lacked the incentives to delay parenthood.

The alienation of youth, especially low income minority youth, is one of the most destructive consequences of the existing inequality, and the society that is unwilling to pay for initial "equal" opportunity soon finds itself having to pay substantially more for child protective services, foster care, public assistance, drug rehabilitation programs, and overcrowded prisons.

Social Security for the Elderly: A Proven Model

The same "social savings" model that has proven so successful in providing for the economic needs of the elderly in the United States could provide the answer to breaking the cycle of poverty for children.

Social Security requires everyone to plan for their retirement by contributing to a "social savings" program during their working years which then provides benefits for them when they retire. Before Social Security the elderly were responsible for setting aside sufficient resources for their retirement. However, because too many individuals failed to do this, substantial poverty existed among the elderly. Although some theorists have viewed Social Security as an unwanted intrusion by government into the affairs of the individual and have urged that it be voluntary (Feldstein, 1974), the success of the program in insuring income protection to the elderly has led to its continued widespread support.

Social Security is a "social" insurance program, as opposed to an insurance program, which means that it serves a collective social purpose. Contributions to Social Security do not go into a special trust fund earmarked for the individual who has made the contribution. Instead, they go into a general fund from which they are distributed to current beneficiaries. The program operates on a pay-as-you-go basis, with retired beneficiaries being paid from contributions collected from the current working generation. Thus, benefits are only marginally related to contributions, and many current beneficiaries receive payments well in excess of what similar contributions to a private system would have entitled them to.[154] Economist Joseph Pechman (1989, 171) points out that Social Security beneficiaries in the United States "as a group receive far larger benefits than those to which the taxes they paid, or that were paid on their behalf, would entitle them." He argues that instead of viewing Social Security as an "insurance" program for old age, it is better to understand it as an "institutionalized compact between the working and non-working generations" (p. 175).

---

154. It has been estimated that the average Social Security recipient receives a benefit worth more than twice what would be expected based on contributions the retiree paid. Schorr (1987, 58) observes, "the average low-paid man retiring in 1982 received a benefit of $371 a month, of which his contributions paid for $105; thus he received a subsidy of $266. An average highly paid man received monthly benefits of $705, of which his contributions had paid for $284; thus he received a subsidy of $421." To correct the popular misconception that Social Security payments represent a fully paid for premium, U.S. Representative Cooper has suggested that Social Security checks be printed in red ink after the recipient has collected all the money he or she paid into the system and the interest it accrued (Broder, 1991).

Social Security thus represents a "social savings" approach to providing income protection for the elderly. There are no efforts to try to make Social Security unattractive or to discourage participation. Quite the contrary, Social Security stipulates universal coverage, providing benefits for all irrespective of their income.

In the United States in 1973, Old Age Assistance (OAA), the last major remaining residual social program for the elderly, was replaced with a social savings program called Supplemental Security Income (SSI), and became a part of the Social Security program. OAA's replacement with SSI signalled the end of the residual approach to social services for the elderly at the federal level. All of the major federal programs for the elderly became *universal* and insured coverage for all regardless of income or "paid in" contributions to Social Security. Today, elderly who are unable to provide for themselves and who would not otherwise be eligible for Social Security are still provided with Social Security payments.[155]

As a social savings program, Social Security provides a guaranteed minimum income for all beneficiaries, while also providing differential benefits related to the contributions the individual has made. Most importantly, Social Security does not have the stigma of a "public assistance" program, but retains the dignity of an "earned pension." Advocates and partisans who fight on behalf of the elderly for improved Social Security benefits are not viewed as asking for charity, only demanding what their constituency has earned. Over the years no other social program has achieved more wide spread public support (Marmor, Mashaw, and Harvey, 1990). Social Security enjoys wide support because it is viewed not as a public assistance program but as an insurance program paid for by the beneficiaries (Aaron, 1982).[156] As Mead (1986) argues, Social Security is popular because it is tied to "work effort."

The situation is in contrast to that of lone-mothers and their children receiving public assistance, who are viewed as people asking for a hand out. Of course, the desire to lend a helping hand, especially to children, is what gives impetus to public assistance programs. As Murray (1984, 235-236) observes, "Most of us want to help. It makes us feel bad to think of neglected children and rat-infested slums, and we are happy to pay for the

---

155. SSI provides a guaranteed minimum income for the elderly and included provisions for the severely disabled for whom it was believed the expectation of work was not reasonable.

156. See Ozawa (1977) for further discussion of the regressive tax component elements of the Social Security program.

thought that people who are good at taking care of such things are out there. If the numbers of neglected children and number of rats seem to be going up instead of down, it is understandable that we choose to focus on how much we put into the effort instead of what comes out. The tax checks we write buy us, for relatively little money and no effort at all, a quieted conscience. The more we pay, the more certain we can be that we have done our part, and it is essential that we feel that way regardless of what we accomplish."

AFDC is funded from general tax revenues and therefore vastly different from Social Security. The lone-mothers and children who benefit from AFDC have made no contributions that might warrant a payment to them. Thus, they are viewed as a "burden" on the back of the already overburdened tax payer. As we have seen, the answer in North America has been to make public assistance so unattractive that those receiving it will want to stop (Jencks, 1993). The paradoxical result, however, has been the development of a public assistance trap with a grip so tight that once people get in, they are rarely able to muster the resources, energy, or will to get out.

The primary victims of this approach are not working age men or lone-mothers, but the children, who grow up in circumstances devoid of hope or opportunity. The result has been a social calamity, whose proportions we are only beginning to appreciate. Although its physical form can be seen in the blighted neighborhoods of most major cities, its impact on the hopes and dreams of the poor, especially poor children, is not so visible. Investing the minimal amount in the development of poor children is unwise in the extreme, since they represent one of society's most valuable human resources (Denison, 1985). The farmer knows the lesson well—you reap what you sow. If you take care of the soil, rotate the crops, provide fertilizers and proper irrigation, the land will provide bountiful crops. But follow a "parched soil" approach—neglect the land, provide minimal irrigation, restrict soil nutrients—and the harvest will be little more than weeds.

The same has been true with respect to young children living in poverty. If we approach poverty among children with the intent of providing only minimal opportunities for their future, can we really blame them for the paths they take? What paths have been open to them? What can such an approach hope to achieve, other than the satisfaction that we have properly "punished" those who are not able or willing to provide for themselves? The approach has not ended poverty in North America nor in any other part of the world. Rather, it has only locked into place those who have fallen into it. A way out must be found.

A Bold Approach: Developing a "Social Savings" Account for Children

An approach like Social Security could also prove successful in protecting children. Just as Social Security requires citizens to prepare for their retirement years by setting up a social savings account, a similar "child's future security" account might be created that would provide a savings account for young persons in order to insure they have the funds necessary to embark successfully on adult life at the age of 18, regardless of the economic situation they are born into. It would provide poor children an opportunity to break free of the cycle of poverty into which they were born.

How It Might Work

Just as Social Security ensures that individuals have money for their retirement through a mandatory "social savings" scheme, the Child's Future Security (CFS) account would ensure that children would have money set aside for their college education (or transition to adulthood). At birth, every child, regardless of the current economic status of their family, would have a custodial account—a "Child's Future Security" account—opened in their name with an initial deposit by the government of $1,000 at a bank or registered brokerage firm selected by the parent. Each year the account would receive an additional $500 deposited by the government from funds collected in the same fashion used by Social Security.

The children's parents could, if they wished, contribute privately to the account, as could the child through his or her earnings, although such contributions would not diminish the government contribution. At age eighteen, the accumulated funds would be made available to the young person for approved career program expenditures, such as college tuition, vocational training, job-readiness programs, and so on.[157] By the time the child reached eighteen, a typical CFS deposit could have an accumulated balance of almost $40,000 (see Figure 11.1).

---

157. The purpose of the Child's Future Security account is to provide young people with the resources needed for effective transition to adulthood. The funds are not for consumer needs and would not be made available for consumer item, but only for purposes that represent an investment in the young person's future.

Figure 11.1 Projected Growth of a Child's Future Security Account

Amount in Account

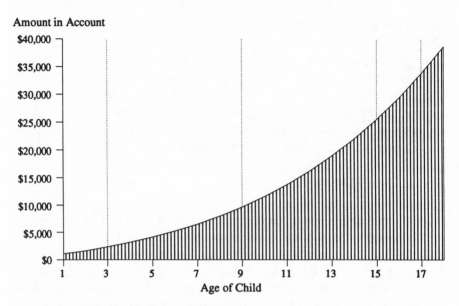

Note: Assumes an annual growth rate of 8 percent.

Costs

Given roughly 4 million births a year in the United States, new CFS accounts would cost an estimated $4 billion annually. Maintaining the annual contribution to the accounts for the other roughly 60 million children under the age of eighteen, would add another $30 billion, for a total annual cost of roughly $34 billion. Following a start-up expense, the program would be funded entirely by children repaying their benefits during adulthood, using a collection mechanism similar to that used by the Social Security Administration, in which a payroll contribution of less than one half of 1 percent would be made by employee and employer.

Parents' Contribution

The cost could be reduced considerably by requiring parents to contribute to the cost of their child's CFS through a graduated tax schedule. For instance, parents with incomes above $30,000 might be asked to contribute at the rate of one percent of all taxable income above $30,000 (with appropriate

Table 11.1 Projected Tax Schedule

Family Income	Tax Payment
$30,000	0
35,000	50
40,000	100
45,000	175
50,000	250
55,000	350
60,000	450
65,000	575
70,000	700
75,000	850
80,000	1,000

adjustments for family composition). The rate of contribution could be increased by one half percent for each additional $10,000 of income (see Table 11.1).

An approach which shared the cost of the Child's Future Security account with parents would fund more than half the total cost of the program. Thus, the remaining cost of the program that would need to be funded through a payroll tax would be less than $15 billion (or less than one half of one percent from both employer and employee).

In Canada, a scheme resembling this already exists. Parents can save money in a tax exempt "Registered Educational Savings Plan" (RESP), which allows parents to contribute up to $1,500 a year fully tax deductible into a custodial account opened in the child's name with a registered security dealer. Funds in the account can be invested in stocks, bonds, mutual funds and money market instruments. Canada's largest bank advises parents that if they contribute the allowable $1,500 a year for 21 years the funds in the account will likely grow to "more than $83,000—more than enough to ensure that your child or grandchild will be able to continue their education." Even though the net cost of the annual contribution is less than $900 for the average family, only a small number of Canadian families have taken advantage of this government subsidized savings plan. Although the law governing the RESP does not exclude poor children, the program is essentially limited to upper class families who have the money to set aside. Thus, those most likely to take advantage of this plan are those least likely to need it, with children from poor families virtually excluded from ever benefiting. For the RESP program to be equitable would require that its provision be guaranteed to all. In essence, this is what the Child's Future Security account achieves.

Because recipients of CFS would repay their benefits through payments made during their working adulthood, the Child's Future Security program represents an approach that, like Social Security, reinforces the broad social reciprocal contract between the generations. Further, the children would likely go on to pay substantially more taxes as productive citizens, and be less likely to incur social costs (i.e., welfare assistance or correctional system costs).[158]

Wealth Builder Approach

Financial well-being has two dimensions—income and wealth—one short term and the other long-term. Income assistance payments that address the short-term income dimension by providing families with money for immediate basic needs such as shelter, food, and clothing, do little to foster long-term accumulation of assets or wealth (Sherraden, 1990). The CFS account is essentially a long term wealth builder, something frequently overlooked by programs that attempt to ameliorate poverty. The account would be managed separately from current income security programs like Social Security or AFDC, with rules developed and administered by a governing board to oversee the program's operation.[159] Ideally, CFS funds would be held in

---

158. The best assurance of a sound Social Security system is a productive work force. Since Social Security is a contract between generations, the approach proposed here would strengthen the overall Social Security program by assuring that the generation coming of age would be able to meet its obligation to the generation retiring. Commenting on the high rate of poverty among Canadian children, Eichler (1988, 49) observes, "The future consequences of neglecting to provide for our young could possibly disrupt the entire society. After all, it is the younger ones who have to produce the goods from which pensions are paid."

159. The needs of children and the elderly are substantially different. Consequently, these programs should be kept separate. The approach proposed here is simply to model current child welfare income security programs along the lines of the successful Social Security program.

custodial accounts at private brokerage firms where they could be invested in stocks, bonds, or mutual funds, in much the same way that retirement funds are invested in Individual Retirement Accounts (IRAs) in the United States or Registered Retirement Savings Plans (RRSPs) in Canada. Parents might select among approved mutual funds in which to invest their child's account balances. The child would be encouraged to participate in the investment decision-making process, perhaps receiving semi-annual statements of their account balance that would reinforce the lessons of saving and investing.[160] By working with their own funds, children would be learning lessons and habits which could serve them in our society throughout their lives. In a sense, the CFS account is conceived more as a "capital building" account than a "savings account" with a view that child thus learn more about investing.

Ideally, responsibility for overseeing the program would be assigned to the child welfare system, where child welfare social workers would provide advice to the parent and child in making investment choices and developing a plan for productive and approved uses of funds in the child's account.

In this manner, the child would establish a meaningful base for accumulating asset wealth and ownership in our economy. The United States and Canada are free enterprise market economies in which virtually all business and industry are privately owned, with small public sector involvement. To participate meaningfully in the nation's wealth individuals must come to know and understand early in their lives the procedures and instruments used to allocate and manipulate ownership and wealth. Today, most young people know very little about stock ownership, what it is, how it works, and the good of it.[161] This is comparable to an island child growing up in Micronesia not knowing how to fish, or a child raised on a ranch in Argentina knowing nothing of cattle. Although many young people in our society may have a passing acquaintance with the language of business and invest-

---

160. The low savings rate in North America has been of particular concern because these savings fund growth and investment. As Thurow (1992, 160) points out, "Of twenty-one industrial countries, no country had a savings rate lower than that of the United States in the late 1980s."

161. Home ownership has been the other major avenue to obtaining a share of the enormous amount of privately held wealth. In the United States the provision of mortgage interest payment deduction from federal income tax has served as a subsidy for home ownership. In 1984, the Federal Reserve reported that the average net worth of a typical family was primarily determined by home ownership. The average net worth of a family that rents was less than $100, whereas the net worth of homeowners was more than $50,000 (Avery et al., 1984a,b).

ment, and may even participate in a stock purchase simulation in school, most never learn the importance of stock ownership in obtaining a share of the productive assets of the nation.

The CFS account would give young people a reason to learn about stocks, bonds and investing because they would have funds to invest. If young people developed better skills and knowledge about investing and saving, the long term collective benefit of their knowledge would be a nation better able to save, invest, and compete in the global marketplace. Because children would "have a stake" in their society, they would learn the importance of saving and investing, and how the free enterprise system in which they live works.[162] It is extremely important that children living in a free market economy not grow up alienated by ignorance of the very instruments of power and wealth that represent ownership in their society (Siegal, 1985).

Finally, the money saved in the CFS accounts would be directly invested in the nation's economy and, thus, would promote increased economic growth and development. The savings and investment this approach would produce, would also increase the nation's savings rate.

Benefits of the Child's Future Security Account Program

The aim of the CFS account is not new. Economists and others have long recognized the value of such an approach (Haveman, 1988; Sherraden, 1990; Thurow, 1992).[163] In 1970, Nobel Prize winning economist James Tobin proposed:

> After high school, every youth in the nation—whatever the economic means of his parents or his earlier education—should have the opportunity to develop his capacity to earn income and to contribute to the society. To this end the federal government could make available to every young man and woman, on graduation from high school and in any case at the age of 19, an endowment of, for example, [roughly $20,000 in 1991 dollars]...

---

162. In this regard, see the recent work on developing a "stake" through an asset-based welfare approach by Sherraden (1991).

163. Thomas Paine argued for a similar approach two centuries ago in his treatise *Agrarian Justice*. Specifically, he argued that every person on their twenty-first birthday "should be entitled to receive fifteen pounds sterling each" (see Agassi, 1991, 453). The funds for this provision were to derive from a 10 percent inheritance tax on estates.

This proposal has a number of important advantages. Individuals are assisted directly and equally, rather than indirectly and haphazardly, through government financing of particular programs. The advantages of background and talent that fit certain young people for university education are not compounded by financial favoritism. Within broad limits of approved programs, individuals are free to choose how to use the money the government is willing to invest in their development. No individual misses out because there happens to be no training courses where he lives, or because his parents' income barely exceeds some permissible maximum. (P. 92)

Lester Thurow (1992, 279) recently proposed a similar approach:

The Social Security system could be expanded beyond health care and pensions for the elderly to include training for the young. Upon birth, every young person would have a training account set up in his [or her] name for use after graduation from high school in which a sum of money equal to the amount of public money that is now spent on the average college graduate (about $17,500) would be deposited. Over their lifetime, individuals could draw upon this fund to pay for university training or to pay their employer for on-the-job skill training. Repayment would occur in the form of payroll tax deductions.

In yet another way, CFS derives from one of North America's oldest pioneer traditions. Like the grubstake provided the prospector a century ago, CFS funds would constitute the resources each young person would need upon graduation from high school to embark upon their future. Like the prospector, the youthful beneficiary would, during the course of his or her adult working life, repay the cost of the grubstake, so that others who followed would continue to benefit.

Building Hope

The most important aspect of this approach may not be its financial benefits, which will be substantial, but its impact on personal and social development. In my view, the psychological and personality development benefits would far outweigh the financial rewards (Coleman, et al., 1966). The most significant role the CFS account program would have would be instilling hope and opportunity in millions of young people who would otherwise have none (Siegal, 1985). Even the poorest children would know that upon graduation from high school opportunity would be waiting for them.

One of the most successful programs to demonstrate the viability of this approach was initiated and funded by Eugene Lang, a self-made millionaire and philanthropist (Ellwood, 1988, 215-216). Lang promised the students of the inner-city Harlem school that he himself had attended that he would pay the cost of a college education for any student who graduated from the school and was subsequently admitted to a college or university. Prior to this time, the school's dropout rate had been close to 50 percent, with few students going on to college—a statistic mirrored in national data (see Figure 10.2). Following Lang's offer, the dropout rate plummeted to barely 5 percent. Nearly all students began graduating, with most of those accepting Lang's offer and continuing on to college. The success of Lang's venture has led to the formation of the "I Have a Dream" Foundation. The program has been replicated in twenty-four cities serving 5,000 young people and financed from private giving (Bowen, 1987; Solomon, 1989).

Staying in School. At 29 percent the United States has one of the highest high school drop out rates in the world. This compares to 6 percent in Japan, 9 percent in Germany, and 20 percent in Canada (Thurow, 1992, 159).[164] The CFS program would go a long way toward reducing this dropout rate, providing young people an incentive to stay in school and discouraging early pregnancy and family formation. Young men and women, despite an impoverished family situation, would know that when they graduated from high school, they would have the resources to attend training school, apprentice training, community college, or a university.[165] If a young woman chose to have a child out of wedlock, she might be required to share the costs of rearing that child using funds from her accumulated CFS account, supplemented with funds from the father's CFS account. Thus, the mother and putative father would understand beforehand that having children before finishing high school or before marriage would severely limit future opportunities. The costs of their behavior would be directly borne by

---

164. Thurow (1992, 40) observes, "in the twenty-first century, the education and skills of the work force will end up being the dominant competitive weapon."

165. Lester Thurow (1992, 52) points out that in the new global economy "the education of the bottom 50 percent of the population moves to center stage." It is not just the education of the management that is required in the new world order, but the education of the whole population (Friedberg, 1988; Solomon, 1989). "In the end the skills of the bottom half of the population affect the wages of the top half. If the bottom half can't effectively staff the processes that have to be operated, the management and professional jobs that go with the processes disappear" (p. 55). Later Thurow (1992, 247) observes, "Japanese high-school students come near the top in any international assessment of achievement, and the nation's ability to educate the bottom half of the high-school class is simply unmatched anywhere in the world."

them. The empirical research suggests that as they became aware of opportunities other than that offered by early parenthood on public assistance, fewer would allow themselves to get trapped.

Promote Entrepreneurship. Young people today have no assurance, even with a college education, that a job will be available for them when they are ready to enter the labor market. With the advance of high technology and the information age combined with the broad reach of global markets, labor market conditions have been changing. Large corporations have been reducing the size of their workforce. Increasing numbers of young people may have to rely on their own initiative and imagination to create opportunities for themselves. They will need to develop new opportunities such as starting their own business or pooling their resources with friends and associates and buying a franchise business. However, starting a business or buying a franchise requires start up capital. One of the important uses of the CFS account funds would be to provide young people who chose to try their hands at entrepreneurship with start up capital. Whatever the young person's choice, the role of the social worker would be to both encourage the young person to stay in school as well as to ensure careful and proper use of the available funds for transition into self-supporting adult roles.

Grubstake. Children living in impoverished homes and blighted neighborhoods have little hope and even less to lose. As they watch television they realize all too well that in a society possessing abundant wealth, they have been dealt a losing hand. It is not surprising that so many are tempted by gang involvement, drug use or drug dealing, and criminal behavior, none of which are effectively countered by any fear of loss. Why, the young person asks, should I worry when I have nothing to lose? The CFS account attempts to change this equation by making even the most impoverished child a stakeholder in society. When they see they have real hope and opportunity, they will realize they have a lot to lose, and yet still more to gain, and will be far more likely to contribute positively toward their community.

Thurow (1992) has pointed out that to make new citizens into productive workers requires substantial investment in the social and economic infrastructure: new schools, additional housing, plant and equipment to support employment, and so on. Thurow estimates that each new citizen born in America will require $20,000 for housing, $20,000 for food, $20,000 for public infrastructure, $100,000 for education, and $80,000 for plant and equipment to permit productive participation in advanced post modern society. He concludes that, "basically each new American will require an investment of $240,000 before he or she is capable of fitting into the American economy as a self-sufficient, average citizen-worker" (p. 206).

The CFS account is essentially an investment in infrastructure development—the infrastructure being our children. It provides the additional marginal investment that would greatly leverage the nearly quarter of a million dollars that will be required for each new citizen.

In many ways, we already do much of what the CFS account proposes through a patchwork of job training programs, higher education training grants, loan programs and loan guarantees. The CFS account would simply consolidate and unify many separate programs into a single approach that would reduce the vast and confusing patchwork of programs with different rules, eligibility requirements and standards. The CFS account puts the young person at the center of control and demands responsible individual action. It is a program designed to provide young people with hope and vision and to assure the resources required to them.

The CFS account would allow young people to start their careers with as little debt as possible. The transition from adolescence to adulthood in a free enterprise economy requires substantial investment. Today, most young persons wanting to attend college or obtain vocational training must have financial assistance. Young people from low-income and middle-income families face a difficult time. While they may be eligible for financial aid programs, such means-tested programs often promote dependency and a reliance on government aid. Further, young people who take on substantial debt to fund their college education too often mortgage their future and much of their hope.[166] The CFS program would free young people from incurring such heavy burdens early in their careers.

Limitations

Limitations to the CFS program do exist. For one, it does not address the current and pressing problems that children may be suffering now: substan-

---

166. The approach proposed here teaches the value of saving and investing. Young people learn how saving permits the building of a capital reserve that can prove useful for future needs. Other approaches to provide funds for college or vocational training that open a "line of credit" encourage the habit of borrowing. Young people learn to borrow and spend only to accumulate debt. Further, this "debtor" approach may result in children believing that they have mortgaged their future once the "credit line" has been fully used. The advantage of the social savings approach is that it encourages the habit of saving and teaches young people about investing. These are lessons and habits that will serve them in the future.

dard housing, poor health, inadequate nutrition, violent surroundings, and ineffective schooling. It may seem insensitive in the face of such urgent needs to focus on building a savings account for future needs. Although the immediate needs of children are vitally important, and should receive priority (as discussed in Chapter 9), we must not neglect long-term, preventative solutions that will eventually get to the root causes. We have seen this with respect to Social Security for the elderly. Like a physician attending a diseased patient, child welfare would be delinquent in its service should it provide only immediate comfort and care while neglecting to search for an ultimate cure. The problem of child poverty will never end unless we adapt long-term solutions addressed to root causes.

The objection can also be made that if children gain money too easily, they will have little appreciation for the labor and toil it represents. This is a crucial issue because if children are able to build substantial savings with little or no effort, they may mistakenly believe that money and savings will always be easy to come by—a lottery in which everyone wins. Money easily gained can become money easily lost. There is no simple solution to this problem. It will be important for schools, parents, and society as a whole to emphasize this value to children, assuring them that the money will have to be repaid through contributions made during their working years. Children would have to know that the CFS funds represent a "compact between the generations," a statement of faith in their future and potential, an investment made by one generation in the future of the next.

Implementation

The CFS account is obviously a long-term solution, and would not immediately end poverty among children. Several years would pass before effects would be felt. One immediate concern would be those children currently too old to effectively participate. One solution might be to phase the program in for all children under six years of age and to make it voluntary for all children over six. All children would have an account opened for them unless they expressly asked not to participate. An educational loan fund, such as has been proposed by President Clinton, could be made available to all children who have not been able to accumulate savings for their adult education and training. Over time, younger children would have accumulated funds in their accounts and thus would need to borrow less. After full implementation, the need for an educational loan fund would likely disappear altogether.

Conclusion

Investing the minimal amount in the development of children, especially children from low-income or poor families, is an unwise investment decision. The future of society is determined by the achievements of its young people. Children who grow up in poverty—about one fifth of all young people in North America—are, through current social programs, being effectively denied both hope and opportunity. The result is despair and resentment against the society in which they have so little stake.

Social Security is a social savings program that guarantees everyone a decent life in their retirement years. It does not allow individuals to risk becoming dependent on society through public assistance during old age. Similarly, the Child's Future Security account represents a "social investment" approach to safeguarding the futures of children. It would guarantee all children the resources required at a critical stage in their lives to make the difficult transition to effective, self-reliant and productive citizenship. It would permit them to realize opportunities in the free enterprise market economy without reference to the economic status of their parents, thereby ensuring all an equal opportunity and a fair start. As with Social Security for the elderly, the CFS account would be paid for by the beneficiaries themselves during their working lives, the assumption being that young people who had the resources to properly prepare themselves for a career or occupation would earn more income and, thus, pay into the program throughout their working life. The program would, within a generation, significantly reduce, even eliminate, poverty among children, at least to the extent we have seen it reduced among the elderly. Many of the social problems attendant upon that poverty would also vanish.

The CFS account does not rely on a residual approach, but attempts to prevent the need for residual services by building a structure that reduces the number of children unable to achieve economic self-reliance. The intent is to lead children to economic self-sufficiency where they can make positive contributions to the collective good.

12

A Vision for the Future

Surprised by the unexpectedly high proportion of cases of cleft palate coming from certain sparsely populated counties in upstate New York... Gentry
responded by doing what public health physicians have done for decades; he
started putting up pins on a map, in this instance a map of New York state,
one pin for each case...When all the pins were in place, they made a pattern
that Gentry found familiar. Where had he seen it before? After some effort,
he remembered. It was in a geology course, on a map of igneous rock forma-
tions...Some of these rocks emit natural radiation, and, as Gentry knew,
radiation had been suspected as a possible source of cleft palate and other
deformities present at birth.

Odd though it may seem, this story has much to tell us about identifying
neighborhoods that are at risk for child maltreatment, for just as cases of
cleft palate can be mapped, and their underlying ecological causes exposed,
so can cases of child abuse and neglect.

J. Garbarino and D. Sherman, *Protecting Children from Abuse and Neglect*

About two decades ago when Garbarino and Sherman examined the distribution of child maltreatment cases in a large Midwestern metropolitan
county they found a remarkable similarity between a map of child maltreatment reports and a map of social and economic conditions.[167] In those
neighborhoods where they found poverty they also found child abuse. Like
poverty, child abuse was essentially confined to those poor neighborhoods.
Garbarino and Sherman (1980, 99) reported, "We found that the five indicators of social conditions accounted for a great deal (80 percent) of the variations in child maltreatment among the neighborhoods."

Since 1975 the number of child abuse reports in the United States has
increased tenfold from less than 300,000 to almost three million a year
(McCurdy and Daro, 1993). The rapidly rising number of child abuse

---

167. Social conditions were defined by three variables: (1) the percent of lone-parent families, (2) the percent of working mothers, and (3) the percent of less-than-one-year residents.
The economic variables were the percent of families with an annual income defined as
"struggling" and the percent with income defined as "comfortable" (Garbarino and Sherman,
1980, 99).

reports in recent decades count actual events. We need to ask why these counts have gone up so sharply in North America at a time when the child population remained relatively unchanged. Perhaps part of the rise can be explained by an increased awareness of the problem and a willingness of the public to report. Yet, there seems to be something more at work here. As we have seen in Chapter 8, the social and economic conditions for children have been getting worse, especially for poor children who account for the vast majority of abuse reports (Martin, 1985; United States Department of Health and Human Services, 1988).

In a sense, child abuse report numbers may serve as an unobtrusive measure of the deterioration of the situation of poor children (Wolock and Horowitz, 1979). In this regard, abused children are a barometer of a wider and more serious problem. The despair of their situation reflects a broader decline of the environment of poor children. These children are raised in families and neighborhoods that lack the resources to properly care for them.

The Rights and Responsibilities of Families

> If a society cannot create broad consensus about who is responsible for raising children and supporting them economically, it will soon have a lot of children for whom nobody takes much responsibility.
>
> Christopher Jencks, *Rethinking Social Policy*

In modern market economies responsibility for raising children has been lodged with families, which are assured broad latitude and privacy in raising and disciplining their young. As the haven for personal loyalty and protection, the family is seen as the ideal setting for ensuring growing children the love and affection that is so essential to their development—a commodity no other institution besides the family can provide. The family also shoulders the responsibility for the economic and material needs of the child. For most families this situation has worked out well. Families with adequate economic resources have been able to craft their own economic futures, which has ensured autonomy and fostered individual initiative.

However, as we have seen, many families in North America lack sufficient resources to properly and adequately raise their children—they live in poverty. The children in these families, consisting usually of a lone-parent, are frequently deprived of the things most other children take for granted: a neighborhood free of drugs, crime, prostitution, and gang violence (Garbar-ino, et al., 1991; Kotlowitz, 1992). They attend schools that are chaotic, underfunded, and reflect the disorganization and decay found in their com-munity (Kozol, 1991). What chance do these children have? What are their odds for success in a competitive free market economy? Can they be expected to grow up believing in the fairness, equity, compassion, and decency of their society?

The Role of Child Welfare

The child welfare system represents and administers our collective respon-sibility for children. What is the role of the child welfare system in a mod-ern high technology society like the United States? Historically, the child welfare system has been guided by a residual perspective which focused on protecting and serving those children most in need who were unable to be properly cared for by their parents. Yet major social change has impacted society rendering this residual approach inadequate.

The Residual Approach

> By the 1890s, child saving strategies had changed radically. Not only did most reformers reject large institutions and advocate placing children with foster parents... they also rejected the notion that children should be taken from their families simply on account of poverty...This emphasis on family preservation reflected a major shift in reform thought. Recall that only a couple of decades earlier, the same people advocated family breakup not just when parents drank, stole, or seemed otherwise immoral and neglectful but, even more, when they were so poor that they had to ask for relief.
>
> Michael Katz, *In the Shadow of the Poorhouse*

The needs of disadvantaged children have been addressed using a residual approach, which identifies and attempts to rescue the most severely disad-vantaged children. As seen in Figure 12.1 child protection services and fam-ily preservation services are on opposite ends of the continuum of residual services. Historically the residual child welfare system has swung between the two competing demands of: (1) protecting children from homes where they are being abused or neglected and (2) making every effort to keep chil-dren with their family even when they are at risk.

Figure 12.1 The Pendulum of Residual Child Welfare Services

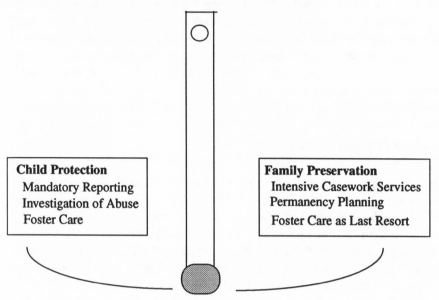

Mandatory child abuse reporting laws transformed the child welfare system into a child protection system during the last two decades. Child abuse reports led to investigations and when serious abuse was found it required children be removed from their homes and placed in foster care. Consequently, there has been a steady increase in the number of children entering into foster care over the decades.

Family Preservation Services

Murphy is the Cook County (Illinois) public guardian, the court appointed lawyer for 31,000 abused and neglected children...Last year, campaigning to rein in one "family preservation" program, Murphy sent every Illinois legislator color autopsy photos of a girl scalded and beaten to death after caseworkers taught her family new disciplinary skills.

Newsweek, April 25, 1994

The increasing number of children entering into foster care has historically led to counter initiatives to reduce this number. Too many children, it was feared, were unnecessarily entering into foster care. In the late 1970s a group of researchers in Washington began reporting on the use of intensive casework services directed at families where children were in imminent need of placement in foster care. The Homebuilders program claimed to have prevented the placement of almost 97 percent of children served. The results were remarkable but viewed with skepticism because of major limitations with the research design (i.e., they did not use a control group). Subsequent research reported in the early 1990s in Washington and Utah also produced supportive results, although not as spectacular as early reports. However, the Washington and Utah studies have also been criticized as "fatally flawed" because of nonresponse in a small control group (N = 27). The promise of intensive casework services to preserve families and prevent removal of a child have led to widespread experimentation and implementation. The family preservation approach has been promoted by major private foundations with substantial funding. The prominence of family preservation will no doubt increase because of the passage of federal budget provisions that allocated 60 million dollars in 1994, rising to 240 million in fiscal 1998 for states to establish family preservation services.

There have been more than thirty published evaluation studies of family preservation programs. On balance most of these studies fail to provide evidence for substantial success of the intensive casework services approach of family preservation. Researchers at the University of Chicago have recently completed the most comprehensive and rigorous evaluation of the family preservation approach (Schuerman, Rzepnicki, Littell, and Chak, 1993). Families were randomly assigned to experimental and control groups at several different sites around the state of Illinois. There were 995 families in the experimental intensive casework services group and 569 families in the routine services control group. The experimental families received on average ten times more contact hours with their caseworker and many of these contacts were with the family in their home. What was the difference between the experimental and control groups? The experimental families were slightly more likely to have their children removed. In addition, the experimental children were more likely to be subsequently reported for abuse. In short, there is no evidence from the most rigorous test to date that "family preservation" is a more effective approach than routine services.

Child Protective Services

Family preservation services are not alone in failing to demonstrate the effectiveness of the residual approach. During the 1970s and 1980s child welfare services in the United States were transformed into child protective services by the enactment of mandatory child abuse reporting laws. As a result of these laws the number of child abuse reports in the United States increased from about 10,000 a year in the early sixties to more than 3,000,000 today. Advocates of the transformation promised that child abuse and child abuse fatalities would decline. Although child abuse reports have increased sharply, there has been no collateral change in child abuse fatalities. Increased child abuse reporting has not reduced child abuse fatalities.

The main effect of increased reporting has been the transformation of child welfare services into a system of child protective services situated on the child rescue end of the residual services continuum. In large measure, the increased emphasis on family preservation in the 1990s has been in response to this overemphasis on protective services during the 1980s—an elixir to the excesses of the child protection approach. As the pendulum swings between these two ends of the residual services continuum major changes in the child welfare system occur but the progress is more often sideways than forward.

Science: The Search for Root Causes

In science there is a search for causal relationships. When a child is abused or neglected, something needs to be done. Primarily it has been child welfare social workers who have provided state intervention to protect children. However, when the numbers continue to rise we need to ask if we are addressing the root causes. The residual approach to child welfare does not go to the root causes of child poverty. The approach is rather like responding to a tuberculosis epidemic by setting up field hospitals, where limited medical care is rationed to those most in need. Such an approach, while helpful to an extent, fails to address the underlying causes of the disease. Years ago significant progress against tuberculosis was not achieved until public health efforts finally produced a vaccine, which went to the root cause of the disease.

Solving Child Poverty

The residual approach simply accepts the view that many children will always be in need or at-risk. At some point, we must realize the futility of responding to what is an epidemic of child poverty by simply redirecting more resources to child abuse protection. With more than 14 million children living in households below the poverty line, and more than 5 million of these living in households below half the poverty line, the problem of children in poverty has outgrown the ability of the residual public child welfare system to deal effectively with it.

At the beginning of the 1990s distinguished social theorists across the political spectrum recognized that child poverty had become the fundamental social problem. Andrew Hacker (1992, 78) observed, "The real problem of our time is that more and more infants are being born to mothers who are immature and poor." Charles Murray (1993, A24) writes, "Every once in a while the sky really is falling, and this seems to be the case with illegitimacy... Illegitimacy is the single most important social problem of our time—more important than crime, drugs, poverty, illiteracy, welfare, or homelessness because it drives everything else." Christopher Jencks (1992, 19) echoes this view, "America's most serious social-policy error [is] the way in which we try to help single mothers. I argue that America does not provide most unskilled single mothers with a socially acceptable strategy for supporting their families. As a result, most have adopted socially unacceptable strategies."

The problem of poverty among lone-parents and their children has become the core social problem in North America. The problem has been cast as the collapse of the family, a plague of illegitimacy, an epidemic of child abuse, and a crisis for children. At the core all stem from the same problem, child poverty. Child poverty will not end without intervention. Yet, there has not been a broad commitment to solving this problem, in part because the problems facing these mothers and their children have been defined within a residual perspective.

It is necessary to rethink collective responsibility for the welfare of children, developing new approaches that acknowledge the limitations of the residual model in coping with widespread poverty among lone-parent families. Child welfare must incorporate a broader structural perspective. To the extent that the problems which children and families face are induced and sustained by external socioeconomic forces and circumstances, they must be approached at that level. It is no longer possible, for example, to separate the issues of income protection for lone-parent families from the issue of child neglect. If lone-parent families are trapped in poverty and have few opportunities to improve their situation, the child welfare system must develop policies and programs to address their circumstances. This means looking to solutions that provide income protection for the family.

Advocates of the residual perspective question the structural approach. Susan Sheehan (1993, 79) captures the basic sentiment:

> The simple remedy one hears proposed most often is that the money spent on foster care—whose wards in New York City have nearly tripled in the past ten years—would be better spent trying to solve its root causes: poverty, drug addiction, and homelessness. Yet experience has shown that these social problems are amenable only to slow, expensive, and hard-thought-out measures. In the meantime, something has to be done to take care of the children.

This is the dilemma of the front-line child welfare social worker who daily confronts the pressing needs of the child, and has little time or patience for broader structural questions. However, if the broader questions are not addressed, the root causes of the problem will remain. Until the root causes are addressed, significant progress in reducing child poverty and neglect will elude the child welfare system.

Government has not taken a residual approach with other groups such as senior citizens or business entrepreneurs. We have seen how effective the Social Security program has been for the elderly in reducing poverty. During the 1960s close to 40 percent of the elderly in the United States lived in households with income below the poverty line (Orshansky, 1967). Thirty years later it has been reduced to less than 10 percent, a decline that can be attributed directly to the structural approach of Social Security. During this same period, virtually no progress was made for children. In fact, the percentage of children in poverty increased in this period from about 15 percent to more than 20 percent.

Like seniors, the business community routinely looks to government to provide an environment conducive to economic opportunity. Government responds because it understands the importance of investing in an economic infrastructure. It paves highways, constructs bridges, lays rail lines, subsidizes the technical training needed for modern high technology, supports research, and provides a host of services required for businesses to compete and survive in a highly competitive global marketplace. Just as we invest in business and industry, so must we invest in society's most vital human resource—its children. Roads must be built that will lead children to opportunity and ensure their success.

Yet, more and more child welfare is being limited to protecting children from physical and sexual assault. If this residual definition of child welfare is accepted, thereby defining the boundaries of our collective responsibility toward children, the residual model will have reached its logical conclusion, in which access to services is restricted to the narrowest category of children in need, the victims of abuse. Child welfare will have abandoned its helping orientation as an ally of the family to become a putative guardian of the child against the parent. For the child welfare profession, and for children, this road is a cul-de-sac.

What is required is a broader understanding of the mechanisms, processes, and causes that lead families and their children into poverty, hopelessness, and despair—and thereby to the attention of the child welfare system. The child welfare system must be viewed as part of the broader public infrastructure designed to nurture and develop the potential of children. Like public schools, public health programs, recreational programs, and community mental health programs, the child welfare system must become, as Callahan (1985, 6) argues, "a system designed to guarantee to children the resources required for their development...by providing supportive, supplementary, and substitutive services...and advocating changes in economic, health, education, and social policies which have a significant impact on their well-being." This can be done only by taking into account the social and economic realities children and families confront.

The Structural Approach

In order to take into account the broader social and economic situation of children and their families, I propose the following as a statement of collective obligation to children as implemented by the child welfare system:

First, the child welfare system must return responsibility for protecting children from severe physical and sexual assault to the police and the courts. One unanticipated consequence of mandatory child abuse reporting laws, especially in the United States, has been to shift responsibility for managing severe physical and sexual assault from the police to child welfare professionals. For child welfare agencies this problem has emerged as their primary responsibility, transforming them into protective service agencies. This development not only prevents the child welfare system from achieving its historic mission of helping disadvantaged and impoverished children and ensuring equal opportunity but also mires the profession in a problem it cannot solve. It is an approach that too often allows criminal physical and sexual assault of children to go unprosecuted and thus fails to protect children from continued harm.

Second, the child welfare system must seek to guarantee an economic safety net for families with children that will ensure a basic level of child care. This would include not only the development of an infrastructure of child development programs, such as free public education and care for all children from birth to age eighteen, but also the institution of policies such as the family and children's allowance, child tax deduction, child tax credit, and child support collection services, all of which would provide a stable, economic structure of support for families, thereby ensuring that they possess the minimal resources to properly care for the children in their custody. Children should not suffer unduly because of the disappointments, limitations, or economic failings of their parents. Neither should they place an overwhelming economic burden on a lone-parent. Instead, they must know that they have a basic level of income security and educational opportunity. That the child welfare system has not been centrally concerned with these issues is perhaps its greatest failing.

Third, the child welfare system must provide an engine of economic opportunity for young people that will allow them to make the most of their lives. In an earlier period providing universal free education was enough. Over time the amount of education provided was extended to include college. Yet education is no longer sufficient or assured. When young people leave home and start on their own in a modern market economy they need economic resources. I have proposed the Child's Future Security (CFS) account as one means by which these resources might be assured. For many young people growing up in poverty, in blighted neighborhoods, in dangerous and hostile environments, the CFS account would provide more than just a glimmer of hope. Young people would know that at a crucial time in their lives they would have the resources to capitalize on the opportunities the free market economy provides. Funds in their CFS account could serve as the fulcrum to achieve the escape velocity required to break out of the cycle of poverty. It is essential that young persons have the training, preparation, and advanced education required for effective participation in our high technology society and the resources needed to obtain these.

The CFS account would target not just deprived children but middle class families as well, who must often make great economic sacrifices when their children leave home, or else watch them founder on treacherous economic shoals. The CFS account represents an investment in human capital tailored to the needs of a free enterprise system that could lead to unprecedented achievement.

Finally, we must adopt a structural perspective that includes a place for residual services but is not limited to them. Historically the emphasis has been on the residual approach, to the virtual exclusion of a structural approach. But no amount of residual services can suffice if the infrastructure for child development crumbles. The infrastructure for many families, especially lone-parent families, has essentially crumbled. For these families no amount of residual services is adequate.

Still, the answer is not found in choosing between a structural or residual approach, but in striking a creative balance between the two.

The child welfare field may not be able to adopt all the necessary policies, lobby for enactment of the legislation, or fund the social programs required to achieve the objectives set forth in a structural approach. Fundamental barriers over which the child welfare profession has little influence stand in the way. Nonetheless, those in the child welfare field must be clear on its direction and on the goals it wants to accomplish. Developing a new perspective is the necessary first step. In the process the child welfare system may be able to do much for children. No doubt, the task will be difficult but there is no task more worthy of the effort.

It may be the nature of the democratic system in a market economy that those with the most wealth can use their advantage to advance their interests, even if it is at the expense of others not so fortunate. The invisible hand of the marketplace may be unable to correct for this exercise of self-interest. Government intervention to level the playing field and protect the interests of the poor and others unable to protect themselves will be required, recognizing that such actions, in the long term, serve the broader good.

The Focus of Public Policy

Just as there is a swing in child welfare service between child protection and family preservation, so there is a larger swing in broad public policy focus between issues of wealth and poverty. The decade of the 1980s belonged to conservative social thinkers whose theories rose to prominence in the English speaking democracies of the West. In Britain Margaret Thatcher ushered in a tough economic conservatism that reduced the role of government, privatized state industries, and promoted an aggressive spirit of capitalism. In the United States Ronald Reagan, with a broad program for bold conservative economic policies unseated an incumbent president. Shortly after Brian Mulroney led conservatives to victory in Canada. The architects of these conservative victories began dismantling what they viewed as generous social programs that encouraged dependency and a plethora of social ills. As never before, the poor and the programs designed to serve them were viewed as barriers to economic progress. Public attention was drawn to the cost of programs for the poor. Meanwhile, the architects of the conservative victory also put in place economic policies designed to unleash the creativity and energies of the asset holders—deregulation of the banking industry and other financial institutions, privatization of state owned industries, relaxation of governmental regulation of commerce, and the weakening of labor unions.

The most important changes involved a shift in tax policy away from taxes on business and industry and progressive personal taxes toward broader taxes on the middle class. In the United States, a fundamental reduction in progressive income tax was achieved. In terms of direct effects, the greatest triumph of these conservative governments was the success in reducing the tax burden on asset holders, those with substantial wealth. The tax savings for families in the upper income brackets rose to more than $100 billion a year by the end of the decade (Phillips, 1993). Reducing taxes on the wealthy, it was argued, would lead to savings which would be used for investment. However, the dramatic tax reductions on the wealthy failed to produce the sustained economic growth needed to provide replacement revenue. While government spending continued, it was financed by increased borrowing, with the overall result that during the decade federal government debts in the United States and Canada increased fourfold. The cost of carrying this debt, in terms of required interest payments, has become an increasing burden carried by all.

Asset holders did not call for conservative governments to create social programs that required new government bureaucracies but for tax policies which favored their economic position. Government programs that depend on agency bureaucracies are unable to take advantage of the efficiencies and inherent nature of the free market. Thus, the task was to promote policies that favor the holding and accumulation of assets. Consequently, the last decade produced enormous gains for asset holders and continued the shift of wealth upward.

In the broad view of economic life the poor, especially poor children, present no threat to the material success of the wealthy. The poor have virtually no asset wealth, and what they possess is so little as to be negligible. The cost of income assistance to the poor through welfare pales in comparison to the total income of the wealthy.

So why should the poor be such a worrisome problem? Perhaps, the issue was not so much the cost of supporting the poor, but rather that focus on the poor diverted attention from policies that sought to substantially reduce taxes on the wealthy and enhance their financial position. The argument against the poor was made to explain, in part, the declining prospects of the middle class, a decline that was occurring primarily because the tax burden was being shifted from the wealthy onto the middle class, not because welfare recipients were increasingly failing to carry their fair share of the work load. The poor had nothing and received little. They became a smoke screen to divert attention from a fundamental change in tax policy that further concentrated wealth at the top.

Currently many people see the poor as the undoing of society. The violence, drugs and the epidemic of children born out of wedlock are seen as pushing society to the brink of disaster. As long as public attention can be riveted on the problems and misbehaviors of the poor, there is no need to examine the vanishing progressivity and inequitable nature of the current tax system that leads to greater concentrations of wealth and income at the top, leaving those at the middle or bottom with less.

Charles Murray, Larry Mead, Milton Friedman, George Gilder, and the other intellectual architects of conservatism painted the canvas of poverty with black faces, with indolent faces, with the faces of depraved and irresponsible women. Now as we enter the third millennium new faces appear on the canvas of poverty—the faces of children. As our eyes meet theirs, it becomes increasingly difficult to look away.

Undoubtedly some conservative theorists have noble intentions and sincerely believe their approach represented the best avenue for the poor as well as the middle class and the wealthy. For more than a decade they have been able to implement and test their approaches in North America and Britain. The result of these policies of limited government involvement has been more, rather than fewer, children living in poverty. The failure of such approaches to make any headway against child poverty requires us to look elsewhere, to explore new directions that break with the outmoded and failed policies of the past.

Achieving Fundamental Reform

Concern with child poverty could galvanize public sentiment in support of child welfare reform. Fundamental child welfare reform along the lines discussed here could provide the seeds for fundamental social advancement. It has happened before (Taylor, 1991). Historian Michael Katz (1986, 113) observed, "Throughout the country, by the 1890s, children had captured the energy and attention of social reformers with an intensity never matched in other periods of American history. Almost overnight, it seemed, children became the symbol of a resurgent reform spirit, the magnet that pulled together a diverse...but very effective coalition." It was this early wave of compassion that led to the development of the public child welfare system in the United States.

Children stand again, as they did a century ago, "as the fulcrum that can move society from an era of material self-absorption to an era of civic-minded government" and collective responsibility for the building the infrastructure required to ensure all children have a fair start and equal opportunity. The momentum for real change has been building. An opportunity to renew our faith in free enterprise and democracy is once again before us. It requires development of an infrastructure that ensures all children a fair start and an equal opportunity. Those of us who have prospered must look into our hearts and realize that, in the final analysis, we each benefit most when all of us have an opportunity.

In her futuristic novel, *The Children of Men*, P.D. James depicts a world without children. The innocence, the awkwardness, the playfulness, the enchanting laughter and untarnished spirit of children are nowhere to be found. It is a stark and dreary landscape where, through a phenomenon resulting in global infertility, hope in the future has evaporated. Women can only cling to dolls and men grasp for meaning in endeavors void of purpose. Humanity marches relentlessly toward the end of its existence.

Global infertility, of course, is not the only way to end our future. The future can simply deteriorate through infertility of hope and opportunity. When millions of children live in impoverished households in blighted neighborhoods, their future is diminished and destroyed before it can blossom. The consequence may come to resemble a landscape scarcely different from that portrayed by P.D. James.

To the extent a society protects and invests in its children, so will it ensure its future. To the extent that it does not, it imperils its existence. As the Committee for Economic Development (1987, 2) urged, "The nation cannot continue to compete and prosper in the global arena when more than a fifth of our children live in poverty and a third grow up in ignorance. And if the nation cannot compete it cannot lead. If we continue to squander the talents of millions of our children, America will become a nation of limited potential. It would be tragic if we allow this to happen."

To rebuild our society, to rebuild our economy, to rebuild our future, we must start with our children, who are our future. The approaches proposed here are suggestions on the directions we can take on the way toward rebuilding our collective vision and commitment to that future. The possibilities of humankind are boundless. We define our horizons by the decisions we make. Acting collectively we can build a fundamentally better future for our children.

Bibliography

Aaron, H. (1982). *Economic effects of Social Security.* Washington, DC: The Brookings Institution.

Abbott, E. (1942). *Social welfare and professional education.* Chicago: The University of Chicago Press.

Adams, O. (1988). Divorce rates in Canada. Statistics Canada, *Canadian Social Trends*, 18-19.

Adams. P. (1992). *Marketing social change: The case of family preservation.* Paper presented at the Annual Program Meeting of the Council on Social Work Education, Kansas City, March 1.

Addams, J. (1902). *Democracy and social ethics.* New York: Macmillan.

Addams, J. (1910). *Twenty years at Hull House.* New York: Macmillan.

Adelson, L. (1961). Slaughter of the innocents: A study of forty-six homicides in which the victims were children. *New England Journal of Medicine* 246:1345-1349.

Administration for Children, Youth, and Families. (1984). *Report to Congress on PL 96-272, The Adoption Assistance and Child Welfare Act of 1980.* Washington, DC: Department of Health and Human Services.

Adoption Assistance and Child Welfare Act of 1980, Public Law 96-272, H.R. 3434, 94 Stat. 500 (June 17).

Agassi, J. B. (1991). The rise of the ideas of the welfare state. *Philosophy of the Social Sciences* 21:444-457.

Agresti, A. (1984). *Analysis of ordinal categorical data.* New York: Wiley.

Aldridge, M. (1990). Social work and the news media-a hopeless case. *British Journal of Social Work* 20:611-625.

Alfaro, J. D. (1988). What can we learn from child abuse fatalities? A synthesis of nine studies. In D. J. Besharov, ed., *Protecting children from abuse and neglect: Policy and practice*, 219-264. Springfield, IL: Charles C Thomas.

Allan, L. J. (1978). Child abuse: A critical review of the research and theory. In J. P. Martin, ed., *Violence in the family.* New York: Wiley.

Allen, M., and Golubock, C. (1985). An emerging legal framework for permanency planning. *Children and Youth Services Review* 7:135-160.

Allen, M., Golubock, C., and Olson, L. (1983). A guide to the Adoption Assistance and Child Welfare Act of 1980. In M. Hardin, ed., *Foster children in the courts*, 575-609. Boston: Butterworth Legal Publishers.

Amacher, K. A., and Maas, H. S. (1985). Children, youth, and social work practice. In S. A. Yelaja, ed., *An introduction to social work practice in Canada*, 217-233. Scarborough, Ontario: Prentice-Hall.

337

American Humane Association. (1977). *Statistics for 1977.* Denver, CO: Author.

American Humane Association. (1978). *National analysis of official child neglect and abuse reporting.* Denver, CO: Author.

American Humane Association. (1979). *National analysis of official child neglect and abuse reporting.* DHEW Publication No. (OHDS) 79-30232. Denver, CO and Washington, DC: U.S. Department of Health, Education, and Welfare.

American Humane Association. (1981). *National analysis of official child neglect and abuse reporting, Annual report, 1980,* Denver, CO: Author.

American Humane Association. (1983). *National analysis of official child neglect and abuse reporting, Annual report, 1981,* Denver, CO: Author.

American Humane Association. (1987). *National analysis of official child neglect and abuse reporting, Annual report, 1985,* Denver, CO: Author.

American Humane Association. (1988). *National analysis of official child neglect and abuse reporting, Annual report, 1986.* Denver, CO: Author.

American Public Welfare Association. (1994). *Responsibility/work/pride: The values of welfare reform.* Washington, DC: Author.

Anderson, E. (1990). *Streetwise: Race, class, and change in an urban community.* Chicago: University of Chicago Press.

Anderson, E. (1994). Looking out for our nation's welfare. *Register Guard,* January, 9:F1 and F4.

Anderson, J. B., and Davidovits, P. (1975). Isotope separation in a "seeded beam." *Science* 187:642-644.

Anderson, R., Ambrosino, R., Valentine, D., and Lauderdale, M. (1983). Child deaths attributed to abuse and neglect: An empirical study. *Children and Youth Services Review* 5:75-89.

Antler, J., and Antler, S. (1979). From child rescue to family protection: The evolution of the child protection movement in the United States. *Children and Youth Services Review* 1:177-204.

Antler, S. (1981). The rediscovery of child abuse. In L. H. Pelton, ed., *The social context of child abuse and neglect* 39-54. New York: Human Sciences Press.

Archard, D. (1993). *Children: Rights and childhood.* London: Routledge.

Armstrong, P., and Armstrong, H. (1984). *The double ghetto.* Toronto: McClelland and Stewart.

Associated Press. (1988). U.S. child support agency given a `C' on report card [quotes Thomas Downey]. *The Register Guard* (Eugene, Oregon), October 15.

Avery, R. B., Elliehausen, G. E., and Canner, G. B. (1984a). Survey of consumer finances, 1983. *Federal Reserve Bulletin,* September, 679-682.

Avery, R. B., Elliehausen, G. E., and Canner, G. B. (1984b). Survey of consumer finances, 1983: A secondary report. *Federal Reserve Bulletin,* December, 857-869.

Bachrach, C. (1986). Adoption plans, adopted children and adoptive mothers. *Journal of Marriage and the Family* 48:243-253.

Bagley, C., and King, K. (1990). *Child sexual abuse: The search for healing.* London: Tavistock/Routledge.

Baker, M. (1985). *What will tomorrow bring? A study of the aspirations of adolescent women.* Ottawa: Canadian Advisory Council on the Status of Women.

Bakwin, H. (1952). Roentgenographic changes in homes following trauma. *Journal of Pediatrics* 42:7-15.

Bakwin, H. (1956). Multiple skeletal lesions in young children due to trauma. *Journal of Pediatrics* 39:7-15.

Baldwin, J. A., and Oliver, J. E. (1975). Epidemiology and family characteristics of severely abused children. *British Journal of Preventive and Social Medicine* 29:205-221.

Bane, M. J., and Jargowsky, P. A. (1988). The links between government policy and family structure: What matters and what doesn't. In A. J. Cherlin, ed., *The changing American family and public policy*, 219-261. Washington, DC: The Urban Institute Press.

Banting, K. G. (1987). *The welfare state and Canadian federalism.* 2d ed. Kingston and Montreal: McGill-Queen's University Press.

Barmeyer, G. H., Alderson, L. R., and Cox, W. B. (1951). Traumatic periostitis in young children. *Journal of Paediatrics* 38:184-190.

Barth, R., Berrick, J. D., and Courtney, M. (1990). *A snapshot of California's families and children: Pursuant to the child welfare reforms of the 1980s.* A presentation to the California Child Welfare Strategic Planning Commission, February 22.

Barth, R. P., and Berry, M. (1987). Outcomes of child welfare services under permanency planning. *Social Service Review* 61:71-90.

Bawden, D. L., and Sonenstein, F. L. (1992). Quasi-experimental designs. *Children and Youth Services Review* 14:137-144.

Bean, P., and Melville, J. (1989). *Lost children of the empire.* London: Unwin Hyman Ltd.

Bebbington, A., and Miles, J. (1989). The background of children who enter local authority care. *British Journal of Social Work* 19:349-368.

Becker, G. (1981). *A treatise on the family.* Cambridge, MA: Harvard University Press.

Beeghley, L. (1983). *Living poorly in America.* New York: Praeger.

Bell, W. (1965). *Aid to dependent children.* New York: Columbia University Press.

Bellamy, D. (1983). Social policy in Ontario. In Ontario Social Development Council, *The province of Ontario, Its social services, A handbook on the human services*, 31-51. Toronto: Ontario Social Development Council.

Bellamy, D., and Irving, A. (1986). Pioneers. In J. C. Turner and F. J. Turner, eds., *Canadian social welfare* 29-49. Dons Mills, Ontario: Collier Macmillan Canada.

Beller, A., and Graham, J. W. (1993). *Small change: The economics of child support.* New Haven: Yale University Press.

Berk, R. A., Campbell, A., Klap, R., and Western, B. (1992). The deterrent effect of arrest in incidents of domestic violence-a Bayesian-analysis of 4 field experiments. *American Sociological Review* 57:698-708.

Berlin, G. (1992). Choosing and measuring interventions. *Children and Youth Services Review* 14:99-118.

Bergquist, C., Szwejda, D., and Pope, G. (1993). *Evaluation of Michigan's Families First program: Summary report.* Lansing, MI: Michigan Department of Social Services.

Berry, M. (1990). *Keeping families together: An examination of an intensive family preservation program.* Unpublished doctoral dissertation. University of California, Berkeley.

Berry, M. (1991). The assessment of imminence of risk of placement: Lessons from a family preservation program. *Children and Youth Services Review* 13:239-256.

Berry, M. (1992). An evaluation of family preservation services: Fitting agency services to family needs. *Social Work* 37:314-321.

Berry, M. (1993). The relative effectiveness of family preservation services with neglectful families. In E. S. Morton and R. K. Grigsby, eds., *Advancing family preservation practice.* 70-98. Newbury Park: Sage.

Besharov, D. J. (1983). *Criminal and civil liability in child welfare work: The growing trend.* Washington, DC: American Bar Association.

Besharov, D. J. (1987). *Defending child abuse and neglect cases: Representing parents in civil proceedings.* DC Superior Court. Washington, DC: Counsel for Child Abuse and Neglect.

Besharov, D. J. (1988a). Introduction. In D. J. Besharov, ed., *Protecting children from abuse and neglect: Policy and practice,* 3-8. Springfield, IL: Charles C Thomas.

Besharov, D. J. (1988b). The misuse of foster care: When the desire to help children outruns the ability to improve parental functioning. In D. J. Besharov, ed., *Protecting children from abuse and neglect: Policy and practice,* 185-206. Springfield, IL: Charles C Thomas.

Besharov, D. J. (1990a). Gaining control of child abuse reports. *Public Welfare* 48:34-40.

Besharov, D. J. (1990b). *Recognizing child abuse.* New York: Free Press.

Besharov, D. J. (1991). Douglas J. Besharov's response to the symposium review by Deborah Daro and Rosina Becerra. *Children and Youth Services Review* 13:306-309.

Besharov, D. J. (1993). Escaping the dole: For young unmarried mothers, welfare reform alone can't make work pay. *Washington Post,* December 12:C3.

Best, J. (1990). *Threatened children: Rhetoric and concern about child-victims.* Chicago: The University of Chicago Press.

Billingsley, A., and Giovannoni, J. M. (1972). *Children of the storm: Black children and American child welfare.* New York: Harcourt, Brace, Jovanovich.

Bishop, Y. M. M., Fienberg, S. E., and Holland, P. W. (1975). *Discrete multivariate analysis: theory and practice.* Cambridge, MA: The MIT Press.

Blenkner, M., Bloom, M., and Nielsen, M. (1971). A research and demonstration project of protective services. *Social Casework* 52:483-499.

Blinder, A. (1982). *The truce in the war on poverty: Where do we go from here?* Paper 3. Washington, DC: National Policy Exchange.

Boehm, B. (1970). The child in foster care. In H. D. Stone, ed., *Foster care in question: A national reassessment by twenty-one experts* 220-227. New York: Child Welfare League of America.

Bolton, F. G., Laner, R., and Gai, D. (1981). For better or worse? Foster parents and foster children in an officially reported child maltreatment population. *Children and Youth Services Review* 3:37-53.

Bourget, D., and Bradford, J. M. W. (1990). Homicidal parents. *Canadian Journal of Psychiatry* 35:233-238.

Bowen, E. (1987). Needy kids, perpetual aid. *Time,* November 30, 70.

Bowlby, J. (1958). The nature of the child's tie to his mother. *International Journal of Psychoanalysis* 39:350-373.

Bowlby, J. (1969). *Attachment and loss. Vol. 1. Attachment.* New York: Basic Books.

Boyle, M. H., Offord, D. R., Hofman, H. G., Catlin, G. P., Byles, J. A., Cadman, D. T., Crawford, J. W., Links, P. S., Rae-Grant, N. I., and Szatmari, P. (1987). Ontario child health study. I. Methodology. *Archives of General Psychiatry* 44:826-832.

Brace, C. L. (1859). *The best method of disposing of pauper and vagrant children.* New York: Wyncoop and Hallenbeck.

Brace, E., ed. (1894). *The life of Charles Loring Brace: Chiefly told in his own letters.* London: S. Low, Marston and Company.

Bradbury, D. E. (1962). *Five decades of action for children.* Washington, DC: U.S. Department of Health, Education, and Welfare, Children's Bureau.

Brazer, H. E. (1967). Tax policy and children's allowance. In E. M. B. Burns, ed., *Children's allowances and the economic welfare of children,* 140-149. New York: Citizen's Committee for Children of New York.

Bremner, R. H., ed. (1971). *Children and youth in America: A documentary history. Vol. II: 1866-1932, Parts one through six.* Cambridge, MA: Harvard University Press.

Briar, S. (1963). Clinical judgment in foster care placement. *Child Welfare* 42:161-169.

Brieland, D. (1965). An assessment of resources in child welfare research. In M. Norris and B. Wallace, eds., *The known and the unknown in child welfare research: An appraisal,* 188-196. New York: Child Welfare League of America.

Brindle, D. (1991). The Orkney affair: A crisis for social work. *Guardian,* April 5:3.

British Medical Journal (1973). Deliberate injury of children. *British Medical Journal* 4:61-62.

Broder, D. (1991). Unless we act now, nation's future looks bleak. *Washington Post,* June 15.

Browning, D., and Evison, I. (1993). The family debate: A middle way. *Christian Century* 110:712-716.

Bruno, F. J. (1957). *Trends in social work, 1874-1956: A history based on the proceedings of the National Conference of Social Work.* New York: Columbia University Press.

Buchan, W. (1783). *Domestic medicine: Or a treatise on the prevention and cure of diseases.* London: Milner.

Burns, E. M. B., ed. (1967). *Children's allowances and the economic welfare of children.* New York: Citizen's Committee for Children of New York.

Burt, M. R., and Bayleat, R. R. (1978). *A comprehensive emergency services system for neglected and abused children.* New York: Vantage Press.

Burt, M. R., and Blair, L. H. (1971). *Options for improving care of neglected and dependent children.* Washington, DC: Urban Institute.

Burt, R. A. (1971). Forcing protection on children and their parents: The impact of Wyman v. James. *Michigan Law Review* 69:1259-1310.

Burtch, B., Pitcher-LaPrairie, C., and Wachtel, A. (1980). Issues in the determination and enforcement of child support orders. *Canadian Journal of Family Law* 3:5-21.

Bush, M. (1987). *Families in distress.* Los Angeles and Berkeley: University of California Press.

Butler, A. (1992). The changing economic consequences of teenage childbearing. *Social Service Review* 66:1-31.

Caffey, J. (1946). Multiple fractures in the long bones of infants suffering from chronic subdural hematoma. *American Journal of Roentgenology* 56:163-173.

Caffey, J., and Silverman, W. A. (1945). Infantile cortical hyperostos: Preliminary report on a new syndrome. *American Journal of Roentgenology* 55:1-16.

Calasanti, T. M., and Bailey, C. A. (1991). Gender inequality and the division of household labor in the United States and Sweden: A socialist-feminist approach. *Social Problem* 38:34-53.

Callahan, M. (1985). Public apathy and government parsimony: A review of child welfare in Canada. In K. L. Levitt and B. Wharf, eds., *The challenge of child welfare*, 1-27. Vancouver: University of British Columbia.

Campbell, D. T., and Stanley, J. C. (1963). Experimental and quasi-experimental designs for research. Chicago: Rand McNally.

Cameron, J. M. (1978). Radiological and pathological aspects of the battered child syndrome. In S. M. Smith, ed., *The maltreatment of children*, 69-81. Baltimore: University Park Press.

Canadian Council on Social Development. (1988). *A choice of futures: Canada's commitment to its children.* Ottawa: Author.

Canadian Press. (1993). Canada's net wealth rises 2%. *Globe and Mail,* November 15, p. B12.

Cassetty, J. (1978). *Child support and social policy.* Lexington, MA: D.C. Heath.

Chambers, D. L. (1979). *Making fathers pay: The enforcement of child support.* Chicago: University of Chicago Press.

Charnley, J. (1955). *The art of child placement.* Ann Arbor: University of Michigan Press.

Chawla, R. K. (1990). The distribution of wealth in Canada and the United States. *Perspectives* 2:29-41.

Chess, W. A., Hale, K., Carroll, K., Baker, D. R., Wilson, M., Spyres, E., and Jayaratne, S. (1993). *The family focus services program: Final report.* Norman, OK: Oklahoma Department of Human Services.

Child Abuse Study Group. (1990). *Taking child abuse seriously.* London: Unwin Hyman.

Children's Bureau. (1980). *Child welfare training: Comprehensive syllabus for a child welfare training program.* DHHS Publication No. (OHDS) 80-30276, Washington, DC: U.S. Department of Health and Human Services.

Children's Defense Fund. (1986). *Preventing adolescent pregnancy: What schools can do.* Washington, DC: Author.

Children's Defense Fund. (1991). *The state of America's children 1991.* Washington, DC: Author.

Children's Defense Fund. (1994). *The state of America's children 1994.* Washington, DC: Author.

Clark, K. B. (1965). *Dark ghetto: Dilemmas of social power.* New York: Harper and Row.

Clarke, A. M., and Clark, C. B. eds. (1976). *Early experience: Myth and evidence.* London: Open Books.

Clarke-Stewart, A. (1993). *Daycare.* Cambridge, MA: Harvard University Press.

Clement, P. F. (1978). Families in foster care: Philadelphia in the late nineteenth century. *Social Service Review* 53:406-420.

Clinton Administration. (1994). Possible elements in the welfare reform proposal: a new vision. (March 22). Washington, DC: Author.

Cohen, J. S., and Westhues, A. (1990). *Well-functioning families for adoptive and foster children: A handbook for child welfare workers.* Toronto: University of Toronto Press.

Cohn, A. H., and Daro, D. (1987). Is treatment too late?: What ten years of evaluative research tell us. *Child Abuse and Neglect* 11:433-522.

Coleman, J. S., Campbell, E. Q., Hobson, C. J., McPartland, J., Mood, A. M., Weinfeld, F. D., and York, R. L. (1966). *Equality of educational opportunity.* Washington, DC: U.S. Government Printing Office.

Coleman, T. (1965). The NSPCC in need. *The Guardian*, February 19, 14.

Collier, W. V., and Hill, R. H. (1993). *Family ties. Intensive family preservation services program. An evaluation report.* New York, NY: New York Department of Juvenile Justice.

Colon, F. (1981). Family ties and child placement. In P. A. Sinanoglu and A. N. Maluccio, eds., *Parents of children in placement: Perspectives and programs*, 241-267. New York: Child Welfare League of America.

Committee for Economic Development. (1987). *Children in need: Investment strategies for the educationally disadvantaged.* Washington, DC: Author.

Congressional Budget Office. (1987). *The changing distribution of federal taxes: 1975-90*, October, table 8, 48. Washington, DC: Author.

Congressional Budget Office. (1992). *Green book.* Washington, DC: Author.

Conway, J. F. (1990). *The Canadian family in crisis.* Toronto: James Lorimer and Company.

Cooper, D. M. (1993). *Child abuse revisited: Children, society and social work.* Buckingham, England: Open University Press.

Corbit, G. (1985). *The hidden unemployables.* Paper delivered at the University of Calgary, January 21.

Corby, B. (1987). *Working with child abuse.* Milton Keynes, England: Open University Press.

Costin, L., and Rapp, C. (1984). *Child welfare policies and practices.* New York: McGraw-Hill.

Costin, L. (1992). Cruelty to children: A dormant issue and its rediscovery, 1920-1960. *Social Service Review* 66:177-198.

Cournand, A., and Meyer, M. (1976). The scientist's code. *Minerva* 14:79-96.

Creighton, S. J. (1984). *Trends in child abuse.* London: National Society for the Prevention of Cruelty to Children.

Cunningham, M. L., and Smith, R. J. (1990). *Family preservation in Tennessee: The home ties intervention.* Knoxville, TN: University of Tennessee Social Work Office of Research and Public Services.

Danziger, S., and Gottschalk, P. (1986). *How have families with children been faring?* Institute for Research on Poverty Discussion Paper 801-806. Madison, WI: University of Wisconsin.

Danziger, S., Jakubson, G., Schwartz, S., and Smolensky, E. (1982). Work and welfare as determinant of female poverty and household headship. *The Quarterly Journal of Economics* 98:519-534.

Danziger, S., and Stern, J. (1990). *The causes and consequences of child poverty in the United States.* Innocenti Occasional Papers, No. 10. Florence, Italy: Spedale degli Innocenti.

Danziger, S., and Weinberg, D. H., eds. (1986). *Fighting poverty.* Cambridge, MA: Harvard University Press.

Darity, W., Jr., and Myers, S., Jr. (1983). Changes in Black family structure: Implications for welfare dependency. *American Economic Review Proceedings* 73:59-64.

Daro, D. (1988). *Confronting child abuse: Research for effective program design.* New York: Free Press.

Daro, D. (1991). Review of *Recognizing child abuse*, by D. J. Besharov, *Children and Youth Services Review* 13:301-304.

Daro, D., and Mitchel, L. (1990). *Current trends in child abuse reporting and fatalities: The results of the 1989 annual fifty state summary.* Chicago: National Committee for the Prevention of Child Abuse and Neglect.

Daro, D., and McCurdy, M. A. (1991). *Current trends in child abuse reporting and fatalities: The results of the 1990 annual fifty state survey.* Working paper No. 808. Chicago: National Committee for the Prevention of Child Abuse.

Dattalo, P. (1991). *The gentrification of public welfare.* Unpublished paper. Richmond, VA: Virginia Commonwealth University.

Dear, R. B. (1989). What's right with welfare? The other face of AFDC. *Journal of Sociology and Social Work* 16:5-43.

DeFrancis, V. (1956). *Child protective services in the United States.* Denver, CO: Children's Division, The American Humane Association.

DeFrancis, V. (1966). *Child abuse legislation: Analysis of mandatory reporting laws in the United States.* Denver, CO: Children's Division, American Humane Association.

DeFrancis, V. (1967). *Child protective services in the United States: A nationwide survey.* Denver, CO: Children's Division, American Humane Association.

Denison, E. F. (1985). *Trends in American economic growth, 1929-1982.* Washington, DC: The Brookings Institution.

DeParle, J. (1992). Why marginal changes don't rescue the welfare system. *The New York Times*, March 1, E3.

Desowitz, R. S. (1987). *The thorn in the starfish.* New York: W.W. Norton.

Dickinson, N. S. (1986). Which welfare strategies work? *Social Work* 32:266-272.

Dingwall, R. (1989). Some problems about predicting child abuse and neglect. In O. Stevenson, ed., *Child Abuse: Professional practice and public policy*, 28-53. London: Havester Weatsheaf.

Dingwall, R., Eekelaar, J., and Murray, T. (1983). *The protection of children: State intervention and family life*. Oxford: Basil Blackwell.

Donnelly, A. H. C. (1991). What we have learned about prevention: What we should do about it. *Child Abuse and Neglect* 15:99-106.

Donnelly, B. P. (1980). *A policy review of California's foster care placement and payment systems*. Report No. S80-6 (May 1980). State of California, Department of Finance, Program Evaluation Unit.

Donzelot, J. (1979). *The policing of families*. New York: Pantheon.

Downs, S., and Taylor, C. (1978). *Resources for training: Permanent planning in foster care*. Portland, OR: Regional Research Institute for Human Services, Portland State University.

Duncan, G. J., and Hoffman, S. D. (1985). Economic consequences of marital stability. In M. David and T. Smeeding, eds., *Horizontal equity, uncertainty and well-being*, 427-470. Chicago: University of Chicago Press.

Duncan, G. J., and Hoffman, S. D. (1989). *Welfare benefits, economic opportunities, and the incidence of out-of-wedlock births among Black teenage girls*, mimeo. Institute for Social Research, University of Michigan, March.

Duncan, G. J., and Rodgers, W. (1991). Has children's poverty become more persistent? *American Sociological Review* 56:538-550.

Duquette, D. N. (1980). Liberty and lawyers in child protection. In C. H. Kempe and R. E. Helfer, eds., *The battered child*, 3d ed. rev. and expanded, 316-329. Chicago: The University of Chicago Press.

Dybwad, G. (1949). The challenge to research. *Child Welfare* 28:9-15.

Eckenrode, J., Powers, J., Doris, J., Munsch, J., and Bolger, N. (1988). Substantiation of child abuse and neglect reports. *Journal of Consulting and Clinical Psychology* 56:9-16.

Edelman, M. W. (1987). *Families in peril: An agenda for social change*. Cambridge, MA: Harvard University Press.

Eichler, M. (1988). *Families in Canada today: Recent changes and their policy consequences*. 2d ed. Toronto: Gage.

Ellwood, D. T. (1986). *Targeting the would-be long term recipient: Who should be served?* report to the U.S. Department of Health and Human Services. Princeton, NJ: Mathematica Policy Research.

Ellwood, D. T. (1988). *Poor support*. New York: Basic Books.

Ellwood, D. T. (1989). *Poverty through the eyes of children*. Unpublished manuscript, John F. Kennedy School of Government, Harvard University, Cambridge, MA.

Ellwood, D. T., and Crane, J. (1990). Family change among Black Americans: What do we know? *Journal of Economic Perspectives* 4:6-84.

Elmer, E. (1967). *Children in jeopardy-A study of abused minors and their families.* Pittsburgh, PA: University of Pittsburgh Press.

Emlen, A. (1974). Day care for whom? In A. L. Schorr, ed., *Children and decent people*, 88-112. New York: Basic Books.

Emlen, A. (1976). *Barriers to planning for children in foster care.* Vol. 1. Portland, OR: Regional Research Institute for Human Services, Portland State University.

Emlen, A., Lahti, J., Downs, G., McKay, A., and Downs, S. (1977). *Overcoming barriers to planning for children in foster care.* Portland, OR: Regional Research Institute for Human Services, Portland State University.

England, H. (1986). *Social work as art: Making sense for good practice.* London: Allen and Unwin.

Epstein, W. M. (1983). Research biases. *Social Work* 28:77-78.

Erikson, E. (1959). *Identity and the life cycle.* New York: International University Press.

Espenshade, T. J. (1979). The economic consequences of divorce. *Journal of Marriage and the Family* 41:615-625.

Evans, P. M. (1992). Targeting single mothers for employment: Comparisons from the United States, Britain, and Canada. *Social Service Review* 66:378-398.

Evans, P. M., and McIntyre, E. (1987). Welfare, work incentives, and the single mother: An interprovincial comparison. In J. S. Ismael, ed., *The Canadian welfare state*, 101-125. Edmonton: The University of Alberta Press.

Ezell, M., and McNeese, C. A. (1986). Practice effectiveness: Research or rhetoric? *Social Work* 31:401-402.

Falconer, N. E., and Swift, K. (1983). *Preparing for practice, The fundamentals of child protection.* Toronto: Children's Aid Society of Metro Toronto.

Faller, K. C. (1981). *Social work with abused and neglected children.* New York: The Free Press.

Faller, K. C. (1985). Unanticipated problems in the United States child protection system. *Child Abuse and Neglect* 9:63-69.

Faller, K. C. (1991). Child welfare policy and practice. *Children and Youth Services Review* 13:1-8.

Faludi, S. (1991). *Backlash: The undeclared war against American women.* New York: Crown Publishers.

Fanshel, D. (1971). The exit of children from foster care: An interim research report. *Child Welfare* 50:65-81.

Fanshel, D. (1976). Discharge and other status outcomes. *Child Welfare* 55:143-171.

Fanshel, D. (1981). Decision-making under uncertainty: Foster care for abused or neglected children. *American Journal of Public Health* 71:685-686.

Fanshel, D., and Shinn, E. (1972). *Dollars and sense in the foster care of children: A look at cost factors.* New York: Child Welfare League of America.

Fanshel, D., and Shinn, E. (1978). *Children in foster care: A longitudinal investigation.* New York: Columbia University Press.

Federal Bureau of Investigation. (1962-1989). *Uniform crime reports for the United States.* Washington, DC: U.S. Department of Justice, Federal Bureau of Investigation.

Fein, E., Maluccio, A. N., Hamilton, J. V., and Ward, D. E. (1983). After foster care: Outcomes of permanent planning for children. *Child Welfare* 62:485-462.

Fein, L. G. (1979). Can child fatalities, end product of child abuse, be prevented? *Children and Youth Services Review* 1:1-53.

Feldman, L. H. (1990). *Evaluating the impact of family preservation services in New Jersey.* New Jersey: Bureau of Research, Evaluation, and Quality Assurance, Division of Youth and Family Services.

Feldman, L. H. (1991). *Assessing the effectiveness of family preservation services in New Jersey within an ecological context.* NJ: New Jersey Department of Human Services, Division of Youth and Family Services.

Feldstein, M. (1974). Social Security, induced retirement, and private savings: New time-series evidence. *Journal of Political Economy* 84:905-926.

Ferguson, D. H. (1961). Children in need of parents: Implications of the Child Welfare League Study. *Child Welfare* 40:1-6.

Fienberg, S. E. (1981). *The analysis of cross-classified categorical data.* Cambridge, MA: The MIT Press.

Finkelhor, D. (1990). Is child abuse over reported? *Public Welfare* 48:22-29.

Firestone-Seghi, L. (1979). Assessing results of the Alameda Project. *Children and Youth Services Review* 1:429-435.

Fischer, J. (1971). *Framework for the analysis of outcome research.* Honolulu: School of Social Work, University of Hawaii.

Fischer, J. (1973). Is casework effective: A review? *Social Work* 18:5-20.

Fischer, J. (1983). Evaluations of social work effectiveness: Is positive evidence always good evidence? *Social Work* 28:74-77.

Fisher, S. H. (1958). Skeletal manifestations of parent induced trauma in infants and children. *8th Medical Journal* 51:956-960.

Fontana, V. J. (1971). *The maltreated child.* Springfield, IL: Charles C Thomas.

Fontana, V. J., and Besharov, D. J. (1979). *The maltreated child: The maltreatment syndrome in children, A medical, legal and social guide.* 4th ed. Springfield, IL: Charles C Thomas.

Forrest, J. D., and Singh, S. (1990). The sexual and reproductive behavior of American women, 1982-1988. *Family Planning Perspectives* 22:206-214.

Forsythe, P. (1992). Homebuilders and family preservation. *Children and Youth Services Review* 14:37-47.

Fraiberg, S. (1977). *Every child's birthright: In defense of mothering.* New York: Basic Books.

Frank, R. H. (1985). *Choosing the right pond: Human behavior and the quest for service.* New York: Oxford University Press.

Franklin, A. W., ed. (1975). *Concerning child abuse.* London: Churchill-Livingstone.

Fraser, M., Pecora, P., and Haapala, D. (1991). *Families in crisis.* New York: Aldine de Gruyter.

French, D. (1949). *The contribution of research to social work.* New York: American Association of Social Workers.

Friedberg, A. (1988). *The weary titan: Britain and experience of relative decline, 1895-1905.* Princeton, NJ: Princeton University Press.

Friedman, M., and Friedman, R. (1979). *Free to choose.* New York: Harcourt Brace Jovanovich.

Frost, N., and Stein, M. (1989). *The politics of child welfare: Inequality, power and change.* New York: Harvester Wheatsheaf.

Furstenberg, F. F., Jr. (1991). As the pendulum swings: Teenage childbearing and social concern. *Family Relations* 40: 127-138.

Furstenberg, F. F., Jr., Brooks-Gunn, J., and Morgan, S. P. (1987). *Adolescent mothers in later life.* New York: Cambridge University Press.

Galbraith, J. K. (1967). *The new industrial state.* Boston: Houghton-Mifflin.

Gambrill, E. (1990). *Critical thinking in clinical practice: Improving the accuracy of judgments and decision about clients.* San Francisco: Jossey-Bass.

Gambrill, E. D., and Stein, T. J. (1981). Decision making and case management: achieving continuity of care for children in out-of-home placement. In A. N. Maluccio and P. A. Sinanoglu, eds., *The challenge of partnership: Working with parents of children in foster care*, 109-139. New York: Child Welfare League of America, Inc.

Garbarino, J. (1991). *No place to be a child: Growing up in a war zone.* Lexington, Mass: Lexington Books.

Garbarino, J., and Carson, B., and Flood, M. F. (1983). A protective service system. *Children and Youth Services Review* 5:49-63.

Garbarino, J., and Sherman, D. (1980). Identifying high-risk neighborhoods. In J. Garbarino, S. H. Stocking, and Associates, eds., *Protecting children from abuse and neglect: Developing and maintaining effective support systems for families*, 94-108. San Francisco: Jossey-Bass.

Garbarino, J., and Stocking, S. H. (1981). The social context of child maltreatment. In J. Garbarino, S. H. Stocking, and Associates, eds., *Protecting children from abuse and neglect: Developing and maintaining effective support systems for families*, 1-14. San Francisco: Jossey-Bass.

Garfinkel, I. (1968). Negative income-tax and children's allowances programs-Comparisons. *Social Work* 13:33-39.

Garfinkel, I. (1992). *Assuring child support: An extension of child security.* New York: Russell Sage Press.

Garfinkel, I., and McLanahan, S. (1986). *Single mothers and their children: A new American dilemma.* Washington, DC: Urban Institute Press.

Garfinkel, I., Meyer, D. R., and Sandefur, G. D. (1992). The effects of alternative child support systems on Blacks, Hispanics, and Non-Hispanic Whites. *Social Service Review* 66:505-523.

Garfinkel, I., and Uhr, L. (1987). A new approach to child support. *The Public Interest* 75:111-122.

Gart, J. J. (1971). The comparison of proportions: A review of significance tests, confidence intervals, and adjustments for stratification. *Review of the International Statistical Institute* 39:148-169.

Gelles, R. J., and Straus, M. A. (1987). Is violence toward children increasing? A comparison of 1975 and 1985 national survey rates. *Journal of Interpersonal Violence* 2:212-222.

Gelles, R. J., and Straus, M. A. (1988). *Intimate violence: The causes and consequences of abuse in the American family.* New York: Simon and Schuster.

General Accounting Office. (1976). *Administration of Children, Youth and Families-Need to better use its research results and clarify its role.* HRD-77-76. Washington, DC: Author.

Gideonse, S. K., and Meyers, W. R. (1988). Why 'workfare' fails. *Challenge* 31:44-49.

Gil, D. (1970). *Violence against children.* Cambridge, MA: Harvard University Press.

Gilbert, N., and Gilbert, B. (1991). *The enabling state: Modern welfare capitalism in America.* New York: Oxford University Press.

Gilder, G. (1981). *Wealth and poverty.* New York: Basic Books.

Gilder, G. (1984). *The spirit of enterprise.* New York: Simon and Schuster.

Giovannoni, J. M. (1982). Prevention of child abuse and neglect: Research and policy issues. *Social Work Research and Abstracts* 18:23-31.

Giovannoni, J. M. (1989). Substantiated and unsubstantiated reports of child maltreatment. *Children and Youth Services Review* 11:299-318.

Giovannoni, J. M., and Becerra, R. (1979). *Defining child abuse.* New York: Free Press.

Giovannoni, J. M., and Billingsley, A. (1970). Child neglect among the poor: A study of parental adequacy in families of three ethnic groups. *Child Welfare* 49:196-204.

Glazer, N. (1974). The schools of the minor professions. *Minerva* 12:346-364.

Glickman, E. (1957). *Child placement through clinically oriented casework.* New York: Columbia University Press.

Godfrey, R., and Schlesinger, B. (1965). *Child welfare services: Winding paths to maturity.* Toronto: Canadian Conference on Children.

Goerge, R. M. (1990). The reunification process in substitute care. *Social Service Review* 64:422-457.

Golden, O. (1992). *Poor children and welfare reform.* Westport, CT: Auburn House Publishing.

Golding, P., and Middleton, S. (1982). *Images of welfare: Press and public attitudes to poverty.* London: Martin Robertson.

Goldstein, H. (1992). If social work hasn't made progress as a science, might it be an art? *Families in Society* 73:48-55.

Goldstein, J., Freud, A., and Solnit, A. (1973). *Beyond the best interests of the child.* New York: Free Press.

Goldstein, J., Freud, A., and Solnit, A. (1979). *Before the best interests of the child.* New York: Free Press.

Goldstein, N. C. (1991). *Why poverty is bad for children.* Unpublished Ph.D. dissertation. Cambridge, MA: Harvard University Press.

Goodman, L. A. (1985). The analysis of cross-classified data having ordered and/or unordered categories: Association models, correlational models, and asymmetry models for contingency tables with or without missing data. *Annals of Statistics* 13:10-69.

Goodwin, L. (1972). Welfare mothers and the work ethic. *Monthly Labor Review* 95:35-37.

Gordon, H. L. (1948, October). Editorial comment: Towards improved services to children. *Child Welfare* 27:7-10.

Gordon, H. L. (1956). Casework services for children. Boston: Houghton-Mifflin.

Gordon, L. (1988). *Heroes of their own lives: The politics and history of family violence, Boston 1880-1960.* New York: Penguin Books.

Gray, J. D., Cutler, C. A., Dean, J. G., and Kempe, C. H. (1977). Prediction and prevention of child abuse and neglect. *Child Abuse and Neglect* 1:45-58.

Greenhouse, S. (1993). If the French can do it, why can't we? *The New York Times Magazine*, November 14, Section 6, 59-62.

Greenland, C. (1987). *Preventing CAN deaths: An international study of deaths due to child abuse and neglect.* London: Tavistock Publications.

Groenveld, L. P., and Giovannoni, J. M. (1977). Disposition of child abuse and neglect cases. *Social Work Research and Abstracts* 13:24-31.

Gruber, A. R. (1978). *Children in foster care: Destitute, neglected, betrayed.* New York: Human Sciences Press.

Guest, D. (1985). *The emergence of social security in Canada,* 2d ed. Vancouver: University of British Columbia Press.

Gwinn, J. L., Lewin, K. W., and Peterson, H. G. (1961). Roentgenographic manifestations of unsuspected trauma in infancy: A problem of medical, social and legal importance. *Journal of the American Medical Association* 176:926-929.

Haanes-Olson, L. (1972). Children's allowance: Their size and structure in five countries. *Social Security Bulletin* 5:17-28.

Hacker, A. (1992). *Two nations: Black and white, separate, hostile, unequal.* New York: Ballantine Books.

Hagan, H. R. (1957). Distinctive aspects of child welfare. *Child Welfare* 36:1-6.

Halper, G. and Jones, M. A. (1981). *Serving families at risk of dissolution: Public preventive services in New York City.* New York: Human Resources Administration, Special Services for Children.

Hampton, R. L., and Newberger, E. H. (1985). Child abuse incidence and reporting by hospitals: Significance of severity, class, and race. *American Journal of Public Health* 75:56-60.

Handler, J. F., and Hasenfeld, Y. (1991). *The moral construction of poverty: Welfare reform in America.* New York: Sage.

Hardicker, P., Exton, K., and Barker, M. (1991). *Policies and practices in preventive child care.* London: Gower.

Harding, N. (1992). The Marxist-Leninist detour. In J. Dunn, ed., *Democracy: The unfinished journey 508BC to AD1993, 155-187.* New York: Oxford University Press.

Harlow, H. (1958). The nature of love. *American Psychologist* 13:673-685.

Harlow, H. (1961). The development of affection patterns in infant monkeys. In B. M. Foss, ed., *Determinants of infant behavior,* Vol. 1. London: Methuen.

Harlow, H. F., and Zimmerman, R. R. (1959). Affectional responses in the infant monkey. *Science* 130:421-432.

Hartman, A. (1971). But what is social casework? *Social Casework* 52:411-419.

Haskins, R., Burnett, C. K., and Dobelstein, A. (1983). *Single parent families: Recommendations for child support.* Chapel Hill: University of North Carolina, Bush Institute for Child and Family Policy.

Haveman, R. (1988). *Starting even: An equal opportunity program to combat the nation's new poverty.* New York: Simon and Schuster.

Hazlitt, H. (1973). *The conquest of poverty.* New Rochelle, NY: Arlington House.

Heineman, M. (1981). The obsolete scientific imperative in social work research. *Social Service Review* 55:371-397.

Helfer, R. (1978). *Report on the research using the Michigan Screening Profile of Parenting (MSPP).* Washington, DC: National Center on Child Abuse and Neglect.

Henggler, S. W., Melton, G. B., and Smith, L. A. (1992). Family preservation using multisystematic therapy: An effective alternative to incarcerating serious juvenile offenders. *Journal of Consulting and Clinical Psychology* 60:953-961.

Hennepin County Community Services Department. (1980). *Family study project: Demonstration and research in intensive services to families.* Minneapolis: Author.

Henriksen, H., and Holter, H. (1978). Norway. In S. Kamerman and A. J. Kahn, eds., *Family policy: Government and families in fourteen countries,* 49-67. New York: Columbia University Press.

Henshaw, S. K., and Van Vort, J. (1989). Teenage abortion, birth and pregnancy statistics: An update. *Family Planning Perspective* 21:85-88.

Hepworth, H. P. (1982). *Trends and comparisons in Canadian child welfare services.* Paper presented at the First Conference on Provincial Social Welfare Policy, University of Calgary, May 5-7.

Hepworth, H. P. (1985). Child neglect and abuse. In K. L. Levitt and B. Wharf, eds., *The challenge of child welfare,* 28-52. Vancouver: University of British Columbia.

Hewlett, S. A. (1991). *When the bough breaks: The cost of neglecting our children.* New York: Basic Books.

Hewitt, C. (1983). Defending a termination of parental rights case. In M. Hardin, ed., *Foster children in the courts,* 229-263. Boston: Butterworth Legal Publishers.

Hiller, H. H. (1991). *Canadian society: A macro analysis.* 2d ed. Toronto: Prentice-Hall.

Holman, B. (1978). *Poverty: Explanations of social deprivation.* London: Martin Robertson.

Holman, B. (1988). *Putting families first: Prevention and child care.* London: Macmillan.

Hornby, H., and Collins, M. (1981). Teenagers in foster care: The forgotten majority. *Children and Youth Services Review* 3:7-20.

Hoshino, G. (1974). AFDC as child welfare. In A. Schorr, ed., *Children and decent people,* 113-141. New York: Basic Books.

Hotschild, A., and Machung, A. (1989). *The second-shift: Inside the two-job marriage.* New York: Penguin.

Howells, J. G. (1975). *Remember Maria.* London: Butterworths.

Howitt, D. (1992). *Child abuse errors: When good intentions go wrong.* New York: Harvester Wheatsheaf.

Howling, P. T., Wodarski, J. S., Kurtz, P. D., and Gaudin, J. M. (1989). Methodological issues in child maltreatment research. *Social Work Research and Abstracts* 25:3-7.

Hunter, W. M., Coulter, M. L., Runyan, D. K., and Everson, M. D. (1990). Determinants of placement for sexually abused children. *Child Abuse and Neglect* 14:407-417.

Huston, A. C. ed. (1991). *Children in poverty: Child development and public policy*. New York: Cambridge University Press.

Hutchison, E. D. (1989). Child protective screening decisions: An analysis of predictive factors. *Social Work Research and Abstracts* 25:9-15.

Hutchison, E. D. (1990). Child maltreatment: Can it be defined? *Social Service Review* 64:61-78.

Hutchison, E. D. (1992). Child welfare as a woman's issue. *Families in Society* 73:67-78.

Hutchison, E. D. (1993). Mandatory reporting laws: Child protective case-finding gone awry? *Social Work* 38:56-63.

Huxley, P. (1986). Statistical errors in the British Journal of Social Work, Volumes 1-14. *British Journal of Social Work* 16:645-58.

Huxley, P. (1988). "Quantitative-descriptive" articles in the British Journal of Social Work, volumes 1-14. *The British Journal of Social Work* 18:189-199.

Ingrassia, M., and McCormick, J. (1994). Why leave children with bad parents? *Newsweek*, April 25: 52-58.

Innis, M. (1991). Women ain't equal yet, baby. *Denver Post*, July 1, editorial page.

Isaacs, S. (1972). Neglect, cruelty, and battering. *British Medical Journal* 2:756-757.

James, P. D. (1993). *The children of men*. New York: Penguin.

Janko, K. S. (1991). *The social construction of child abuse: A qualitative investigation of child maltreatment*. Unpublished Ph.D. dissertation, University of Oregon.

Jaudes, P. K., and Morris, M. (1990). Child sexual abuse: Who goes home? *Child Abuse and Neglect* 14:61-68.

Jencks, C. (1992). *Rethinking social policy: Race, poverty, and the underclass*. Cambridge, MA.: Harvard University Press.

Jenkins, S., and Norman, E. (1972). *Filial deprivation*. New York: Columbia University Press.

Jenkins, S. (1974). Foster care. In A. Schorr, ed., *Children and decent people*, 24-52. New York: Basic Books.

Jenkins, S., and Norman, E. (1975). *Beyond placement: Mothers view foster care*. New York: Columbia University Press.

Jenkins, S., and Sauber, M. (1966). *Paths to child placement*. New York: Community Council of Greater New York.

Jeter, H. R. (1960). *Children who receive services from public child welfare agencies.* Washington, DC: Children's Bureau.

Jeter, H. R. (1963). *Children, problems and services in child welfare programs.* Washington, DC: Children's Bureau.

Johnson, C. M., Sum, A. M., and Weill, J. D. (1988). *Vanishing dreams: The growing economic plight of America's young families.* Washington, DC: Children's Defense Fund.

Johnson, C. M., Miranda, L., Sherman, A., and Weill, J. D. (1991). *Child poverty in America.* Washington, DC: Children's Defense Fund.

Johnson, D., and Fein, E. (1991). The concept of attachment: Applications to adoption. *Children and Youth Services Review* 13:397-412.

Johnson, H. (Spring 1988). Wife abuse. Statistics Canada, *Canadian Social Trends,* 17-22.

Johnson, H., and Chisholm, P. (Autumn 1989). Family homicide. Statistics Canada, *Canadian Social Trends,* 17-18.

Jones, M. A., Neuman, R., and Shyne, A. (1976). *A second chance for families: Evaluation of a program to reduce foster care.* New York: Child Welfare League of America.

Jones, A., and Rutman, L. (1981). *In the children's aid: J.J. Kelso and child welfare in Ontario.* Toronto: University of Toronto Press.

Jones, C. A., Gordon, N. M., and Sawhill, I. V. (1976). *Child support payments in the United States.* Washington, DC: Urban Institute.

Kadushin, A. (1959). The knowledge base of social work. In A. J. Kahn, ed., *Issues in American social work,* 39-79. New York: Columbia University Press.

Kadushin, A. (1965). Introduction of new orientations in child welfare research. In M. Norris and B. Wallace, eds., *The known and the unknown in child welfare research: An appraisal,* 28-39. New York: Child Welfare League of America.

Kadushin, A. (1967). *Child welfare services.* 1st ed. New York: Macmillan.

Kadushin, A. (1976). *Emotional abuse.* Unpublished paper presented at a joint U.S. National Center on Child Abuse and Neglect and National Institute of Mental Health Workshop on Emotional Maltreatment, Houston, Texas, April.

Kadushin, A., ed. (1970). *Child welfare services: A sourcebook.* New York: Macmillan.

Kadushin, A. (1978). Child welfare strategy in the coming years: An overview. In F. Farro, ed., *Child welfare strategy in the coming years,* 1-50. Children's Bureau (OHDS) 78-30158. Washington, DC: U.S. Department of Health, Education, and Welfare.

Kadushin, A., and Martin, J. A. (1981). *Child abuse: An interactional event.* New York: Columbia University Press.

Kadushin, A., and Martin, J. A. (1988). *Child welfare services*. 4th Edition. New York: Macmillan.

Kahn, A. J. (1956). Facilitating social work research. *Social Service Review* 30:331-343.

Kahn, A. J., ed. (1973). *Shaping the new social work*. New York: Columbia University Press.

Kahn, A. J. (1976). Social service delivery at the neighborhood level: Experience, theory and fads. *Social Service Review* 50:23-56.

Kahn, A. J., and Kamerman, S. B. (1975a). *Not for the poor alone*. Philadelphia: Temple University Press.

Kahn, A. J., and Kamerman, S. B. (1975b). *Social policies in the United States: Policies and programs*. Philadelphia: Temple University Press.

Kamerman, S. B., and Kahn, A. J., eds. (1978). *Family policy: Government and families in fourteen countries*. New York: Columbia University Press.

Kamerman, S. B., and Kahn, A. J. (1983). *Income transfers for families with children: An eight country study*. Philadelphia: Temple University Press.

Kamerman, S. B., and Kahn, A. J., eds. (1988a). *Child support: From debt collection to social policy*. Newbury Park, CA: Sage.

Kamerman, S. B., and Kahn, A. J. (1988b). *Mothers alone: Strategies for a time of change*. Dover, MA: Auburn House Publishing.

Kamerman, S. B., and Kahn, A. J. (1990). Social services for children, youth and families in the United States. Special Issue of *Children and Youth Services Review* 12:1-184.

Kaplan, D., and Reich, R. (1976). The murdered child and his killers. *American Journal of Psychiatry* 133:809-813.

Karpf, M. J. (1931). *The scientific basis of social work*. New York: Columbia University Press.

Katz, M. H., Hampton, R. L., Newberger, E. H., Bowles, R. T., and Snyder, J. C. (1986). Returning children home: Clinical decision making in cases of child abuse and neglect. *American Journal of Orthopsychiatry* 56:253-263.

Katz, M. B. (1986). In the shadow of the poorhouse. New York: Basic Books.

Kempe, C. H., and Silver, H. (1959). The problem of parental criminal neglect and severe abuse of children. *AMA Journal of Diseases of Children* 98:528.

Kempe, R. S., and Kempe, C. H. (1978). *Child abuse*. New York: Open Books.

Kempe, C. H., Silverman, F., Steele, B., Droegmueller, W., and Silver, H. (1962). The battered-child syndrome. *Journal of the American Medical Association* 181:17-24.

Kendrick, M. (1990). *Nobody's children: The foster care crisis in Canada*. Toronto: Macmillan of Canada.

Kessler-Harris, A. (1982). *Out to work: A history of wage-earning women in the United States*. New York: Oxford University Press.

Keynes, J. M. (1964). *The general theory of employment, interest and money.* New York: Harcourt, Brace and World.

Kimura, M. (1965). Some recent advances in the theory of population genetics. *Japanese Journal of Human Genetics* 10:43-48.

King, M. L., Jr. (1963). *Why we can't wait.* New York: Harper and Row.

Kinney, J. M., Haapala, D., and Booth, C. (1991). *Keeping families together: The Homebuilders Model.* Hawthorne, NY: Aldine de Gruyter.

Kinney, J. M., Madsen, B., Fleming, T., and Haapala, D. (1977). Homebuilders: Keeping families together. *Journal of Clinical and Counseling Psychology* 43:667-673.

Kline, D., and Overstreet, H. (1972). *Foster care or children: Nurture and treatment.* New York: Columbia University Press.

Knitzer, J., Allen, M. A., and McGowan, B. (1978). *Children without homes.* Washington, DC: Children's Defense Fund.

Koring, P. (1994). Taxpayers are Major's main squeeze: After 15 years of Tory government, the rich are richer and the poor are poorer. *Globe and Mail*, February 2: A1-A2.

Kostash, M. (1987). *No kidding: Inside the world of teenage girls.* Toronto: McClelland and Stewart.

Kotlowitz, A. (1991). *There are no children here: The story of two boys in the Other America.* NY: Doubleday.

Kozol, J. (1991). *Savage inequalities: Children in America's schools.* New York: Crown Books.

Krugman, P. R. (1992). *The age of diminished expectations: U. S. economic policy in the 1990s.* Cambridge, MA: MIT Press

Kuhn, T. S. (1962). *The structure of scientific revolutions.* Chicago: The University of Chicago Press.

Kunzel, R.G. (1993). *Fallen women, problem girls: Unmarried mothers and the professionalization of social work, 1890-1945.* New Haven, CT: Yale University Press.

Labor Trends, August 1990.

Landsman, M. J. (1985). *Evaluation of fourteen child placement prevention projects in Wisconsin, 1983-1985.* Iowa City, IA: National Resource Center on Family Based Services.

LaRoe, R., and Pool, J. C. (1988). Gap grows between rich, poor. *Columbus Dispatch*, July 16.

Lealman, G. T., Haigh, D., Phillips, J. M., Stoan, J., and Ord-Smith, C. (1983). Prediction and prevention of child abuse-An empty hope. *Lancet* 8339:1423-1424.

Lefaucheur, N., and Martin, C. (1993). Lone parent families in France: Situation and research. In J. Hudson and B. Galaway, eds., *Single parent families: Per-*

spectives on research and policy, 31-50. Toronto: Thompson Educational Publishing.

Leiby, J. (1978). *A history of social welfare and social work in the United States.* New York: Columbia University Press.

Lemov, P. (1989). Bringing children of the underclass into the mainstream. *Governing*, June, 34-39.

Levine, R. S. (1973). Caveat parens: A demystification of the child protection system. *University of Pittsburgh Law Review* 35:1-52.

Levitan, S. A. (1990). *Programs in aid of the poor.* Baltimore, MD: The John Hopkins University Press.

Levitt, K. L., and Wharf, B., eds. (1985). *The challenge of child welfare.* Vancouver: University of British Columbia.

Levy, F. (1987). *Dollars and dreams: The changing American income distribution.* New York: W. W. Norton and Company.

Lewis, A., and Schneider, W. (1985). Hard times: The public on poverty. *Public Opinion* 7:2-7.

Lewis, R. (1994). Application and adaptation of intensive family preservation services to use for the reunification of foster children with their biological parents. *Children and Youth Services Review* 16: forthcoming.

Liljestrom, R. (1978). Sweden. In S. Kamerman and A. J. Kahn, eds., *Family policy: Government and families in fourteen countries*, 19-48. New York: Columbia University Press.

Lindblom, C. E., and Cohen, D. K. (1979). *Usable knowledge: Social science and social problem solving.* New Haven: Yale University Press.

Lindsey, D. (1978). *The scientific publication system in social science: A study of the operation of leading professional journals in psychology, sociology and social work.* San Francisco: Jossey-Bass.

Lindsey, D. (1982). Achievements for children in foster care. *Social Work* 27:491-496.

Lindsey, D. (1991a). Adequacy of income and the foster care placement decision: Using an odds ratio approach to examine client variables. *Social Work Research and Abstracts* 28:29-36.

Lindsey, D. (1991b). Building a great public university: The role of funding at British and American universities. *Research in Higher Education* 32:217-244.

Lindsey, D. (1991c). *Does increased reporting reduce child abuse fatalities? An examination of national statistics.* Unpublished manuscript. School of Social Welfare, University of California, Berkeley.

Lindsey, D. (1991d). Factors affecting the foster care placement decision: An analysis of national survey data. *American Journal of Orthopsychiatry* 61:272-281.

Lindsey, D. (1991e). Reliability of the foster care placement decision: A review. *Research in Social Work Practice* 2:65-80.

Lindsey, D., and Kirk, S. A. (1992). The role of social work journals in the development of a knowledge base for the profession. *Social Service Review* 66: 295-310.

Lindsey, D., and Ozawa, M. N. (1979). Schizophrenia and SSI: Implications and problems. *Social Work* 24:120-126.

Lis, E. F., and Frauenberger, G. S. (1950). Multiple fractures associated with subdural hematoma in infancy. *Paediatrics* 6:890-892.

Longfellow, C. (1979). Divorce in context: Its impact on children. In G. Levinger and O. C. Moles, eds., *Divorce and separation: Context, causes, and consequences*, 287-306. New York: Basic Books.

Love, R., and Poulin, S. (1991). Family income and inequality in the 1980s. *Perspectives* 3:51-57.

Low, S. (1958). *Staff in public child welfare programs-1956, with Trend Data 1946-1956.* Children's Bureau Statistical Series, No. 41. Washington, DC: U.S. Children's Bureau.

Lyle, C. G., and Nelson, J. (1983). *Home based vs. traditional child protective services: A study of home based services demonstration project in the Ramsey County Community Human Services Department.* Unpublished paper. St. Paul, MN: Ramsey County Community Human Services Department.

Lynch, M. A. (1985). Child abuse before Kempe: An historical literature review. *Child Abuse and Neglect* 9:39-54.

Maas, H. S., and Engler, Jr., R. E. (1959). *Children in need of parents.* New York: Columbia University Press.

MacDonald, M., and Sawhill, I. V. (1978). Welfare policy and the family. *Public Policy* 26:89-119.

Magura, S. (1981). Are services to prevent foster care effective? *Children and Youth Services Review* 3:193-212.

Mahoney, K., and Mahoney, M. J. (1974). Psychoanalytic guidelines for child placement. *Social Work* 19:688-696.

Mahoney, M. J. (1976). *The scientist as subject.* Cambridge, MA: Ballinger.

Malthus, T. R. (1941). *Essay on the principle of population.* [first published in 1798]. New York: E.P. Dutton.

Maluccio, A. N., and Sinanoglu, P. A. (1981). *The challenge of partnership: Working with parents of children in foster care.* New York: Child Welfare League of America.

Mandell, N. (1988). The child question: Links between women and children in the family. In N. Mandell and A. Duffy, eds., *Reconstructing the Canadian family: Feminist perspectives*, 49-81. Toronto: Butterworths.

Margolin, L. (1992). Deviance on record: Techniques for labeling child abusers in official documents. *Social Problems* 39:58-70.

Marie, A. (1954). Hematome sousdural du nourrisson associe a des fractures des membres. *Semaine hospitale Paris* 30:1757.

Marmor, T. R., Mashaw, J. L., and Harvey, P. L. (1990). *America's misunderstood welfare state: Persistent myths, enduring realities.* New York: Basic Books.

Marquezy, R. A., Bach, C., and Blondeau, M. (1952). Hematome sousdural et fractures multiplas des os longs chez un nourrisson de N. mois. *Archives Francaises de Pediatrie* 9:526-000.

Marshall, W., and Kamarck, E. C. (1993). Replacing welfare with work. In W. Marshall and M. Schram, eds., *Mandate for change,* 217-236. New York: The Berkley Publishing Group.

Martin, M. (1985). Poverty and child welfare. In K. L. Levitt and B. Wharf, eds., *The challenge of child welfare,* 53-65. Vancouver: University of British Columbia.

Mason, J., Wodarski, J. S., and Parham, J. (1985). Work and welfare: A reevaluation of AFDC. *Social Work* 33:197-203.

Massey, D. S., and Denton, N. A. (1993). *American apartheid: Segregation and the making of the underclass.* Cambridge, MA: Harvard University Press.

Matza, D. (1964). *Delinquency and drift.* New York: Wiley.

Maxwell, N. L. (1990). Changing female labor-force participation—Influences on income inequality and distribution. *Social Forces* 68:1251-1266.

McCabe, A. (1967). *The pursuit of promise.* New York: Community Service Society.

McCurdy, M. A., and Daro, D. (1993). *Current trends in child abuse reporting and fatalities: The results of the 1992 annual fifty state survey.* Chicago: National Committee for the Prevention of Child Abuse.

McDonald, T., and Marks, J. (1991). A review of risk factors assessed in child protective services. *Social Service Review* 65:112-132.

McDonald, W. R., and Associates. (1992). *Evaluation of AB 1562 in-home care demonstration projects: Final report.* Sacramento, CA: Author.

McGowan, B. G. (1990). Family-based services and public policy: Context and implications. In J. K. Whittaker, et al., eds., *Reaching high risk families: Intensive family preservation services in human services,* 65-87. Hawthorne, NY: Aldine de Gruyter.

McGowan, B., and Meezan, W., eds. (1983). *Child welfare.* Itasca, IL: Peacock Publishing.

McLanahan, S. (1988). The consequences of single parenthood for subsequent generations. *Focus* 11:16-21.

McLanahan, S., and Garfinkel, I. (1993). Single mothers in the United States: Growth, problems and policies. In J. Hudson, and B. Galaway, eds., *Single parent families: Perspectives on research and policy,* 15-29. Toronto: Thompson Educational Publishing.

Mead, L. M. (1986). *Beyond entitlement: The social obligations of citizenship.* New York: Free Press.

Mead, L. M. (1985). The hidden jobs debate. *The Public Interest* 95:40-58.

Mech, E. (1970). Decision analysis in foster care practice. In H. D. Stone, ed., *Foster care in question*, 26-51. New York: Child Welfare League of America.

Meezan, W., and McCroskey, J. (1993). *Family centered home based interventions for abusive and neglectful families in Los Angeles.* Unpublished paper. Los Angeles: University of Southern California School of Social Work.

Meissner, M. (1975). No exit for wives: Sexual division of labour and the cumulation of household demands. *Canadian Review of Sociology and Anthropology* 12:424-439.

Mendelson, M. (1987). Can we reform Canada's income security system? In S. B. Steward, ed., *The future of social welfare systems in Canada and the United Kingdom*, Proceedings of a Canada/UK Colloquium, Oct. 17-18, 1986-1987. Halifax: Institute for Research on Public Policy.

Metcalf, C. E., and Thornton, C. (1992). Random assignment. *Children and Youth Services Review* 14:145-156.

Meyer, C. H. (1984). Can foster care be saved? *Social Work* 29:499.

Meyer, H. S., Borgatta, E., and Jones W. (1965). *Girls at vocational high: An experiment in social work intervention.* New York: Russell Sage Foundation.

Michigan Department of Social Services. (1993). *Report to the House Appropriations Subcommittee on Social Services, May 25.* Lansing, MI: Author.

Miller, D. S. (1959). Fractures among children - 1, parental assault as causative agent. *Minnesota Medicine* 42:1209-1213.

Mitchell, C., Tovar, P., and Knitzer, J. (1989). *The Bronx Homebuilders program: An evaluation of the first 45 families.* New York: Bank Street College of Education.

Mlyniec, W. J. (1983). *Prosecuting a termination of parental rights case. In M. Hardin, ed., Foster children in the courts, 193-228.* Boston: Butterworth Legal Publishers.

Mnookin, R. H. (1973). Foster care: In whose best interest? *Harvard Educational Review* 43:599-638.

Mnookin, R. H. (1985). *In the interest of children: Advocacy, law reform, and public policy.* San Francisco: Freeman.

Montgomery, S. (1982). Correspondence. *British Journal of Social Work* 12:669-672.

Moore, K. A., Nord, C. W., and Peterson, J. L. (1989). Non-voluntary sexual activity among adolescents. *Family Planning Perspectives* 21:110-114.

Morris, M., and Williamson, J. W. (1987). Workfare: The poverty/dependence trade-off. *Social Policy* 18:13-16, 49-50.

Moynihan, D. P. (1965). *The Negro family: The case for national action.* Washington, DC: Office of Policy Planning and Research, U.S. Department of Labor.

Moynihan, D. P. (1973). *The politics of a guaranteed annual income: The Nixon administration and the Family Assistance Plan.* New York: Random House.

Moynihan, D. P. (1981). Children and welfare reform. *Journal of the Institute for Socioeconomic Studies* 6:1-8.

Moynihan, D. P. (1986). *Family and nation.* San Diego: Harcourt, Brace Jovanovich.

Moynihan, D. P. (1990). Towards a post-industrial social policy. *Families in Society* 71:51-56.

Mullin, E., Chazin, R., and Feldstein, D. (1970). *Preventing chronic dependency.* New York: Community Service Society.

Mullen, E. J, and Dumpson, J. R., eds. (1972). *Evaluation of social intervention.* San Francisco: Jossey-Bass.

Munroe-Blum, H., Boyle, M. H., Offord, D. R., and Kates, N. (1989). Immigrant children- psychiatric disorder, school performance and service utilization. *American Journal of Orthopsychiatry* 59:510-519.

Murray, C. (1984). *Losing ground.* New York: Basic Books.

Murray, C. (1993). The coming white underclass. *The Wall Street Journal*, Friday, October 29.

Myrdal, G. (1944). *An American dilemma.* New York: Harper and Brothers.

Nagi, S. Z. (1977). *Child maltreatment in the United States: A challenge to social institutions.* New York: Columbia University Press.

Nasar, S. (1992). The 1980s: A very good time for the very rich. Data show the top 1% got 60% of gain in decade's boom. *New York Times*, March 5, p. A1 and C13.

Nasar, S. (1994). Economics of equality: A new view. *New York Times*, January, 8, p. A17 and 26.

National Black Child Development Institute. (1989). *Who will care when parents don't? A study of Black children in foster care.* Washington, DC: Author.

National Center for Children in Poverty. (1990). *Five million children: A statistical profile of our poorest young citizens.* New York: Author, School of Public Health, Columbia University.

National Center for Comprehensive Emergency Service to Children. (1976). *Comprehensive emergency services training guide.* 2d ed. Nashville, TN: Author.

National Center on Health Statistics. (1989). *Vital statistics of the United States, Vol. II. Mortality, Part A.* Washington, DC: U.S. Department of Health and Human Services.

National Commission on Children. (1991). *Beyond rhetoric a new American agenda for children and families: Final report of the National Commission on Children.* Washington, DC: Author.

National Council on Welfare. (1985). *Opportunity for reform, a response by the National Council of Welfare to the consultation paper on child and elderly benefits.* Ottawa: Minister of Supply and Services Canada.

National Council on Welfare. (1989). *Social spending and the next budget.* Ottawa: Health and Welfare Canada.

National Council on Welfare. (1993). *Poverty profile update for 1991.* Ottawa: Author.

Native Council of Canada. Crime and Justice Commission. (1978). *Metis and non-status Indians.* Ottawa: Supply and Services Canada.

Nelson, B. J. (1984). *Making an issue of child abuse: Political agenda setting for social problems.* Chicago: University of Chicago Press.

Nelson, K., Emlen, A., Landsman, M. J., and Hutchinson, J. (1988). *Factors contributing to success and failure in family-based child welfare services: Final report.* Iowa City: National Resource Center on Family Based Services, University of Iowa School of Social Work.

Nelson, K., and Landsman, M. J. (1992). *Alternative models of family preservation: Family-based services in context.* Springfield, IL: Charles C. Thomas.

Noble, B. P. (1993). Worthy child-care pay scales. *The New York Times,* April 18, Section F, p. 25.

Norman, A. J., and Glick, P. C. (1986). One-parent families: A social and economic profile. *Family Relations* 35:9-17.

Norris, M., and Wallace, B. eds. (1965). *The known and the unknown in child welfare research: An appraisal.* New York: Child Welfare League of America.

Noyes, P. (1991). *Child abuse—A study of inquiry reports.* London: HMSO.

Nunnally, J. C. (1961). *Popular conceptions of mental health.* New York: Holt, Rinehart, and Winston.

Offord, D. R., Boyle, M. H., Szatmari, P., Rae-Grant, N. I., Links, P. S., Cadman, D. T., Byles, J. A., Crawford, J. W., Munroe-Blum, H., Byrne, C., Thomas, H., and Woodward, C. A. (1987). Ontario child health study: II. Six-month prevalence of disorder and rates of service utilization. *Archives of General Psychiatry* 44:832-836.

O'Higgins, M. (1988). The allocation of public resources to children and the elderly in OECD countries. In J. Palmer, T. Smeeding, and B. B. Torrey, eds., *The vulnerables: Americas's young and old in the industrial world,* 214-222. Washington, DC: Urban Institute Press.

O'Higgins, M., Schmaus, G., and Stephenson, G. (1985, June). *Income distribution and redistribution: A microdata analysis of seven countries.* Luxembourg Income Study, Working Paper No. 3.

Olson, I. (1970). Some effects of increased aid in money and social services to families getting AFDC grants. *Child Welfare* 49:94-100.

Ontario. (1979). *The family as a form for social policy.* Toronto: Provincial Secretary for Social Development.

Orshansky, M. (1965). Counting the poor: Another look at the poverty profile. *Social Security Bulletin* 28:3-29.

Orshansky, M. (1967). Who was poor in 1966? In E. M. B. Burns, ed., *Children's allowances and the economic welfare of children,* 19-57. New York: Citizen's Committee for Children of New York.

Ozawa, M. N. (1977). Social insurance and redistribution. In A. Schorr, ed., *Jubilee for our times: A practical program for income equality,* 123-177. New York: Columbia University Press.

Ozawa, M. N. (1991a). Child welfare programs in Japan. *Social Service Review* 65:1-21.

Ozawa, M. N. (1991b). Unequal treatment of children by the Federal government. *Children and Youth Services Review* 13:255-268.

Ozawa, M. N. (1993). America's future and her investment in children. *Child Welfare* 72:517-529.

Packman, J. (1981). *The child's generation.* London: Blackwells/Robertson.

Packman, J. (1975). *The child's generation: Child care policy from Curtis to Houghton.* London: Blackwell.

Packman, J., Randall, J., and Jacques, N. (1986). *Who needs care? Social work decisions about children.* Oxford: Basil Blackwell.

Page, R. M. (1987). Child abuse: The smothering of an issue-A British perspective. *Children and Youth Services Review* 9:51-65.

Palmer, S. E. (1971). The decision to separate children from their natural parents. *Social Work* 39:82-87.

Parton, N. (1985). *The politics of child abuse.* London: Macmillan.

Passell, P. (1992). *Economic scene.* New York Times, February 12.

Pate A. M.,and Hamilton, E. E. (1992). Formal and informal deterrents to domestic violence: The Dade county spouse assault experiment. *American Sociological Review* 57:691-697.

Pavetti, L. (1993). *The dynamics of welfare and work: Exploring the process by which women work their way off welfare.* Unpublished doctoral dissertation, Harvard University.

Pearce, D. (1990). Welfare is not for women: Why the War on Poverty cannot conquer the feminization of poverty. In L. Gordon, ed. *Women, the state, and welfare.* Madison, WI: The University of Wisconsin Press.

Peckham, C. S., and Jobling, M. (1975). Deaths from non-accidental injuries in childhood. *British Medical Journal* 2:686.

Pechman, J. A. (1989). *Tax reform, the rich and the poor.* Washington, DC: The Brookings Institution.

Pecora, P. J., Fraser, M. W., and Haapala, D. A. (1991). Client outcomes and issues for program design. In K. Wells and D. Biegel, eds., *Family preservation services: Research and evaluation.* 3-32. Newbury Park: Sage.

Pecora, P. J., Fraser, M. W., and Haapala, D. A. (1992). Intensive home-based family preservation services: An update from the FIT project. *Child Welfare* 71:177-188.

Pelton, L. H. (1981). Child abuse and neglect: The myth of classlessness. In L. H. Pelton, ed., *The social context of child abuse and neglect,* 23-38. New York: Human Sciences Press.

Pelton, L. H. (1989). *For reasons of poverty: A critical analysis of the public child welfare system in the United States.* New York: Praeger.

Pelton, L. H. (1991). Beyond permanency planning: Restructuring the public child welfare system. *Social Work* 36:337-434.

Pelton, L. H. (1992). A functional approach to reorganizing family and child welfare interventions. *Children and Youth Services Review* 14:298-304.

Phillips, K. (1990). *The politics of rich and poor: Wealth and the American electorate in the Reagan aftermath.* New York: Random House

Phillips, K. (1993). *Boiling point: Republicans, Democrats and the decline of middle-class prosperity.* New York: Random House

Phillips, M. H., Haring, B. L., and Shyne, A. W. (1972). *A model for intake decisions in child welfare.* New York: Child Welfare League of America.

Phillips, P., and Phillips, E. (1983). *Women and work: Inequality in the labour market.* Toronto: Lorimer.

Philp, M. (1994a). Liberals facing a heavy load of welfare work. *Globe and Mail,* January, 19, A1 and A4.

Philp, M. (1994b). Welfare shatters dreams of a better life. *Globe and Mail,* January, 21, A1 and A8.

Picton, C., and Boss, P. (1981). *Child welfare in Australia: An introduction.* Sydney: Harcourt Brace Jovanovich.

Pierce, W. (1992). Adoption and other permanency considerations. *Children and Youth Services Review* 14:61-66.

Pike, V. (1976). Permanent planning for foster children: The Oregon Project. *Children Today* 5:22-25.

Pike, V., and Downs, S. (1977). *Permanent planning for children in foster care: A handbook for social workers,* DHEW Publication No. (OHD) 77-30124. Washington, DC: U.S. Government Printing Office.

Pine, B. A. (1986). Child welfare reform and the political process. *Social Service Review* 60:339-360.

Polakow, V. (1993). *Lives on the edge: Single mothers and their children in the other America.* Chicago: The University of Chicago Press.

Powers, E., and Witmer, H. L. (1951). *An experiment in the prevention of delinquency-The Cambridge Somerville youth study.* New York: Columbia University Press.

Pritchard, C. (1992). Children's homicide as an indicator of effective child protection: A comparative study of Western European Statistics. *British Journal of Social Work* 22:663-684.

Proch, K., and Howard, J. A. (1986). Parental visiting of children in foster care. *Social Work* 31:178-181.

Pryor, R. C. (1991). *New York State Central Register reporting highlights, 1974-1990.* Albany, NY: State Central Register for Reports of Child Abuse and Maltreatment.

Radbill, S. X. (1974). History of child abuse and infanticide. In R. E. Helfer and C. H. Kempe, eds., *The battered child,* 3-21. Chicago: The University of Chicago Press.

Ravetz, J. (1971). *Scientific knowledge and its social problems.* London: Oxford University Press.

Rainwater, L., and Yancey, W. L. (1967). *The Moynihan report and the politics of controversy.* Cambridge, MA: MIT Press.

Regional Research Institute for Human Services (1978). *Permanent planning in foster care: Resources for training and a guide for program planners.* Portland, OR: Author.

Reid, J. H. (1959). Action called for—recommendation. In H. S. Maas and R. E. Engler, *Children in need of parents,* 378-397. New York: Columbia University Press.

Reid, W. J., and Hanrahan, P. (1981). The effectiveness of social work: Recent evidence. In E. M. Goldberg and N. Connelly, eds., *Evaluative research in social care: Papers from a workshop on recent trends in evaluative research in social work and the social services,* May 1980, 9-20. London: Heinemann.

Reimer, D.R. (1988). *The prisoners of welfare: Liberating America's poor from unemployment and low wages.* New York: Praeger.

Rein, M., Nutt, T. E. and Weiss, H. (1974). Foster family care: Myth and reality. In A. Schorr, ed., *Children and decent people,* 24-52. New York: Basic Books.

Rein, M., and Rainwater, L. (1978). Patterns of welfare use. *Social Service Review* 52:511-534.

Rejda, G. E. (1970). Family allowances as a program for reducing poverty. *Journal of Risk Insurance* 37:539-554.

Report on Business Magazine (1993). 1993 in Figures. Supplement to *Globe and Mail,* January, 94-98.

Richmond, M. E. (1986). *The friendly visitor: General suggestions to those that visit the poor.* Philadelphia: Society for Organizing Charity.

Richmond, M. E. (1912). *Relation of output to intake.* Charity Organization Bulletin, New Series, 3 (9).

Richmond, M. E. (1917). *Social diagnosis.* New York: Russell Sage Foundation.

Ringen, S. (1985). *Difference and similarity: Two studies in comparative income distribution.* Stockholm: The Swedish Institute for Social Research.

Ringwalt, C., and Caye, J. (1989). The effects of demographic factors on perceptions of child neglect. *Children and Youth Services Review* 11:133-144.

Rodham, H. (1977). Children's policies: Abandonment and neglect. *The Yale Law Journal* 86:1522-1531.

Rose, S. J. (1992). *Social stratification in the United States.* New York: The New Press.

Ross, D. P., and Shillington, R. (1989). *The Canadian fact book on poverty, 1989.* Ottawa: Canadian Council on Social Development.

Ross, H. L., and Sawhill, I. V. (1975). *Time of transition: The growth of families headed by women.* Washington, DC: The Urban Institute.

Rossi, P. H. (1987). The iron law of evaluation and other metallic rules. In J. Miller and M. Lewis, eds., *Research in social problems and public policy,* Vol. 4, 3-20. Greenwich, CT: JAI Press.

Rossi, P. H. (1992a). Assessing family preservation programs. *Children and Youth Services Review* 14:77-97.

Rossi, P. H. (1992b). Strategies for evaluation. *Children and Youth Services Review* 14:167-191.

Rossi, P. H. (1994). Review of "Families in Crisis." *Children and Youth Services Review* 16: forthcoming.

Rossi, P., and Wright, J. D. (1984). Evaluation research: An assessment. *Annual Review of Sociology* 10:331-352.

Rowe, J., and Lambert, L. (1973). *Children who wait.* London: Association of British Adoption and Fostering Agencies.

Rubin, A. (1985). Practice effectiveness: More grounds for optimism. *Social Work* 30:469-476.

Rubin, A. (1986). Tunnel vision in the search for effective interventions: Rubin responds. *Social Work* 31:403-404.

Rusk, J. (1994). Too many children losing out. *Globe and Mail,* May 10: A7.

Rutter, M. (1972). *Maternal deprivation reassessed.* London: Penguin.

Ryan, T. J. (1972). *Poverty and the child: A Canadian study.* Toronto: McGraw-Hill Ryerson.

Rzepnicki, T. L., and Stein, T. J. (1985). Permanency planning for children in foster care: A review of projects. *Children and Youth Services Review* 7:95-108.

Sarri, R., and Finn, J. (1992a). Child welfare policy and practice: Rethinking the history of our certainties. *Children and Youth Services Review* 14:219-236.

Sarri, R., and Finn, J. (1992b). Introduction to special issue on child welfare policy and practice: Rethinking the history of our certainties. *Children and Youth Services Review* 14:213-216.

Sawyer, M. (1976). *Income distribution in OECD countries, OECD Economic Outlook-Occasional Studies.* Paris: Organization for Economic Cooperation and Development.

Scannapieco, M. (1994). Home-based services program: Effectiveness with at-risk families. *Children and Youth Services Review* 16: forthcoming.

Schafer, R., and Erickson, S. D. (1993). Evolving family preservation services: The Florida experience. In E. S. Morton and R. K. Grigsby, eds., *Advancing family preservation practice.* 56-69. Newbury Park: Sage.

Schloesser, P., Pierpont, J., and Poertner, J. (1992). Active surveillance of child abuse fatalities. *Child Abuse and Neglect* 16:3-10.

Schneider, P. (1987). Lost innocents: The myth of missing children. *Harpers*, February, 47-53.

Schnell, R. L. (1987). A children's bureau for Canada: The origins of the Canadian Council on Child Welfare, 1913-1921. In A. Moscovitch, and J. Albert, eds., *The benevolent state: The growth of welfare in Canada*, 95-110. Toronto: Garamond Press.

Schorr, A. L. (1966). *Poor kids.* New York: Basic Books.

Schorr, A. L., ed. (1974). *Children and decent people.* New York: Basic Books.

Schorr, A.L. (1986). *Common decency.* New Haven, CT: Yale University Press.

Schorr, L. B., with Schorr, D. (1989). *Within our reach: Breaking the cycle of disadvantage.* New York: Anchor, Doubleday.

Schram, S. F. (1991). Welfare spending and poverty: Cutting back produces more poverty, not less. *The American Journal of Economics and Sociology* 50:129-141.

Schram, S. F., and Wilken, P. H. (1989). It's no 'Laffer' matter: Claim the increasing welfare aid breeds poverty and dependency fails statistical test. *American Journal of Economics and Sociology* 48:203-217.

Schram, S. F., Turbett, J. P., and Wilken, P. H. (1988). Child poverty and welfare benefits: A reassessment with state data of the claim that American welfare breeds dependence. *American Journal of Economics and Sociology* 47:409-422.

Schuerman, J. R., Rzepnicki, T. L., and Littell, J. H. (1991). From Chicago to Little Egypt: Lessons from an evaluation of a family preservation program. In K. Wells and D. Biegel, eds., *Family preservation services: Research and evaluation.* 33-46. Newbury Park: Sage.

Schuerman, J. R., Rzepnicki, T. L., Littell, J. H., and Budde, S. (1992). Implementation issues. *Children and Youth Services Review* 14:193-206.

Schuerman, J. Rzepnicki, T. L., Littell, J. H., and Chak, A. (1993). *Evaluation of the Illinois Family First Placement Family Preservation Program: Final Report.* Chicago, IL: Chapin Hall Center for Children.

Schuerman, J. R., and Vogel, L. H. (1986). Computer support of placement planning: The use of expert systems in child welfare. *Child Welfare* 65:531-543.

Schwab, J. A., Bruce, M. E., and McRoy, R. G. (1984). Matching children with placements. *Children and Youth Services Review* 6:359-368.

Schwab, J. A., Bruce, M. E., and McRoy, R. G. (1986). Using computer technology in child placement decisions. *Social Casework* 67:359-368.

Schwartz, I. M., and AuClaire, P. (1989). Intensive home-based service as an alternative to the out-of-home placement: The Hennepin county experience. Unpublished paper.

Schwartz, I. M., AuClaire, P., and Harris, L. J. (1991). Family preservation services as an alternative to the out-of-home placement of adolescents: The Hennepin county experience. In K. Wells and D. Biegel, eds., *Family preservation services: Research and evaluation.* 187-206. Newbury Park: Sage.

Scott, P. D. (1973). Fatal battered baby cases. *Medicine, Science and the Law* 13:197-206.

Scott, P. D. (1978). The psychiatrist's viewpoint. In S. M. Smith, ed., *The maltreatment of children,* 175-203. Baltimore, MD: University Park Press.

Sedlak, A. (1989). *The supplementary analyses of data on the national incidence of child abuse and neglect.* (p. 2-2, Table 2-1). Rockville, MD: Westat.

Sedlak, A. (1991). *The supplementary analyses of data on the national incidence of child abuse and neglect.* Revised August 30, 1991. Rockville, MD: Westat.

Segal, S. P. (1972). Research on the outcomes of social work therapeutic interventions: A review of the literature. *Journal of Health and Social Behavior* 13:3-17.

Segalman, R., and Basu, A. (1981). *Poverty in America: The welfare dilemma.* Westport, CT: Greenwood Press.

Select Committee on Children, Youth and Families. (1987). *Abused children in America: Victims of official neglect.* U.S. House of Representatives, Washington, DC: U.S. Government Printing Office.

Select Committee on Children, Youth, and Families. (1989a). *No place to call home: Discarded children in America.* U.S. House of Representatives. Washington, DC: U.S. Government Printing Office.

Select Committee on Children, Youth, and Families. (1989b). *U.S. children and their families: Current conditions and recent trends, 1989.* U.S. House of Representatives. Washington, DC: U.S. Government Printing Office.

Sewell, S. R. (1976). *Compliance with child support obligations.* Unpublished paper. University of Texas Law School.

Sharpe, R., and Lundstrom, M. (1991). SIDS sometimes used to cover up child abuse deaths. *USA Today,* January 10, 2.

Sheldon, B. (1986). Social work effectiveness experiments: Review and implications. *British Journal of Social Work* 16:223-242.

Sherman, L. W.,and Berk, R. A. (1984). The specific deterrent effects of arrest for domestic assault. *American Sociological Review* 49:261-272.

Sherman, L. W., and Smith, D. A. (1992). Crime, punishment, and stake in conformity: Milwaukee and Omaha experiments. *American Sociological Review* 57:680-690.

Sherraden, M. (1990). Rethinking social welfare: Towards assets. *Social Policy* 7:37-43.

Sherraden, M. (1991). *Assets and the poor: A new American welfare policy.* New York: M. E. Sharpe.

Shyne, A. W., and Schroeder, A. G. (1978). *National study of social services to children and their families.* (DHEW Publication No. OHDS 78-30150). Washington, DC: United States Children's Bureau.

Siegal, M. (1985). *Children, parenthood, and social welfare: In the context of developmental psychology.* Oxford: Oxford University Press.

Silverman, F. N. (1953). The Roentgen manifestations of unrecognized skeletal trauma in infants. *American Journal of Roentgenology* 69(1):413-427.

Sinanoglu, P. A. (1981). Working with parents: Selected issues and trends as reflected in the literature. In A. N. Maluccio and P. A. Sinanoglu, eds., *The challenge of partnership: Working with parents of children in foster care*, 3-21. New York: Child Welfare League of America, Inc.

Sisman, H. (1990). One of the saddest jobs on earth. This World section of *The San Francisco Chronicle*, November 4, 13-16.

Smeeding, T. (1991). *Cross national perspectives on income security programs.* Testimony before the U.S. Congress Joint Economic Committee, September 25.

Smeeding, T. (1992). Why the United States anti-poverty system doesn't work very well. *Challenge* 35:30-35.

Smith, A. (1937). *An inquiry into the nature and cause of the wealth of nations.* [first published in 1776]. New York: Modern Library.

Smith, M. J. (1950). Subdural hematoma with multiple fractures. *American Journal of Roentgenology* 6:343-344

Solicitor General of Canada (1989). *Family violence.* Liason 15:4-13.

Solomon, J. (1989). Managers focus on low-wage workers. *Wall Street Journal*, May 9, B1.

Somander, L. H. K., and Ramner, L. M. (1991). Intra-and-extra familial child homicide in Sweden, 1971-1980. *Child Abuse and Neglect* 15:45-55.

Sosin, M. R., Piliavin, I., and Westerfelt, H. (1991). Toward a longitudinal analysis of homelessness. *Journal of Social Issues* 46:157-174.

Smith, P. B., and Poertner, J. (1993). Enhancing the skills of adolescents as individuals and as parents. *Children and Youth Services Review* 15:275-280.

Specht, H. (1990). Social work and the popular psychotherapies. *Social Service Review* 64:345-357.

Spector, M., and Kitsuse, J. I. (1977). *Constructing social problems.* Menlo Park: Cummings.

Spencer, J. W., and Knudsen, D. D. (1992). Out-of-home maltreatment: An analysis of risk in various settings for children. *Children and Youth Services Review* 14:485-492.

Stanley, T. J. (1988). Marketing to the affluent. Homewood, IL: Dow Jones-Irwin.

Stapleford, F. N., and Lea, N. (1949). Social work looks at Parliament. *Canadian Welfare* 24:20-21.

Stark, E. (1992). Framing and reframing battered women. In E. Buzawa and C. Buzawa, eds., *Domestic violence: The criminal justice response,* 271-292. Dover, MA: Auburn House.

Starr, P. (1982). *The social transformation of American medicine.* New York: Basic Books.

Starr, R. H. (1982). *Child abuse prediction: Policy implications.* Cambridge, MA: Harper and Row, Ballinger Publishing.

Statistics Canada. (1985). *Women in Canada: A statistical report.* Ottawa: Supply and Services.

Statistics Canada. (1987). *Income distributions by size in Canada, 1987,* Catalogue No. 13-207. Ottawa: Supply and Services.

Stein, T. J. (1985). Projects to prevent out-of-home placement. *Children and Youth Services Review* 7:109-122.

Stein, T. J. (1991a). *Child welfare and the law.* New York: Longman.

Stein, T. J. (1991b). Personal communication, September 11.

Stein, T. J., Gambrill, E. D., and Wiltse, K. T. (1978). *Children in foster homes: Achieving continuity of care.* New York: Praeger Publishers.

Stein, T. J., and Gambrill, E. D. (1976). *Decision making in foster care-A training manual.* Berkeley, CA: University Extension Publications.

Stein, T. J., and Rzepnicki, T. L. (1984). *Decision-making in child welfare services: Intake and planning.* Hingham, MA: Kluwer-Nijoff Publishing, Kluwer Academic Publications.

Steiner, G. Y. (1976). *The childrens' cause.* Washington, DC: Brookings Institution.

Straus, M., Gelles, R., and Steinmetz, S. (1980). *Behind closed doors: Violence in the American family.* Garden City, NY: Doubleday.

Straus, M., and Gelles, R. (1986). Societal change and change in family violence from 1975-1985 as revealed by two national surveys. *Journal of Marriage and the Family* 48:465-479.

Stuart, A. (1986). Rescuing children: Reforms in the child support payment system. *Social Service Review* 60:201-217.

Sussman, A., and Cohen, S. (1975). *Reporting child abuse and neglect: Guidelines for legislation.* Cambridge, MA: Ballinger Publishing.

Szykula, S. A., and Fleischman, M. J. (1985). Reducing out-of-home placements of abused children: Two controlled field studies. *Child Abuse and Neglect* 9:277-283.

Tatara, T. (1983). *Characteristics of children in substitute and adoptive care.* Washington, DC: Voluntary Cooperative Information System, American Public Welfare Association.

Tatara, T., and Pettiford, E. K. (1985). *Characteristics of children in substitute and adoptive care.* Washington, DC: Voluntary Cooperative Information System, American Public Welfare Association.

Taylor, P. (1991). Tax cuts can help our kids: Relief for families benefits society. *Washington Post,* June 16, 1B.

Testa, M. F., and Goerge, R. M. (1988). *Policy and resource factors in the achievement of permanency for foster children in Illinois.* Unpublished paper. Chapin Hall Center for Children at the University of Chicago, Chicago.

Theiman, A. A., Fuqua, R., and Linnan, K. (1990). *Iowa family preservation three year pilot project: Final evaluation report.* Ames, IA: Iowa State University.

Theis, S. (1924). *How foster children turn out.* New York: State Charities Aid Association.

Thomlison, R. J. (1984). Something works: Evidence from practice effectiveness studies. *Social Work* 29:51-56.

Thurow, L. C. (1975). *Generating inequality: Mechanisms of distribution in the U.S. economy.* New York: Basic Books.

Thurow, L. C. (1987). *Declining American incomes and living standards.* New York: Economic Policy Institute.

Thurow, L. C. (1992). *Head to head: The coming economic battle among Japan, Europe, and America.* William Morrow and Company.

Titmuss, R. (1968). *Commitment to welfare.* New York: Pantheon Books.

Tobin, J. (1968). Raising the incomes of the poor. In K. Gordon, eds., *Agenda for the nation: Papers on diplomatic and foreign policy issues,* 77-116. Washington, DC: The Brookings Institution.

Tobin, J., Wu, D. Y. H., and Davidson, D. (1989). *Preschool in three cultures: Japan, China and the United States.* New Haven: Yale University Press.

Todd, A. J. (1919). *The scientific spirit in social work.* New York: Macmillan.

Torczyner, J., and Pare, A. (1979). The influence of environmental factors on foster care. *Social Service Review* 53:358-377.

Trotzkey, E. (1930). *Institutional care and placing-out.* Chicago: Marks Nathan Jewish Orphan Home.

Turner, D., and Shields, B. (1985). The legal process of brining children into care in British Columbia. In K. L. Levitt and B. Wharf, eds., *The challenge of child welfare*, 108-124. Vancouver: University of British Columbia.

Tyler, A. H., and Brassard, M. R. (1984). Abuse in the investigation and treatment of intrafamiliar child sexual abuse. *Child Abuse and Neglect* 8:47-53.

Underhill, E. (1974). The child and his surroundings. The strange silence of teachers, doctors and social workers in the face of cruelty to children. *International Child Welfare Review* 21:16-21.

United States Advisory Board on Child Abuse and Neglect. (1990). *Child abuse and neglect: Critical first steps in response to a national emergency.* Washington, DC: Author.

United States Advisory Board on Child Abuse and Neglect. (1991). *A caring community: Blueprint for an effective federal policy on child abuse and neglect.* Washington, DC: Author.

United States Bureau of the Census. (1987). *Child support and alimony, 1985.* Current population reports, Series P-23, No. 152. Washington, DC: Author.

United States Bureau of the Census. (1987). *Money income of households, families and persons in the United States: 1987.* Washington, DC: Author.

United States Congress, Subcommittee on Fiscal Policy of the Joint Economic Committee. (1974). *Income security for Americans: Recommendations of the public welfare study.* December 5. Washington, DC: U.S. Government Printing Office.

United States Department of Health and Human Services, National Center on Child Abuse and Neglect. (1981). *Study findings: National study of the incidence and severity of child abuse and neglect.* DHHS Publication No. (OHDS) 81-30325. Washington, DC: U.S. Government Printing Office.

United States Department of Health and Human Services, National Center on Child Abuse and Neglect. (1988). *Study findings, study of national incidence and prevalence of child abuse and neglect*, 5-29. Washington, DC: U.S. Government Printing Office.

United States General Accounting Office. (1989). *Children and youths: About 68,000 homeless and 186,000 in shared housing at any given time.* Washington, DC: U.S. Government Printing Office.

United States House of Representatives. (1981). *Missing children's act.* Hearings held by the Subcommittee on Civil and Constitutional Rights, Committee on the Judiciary. 97th Congress, 1st session, 18, November 30.

United States Senate. (1983). *Child kidnapping.* Hearings held by the Subcommittee on Juvenile Justice, Committee on the Judiciary. 98th Congress, First session, February 2.

University Associates (1992). *Evaluation of Michigan's Families First program: Summary of results.* Lansing, MI: Author.

University Associates (1993). *Evaluation of Michigan's Families First program: Summary report.* Lansing, MI: Author.

Vasaly, S. M. (1976). *Foster care in five states: A synthesis and analysis of studies from Arizona, California, Iowa, Massachusetts, and Vermont.* Washington, DC: Social Research Group, George Washington University.

von Hoffman, N. (1985). Pack of fools. *New Republic* 193:9-11.

Wald, M. (1975). State intervention on behalf of 'neglected' children: A search for realistic standards. *Stanford Law Review* 27:985-1040.

Wald, M. (1976). State intervention on behalf of 'neglected' children: Standards for removal of children from their homes, monitoring the status of children in foster care, and termination of parental rights. *Stanford Law Review* 28:625-706.

Wald, M. (1980). Thinking about public policy toward abuse and neglect of children: A review of *Before the best interests of the child. Michigan Law Review* 78:645-693.

Wald, M. S. (1988). Family preservation: Are we moving too fast? *Public Welfare* 46:33-37.

Wald, M. S., Carlsmith, J. M., and Leiderman, P. H. (1988). *Protecting abused and neglected children.* Stanford, CA: Stanford University Press.

Wald, M. S., and Woolverton, M. (1990). Risk assessment: The emperor's new clothes? *Child Welfare* 69:483-511.

Wall Street Journal (1985). May 9, p. 1.

Wall Street Journal (1991). Wealth of U.S. households stayed flat. January 11.

Wallerstein, J. S., and Kelly, J. B. (1979). Children and divorce: A review. *Social Work* 24:468-475.

Weber, M. (1958). *The Protestant ethic and the spirit of capitalism.* New York: Scribner.

Weitzman, L. J. (1985). *The divorce revolution: The unexpected social and economic consequences for women and children in America.* New York: Free Press.

Welch, W. M. (1994). Two-thirds back a costly welfare overhaul: Many fear cheating is widespread. USA Today, April 22: 7A.

Wells, K., and Biegel, D. E., eds. (1991). *Family preservation services: Research and evaluation.* Newbury Park, CA: Sage.

Wells, K., and Whittington, D. (1993). Child and family functioning after intensive family preservation services. *Social Services Review* 67:55-83.

Wenocur, S., and Reisch, M. (1989). *From charity to enterprise: The development of American social work in a market economy.* Urbana: University of Illinois Press.

Weston, J. T. (1974). The pathology of child abuse. In R. E. Helfer and C. H. Kempe, eds., *The battered child,* 2d ed., 61-86. Chicago: University of Chicago Press.

Wharf, B. (1985a). The challenge of child welfare. In K. L. Levitt and B. Wharf, eds., *The challenge of child welfare,* 290-301. Vancouver: University of British Columbia.

Wharf, B. (1985b). Preventive approaches to child welfare. In K. L. Levitt and B. Wharf, eds., *The challenge of child welfare,* 200-217. Vancouver: University of British Columbia.

Wheeler, C.E. (1992). Intensive family support services: Catalyst for systems change. Sacramento, CA: Walter R. McDonald and Associates.

Wheeler, C.E., Reuter, G., Struckman-Johnson, D., and Yuan, Y.T. (1992). *Evaluation of the State of Connecticut intensive family preservation services: Phase V annual report.* Sacramento, CA: Walter R. McDonald and Associates.

White, B. (1975). *The first three years of life.* New York: Avon.

White, K. R. (1976). A study of alimony and child support rulings with some recommendations. *Family Law Quarterly* 10:75-91.

Wilensky, H. L., and Lebeaux, C. N. (1958). *Industrial society and social welfare.* New York: Russell Sage Foundation.

Will, G. (1988). What Dukakis should be saying. *Washington Post,* September 15.

Will, G. (1991). Society challenged to break poverty cycle that traps kids. The *Register Guard* (Eugene, Oregon), B2.

Willems, D. N., and DeRubeis, R. (1981). The effectiveness of intensive preventive services for families with abused, neglected, or disturbed children: Hudson county project final report. Trenton, NJ: Bureau of Research, Division of Youth and Family Services.

Wilson, J. (1990). U. S. child abuse shame increases as poverty grips more children. *Register Guard* (Eugene, Oregon), November 20, 10A.

Wilson, J. O. (1985). *The power economy.* Boston: Little, Brown, and Company.

Wilson, W. J. (1987). *The truly disadvantaged: The inner city, the underclass, and public policy.* Chicago: The University of Chicago Press.

Wilson, W. J., and Neckerman, K. M. (1987). Poverty and family structure: The widening gap between evidence and public policy issues. In S. H. Danziger and D. H. Weinberg, eds., *Fighting poverty,* 232-259. Cambridge: Harvard University Press.

Wiltse, K. (1976). Decision making needs in foster care. *Children Today* 5:1-5.

Wires, E. W., and Drake, E. W. (1952). Use of statistics in testing practice. *Child Welfare* 31:17-18.

Wolins, M, and Piliavin, I. (1964). *Institution of foster family: A century of debate.* New York: Child Welfare League of America.

Wolock, I., and Horowitz, B. (1979). Child maltreatment and material deprivation among AFDC recipient families. *Social Service Review* 53:175-194.

Wood, S., Barton, K., and Schroeder, C. (1988). In-home treatment of abusive families: Cost and placement at one year. *Psychotherapy* 25:409-414.

Woolley, P. V., and Evans, W. A. (1955). Significance of skeletal lesions in infants resembling those of traumatic origin. *Journal of the American Medical Association* 181:17-24.

World Health Organization (1974-1990). *World health annual statistics (1974-1990)*. Geneva: World Health Organization.

Yuan, Y. T., McDonald, W. R., Wheeler, C. E., Struckman-Johnson, D., and Rivest, M. (1980). *Evaluation of AB 1562 in-home care demonstration projects: Final report*. Sacramento: Walter R. McDonald and Associates.

Yuan, Y. T. (1990). *Evaluation of AB 1562 in-home care demonstration projects*. Volumes I and II. Sacramento, CA: Walter R. MacDonald and Associates.

Zietz, D. (1964). *Child welfare: Principles and methods*. New York: John Wiley.

Zigler, E. (1979). Controlling child abuse in America: An effort doomed to failure? In R. Bourne and E. H. Newberger, eds., *Critical perspectives on child abuse*, 171-213. Lexington, MA: Lexington Books.

Zill, N., Moore, K., and Steif, T. (1989). *Progress report: Analysis of employment-related characteristics of AFDC mothers in national survey data bases*. Unpublished paper. Washington, DC: Child Trends, Inc.

Zill, N., and Rogers, C. C. (1988). Recent trends in the well-being of children in the United States and their implications for public policy. A. J. Cherlin, ed., *The changing American family and public policy*, 31-115. Washington, DC: The Urban Institute Press.

Author Index

Subject Index